Presented to [illegible] War memorial by [illegible] May 1928.

~~106~~

~~CENTRAL COMMITTEE FOR JEWISH EDUCATION.~~

JEWISH MEMORIAL COUNCIL.

THE

Council of [illegible]

War Memorial

THE JEWS IN EGYPT
AND IN PALESTINE

OXFORD UNIVERSITY PRESS
LONDON EDINBURGH GLASGOW NEW YORK
TORONTO MELBOURNE CAPE TOWN BOMBAY
HUMPHREY MILFORD
PUBLISHER TO THE UNIVERSITY

2240

THE JEWS IN EGYPT AND IN PALESTINE UNDER THE FĀṬIMID CALIPHS

A CONTRIBUTION TO
THEIR POLITICAL AND COMMUNAL HISTORY
BASED CHIEFLY ON GENIZAH MATERIAL
HITHERTO UNPUBLISHED

BY

JACOB MANN, M.A., D.Lit. (Lond.)

VOLUME I

OXFORD UNIVERSITY PRESS
HUMPHREY MILFORD
1920

THESIS APPROVED FOR THE DEGREE OF DOCTOR OF LITERATURE IN THE UNIVERSITY OF LONDON

TO

THE VERY REVEREND THE CHIEF RABBI

JOSEPH H. HERTZ

M.A., PH.D., HONORARY D.H.LITT.

CONTENTS

INTRODUCTION

'THE stone which the builders rejected has become the chief corner-stone.' A feeling similar to that of the Psalmist takes hold of one who explores the remarkable literary finds brought to light from the obscurity of the Cairo Genizah. Documents and letters, poems and compositions in Hebrew and Arabic, which the contemporaries preserved for some time after perusal and then regarded as useless, assigning them to the lumber-room of a synagogue only out of sheer piety, become now the foundation upon which the history of the Jews in Egypt and in Palestine, from 950 C.E. and onwards, is to be based. The attempt is made here to reconstruct the life of these Jewries from the beginning of the Fāṭimid reign in Egypt (969 C.E.) till about the time of Maimonides, who died at the end of the year 1204 C.E. A large number of Genizah fragments, still unpublished, form the basis of this work.

No claim is put forward of having exhausted all the available material. As with the nation of Israel, so with its literature—'scattered and separated among the peoples'. Thus it came about that the Genizah MSS. found their way into numerous libraries, public and private, on both hemispheres. Even those Genizah Collections to which I have had access—and they were the most important—could not be completely explored. The task of examining the many thousands of fragments and extracting all the historical data they contain, requires many years of labour, and cannot be undertaken by one person. But how appropriate is the saying of the Rabbis: 'The work is not for thee alone to finish; but thou art not free to desist from it.' My chief aim was to produce a skeleton of the contemporary history of the Egyptian and the Palestinian Jewries. Persons and events had to be brought into chronological order and sequence. It is my sincere hope that, as more of the Genizah fragments see the light of publication, the skeleton presented here will likewise clothe itself in flesh and blood and approach the stage of completion.

By the nature of our task, a great deal of spade-work was necessary as we proceeded from period to period. Where so much was hitherto unknown, details had to be discussed at length, data already known put into their proper setting and many errors, hitherto maintained, rectified. Contemporary Egyptian history had of course to be drawn upon in order to elucidate what the new material gave us. It was found advisable to arrange the new fragments and other data in appendices[1] to the chapters in order to preserve in the latter a more or less coherent narrative. Yet even this device did not always make it possible to keep up the proper sequence of events. Here and there it was necessary to anticipate what was to be considered later on or to make up for arrears.

The first five chapters incorporate all the new material at our disposal. The last chapter deals with the communal organization of the Jewries in Egypt and in Palestine, summarizing, and also supplementing what was to be learned from the preceding investigations.

Four Genizah Collections in this country supplied the new material given here. The most fruitful was the famous Taylor-Schechter Collection at the Cambridge University Library. My deep gratitude is due, and hereby tendered, to the staff of the Library for the facilities very kindly granted to me when examining the Genizah fragments. Of considerable importance was the collection of Elkan N. Adler, Esq., M.A., London. This well-known scholar has placed me under great obligation for his ready permission to use his valuable MSS. My best thanks are finally due to the staffs of the British Museum and of the Bodleian Library for many courtesies shown to me in the course of my work.

[1] They are cited in the following pages as Appendix A. = A. A. (to Ch. I); Appendix B. = A. B. (to Chaps. II and III); Appendix C. = A. C. (to Ch. IV); Appendix D. = A. D. (to Ch. V).

The fragments are cited in the following pages as T.-S. = Taylor-Schechter Collection, Cambridge; MS. Adler = Collection of Mr. E. N. Adler; Oxford MS. Heb. = Hebrew MSS. at the Bodleian, Oxford; Bodl. = Neubauer-Cowley, *Catalogue of Hebrew MSS. at the Bodleian*, vols. I and II; Or. = Oriental MSS. at the British Museum, London.

∴

A work of this kind, with no special appeal to the reading public at large, is not eagerly sought after by publishers, when the cost of production has increased by leaps and bounds. It was found necessary to divide the work, and publish first the results. The Genizah material, as arranged in the Appendices, forming the basis of the whole treatise, though ready for the press, had to be kept over for a second volume, which, it is to be hoped, will appear in the near future. A full Index will then be added.

It is my pleasant duty to express my heartfelt thanks to Robert Mond, Esq., M.A., F.R.S.E., who helped this volume to see the light of publication.

My gratitude to the Very Rev. the Chief Rabbi, who took a keen interest in my work while in the course of preparation, is expressed in the Dedication that precedes these lines.

J. M.

LONDON, *July*, 1919.

CORRIGENDA

Pp. 20 (ll. 6, 18, and 38), 21 (ll. 29 and 34), 22 (ll. 14 and 23), 136 (l. 32), and 150 (l. 14). *For* Kzāz *read* Ḳazzāz, 'the silk merchant'.

Pp. 20 (l. 23) and 22 (ll. 1, 7, and 13). *For* 'Adiyyah *read* 'Adayah.

P. 23, l. 20. *For* 'Abū'l . . . al-Kmudi *read* Abū'l . . . al-Ḳumūdi.

P. 82, l. 1. *For* אלתפלפל (so in the manuscript) *read* אלמפלפל, al-Mufalfal.

P. 82, l. 4. *For* אבן אונת *read* אבן אוכֿת, 'the nephew of' Sham'ān.

P. 82, l. 13. *For* for *read* concerning.

Pp. 96 (l. 17), 192 (l. 13), 196 (l. 5), and 220, note 1, l. 12. *For* Parnes *read* Parnās.

P. 97, note 3, l. 1. *For* Saḥlan *read* Sahlan.

P. 101, l. 10 from bottom. *For* Bet Sin *read* Bet-Dīn.

P. 112, l. 12. *For* high *read* firm.

P. 150, l. 14 from bottom. *For* Mumal *read* Mu'ammil.

P. 154, l. 9. *For* Ibn Aktabū'l-Syād *read* Ibnu-uḥti (i. e. the nephew of) Abū'l Siyād.

P. 154, l. 14. *For* Renown *read* Treasure.

P. 168, l. 9. *For* Ṣajīr *read* Ṣaġīr.

P. 205, l. 15 from bottom. *For* Ḥabrim *read* Ḥaberim.

LIST OF MANUSCRIPTS USED

AS ARRANGED IN THE APPENDICES TO BE PRINTED IN VOL. II

APPENDIX A (to Ch. I).

A. A. 1 = T.-S. 32. 4
2 = Oxford MS. Heb. d. 36, fols. 9–10 (cp. Bodl. 2776[3]), and a small paper leaf in T.-S. Box K 8
3 = Oxford MS. Heb. d. 75, fol. 15
4 = T.-S. 16. 68
5 = Extracts from several MSS.
6 = Or. 5560, A, fol. 1
7 = Or. 5557, P, fols. 55-56, and T.-S. 8 J 31[10]
7[a] = Oxford MS. Heb. b. 11, fol. 8 (cp. Bodl. 2874, 8[a])
8 = Oxford MS. Heb. e. 95, fol. 54, Or. 5560, A, fols. 5 and 6, and T.-S. 8 J 34[3]
9 = T.-S. 8 K 10
10 = Oxford MS. Heb. a. 3, fol. 21 (cp. Bodl. 2873[21])
11 = T.-S. 18 J 4[5]
12 = T.-S. 13 J 11[7] and 22[21]
13 = T.-S. 8 G 7[1]
14 = Extracts from Or. 5554, A, fols. 28-29, and Oxford MS. Heb. e. 74, fols. 59-60 (cp. Bodl. 2862[21])
15 = *The Gaonic family of Ben-Meir.* Extracts from T.-S. 13 J 1[2]; MS. Adler 2952; T.-S. 8 K 20[3], 13 J 16[16], 8 J 8[6] and 10 J 26[8]
16, I = Extracts from a loose leaf in MS. Adler 2805 and from two paper leaves in T.-S. Box K 6
16, II = Two leaves in MS. Adler 4009
A. A. 16, III = Oxford MS. Heb. d. 76, fol. 50
16, IV = Extracts from MS. Adler 223
17 = *The Gaonic family of Ebyatar Hakkohen.* Or. 5557, A, fol. 7, verso, and Oxford MS. Heb. c. 50, fol. 11. Extract from MS. Adler 3011, fol. 1
18 = T.-S. 13 J 14[10]
19 = T.-S. 13 J 26[16] and extract from Oxford MS. Heb. a. 2, fol. 3 (cp. Bodl. 2805[a.b])
20 = T.-S. 12. 16
21 = A paper leaf; MS. Adler
22 = A paper leaf; MS. Adler
23 = A vellum leaf; MS. Adler and an extract from T.-S. 20. 97

APPENDIX B (to Chaps. II and III).

A. B. 1 = T.-S. 13 J 10[12]
2 = T.-S. 13 J 18[1] and an extract from Or. 5542, fol. 6
3 = Oxford MS. Heb. d. 65, fol. 40 (cp. Bodl. 2877[40])
4 = T.-S. 13 J 13[21]
5 = T.-S. 13 J 31[8]
6 = T.-S. 13 J 23[12]
7 = T.-S. 13 J 14[5]
8 = T.-S. 13 J 15[14]
9 = T.-S. 13 J 31[5]
10 = Extracts from Or. 5544, fol. 8, and Oxford MS. Heb. a. 3, fol. 17 (cp. Bodl. 2873[17])
11 = T.-S. 13 J 19[18] and extracts
12 = T.-S. 13 J 14[20]
13 = T.-S. 13 J 20[25]

A. B. 14 = A loose leaf in MS. Adler 2804
15 = MS. Adler 2804, fol. 7
16 = T.-S. 13 J 24^{11}
17 = A paper leaf; MS. Adler
18 = T.-S. 16. 251
19 = T.-S. 16. 374
20, I and II = Numerous extracts from MSS.
20, III = *Ṣahlan b. Abraham as liturgical writer.* T.-S. 10 K 20^{5} and extracts
21 = A paper leaf in MS. Adler 2804
22 = T.-S. 13 J 18^{28}
23 = T.-S. 13 J 20^{13}
24 = T.-S. 13 J 17^{4}
25 = T.-S. 8 J 21^{6}
26 = T.-S. 13 J 21^{19}
27 = T.-S. 10 J 10^{9}
28 = MS. Adler 2804, fol. 2
29 = T.-S. 13 J 14^{23}
30 = A paper leaf; MS. Adler, and extracts.
31 = Extracts from MS. Adler 2804, fol. 1; T.-S. 18 J $4^{15.25}$, 13 J 14^{16}
32 = T.-S. 12. 80
33 = T.-S. 12. 247
34 = T.-S. 13 J 11^{9}
35 = T.-S. 13 J 9^{2}
36 = T.-S. 13 J 17^{1} (now printed in *J. Q. R.*, N. S., IX, 415)
37 = Or. 5346
38 = T.-S. 13 J 15^{1}
39 = T.-S. 13 J 14^{18}
40 = T.-S. 20. 181
41 = T.-S. 10 J 12^{17}
42 = T.-S. 13 J 16^{14}
43 = T.-S. 13 J 13^{14}
44 = Oxford MS. Heb. c. 28, fol. 8 (cp. Bodl. 2876^{8})
45 = T.-S. 18 J 4^{17}
46 = T.-S. 13 J 23^{11}
47 = T.-S. 18 J 4^{26}
48 = T.-S. 16. 275
49 = MS. Adler 2804, fol. 8
50 = T.-S. 12. 217
51 = MS. Adler 2804, fol. 3, and extract from Oxford MS. Heb. a. 3, fol. 3 (cp. Bodl. 2873^{3})

A. B. 52 = T.-S. 13 J 26^{23}
53 = T.-S. 13 J 31^{7}
54 = A loose leaf in MS. Adler 2804
55 = MS. Adler 2804, fol. 6
56 = T.-S. 13 J 13^{18}
57 = T.-S. 13 J 10^{22}
58 = T.-S. 13 J 33^{12}
59 = Oxford MS. Heb. c. 28, fol. 9 (cp. Bodl. 2876^{9})
60 = T.-S. 13 J 23^{19}
61 = T.-S. 13 J 23^{1}
62 = Oxford MS. Heb. c. 50, fol. 21
63 = MS. Adler 2804, fol. 4
64 = T.-S. 10 J 14^{8}
65 = T.-S. 13 J 15^{11}
66 = T.-S. 13 J 31^{1}
67 = T.-S. 10 J 15^{10}
68 = T.-S. 8 J 20^{1}, and extracts
69 = T.-S. 10 J 9^{25}
70 = A loose leaf in MS. Adler 4020
71 = Oxford MS. Heb. d. 66, fol. 69 (cp. Bodl. 2878^{69}), and T.-S. 13 J 30^{3}
72 = Oxford MS. Heb. f. 39, fols. 29^{b} and 30^{a} (cp. Bodl. 2732)

APPENDIX C (to Ch. IV).

A. C. 1 = T.-S. 13 J 26^{11}
2 = T.-S. 18 J 3^{9}
3 = A loose leaf in MS. Adler 2804
4 = A paper leaf; MS. Adler
5 = A paper leaf, MS. Adler, and an extract from Oxford MS. Heb. c. 28, fol. 59 (cp. Bodl. 2876^{59})
6 = A paper leaf; MS. Adler
7 = T.-S. 13 J 11^{5}
8 = T.-S. 13 J 26^{1}
9 = T.-S. 13 J 13^{17}
10 = A paper leaf; MS. Adler
11 = A letter printed by Harkavy in *Oṣar Ṭob*, 1878, 077–81, where the date is given as 1188 C. E., but really written between 1051–62 C. E.

A. C. 12 = Or. 5544, fol. 1, and Oxford MS. Heb. e. 74, fols. 71ª–72ª (cp. Bodl. 2862[26 b])
13 = T.-S. 13 J 1[8], 16. 248, 13 J 23[13], 26[3]; T.-S. 16. 18, 13 J 19[19], and extracts
14 = 13 J 19[15]
15 = 13 J 16[18]
16 = MS. Adler 2806, fol. 5, and several extracts
17 = T.-S. 13 J 21[21] and several extracts
18 = T.-S. 20. 94
19 = T.-S. 13 J 25[21], 10[11]
20 = Several extracts from MSS. concerning Nesiim
21 = *Karaite Nesiim*. T.-S. 8 K 22[2.3], and extracts from Oxford MS. Heb. a. 3, fol. 42 and d. 66, fols. 49ᵇ–50ª (cp. Bodl. 2873[42], 2878[49.50]); T.-S. 20. 179, 13 J 11[3]
22 = MS. Adler 3765, fol. 1
23 = MS. Adler 3765, fol. 3, and T.-S. 6 J 3[14]
23ª = Oxford MS. Heb. d. 79, fol. 34
24 = T.-S. 12. 109, and several extracts
24ª = Oxford MS. Heb. a. 3, fol. 43 (cp. Bodl. 2873[43 a])
25 = Extracts from T.-S. 13 J 15[23], and other MSS.
25ª = Several extracts from MSS.
26 = T.-S. 20. 106
26ª = T.-S. 10 J 24[1]
27 = Or. 5557, N, fol. 13
28 = Several extracts from MSS.
29 = Or. 5535
30 = MS. Adler 2806, fols. 3, 4, and 2 (this is the proper sequence of the pages)
31 = T.-S. 20. 141
32 = T.-S. 13 J 16[17]

APPENDIX D (to Ch. V).

A. D. 1 = T.-S. 13 J 11[2]
2 = T.-S. 12. 338
2ª = Oxford MS. Heb. c. 13, fol. 20 (cp. Bodl. 2807[16])
A. D. 3 = A leaf in T.-S., Box K 15; Oxford MS. Heb. c. 28, fol. 6 (cp. Bodl. 2876[6]), and several extracts
4 = Numerous extracts from MSS.
5 = Oxford MS. Heb. c. 28, fol. 41 (cp. Bodl. 2876[41])
6 = T.-S. 13 J 15[4], and Oxford MS. Heb. c. 28, fol. 70 (cp. Bodl. 2876[70])
7 = T.-S. 10 J 14[19]
7ª = Oxford MS. Heb. e. 74, fols. 57–58 (cp. Bodl. 2862[20])
8 = T.-S. 32. 8, and extracts
9 = Oxford MS. Heb. d. 68, fols. 27–30 (cp. Bodl. 2836[10])
10 = Or. 5554, B, fols. 21–22, and Oxford MS. Heb. a. 3, fol. 22 (cp. Bodl. 2873[22])
11 = Several extracts from MSS.
12 = T.-S. 20. 114.
13 = Oxford MS. Heb. c. 28, fol. 35 (cp. Bodl. 2876[35])
14 = Numerous extracts concerning Maṣliaḥ Gaon
15 = MS. Adler 2806, fol. 9
16 = Oxford MS. Heb. c. 28, fol. 16 (cp. Bodl. 2876[16], where wrongly described)
17 = *The family of the Nagid Samuel b. Ḥananya*. Oxford MS. Heb., f. 56, fol. 122 and f. 61, fol. 46 (cf. Bodl. 2821[35] and 2855[8]), and numerous extracts
18 = T.-S. 10 J 9[14]
19 = T.-S. 8 J 17[18]
19ª = 10 K 20[1]
20 = *The family of the Gaon Sar Shalom Hallevi*. Numerous extracts from MSS.
21 = A loose leaf in MS. Adler 4020
22 = T.-S. 13 J 31[3]
23 = T.-S. 13 J 20[18]
24 = T.-S. 13 J 20[3], and a leaf in MS. Adler 2738
25 = T.-S. 10 J 14[1], 8 J 33[4], and extracts
26 = T.-S. 13 J 11[4]
27 = T.-S. 13 J 20[9]
28 = T.-S. 13 J 21[10]

A. D. 29 = *The period of Maimonides.* Numerous extracts from MSS.
30 = T.-S. 18 J 4^{20}
30^{a} = A leaf in T.-S., Box J 2
31 = T.-S. 13 J 9^{9}
32 = Several extracts

A. D. 33 = *Abraham Maimuni and his descendants.* Several extracts from MSS.
34 = Contains a critical examination of printed MSS. relating to Abraham Maimuni
35 = Numerous extracts from MSS.

LIST OF ABBREVIATIONS

Arab. Lit. = *Arabische Literatur der Juden*, by M. Steinschneider.
Gr. = Graetz, *Geschichte der Juden.*
H. B. = *Hebräische Bibliographie.*
J. E. = *Jewish Encyclopedia.*
J. Q. R. = *Jewish Quarterly Review.*
J. Q. R., N. S. = *Jewish Quarterly Review*, New Series.
J. R. A. S. = *Journal of the Royal Asiatic Society.*
L. P. = Lane-Poole, *History of Egypt in the Middle Ages*, second edition, 1914.
Ltgsch. synag. Poesie = *Literaturgeschichte der synagogalen Poesie*, by Leopold Zunz.
Mtschr. = *Monatsschrift für Geschichte u. Wissenschaft des Judentums.*
Neub., *Med. Jew. Chron.* = Neubauer, *Mediaeval Jewish Chronicles.*
Pozn. = Poznański.
R. É. J. = *Revue des Études Juives.*
Wüst. = Wüstenfeld, 'Geschichte der Fatimiden-Chalifen' in *Abhandlungen der Königlichen Gesellschaft der Wissenschaften zu Göttingen.*
Z. A. = *Zeitschrift für Assyriologie.*
Z. D. M. G. = *Zeitschrift der Deutschen Morgenländischen Gesellschaft.*
Z. f. H. B. = *Zeitschrift für hebräische Bibliographie.*
Z. D. P. V. = *Zeitschrift des Deutschen Palästina-Vereines.*
ל"ק = לקוטי קדמוניות, by S. Pinsker.

A. M. = Anno Mundi.
A. H. = Anno Hegirae.
C. E. = Common Era.
Sel. = Seleucid Era.
d. = dīnār.

CHAPTER I

From the Conquest of Egypt by Jauhar (969 C. E.) *to the end of al-Ḥakim's reign* (1021 C. E.).

(1) THE history of the Jews in Egypt since the Arab conquest (639–41) till Jauhar's entry into Fusṭāṭ at the head of the Fāṭimid army (969) is almost entirely shrouded in obscurity. The earliest reference to the Jews in Fusṭāṭ, so far known, is a document of the year 750 C. E.[1] But very little indeed do we know of the life of the important Egyptian Jewry during more than three centuries. The vicissitudes of the country during this period are concisely arrated by Lane-Poole in his *History of Egypt in the Middle Ages*.[2] The Jews no doubt were treated in the same manner as the other non-Muslim inhabitants, the people of the tribute (*ahl al-dhimma*). Only a few stray details concerning the Jews can be gathered. When Alexandria surrendered to 'Amr ibn al-'Aṣī in 641, one of the conditions of the capitulation was that the Jews (who doubtless helped to furnish the tribute-money) should be allowed to remain in the city. Their number is reported to have been 40,000, while 70,000 fled before the occupation.[3] The Jews in Egypt used to be distinguished in this period by a different dress. This is evident from the following story which we read in the *History of the Patriarchs of the Coptic Church of Alexandria* (in Graffin-Nau, *Patrologia Orientalis*, V, 1910, 15–16). Samad, the governor of a castle at Alexandria, summoned John, Patriarch in 677–86 C. E., 'before him and threatened him with many threats, and brought him *the garments of a Jew*, and swore that if he would not pay the sum of money that he had first required of

[1] See *J. Q. R.*, XVII, 426–30; cp. N. S., VII, 477.

[2] Second edition, 1914, pp. 1–91, to be cited here as L.-P.

[3] L.-P. 11; Wüstenfeld, *Die Statthalter von Ägypten zur Zeit der Chalifen*, p. 11 (in *Abhandlungen der Königl. Gesellschaft der Wissenschaften zu Göttingen*, vol. 20).

him, he would clothe him with those garments and defile his face with ashes and lead him round the whole city'. 'Some Jews started a litigation against Ibn Ḥujairah (a judge who held office about 716 C.E.) before ʿOmar b. ʿAbd 'l-ʿAzīz and claimed that he had taken money from them.'[1] When the Byzantines landed at Damietta (May 22, 853) they slew a large number of Muslims in the town, while the women and children and the protected people (i.e. Jews and Christians) were carried into captivity.[2]

We have to pass on to the reign of Aḥmad ibn Ṭūlūn (868–84) to glean some further information about the Egyptian Jews. Masʿudi reports of a religious disputation held in the presence of this ruler between his Jewish physician and a Copt, a Jacobite Christian.[3] The Patriarch of the Copts, Michael, had to sell to the Jews a church in Fusṭāṭ in order to pay the sum demanded from him by Ibn Ṭūlūn, as we read in the *Churches and Monasteries of Egypt* (attributed to Abū Saliḥ, translated by Evetts in *Anecdota Oxoniensia*, Semitic Series, VII, 1895, p. 136). 'At the upper end of this ground there is a cemetery of the Jews and Samaritans, and when they come near the Christian cemetery they see the sign of the Cross, and then they return to that part of the ground which Anbā Michael, the 56th patriarch, sold to the Jews, at the time when Aḥmad ibn Ṭūlūn extorted money from him. This patriarch also sold a church to the Jews in the Ḳaṣr ash-Shamaʿ, besides the property of the churches at Alexandria, and the herds of camels of the monks of the monastery of Saint Macarius.' The church was subsequently converted into a synagogue (note 3). Cp. also Wüstenfeld, *Macrizi's Geschichte der Copten*, 6. When he began building the Square in the capital (in about 870) he commanded the Jewish and the Christian cemeteries to be destroyed. Before his death, when his illness was growing worse, the people were ordered to pray for him, Jews and Christians were also present, but they were separated from the Muslims.[4]

(2) Almost next to nothing is known of the spiritual condition of the Egyptian Jewry. We only hear of the famous

[1] Al-Kindi in his *Governors and Judges of Egypt* (cited in *J. Q. R.*, N. S., VI, 436).

[2] Ibid., *l. c.* (cited in *Byzantinische Zeitschrift*, XXII, 390–91).

[3] This passage from Masʿūdi's *Les Prairies d'or* is cited by Steinschneider in *H. B.*, IX, 26–28; see also *Z. D. M. G.*, XLII, 597–98.

[4] Ibid. (in *J. Q. R.*, N. S., *l. c.*).

Mashallah (770–820), one of the first and most important Arab astrologers, who was probably an Egyptian.[1] But it can be gathered that towards the end of the ninth century the study of Hebrew and Jewish literature was well cultivated in Egypt. Sa'adya was already a scholar of renown when he left Fayyūm for Babylon. He must have had favourable opportunities in his native country for obtaining comprehensive as well as profound Jewish knowledge. Another prominent countryman was the celebrated court physician Isaac Israeli in Ḳairowān.[2] Egyptian Jewry no doubt received spiritual guidance from the Babylonian Geonim and their academies, though it cannot be ascertained to what extent (see *J. Q. R.*, N. S., VII, 477 ff.). On the other hand, the Babylonian schools in their turn obtained a good deal of material support, especially from the numerous Babylonian co-religionists that resided in Egypt. Already in the document of 750, referred to above, we find a Bagdād Jew at the head of the Fusṭāṭ community.[3] A letter from the Pumbedita Gaon, Nehemiah (961–68), to this congregation has recently been edited by me (*J. Q. R.*, N. S., VIII, 343 ff.). This is nearly all we know of Jewish-Egyptian affairs up to the occupation of the country by the Fāṭimids.[4]

By reason of close proximity Palestine had of yore close connexions with the rich land of the Nile. During the Arab dominion

[1] See Steinschneider, *Arab. Literatur der Juden*, § 18.

[2] Ibid., § 28.

[3] Though this Bagdād cannot be that of al-Manṣūr, founded in 761 C. E.; see *J. Q. R.*, N. S., VII, 465.

[4] A number of Hebrew Papyri fragments from Egypt, dating from about 400 C. E. and onwards, have hitherto been published by Dr. Cowley, *Journal of Egyptian Archaeology*, II, 1915, 209–13; *J. Q. R.*, XVI, 1–8; Steinschneider, *Zeitschrift für aegypt. Sprache*, 1879, 93–6; *Magazin*, VI, 250–54; Kauffmann and Müller, *Mitteilungen Papyrus Erzherzog Rainer*, I, 38–44. But they yield very little material of historical interest. A papyrus in the first-mentioned publication (p. 210) begins: (1) מן ראשי הכנסת[ומן אחיכם (2) בני הכנסת שבמ[צרים (3) אניכה ראש הכנ[סת . . . (4) ולזקני הכנסת ול[כל . . . (5) הקה׳ הקדוש . . . If the reading שבמ[צרים] (l. 2) be correct, the fragment would date from the Muhammedan period when Miṣr (מצרים) was the usual name for Fusṭāṭ. But another place beginning with מ׳ can be meant here. Another fragment (*l. c.* 212 b), no doubt from the pre-Muhammedan (i. e. Byzantine) period begins, (1) . . . מן אושיא בן י[צחק . . . (2) . . . קראום לראשי ה[כנסת . . . (3) . . . ו . . ולפרוסטטין. Dr. Cowley remarks that פרוסטטין = *προστάται* is a new word equivalent to Parnasim; אושיא = אושעיא.

they became the more so after Ibn Ṭūlūn, the powerful viceroy of Egypt, occupied Syria in 878. Since then this province, which included Palestine, became, with brief intermissions, a dependency of Egypt.[1] The Palestinian Jews had thus on many occasions to appeal for help to their Egyptian brethren. The latter were on the whole more numerous and prosperous, wielding much influence. The seat of the government being in Fusṭāṭ, the Jewry of the Holy Land would bring their political grievances to the notice of their influential co-religionists that resided in the Egyptian capital, requesting them to intervene on their behalf. Moreover, the Palestinian academy, which most likely existed during the whole period, as will be shown farther on, undoubtedly was a spiritual factor of some weight on the Egyptian Jews.

(3) In 969 Jauhar conquered Egypt for his master, the Fāṭimid Caliph al-Moʿizz. This dynasty reigned over the country for two centuries (till the death of al-ʿĀḍid in 1171). The conquest must have brought about a tremendous change for the Jews. If the Aḥimaʿaṣ Chronicle is to be given full credence, they had a powerful advocate at the court of al-Moʿizz. It was Palṭiel who organized the occupation of the country and who remained the trusted Wezīr of this ruler as well as of his son al-ʿAzīz. Moreover, if the identification of Palṭiel with Jauhar be correct, the Jews must have reaped great advantages from the change of rule in Egypt.[2] But it is remarkable that so far nothing has been found in the Genizah MSS. which could shed light on the important and romantic personality of Palṭiel.

The highly-placed Jews in the state must have been a cause of constant chagrin to fanatical Muslims. It is appropriate to cite here an interesting passage from Kremer, *Culturgeschichte des Orients* (I, 188; cp. *H.B.*, XVII, 68–9), 'Some Muhammedan lawyers permitted the employment of non-Muslims for the post of a subordinate Wezīr. The Shiʿite dynasty of the ʿObeidites (the Fāṭimids), who ruled over Ifrikiyya and afterwards over Egypt, acted upon this decision and allowed a Jew to be Wezīr. A contemporary poet in Egypt alludes to this in the following verses, which testify to the keenness and enterprise

[1] L.-P. 158 ff.; cp. pp. 66–7, 72–8, 82–9.
[2] For the latest discussion of this problem see Marx, *J.Q.R.*, N.S., I, 78–85.

of the Jews: "The Jews of our times reached the goal of their desire and came to rule. Theirs is the dignity, theirs the money! Councillors of the state and princes are made from them. O people of Egypt! I give you advice: Become Jews, for Heaven has become Jewish".'

(4) The renegade Jew, Jacob ibn Killis, a native of Bagdād, occupied a very high position in the state. He accompanied in 942 his father to Ramlāh, where he stayed for some time and became a commercial agent. Unsuccessful in this capacity, he went to Fusṭāṭ, where the ruler Kāfūr noticed his abilities and retained his services. After his conversion to Islām in 966 he became a high official. But the exactions of his jealous superior, Ibn Furāt, forced him, after Kāfūr's death, to leave Egypt. He proceeded to al-Mo'izz in Ifrikiyya, where he joined the Jews at the Caliph's court. Jacob brought the chaotic conditions prevailing at that time in Egypt to the Caliph's notice, who was thus confirmed in his resolve to conquer the fertile country of the Nile. Naturally his services were rewarded when al-Mo'izz attained the aim of his life. In 973 the court was transferred from Ḳairowān to Cairo, where the Caliph spent the last two years of his life. Jacob ibn Killis shared with 'Asluj the land administration. The next ruler, al-'Azīz, appointed him Wezīr in 978–9. This position Jacob occupied till his death in 991. He seems to have adopted a friendly attitude towards his former co-religionists. It is even said that he died a Jew and was only outwardly a Muslim. But Muhammedan writers deny the assertion.[1]

A Christian source, which makes Jacob to have been already the Wezīr of al-Mo'izz, relates of frictions between him and the Coptic Patriarch Abraham (Leroy, *Histoire d'Abraham le Syrien, patriarche copte d'Alexandrie*, in *Revue de l'Orient Chrétien*, 1909, 380 ff.). Al-Mo'izz is stated to have been much attached to this Patriarch. The Caliph had a Wezīr, Jacob ibn Khalis, who came with him from the West and who embraced Islām. This Wezīr had a Jewish friend, Moses, who received large gifts from the sovereign and became very wealthy through his friendship with the chief minister of the state. This Moses envied the favour

[1] See Steinschneider, *H. B.*, VIII, 118–22, 140–46, and *Arab. Liter.*, § 60; De Goeje, *Z. D. M. G.*, LII, 77; L.-P. 101. See also Wüstenfeld, *Die Statthalter von Ägypten*, IV, 51 (in *Abhandlungen*, Göttingen, vol. 21).

shown by al-Moʿizz to the Patriarch. Once a religious dispute took place between this Moses and a certain prelate Severus in the presence of the Caliph, the Wezīr, and the Patriarch. Severus, who was the latter's mouthpiece, used insulting language about the Jews in general and Moses in particular. Since then Jacob ibn Killis bore enmity towards the Patriarch.

This Jewish friend of the Wezīr is probably identical with Mūsa b. al-Razzan (al-Aïzar or Azar, probably corrupt from Elʿazar), a famous doctor in the service of al-Moʿizz, who also retained the services of Mūsa's sons Isḥāḳ and Ismaʿīl. The former's son, Jacob, also acted as physician to this ruler. Another contemporary doctor was Abū Zakaraya b. Sada.[1]

The Samaritans also report that their sect were favourably treated by al-Moʿizz. He appointed as governor of Ramlāh a certain Abū-ʿAbdallah from Bagdād, who honoured the Samaritans. This governor took into his service a certain Samaritan ha-Taḳvi b. Isaac (styled by the people 'The Saviour' המושיע). Ha-Taḳvi's son, Abraham, seems to have also been a high state-official in Ramlāh.[2]

[1] See Loeb, *Magazin*, VII, 102–3; Steinschneider, *Arab. Lit.*, § 55; Poznański, *Mtschr.*, XLIX, 48–9, no. 10.

[2] This seems to be the substance of the rather confused account in the *Chronique Samaritaine* (edited by Neubauer, *Journal Asiatique*, 6ième série, vol. 14, 1869, p. 408). בימיו מלך סרים מבניו דכוש מצרים וארע פלשתים (i. e. Kāfūr) ובכלול יומיו אתא מעד והוא אלמעז (al-Moʿizz) . . . ומלך ארץ מצרים ואתו ליד פאסטון (= Filastin) היא מדינת אלרמלה ואתא גבר עמיר מן מדינת קנת ושמה אבו עבד אללה ואוקר לכל שמראי ובלש מנון גבר לתשמשתה ואלא אשקח (= אשכח) מלוא בתשמישתה אלא גבר טב מן בית אפרים ושמה התקוי בן יצחק אנדתה ושמתה שם עממאי המושיע ודער (= ודייר) בכפר צפריה ועבד באדה כל מלכות פלשתים. Neubauer, p. 446, note 4, remarks to Abū-ʿAbdallāh, 'c'est Azīz, le successeur de Möez.' But this is hardly possible, as the chronicler would not have called al-Moʿizz's son a person 'from Bagdād'. The *Nouvelle Chronique Samaritaine* (edited by Adler and Seligsohn, *R.É.J.*, XLV, 253) does not mention al-Moʿizz at all. It states: בימי כהנתו בא המלך סרים והוא מן כושי מצרים וימלוך את ארץ מצרים ואת ארץ פלשתים וילכוד את כל הערים ויאהב את עדת בני ישראל השמרים ואחרי כן בא אל הארץ הזאת איש שמו עמיר והוא מיושבי עיר בגדאד ושמו עבדאללה והוא היה יאהב את עדת בני ישראל השמרים ועשה עמם כל טוב וחסד ויקח לו מהם איש לשרת ושמו התקוי בן יצחק מבית אפרים ויפקידהו על כל אשר לו וישם את כל עובדי המשפט בידו וימשול עבדאללה את כל ערי ארץ פלשתים ויפקוד עליה התקוי בן יצחק הזוכיר. About ha-Taḳvi's son, . . .

I

(1) The new Genizah material, which is given here, furnishes data for the close of the reign of the second Fāṭimid Caliph of Egypt, al-ʿAzīz (975–96). Palṭiel is supposed to have died at the beginning of the Caliph's reign.[1] Till 991 Ibn Killis occupied the Wezīrate and was the monarch's right-hand man. During his period of office Egypt enjoyed tranquillity and prosperity. About four years after his death a Christian, ʿĪsā b. Nestorius, became Wezīr in Cairo for about a year and ten months. His chief deputy was the Jew Menasse, who carried on his duties in Damascus, the capital of the province of Syria. The following is the account given by Wüstenfeld in his history of the Fāṭimid Caliphs.[2] ʿĪsā was hard-hearted and an usurer who grasped for himself every lucrative business, and augmented very much the taxes. He favoured his co-religionists and placed them in the important offices of state, while removing the former Muslim secretaries and tax-collectors. As his chief deputy in Syria he chose a Jew, Menasse b. Ibrāhīm, who showed there the same regard for the Jews as ʿĪsā did for the Christians in Egypt, by reducing their taxes and appointing them as officials. Thus the followers of these two religions ruled the state. This caused great indignation amongst the Muslims. As a result of their protests, the Caliph ordered the arrest of ʿIsā and his Christian assistants. He also sent word to Syria to take hold of Menasse and the Jewish tax-collectors and hand over the administration of the province to Muhammedan officials. But ʿĪsā was soon restored to his dignity through the interventior of the Caliph's daughter.

What happened to Menasse is not clear. Wüstenfeld in his account simply repeats his Arabic sources, whose authors were naturally hostile both to ʿĪsā and Menasse. They are accordingly portrayed in rather unfavourable colours. Some chroniclers even

see Neubauer, *l.c.*, p. 409, התקוי ובנו אברהם ואנדה אבו עבד אלה למדינת פאסון והיא אלרמלה ועבד באדה כל ארעתה והוליד בר וקרא שמו רוח.

[1] Cp. Kaufmann, *Z. D. M. G.*, LI, 441–2.

[2] *Geschichte der Fatimiden-Chalifen* in 'Abhandlungen der Göttinger Königlichen Gesellschaft der Wissenschaften', vol. 27, Abt. II, 64–6, to be cited here as Wüst.—'Wüstenfeld's work is only a *résumé* of sources, but no history'—C. H. Becker. *The Cambridge Mediaeval History*, II, 764.

maintain that al-Moʿizz had both these dignitaries crucified (so Jamal ad-Dīn ibn Tughri-Bardi).[1] But this is evidently incorrect. ʿĪsā resumed his office soon after his arrest. At the beginning of al-Ḥakim's reign he lost his life (7th Muḥarram, 387 A. H.).[2]

We are now able to give new information about Menasse from Jewish sources. His full name was Menasse b. Ibrāhīm al-Ḳzāz.[3] Graetz, following Bar Hebraeus, erroneously styles him Menasse ibn Kazra, just as he makes both him and ʿĪsā to have been the Caliph's representatives at Damascus.[4] The first fragment of Appendix A (to be designated as A. A.) contains a long poem addressed to Menasse's son ʿAdiyyah. He is described as a secretary (Kātib, Sopher) of great dignity, a friend of princes and rulers. He is respected by his co-religionists for his charity and generosity (l. 31 ff.). We find him in Damascus taking the part of the opponents of Solomon b. Yehuda, the Gaon of Jerusalem, as will appear in the third chapter. In the corresponding fragment (given in Appendix B = A. B. No. 57, l. 9) he is mentioned as ʿAdi b. Menasse known as b. al-Ḳzāz.[5]

The chief interest, however, lies here in the eulogy of his late father Menasse (A. A. 1, l. 16). The Wezīr's greatness is described in lines 2–28. They probably contain a great deal of exaggeration. Their author, it should be borne in mind, requires the assistance of ʿAdiyyah. Yet the panegyrics certainly contain a substratum of truth. Menasse was a general like Joab b. Ṣeruyah, and his banner shone with royal splendour. His name was 'healing and life' to his people, who greatly rejoiced at his dignity. The enemies of the Jews could achieve none of their evil designs owing to Menasse's protection. His authority extended to Damascus, Aleppo, Tyre, Sidon, and Ramlāh. A

[1] Ed. Carlyle, *Arab.*, p. 5, top, ثم صلبهم. Cp. also Gottheil, *Z. A.*, XXVI, 205, who cites other sources.

[2] So Wüst. 71; see L.-P. 124, and especially De Sacy, *Religion des Druses*, I, cccii, note 3.

[3] Ibn al-Athīr, s. ann. 380, 386, mentions only Menasse b. Ibrāhīm (cp. Goldziher, *J. Q. R.*, XV, 74). But the Kunya al-Ḳzāz is verified by the Genizah fragments given here.

[4] *Geschichte der Juden*, vol. V, 369–70, 4th edition, to be cited as Gr. v[4].

[5] For the name al-Ḳzāz, cp. T.-S. 24. 44 (cited by Worman, *J. Q. R.*, XVIII, 26), which mentions אלדא[ר אלמערופה] בסלאמה אליהודי אלקזאז and Bodl. 2805[9]: אבו אלפצ[ל] אלקזאז בן אבו אלבראכת הידוע בן אלמקדסי mentioned in a will dated 1189 C. E.

number of Arab tribes were humiliated by him. But he looked after the interests of his co-religionists. He made the children of Aaron and David rejoice and gladdened the heart of the sons of the congregation of the Levites (l. 24). He probably supported the Palestinian Geonim, some of whom were then of priestly descent, as will be shown hereafter.[1] By the expression 'the children of David' may be meant those Geonim who claimed Davidic origin. But also the Nesiim (Patriarchs), of whom we shall hear anon, may have benefited by Menasse's bounty. It is expressly stated that he 'departed from his community in good fame' (l. 28); this seems to disprove the report of his execution, as found in the Arab chroniclers.

Whether Menasse's authority extended to all the places mentioned in the above eulogy is difficult to ascertain. The sway of the Fāṭimids over Syria was never stable and complete. Frequent insurrections occurred in this province and on several occasions order had to be restored by armies dispatched from Egypt. Menasse's régime, as deputy of the Wezīr 'Īsā b. Nestorius, could not have lasted long. About the year 1000 C.E. things were serious indeed for the Fāṭimid rule and the 'Alid cause in Syria. The new Caliph, al-Ḥakim, had to equip an army under 'Alī ibn Ja'far ibn Fellaḥ, which was sent to Damascus in order to suppress the rebellion.[2] The conservative inhabitants of Damascus, the former capital of the 'Omeyyads, were the bitterest foes of 'Ali's descendants, and would submit only by force to a Fāṭimid ruler.

But Menasse's brief management of affairs in Syria and Palestine must have been beneficial to the Jews. About forty years later, the days of Ibn al-Ḳzāz were still cherished by the Damascus Jews as a glorious time for them. In a letter from the Gaon Nathan b. Abraham, a contemporary of Solomon b. Yehuda (given in A. B. No. 72, l. 25 f.), it is mentioned that the people of Damascus celebrated the feast of Purim 'the like of which they did not since the days of Ibn al-Ḳzāz'. His son

[1] A small fragment (in T.-S., Box K 16) contains the following three lines in early hand-writing, (1) לא יכזבו מימיו ישא שלום משע[ר] (2) הישיבה האהרונית הנעזר בשם אלהי יעקב ומכלל (3) סיעתנו ומקהלותינו כי בחמלת צורנו הנודה. The writer is probably a Palestinian Gaon, and also priest.

[2] Cp. especially Hartmann, *Z. D. P. V.*, XXIV, 1901, 56 ff.

ʿAdiyyah remained in this city, where he held an influential position as a Kātib. We find him wielding authority in a dispute in which Solomon b. Yehuda and his academy were involved, as will be shown in a later chapter. He had two sons, Samuel and Ishmael, who are mentioned in our poem as dignitaries (ll. 40–41). The author of this eulogy is unknown. He solicits ʿAdiyyah for support, thereby enabling him to return to his father, who would join him in proclaiming the generosity of their benefactor (ll. 57–58). It seems that they were both people of scholarly standing. It is possible that they belonged to the Palestinian school. The MS. is evidently the original. How it found its way to the Genizah is difficult to say. Perhaps some of ʿAdiyyah's descendants settled in Egypt. We have seen above that the name al-Ḳzāz occurs in other Genizah fragments.

(2) Having established the full name and status of our Menasse, we are able to identify a portion of a Diwān by a contemporary poet. The second number of A. A. contains poems in old handwriting, probably of the end of the tenth century and thus presenting the author's own copy. There is a gap between fols. 9 and 10.[1] There are in all eighteen poems, five of which are incomplete. Poem VI has the superscription, 'And he (the poet) wrote to Abū Sulaiman complaining about the delay of an answer from Menasse b. Ibrāhīm al-Ḳzāz to an eulogy'. The poet is indignant that his beautiful verses, so skilfully wrought, had no effect on this high dignitary. He expected that Menasse would send a reply and benefit the author. The poems fully deserve the praise bestowed upon them by their writer. He uses already with great ease the Hebrew metre, which in Saʿadya's time was quite unknown and is supposed to have originated with Dunāsh b. Labrāṭ.[2]

Our poet lived towards the end of the tenth century and probably resided in a Syrian city. It is difficult to ascertain his identity. At first sight one might identify him with ʿAlvan b. Abraham, some of whose poems were published by Davidson

[1] Two poems of this Diwān are also to be found in another fragment in T.-S., Box K 8.

[2] Cp. Brody, *Studien zu den Dichtungen Jehuda ha-Levi's*, 10 ff. In reality the metre must have been introduced by a school of poets in the Orient, and Dunāsh was the first to make it known in Spain. Compared to our poet here, his handling of the metre is still amateurish.

(*J. Q. R.*, N.S. II, 221 ff.). One of these is addressed to a certain Ḥananya. As will be shown at the end of this chapter, this scholar was the 'Father' of the Palestinian academy under Joshiah Gaon, whose date is known from a document of 1015 C.E. The chronology would thus be no obstacle. ʿAlvan apparently lived somewhere in Syria. But a comparison of the two sets of poems militates against this identification. The poems discussed here are decidedly superior both in diction and in thought. Two kinds of metre are used, the Wafir, employed by preference by most Jewish poets, and the Hazaj.[1] In the MS. the lines run on. Only the hemistichs are divided by colons (:). Here and there words are vocalized. The poems are given in the Appendix in the usual way with full vocalization. They fully deserve publication because, in addition to their age and beauty of diction, they introduce us to several personages of the close of the tenth century about whom nothing was known previously.

Of the first poem only a few words are preserved, and its character cannot be ascertained. No. II is addressed to ʿAbū'l-Faraj Joshuʿa al-Kmudi. He is praised as the 'crown of his people and the glory of his community' whom our lord made his representative, to pray to God for his people. He also chose him as leader (ראש) to Israel (ll. 2–5). Probably our Joshuʿa was a Ḥazzan and had also the title of Rosh (= ראש הפרק, see *infra*, p. 269 f.). But who is the person who appointed him? He is called 'our lord whom the whole people praise, that there is none like him in the diaspora. They compare him to God's angel.' It is he that made Joshuʿa 'a dignitary (נגיד) amidst his people as Moses did to Joshua his minister' (l. 6 ff.). Either this chief authority was the Egyptian Nagid, or, less likely, the Babylonian Exilarch. Perhaps he is to be identified with one of the Nesiim of whom the other poems speak. Where Joshuʿa held office is entirely unknown.

Poem III, written to Samuel b. al-Lebdi,[2] expresses beautifully

[1] Cp. Halper, *J. Q. R.*, N.S., IV, 198 ff., 212–13.

[2] Probably of Lebda, on the North-African coast, east of Tripoli. This name occurs in documents of 1093 and 1102 (Bodl. 2878[66] and *R. É. J.*, LVI, 233), אלשיך אבו יעקב מר' יוסף בר מר' דויד אללבדי; MS. Adler 2594 contains also a document of 1102 C.E. wherein יוסף דידיע בן אללבדי is mentioned. It seems that this coast-town had a Jewish community in the tenth and eleventh centuries.

sentiments of sympathy with a sick friend. The poet laments his own illness, which prevents him from visiting his bedridden friend. 'I am ill and you too, and between us a day's journey and inaccessible wastes. My heart flies to thee like eagles, but my feet are chained so that I cannot visit thee' (ll. 10–11). This Samuel is entirely unknown. In No. IV our poet complains about his having to leave a great scholar, X. b. David, whom 'God relegated to explain the obscurities of the law and to elucidate the secret of the statute' (l. 9) The identity of this scholar is also obscure. The next poem (V) is addressed to the same person. Our poet rates him for not keeping his promises to him. This does not become a man of his type. He is styled נגידי (l. 5). Our writer concludes in a charming manner, 'As long as you live I shall claim my vows (i.e. the vows of thy friendship due to me), and when I die, I shall bequeath them to my children'.

Poem VI is about Menasse, who did not treat our author as he deserved. It is addressed to Abū Sulaiman, who advised him to send Menasse a letter of eulogy and thereby be rewarded. As no answer came, the poet writes indignantly, 'Is this the man whom people everywhere meet with pomp? His promises are like a passing shadow. The seeker of his assistance finds the doors of his house closed' (ll. 4, 10–11). Here we find Menasse spoken of disparagingly. Abū Sulaiman is unknown to me. He was apparently our poet's patron. On Purim he sent him presents for which he composed a poem of thanks (No. VII), of which the beginning only is preserved.

Between fols. 9 and 10 there is a gap. Thus the beginning of Poem VIII is missing. It is composed in honour of a Nasi. 'Our congregation greatly rejoiced on that day with this lord Ṣemaḥ (literally: "causing to sprout the best of sprouts"), and we were pleased when beholding (the people) speaking of the greatness of our Nasi, the anointed one' (ll. 2–3). A Nasi Ṣemaḥ of the end of the tenth century is unknown. He is hardly identical with the Ḳaraite Nasi Ṣemaḥ in Fusṭāṭ who is mentioned in a document of 1036 C.E. (given in Appendix C, No. 21, 1); it is unlikely that a Rabbinite, as our poet was,

Probably (אל)לכדי? in Steinschneider's list (*J. Q. R.*, XI, 132) should read (אל)לבדי.

would have thus eulogized a Ḳaraite descendant of David. In the next composition (No. IX) he laments his separation from a Rabbi Nissim, to whom he was much attached. In No. X he takes up the defence of one of his friends against certain people. One of the Nesiim (בעץ̇ אלרוסא) receives compliments in the next poem (No. XI). His name is illegible. He is styled 'the prince of God, the son of His anointed one' (i.e. King David, l. 4).

Abū Sulaiman, the poet's intimate friend, is ill. It seems that he became blind. This forms the subject of No. XII. Though still young, Abū Sulaiman is a light created by God to illumine the path of his people. 'His spear is wisdom, his weapons the pen and the reed.' The death of a Nasi's son, called b. 'Aubal, is lamented in No. XIII. We know now of a Jacob b. 'Aubal at Fusṭāṭ, a great supporter of the Babylonian schools, who lived at this time. After him his son Joseph looked after the interest of the academies.[1] But these benefactors are not mentioned as having descended from David. Perhaps our poet does not mean an actual Nasi when styling the dead young man 'the son of my people's prince'. On this assumption, a brother (or son) of the above Jacob b. 'Aubal may be lamented here. He evidently died when still young (cp. l. 10). The remainder of the poems are addressed to anonymous persons. Interesting is No. XV, which is an ironical composition thanking for presents. The poet expected substantial support but received a cheese. For such gifts in kind on a more generous scale, there exists a poem of thanks by Yehuda Hallevi to the Nasi Ibrāhīm b. Barūn.[2] Poem XVIII is to an anonymous friend whose relations to the writer seem to have become strained. Expressing his grief, the latter appeals in a touching manner for a renewal of their intercourse.

All these poems are of a personal character and touch upon no general theme such as love, the state of Israel, God's rule of the world. But we possess only a part of the Diwān and it is impossible to ascertain how it was arranged. The persons referred to in the above poems probably resided either in Egypt or in Syria. Damascus and Aleppo must have had considerable

[1] *J. Q. R.*, N. S., VIII, 350, 357–8.

[2] Diwān, ed. Brody, I, p. 7, no. 7, ע״ד הנשיא אבו אברהים [בן] ברון אחרי שלחו לו ממאלקה שקדים וצמוקים תאנים ואתרוגים.

Jewish communities. One of the seven gates of the latter town was called Bāb al-Yahūd.[1] Very little is known of the state of affairs in the Syrian Jewry soon after Menasse's period of office (see, however, *infra*, p. 72 f.). The above poems introduce us to Nesiim, scholars and communal leaders whose activities will become, let us hope, better known by further Genizah finds.

II

(1) Both on account of numbers and influence, the Egyptian Jewry held a predominant position amongst their brethren, residing in the Fāṭimid empire. But, unfortunately, the Genizah has so far preserved very little material about the internal affairs of this community up to about 1000 C.E. A few names of scholars and communal leaders of the second half of the tenth century have come down to us. Elḥanan, the father of the famous Rabbi Shemarya, was probably Rosh in Fusṭāṭ in the time of Nehemiah, Gaon of Pumbedita (961–8). But what the dignity of Rosh really denoted is obscure. It will be discussed more fully farther on. About the year 1000 there lived in Fusṭāṭ Jacob b. ʿAubal and his son Joseph, who were the representatives of the Babylonian academies in this country. They are both styled Alluf and Rēsh-Kallah. Probably they belonged to the Babylonian section in Fusṭāṭ. But the outstanding scholar of the time was undoubtedly Shemarya b. Elḥanan. As we have seen elsewhere, he studied at Pumbedita under Sherira and was 'head of the row of the Nehardeans' at the school. Together with his colleagues Hushiel, the father of Ḥananel, Moses and his son Ḥanok, (the famous 'Four Captives'), he went on a mission to North Africa and Europe on behalf of the academy. He was captured on board ship and ransomed at Alexandria, probably in 970 C.E. Shemarya apparently visited the school of Pumbedita no more but settled

[1] So Muḳaddasi, 985 C.E. The Persian traveller Naṣīr-i-Khusrau, who visited the city in 1047 C.E., mentions only four gates, one of which is the Jewish Gate (see Le Strange, *Palestine under the Moslems*, pp. 361–2). It was called so because the Jewish quarter was on its inner side, and the Jewish cemetery on its outer (see Kremer, *Sitzungsberichte der Wiener Akad. der Wissenschaften, histor.-philos. Klasse*, IV, 226).

in Fusṭāṭ. Sherira and Hai corresponded with him in 991.[1] In the course of our remarks here it will be shown that his funeral took place on the last day of the year 1011. We may therefore assume that Shemarya's activity in Fusṭāṭ lasted for about forty years.

The praises of Shemarya were sung by several writers. Hitherto compliments bestowed upon him by Sherira and Hai were known.[2] Ḥushiel, the father of Elḥanan, eulogized the Egyptian Rabbi from Ḳairowān.[3] But his fame spread even to Spain. No less a person than Dunāsh b. Labrāṭ made his muse sing in honour of our scholar. A. A. 3 contains a poetical preamble of a letter by Dunāsh to Shemarya b. Elḥanan. Unfortunately the letter itself has not been preserved. Only the introductory poem is at our disposal. It is in the same metre as the poem דעה לבי חכמה at the beginning of Dunāsh's refutations against Menaḥem b. Sarūḳ.[4] The Rabbi is compared to a sea of wisdom and all intellectual qualities. A great authority with an equal reputation, he is a fount of living instruction. Everybody has leisure, not so our scholar. Generous to students and sages, he is the grace of the two academies by his good counsel. It is doubtful whether both the Sura and the Pumbedita schools are meant, or only the latter in addition to the Palestinian academy. The second alternative is more probable. As we shall see presently, Samuel the 'Third' (השלישי) of the Palestine school was a great friend of Shemarya's. Dunāsh concludes that our Rabbi was zealous for God's cause and built schools. Here very likely his own academy in Egypt is meant.

Shemarya must have been a celebrated preacher. This is evident from a letter from Samuel the 'Third' to him (A. A. 4). It is written for the purpose of introducing a disciple of Samuel's, Nathan b. Abraham (b. Saul), who is going to Egypt to claim the inheritance left by his father, who died there. Samuel requests the Rabbi to interest himself in this young student. He is probably identical with the later Gaon and Nathan b. Abraham, a hitherto unknown contemporary of Solomon

[1] All this is based on my remarks in *J. Q. R.*, N. S., VIII, 343 ff.; IX, 168 ff.

[2] *J. Q. R.*, VI, 222–3, and N. S., VIII, 352–3; also *Saadyana*, No. XLVII (*J. Q. R.*, XIV, 494, l. 85 ff.).

[3] *J. Q. R.*, XI, 643–50.

[4] Ed. Filipowski, p. 1; Brody and Albrecht, שער השיר, pp. 3–5.

b. Yehuda. A few of his letters are discussed at the end of the third chapter. In his epistle, Samuel praises Shemarya for the excellency of his sermons, discourses, decisions, and explanations. He is further commended for having founded a school for the study of the Torah, where his congregations eagerly imbibe his instruction. There is undoubtedly much flattery and exaggeration in all these praises of our Egyptian scholar, as was the fashion of the time in Muslim countries. Yet a genuine substratum remains which was certainly due to the Rabbi's great merits.

(2) Samuel the 'Third' b. Hoshana, as his full name was, is known as a liturgical writer. The data about him are collected in A. A. 5. Though attached to the academy, he seems to have presided over the Bet-Dīn at Damascus. His son, Abraham, is a signatory to a document of divorce, dated 1022 C.E., at Ramlāh. But it cannot therefrom be ascertained whether his father was then still alive. In a letter to Abraham b. Isaac Hakkohen, a very influential physician in the period of Solomon b. Yehuda (*infra*, p. 84 ff.), Abraham mentions his father as already departed from this life (נ״ע). Samuel must have been an intimate friend of Shemarya. We find him in Fusṭāṭ during the days of mourning for his famous friend.

As will be presently shown, this happened in the first days of 1012. Let us first discuss A. A. 6. It forms a very damaged part of a letter by some unknown writer who was present at the demise of the Rabbi and evidently belonged to his intimate circle. He passed through many vicissitudes. For two years and five months he was probably away in the Magreb (modern Algiers and Morocco). During his absence, the Caliph's messenger inquired after him, evidently having some monetary claim against him. On his return to Fusṭāṭ, he lost three sons who fell victims to the plague that raged in the city. On account of this he stopped there for some time (ll. 1–9). The author of our fragment seems to have been a traveller on his way from the West to some unknown destination. Meanwhile Shemarya became ill and died. As we shall read later on, Elḥanan, his son, was then at Damascus. During the days of mourning Samuel 'the Third' arrived and a great memorial service was held. Probably the Palestinian scholar preached the sermon. Meanwhile denunciations to the Caliph resulted in the arrest of the writer as well as of Samuel, together with twenty-three other people. The prisoners were in danger of their lives. But subsequently they were released in honour. When the letter was written (or more likely copied) Samuel 'the Third' was no longer alive. He is therefore mentioned with ז״ל after his name (l. 11).

(3) The events in connexion with the arrest and the release of these Jews will presently be described. But prior to this A. A. 7 should be discussed. It contains three elegies, skilfully written, using Biblical verses, on the death of some great scholar. The third composition is found partly in two manuscripts. This shows that it was known to more than one person. Internal evidence strengthens me in the belief that the lamented scholar is none else but Shemarya. And I incline to think that the author of the elegies was Samuel 'the Third', who is known as a writer of liturgical compositions. No metre is employed, but the strophes have both internal and external rhyme. Only three strophes have been preserved of the first elegy. It is alphabetical and extends to the letter *kāf*; hence in all eleven strophes. The dead scholar is called 'the unique person of the generation' for whom the disciples mourn. He instructed them in the Torah gratuitously (l. 3 ff.). The second poem has the heading 'Another one (*sc.* composition) by him ז״ל' (referring to the author who was no longer alive when this MS. was written). The strophes are preceded by two lines, 'Behold the sound of bitter cry from the daughter of my people at Ṣoʿan (i.e. Fusṭāṭ).[1] Is not the Rabbi (הרב, as Shemarya is styled by Dunāsh and other correspondents) in her midst or has he gone to the grave?' Eight strophes follow in alphabetical order; of letter ח only the first line is preserved. There is a gap between fols. 55 and 56. It is therefore unknown how far this elegy extended. The first strophe need not be taken to mean that the departed scholar was a priest. This would dispose of our identification with Shemarya, since he is never styled a Kohen. The author merely enumerates the representatives of the Torah, viz. priest, wise man, and Rabbi (איה כהן ותורתו · וחכם ועצתו · ורב ומשנתו).[2] The latter is of primary importance. He is the lamented scholar. The disciples

[1] For Ṣo'an = Fusṭāṭ, cp. Worman, *J. Q. R.*, XIX, 726.

[2] The line is obviously modelled after Jer. 18. 18.

are bidden to put on mourning because 'the light of the land has departed and a breach has been made in Ṣoʿan; the Rabbi has been snatched away and the Western light[1] extinguished' (strophes 3 and 4). Letter א is missing from the third elegy, which is also alphabetical. It extends to letter מ. Of these letters ל–מ are found in two copies. Therein the Palestinian Jews are summoned to mourn for the great dead who taught Bible, Mishnah, Tosaphot (i.e. Tosiphtot), and Talmud. The profoundest tractates he could explain. Who will replace him? Egypt is confused and Palestine trembles. The Palestinian academy vies with the Babylonian school in the expression of mourning, because their crown has departed (strophes 8–10). This proves that the late Rabbi was a favourite of the schools of both countries. It corresponds exactly to the position of Shemarya b. Elḥanan, eulogized alike by Sherira and Hai on the one hand, and by Samuel 'the Third' of Palestine on the other. Moreover, till Maimonides, Egypt possessed no authority of such standing as described in our elegies. No literary production by Shemarya has so far been preserved. Nor do we possess any letter from him.[2] We can only estimate him from the opinions of other people. And these form one uninterrupted song of praise and eulogy.

(4) To return now to the arrest of the twenty-three Jews in Fusṭāṭ and their subsequent release. It must have been a serious affair involving the safety of the whole Egyptian Jewry. It gave rise to a Megillah which I have found in two versions (A. A. 8 and 9). Each of them is extant in two MSS. A happy combination of fragments renders it possible to fix the events at the beginning of Shevaṭ, 4772 A. M., and thus establish Shemarya's year of death. The late Dr. Neubauer published in *J. Q. R.*, IX, 24–6, an Egyptian fragment, forming a part of a Megillah, wherein al-Ḥakim, the mad Caliph, notorious for his persecutions of Jews and Christians alike, is praised and eulogized. As the occasion which gave rise to this scroll was unknown, futile speculations were made about it by Kaufmann

[1] נר מערבי. From the point of view of a Palestinian, Egypt was in the West. Likewise in a letter by Solomon b. Yehuda (given in A. B., no. 5, l. 16, see p. 83) the Egyptian communities are called קהלות המערב.

[2] Cp., however, A. A. 7[a].

(*Z. D. M. G.*, LI, 442–3). Neubauer failed to point out that between fols. 1 and 2 there was a gap, nor did Kaufmann notice it. A. A. 9 has preserved more of this Megillah, and thus mutually some gaps are filled up. It consisted of 76 verses. In all about 33 verses are extant, and one half is still missing. A. A. 8 presents another version of this scroll. 35 verses of it are preserved. Both copies of A. A. 9 are provided with vowels and accents and are divided into verses just as the Bible text (see A. A. 7^b).[1]

Combining both versions, we have the following account. A great multitude of Jews assembled to do the last honour to Shemarya (A. A. 8, beginning, evidently refers to him, as we know from A. A. 6). While they followed the bier to the cemetery, the Muslim mob abused the Jews and pelted them with stones. The agitators denounced the Jews to the authorities. The charges seem to have been connected with taxes. The governor sent constables to meet the Jews who were returning from the funeral, and arrest them. Many fled, while others escaped by bribery. Twenty-three people were caught, among them Samuel 'the Third' b. Hoshana. They were imprisoned in two jails. This took place on Shevaṭ 3rd, 4772 A. M. = 1323 Sel. = 943 since the destruction of the Temple (Dec. 31st, 1011). On the following morning the prisoners were led to the place of execution. On their route the streets teemed with fanatical crowds of Muslims, who jeered at and reviled these unfortunate and innocent people. They would have been summarily executed had not meanwhile the order been given to lead the prisoners to the Caliph's court and confine them in the prison situated there. On that day the situation was still critical. All the Jews in Miṣraim (Fusṭāṭ) were in great distress and had to hide for safety. The Muslim populace meant to massacre all the Jews. A fast-day was observed and the Jews resolved to appeal on the

[1] The author of this Megillah was probably Samuel b. Hoshana, one of the victims of the persecution. A leaf in T.-S., Box K 6, verso (recto blank), begins: הדא מגלה אלפהא | שמואל השלישי בר | הושענא נבע קאלהא | במצר פי זמאן אלמלך | אלפאטמי אלחאכם | באמר אללה 'This Scroll Samuel the Third b. Hoshana composed in Fusṭāṭ in the time of the Fāṭimid king al-Ḥakim bi-amrillah.' Then a few lines in Jewish Arabic, written and vocalized with red ink follow. This fragment seems to be from an Arabic version of our Megillah.

following morning, Shevaṭ 5th, to the Caliph for mercy. They appeared in a procession before the court and implored the ruler. A re-examination of the accusations took place and their baselessness proved. Out of 200 supposed witnesses only four could give any evidence at all. The prisoners were thereupon released. A certain Ḥazzan, Puṭiel, organized a procession of Jews who acclaimed the Caliph at the court, and then marched through the streets of Fusṭāṭ, finally proceeding to the 'great synagogue', where the Hallel was recited. Three scrolls of the Torah were taken out for reciting the king's prayer. It was then instituted to commemorate the event every year, from Shevaṭ 3rd–5th. The Jews directly affected were to fast all the three days, but the rest of the people only on the day of arrest. It was to be announced on the previous Sabbath that all the Jews of Egypt (Fusṭāṭ) should assemble in fast to thank God and praise the Caliph. The report further mentions that when the accusations levelled against the Jews became known in the small places and the villages around Fusṭāṭ, among the garrisons of the commerce-routes and also in Alexandria, they were threatened with massacre. The Caliph had to send word that this agitation should be stopped. The local Jews assembled in fast and resolved to keep Monday and Thursday (of that week) annually as fast-days. The actual charge brought against the Jews is still obscure. Charges of taxation frauds, even if levelled against twenty-three people, are not likely to cause such a grave crisis as described in our scrolls. Unfortunately both versions are defective at the beginning. The atmosphere in Cairo-Fusṭāṭ must have been charged with hostility to non-Muslims. We are in the time of the fanatic persecutions of al-Ḥakim, which will be discussed presently. The large number of Jews assembled at Shemarya's funeral, combined with specious charges multiplied and exaggerated by gossip of a fanatical crowd, must have caused the brewing storm to burst.

(5) The Caliph al-Ḥakim is greatly praised in both versions for his management of the state and the equity of his rule. Evidently the notorious persecutions of the Jews had not begun yet. The following is the account of Lane-Poole (126–7), 'During the first ten years of (al-Ḥakim's) reign (996–1006) the Christians and the Jews enjoyed the immunity and even the

privileges which they had obtained under the tolerant rule of al-ʿAzīz;[1] but as time went on they came in for their share of irrational persecution. In public they were forced to wear black robes by way of livery; and in the baths, where one man without clothes is very like another, the naked Christians were compelled to distinguish themselves by wearing large and heavy crosses, while the Jews had to wear bells, or in the street display a wooden image of a calf, in pleasing allusion to a discreditable episode in their early history.[2] Next a general order was issued for the destruction of all the Christian churches in Egypt and the confiscation of their lands and property; the work of demolition went on for at least five years (1007–12).' No details are given either by Lane-Poole or by Wüstenfeld (*l.c.* 69 ff.) about the destruction of the Jewish synagogues. But Maḳrizi relates that in Cairo the district of Jaudariyya was once inhabited by the Jews. But when al-Ḥakim learned that the Jews, when amongst themselves, used to assemble and sing defamatory verses about Islām, he ordered one night the gates of the quarter to be closed and set the whole on fire. The synagogue of this district was burnt (cp. Schreiner, *Z.D.M.G.*, XLV, 298–9).[3]

[1] In al-Ḥakim's employ was the Jewish physician al-Ḥaḳīr al-Nafiʿ (see Poznański, *Mtschr.*, XLIX, 49).

[2] The date of these orders cannot be exactly ascertained from the sources (see especially De Sacy, *l.c.*, CCCIX, note 1). Ibrahim b. Wasifshah reports that the Caliph assigned to the Jews a special quarter near the gate of Zawila (Zuweila), in order that they should not mix amongst Muslims.

[3] Also Kalḳashandi (*Geographie u. Verwaltung von Ägypten*, translated by Wüstenfeld, *Abhandlungen der Gesellschaft der Wissenschaften*, Göttingen, vol. 25, 73) writes, 'The street al-Jaudariyya was inhabited by Jews till al-Ḥakim was informed that they oppressed the Muslims and reviled the Muhammedan religion. So one night he shut their doors and had them burned in the quarter. Afterwards the Jews inhabited the street of al-Zuweila.' Interesting is the account of Joseph Sambari, the Egyptian chronicler of the sixteenth century (printed by Gottheil, *O. T. and Semitic Studies in memory of W. R. Harper*, II, 365, note 62, from a Paris MS.): והרס בתי כנסיות של היאודים ולאחר ז׳ ימים חזר אותם לדתם איש איש על עבודתו ועל משאו ובנה פעם שנית הכנסיות שלהם ובליל פסח שרף היאודים במחוז שלהם נקרא אלגודרייא · והסיבה שהיה עובר בהחבא בליל פסח ושמע קול היאודים מקרים את ההגדה לבניהם ומפרשים להם בלשון ערבי · ויהי כאשר שמע שהיו אומרים וימות (וימת r.) מלך מצרים ויאנחו בני ישראל חשב שהיו מקללים אותו שימות · ויחר אפו עליהם ויאמר להם למה שלמתם רעה תחת טובה · זה הדבר אשר החזרתי אותם (אתכם r.) לדתם · ותנתן דת על היאודים

From the praises bestowed upon al-Ḥakim in the above 'scrolls' we can gather that till 1012 the Jews had not yet experienced to the full the Caliph's savage whims. On the contrary, he is commended for the great reforms he introduced in the country. He purified the law-courts and was his own Wezīr. A positive proof that the synagogues were not destroyed before 1012 we have in the mention made of 'the great synagogue' (בית הכנסת הגדולה) of Fusṭāṭ where the Jews assembled on Shevaṭ 5th to celebrate their deliverance (A. A. 8, fol. 6 recto, ll. 14–15). The capital of the empire would have certainly been the first place for the Caliph's decree of demolition to be carried out. But the order was soon to be issued. This we learn from A. A. 10, being a letter from Elḥanan b. Shemarya to Jerusalem. He writes that when his father died he was kept in Damascus, stricken with disease. Also the roads were dangerous for travelling. After some time, when things were less critical, he set out on his journey home. On the way his caravan encountered brigands and they barely escaped with their lives. They also met with accidents on their sea voyage and also along the Nile. Having arrived in Fusṭāṭ, Elḥanan set about to manage the school of his father. He assembled the people on a Sabbath and exhorted them to put aside strife and preserve unity. But soon the persecutions began. Synagogues were destroyed, scrolls of the Law torn up and Bible copies trampled upon. 'We put on dark (garments) and went about in mourning. They put on our loins (signs of) oppression' (מועקות, ll. 31–9). I think there is here an allusion to the special marks which the Jews had to wear on their garments. Elḥanan further states that many Jews became apostates and adopted Islām. Unfortunately the letter breaks off here. It is very likely a copy of the original epistle sent to

אשר במצרים וסגר המחוז שלהם ושרף אותם בלילה אחד והנשארים ברחו ונמלטו ומזה הסיבה החרימו חכמי מצרים שלא ילמדו עוד את בניהם בלשון אלשרח. That since then Arabic was no longer used as the language of religious instruction is hardly credible, as this was the native tongue of the Jews in Egypt. The masses of the people were certainly more familiar with Arabic than with Hebrew. Sambari himself (in Neub., *Med. Jew. Chron.*, I, 116) writes how the Nagid used to read on the last day of Tabernacles (שמחת תורה) the first chapter of Genesis with the translation into Aramaic and Arabic (ומתרגם כל פסוק בלשון תרגום וערבי). This custom continued to the time of Maimonides.

Jerusalem. Hence it is found in the Cairo Genizah. But the handwriting is that of Elḥanan's, as the other letters that follow show. Elḥanan has thus kept copies of the letters he sent to his correspondents.

Of these apostate Jews during the persecutions of al-Ḥakim, Elḥanan speaks also in a poem (published by Davidson, *J.Q.R.*, N.S., IV, 56-60). But on the other hand there were brave Jews who staunchly kept to their faith, and many of them preferred exile. They went even as far as Yemen and the Byzantine dominions.[1] This is borne out by the account given by De Sacy (*l.c.* CCCLIX). In 403 A.H. (1012) the persecution of the Jews and the Christians became most violent and general. The former were ordered to wear in the streets blocks of wood weighing 5 lb. suspended from their neck. The destruction of the churches in Egypt and in Syria was carried out more strictly than before. (The demolition of the synagogues probably began in that year.) In the following year (404 A.H.) the laws against 'the people of the tribute' were made more grievous. But a privilege was granted to those who neither wanted to submit to them nor to adopt Islām, to leave the country for the Greek territories or for Nubia and Abyssinia, and a large number availed themselves of this permit. Towards the end of his reign al-Ḥakim became more tolerant. In 408 A.H. Jews and Christians were granted liberty of conscience (this date is not certain because according to some it was in 411 A.H., the last year of the Caliph's reign, see *l.c.* CCCXCVI-IX). In 1020 all those that adopted Islām were allowed to return to their

[1] P. 56: (9) בגדו מסורת אבתם · בידם מסיני מסורים · (10) יען להג הרבה
ועמל ויגיעת בשרים . . . (30) בנים בלא אמן, בנים סכלים, מרים (31) חלפו
עברו חק, ברית עולם מפירים. On the other hand, those that studied the Torah,
(19) במוסר אביהם תכו, גולים כפרים וערים . . . (21) גלמם חרב שזופים ·
לחוקי חרב מתקדרים . . . (41) מסרו עצמם יקרים, לבאים להאיר מעברים ·
(42) מי מהם בחרב · מי גופים מתכברים (43) נכרכים לוטים ספרים · כלים
בעשן כברים . . . (46) סעו ותלמודם בידם והניחו יתרם לנצרים (50) הכינו להכ
צד ברומה ותימן וקדריב. See Davidson's exposition of the poem (pp. 54-5). His identification with the persecutions of al-Ḥakim is correct. Only, following Graetz (V^4, 388), he takes them to have lasted from 100-820. We know now that those against the Jews began only in 1012.

former religion. In seven days 6,000 renegade Christians abjured their adopted faith. No doubt the Jews acted similarly (see also Wüst., *loc. cit.*, 106 ff., 115–16).

It seems to me that Sambari's account (above, p. 33, note 3) should be understood in this way. The reading 'seven days' is obviously absurd. Most likely read 'seven years'. Accordingly during seven years the destruction of the Jewish synagogues went on. After this period the Jews were allowed to return to their religion and rebuild their houses of prayer. The last cruel act of the Caliph was the burning of the Jewish quarter of al-Jaudariyya. According to Sambari this happened on a Passover night. Just as the churches, the synagogues were pulled down not only in Egypt but in Palestine and in Syria, as we learn from letters discussed in the next section of this chapter.[1]

How the Jewish communities in Egypt fared during this sad time is not fully known, but the Genizah has preserved documents drawn up at Fusṭāṭ in the years 1016–18. It is evident that the congregation kept up its organization, though under difficulties. We find in one of them Ephraim b. Shemarya, afterwards the famous head of the Palestinian community at Fusṭāṭ, declaring before a magistrate that 'we are Jews' and have a court of our own.[2] Documents dated Fusṭāṭ, Tishri, 1328 Sel. (1016 C. E.) and Sivan 1329 Sel. (1018 C. E.) are signed

[1] Sambari (in Neub., *Med. Jew. Chron.*, I, 137, top) writes about the synagogues of Fusṭāṭ: ושתי הכנסיות אחרות של רבנים הם במחוז הנקרא קצר אלשמע הא׳ מכנין אותה אלעראקיין . . . והב׳ . . . מכנין אותה כנסת אלשאמיין . . . ונבנית בשנת שלו היא שנת תשפח (r. תשפה) ליצירה. There is little doubt that there existed in Fusṭāṭ a synagogue of the Palestinians before 1025. Sambari evidently refers to the one rebuilt after the demolitions during the persecutions. It was finished in 1025. Also a Ḳaraite synagogue in Fusṭāṭ was destroyed (see Gottheil, *J. Q. R.*, XIX, 510–12). As to a synagogue in Alexandria, see *infra*, p. 89, note 1.

[2] Bodl. 2834[23] (printed by Pozn., *R. É. J.*, XLVIII, 171–2), l. 16 ff., השיב אפרים זה . . . אדוני שקר הדבר לא כן הוא כי יהודים אנחנו ויש . . . ים עד שיתועדו ויראו בעסקינו. It seems that Ephraim claimed that the Jews had judges (or elders) of their own who met to investigate their lawsuits (see also *J. Q. R.*, N. S., X, 139). The document is signed by (read טליון) שמואל הכהן בר עליון, Joseph b. Benjamin, Yehuda b. Ḥadid, X. Hakkohen b. Abraham. These people were probably the 'elders' of the Palestinian community, acting in the capacity of Dayyanim. Samuel Hakkohen b. (Ab) Ṭalion was later on head of this community (see *infra*, p. 95 f.).

by Jacob b. Joseph (Ab)-Bet-Dīn (T.-S. 13 J 1 $^{3\cdot 4}$), who seems to have been the local Rabbi. He left Egypt, probably owing to the persecutions, and settled in Aleppo. At the head of the community he is mentioned in a document dated Marḥeshvan, 4789 A. M. (1028 C. E.).[1]

Lane-Poole (p. 127) writes that 'many Christians, especially among the peasantry, to escape persecution, accepted the Muhammedan religion; and the office where the declarations of conversion were received on two days in a week was besieged with applications, insomuch that some of these eager proselytes were trampled to death in the crush. Such as remained true to their faith were subjected to various humiliations, and forbidden to ride horses, to keep Muslim servants, to be rowed by Muslim boatmen, or to purchase slaves.' Undoubtedly this was also the case with the Jews, as we have seen above (pp. 34–5). We may assume that the majority of them submitted to all these indignities and restrictions rather than prove faithless to their God. Those that could leave the country emigrated to more tolerant lands. Probably after 1020 most of them returned. A number of Jews adopted Islām, in most cases, no doubt, only outwardly. When al-Ḥakim rescinded his edicts, they must have openly rejoined their former co-religionists. Graetz (*l. c.*) states that in

[1] See the letter to him from Tyre in Wertheimer's גנזי ירושלם, III, 15^{a}–16^{a} = Bodl. 2873^{37}. Our Jacob was also the recipient of the interesting letter from Elijah Hakkohen b. Abraham (printed by Schechter in *Berliner Festschrift*, Hebr. part, 110–12). The writer was not president of the Fusṭāṭ Bet-Dīn, as Schechter assumes, but perhaps lived in Palmyra (for נכתב בסדמוד כֹבֹ להיום (p. 110, l. 5), it appears to me that נכתב בתדמור כֹדֹ לחודש should be read). Benjamin of Tudela found there a considerable community numbering about 2,000 people (*Itinerary*, ed. Adler, 31–2). And indeed the writer of the epistle mentions that he ministers to three congregations, including a Ḳaraite one. Our Jacob was then already in Aleppo. But Elijah recalls in his epistle the kindness his friend showed to him, and to his son, during their stay in Fusṭāṭ (במצרים, l. 18; cp. also *J.Q.R.*, N.S., X, 143). Finally, MS. Adler 1267, fol. 1, contains a letter from Meir הכהן והמלמד b. Menaḥem to Jacob החבר b. יוסף אב בית דין בס[נה]דרין גדולה (verso). In the epistle Jacob as well as the Aleppo congregation (כל הקהל הקודש הדרים במדינת צובה) are greeted. There is no doubt that our Jacob is meant here. We thus learn that his father was Ab of the סנהדרין גדולה, i. e. the academy (probably of Palestine). He was no longer alive in 1016 (as the document cited *infra*, p. 38, note 1, shows). Accordingly he was probably 'Father' under the Gaon Samuel Hakkohen b. Joseph (cp. *infra*, p. 71).

1014 the Jews and the Christians were expelled from the country. This is now disproved, as regards the former, by the fact that we find in 1016 Jews in Fusṭāṭ inhabiting their own quarter, Ḳaṣr ash-Shama' (see Pozn., *l. c.*, 146). Indeed Maḳrizi (in Wüstenfeld, *Geschichte der Copten*, 66) reports that when al-Ḥakim ordered all the Jews and the Christians to emigrate from Egypt to the Greek cities, they came together before the castle at Cairo, asked for protection and referred to the promise (of tolerance) given to them by the Amir of the Muslims. The Caliph thereupon cancelled their expulsion.

(6) In conclusion of this section additional information about Elḥanan b. Shemaya will be discussed. He remained in Fusṭāṭ during the grave crisis through which Egyptian Jewry passed.[1] He was probably unable to maintain his father's school. A few more of his letters are dealt with here. A. A. 11 is addressed to Damascus. It is evident from the many corrections that the fragment, in Elḥanan's handwriting, is only a draft of the original epistle. The sad news reached him of his son-in-law having been drowned while travelling on business. The daughter remained a widow in Ḳairowān in a strange land. It is not clear whether her husband was a native of this town. But their home was probably there (cp. also *J. Q. R.*, N. S., VIII, 356, note 56). In requesting support from his correspondents, Elḥanan states that he made it his rule never to demand assistance from the Caliph till he offers it on his own account. We thus gather the important information that Elḥanan was sometimes the recipient of the sovereign's bounty. This is quite in accordance with the favourable position of the Jews in Egypt prior to al-Ḥakim's persecutions. As principal of the Fusṭāṭ school, Elḥanan (and

[1] The document, dated 1016 C. E. (T.-S. J 1³, see above, pp. 36–7), is signed by

יעקב בירבי יוסף בית דין נ̇נ̇

שלמה בר פשאט   יוסף בן ישראל

אברהם בירבי איוב משה בר עלון

נכתבה עדותו על פיו

זו עדות [כת]ורה אלחנן ראש הסדר בירבי

This shows clearly that Elḥanan remained in Fusṭāṭ during the persecutions. One of the signatories, Joseph b. Israel, is probably identical with Joseph b. Israel of Tustar, the brother of Sahl, and uncle of the two prominent brothers, Abū Sa'ad and Abū Naṣr (see *infra*, pp. 81, 122, note 1, and 150).

very likely his father and grandfather) received a grant from the government. Likewise Joshiah, the contemporary Gaon of Palestine, was maintained by the state, as will be seen farther on. Thereby the schools and their directors gained much in prestige. The constant appeals to the communities for support, as became—forsooth by dire necessity—the practice of the Palestinian Geonim since Joshiah (see farther on) no less than that of the Babylonian Geonim, were hardly conducive to enhance the dignity of the centre of Jewish learning in the eyes of the people. Yet, in truth, the Jewries of all countries contributed generously and freely to the upkeep of the seats of learning in Babylon and in Palestine.

Elḥanan's friends in Damascus were Abraham Ḥazzan, Ephraim and Samuel Hakkohen. He probably made their acquaintance during his stay there in 1012. A. A. 12 is a small epistle addressed to the congregants of the synagogue situated in the house of a certain Mauhub. Elḥanan sends them greetings on Purim and reminds them of the duty of giving presents to the poor. His former letters begin with his name and title. Here only Rosh Hasseder forms the heading, as the letter was local and his handwriting well known. Perhaps owing to the shortage of synagogues after their demolition, prayers were read in private houses. The synagogue in Mauhub's house had a Ḥazzan (Ḥusain) and seems to have been more than a so-called private מנין.[1]

In all the letters known to us, Elḥanan styles himself Rosh Hasseder, or more fully ראש הסדר שלכל ישראל, while his father held the dignity of Ab-Bet-Dīn, שלכל ישראל (cp. *J. Q. R.*, N. S., VIII, 344, in A. A. 10 we have שמריה אב). Only Bodl. 2805[15] contains a legal document signed by אלחנן בית דין בירבי שמריה. Poznański (אנשי קירואן, No. 11, end) maintains that Elḥanan was Ab-Bet-Dīn. But it is far from certain whether he ever held this dignity. He was still Rosh Hasseder in 1020/1. This can be gathered from a somewhat obscure Genizah fragment (published

[1] Perhaps owing to the demolition of the synagogues worshippers met in private houses. It may be that the members of a destroyed synagogue held services in Mauhub's house, where the Reader officiated. A document of 1038 mentions a synagogue of the Rabbinites in Fusṭāṭ as having been in the possession of Musa ibn Ya'ḳūb, the Caliph's physician, for more than forty years (*infra*, p. 83). Accordingly it was not destroyed during the persecutions of 1012–20. Probably it was attached to his private residence, and in this way escaped demolition.

by Kamenetzky, *R. É. J.*, LV, 49–51). A certain person takes the part of the Palestinian Gaon against Elḥanan. The latter wrote to the former not to make any innovation till he shall have received the title of Ab (לבל יחדש דבר עד אשר יקבנו בשם אבות). The expression may also mean, ‘till he (the Gaon) will name him by the title of his fathers’, i.e. that of Ab-Bet-Dīn held by Shemarya. Elḥanan stated that he had arranged a regular course of study, probably in Fusṭāṭ continuing his father's school, and that a certain Barhūn (= Abraham, perhaps Abraham b. Sahlān ?, see *infra*, p. 96 f.) was his assistant. The epistle emanates perhaps from a member of the Palestinian academy, who was, however, familiar with the affairs of Hai's school at Bagdād, where he seems to have stayed for some time. Elḥanan is described as a superficial scholar full of vain boastings. The letter was probably addressed to Yehuda Alluf of Ḳairowān (see about him Pozn., *loc. cit.*, No. 22).[1]

[1] *R. É. J.*, *l. c.*, l. 1 ff.: יהודה אלוף בישיבה שלגולה ותמה אני ממר אלחנן ראש הסדר כי בא ממנו כתָב אל שער הישיבה הגיד לו (read בו) כי שלח כתב אל מרנו גאון צבי יחי לעד הזהירו לבל יחדש דבר עד אשר יקבנו בשם אבות הלא ידע אם לא שמע כי לא יוכל להתערב [בדבר זה] זולתי קדושי ארץ . . הלא ידע מעשיו מפורסמין בצובה ובדמשק וארץ כנען ואולם שררה הוא מבקש והיא בורחת מהימנו וגם נם כי קבע (cp. *R. É. J.*, LVI, 256) פרק וכי ברהון עמד על ראשו בהגדה ושבועה כי כל יושבי האדמות לא ידעו מנהג הפרקים קל וחומר מנהג הישיבה מאי זה מקום ידעו מן הגורן או מן היקב הלא השימוש יתר מן הלימוד וגם חכמי הישיבה מזכירים בכל עת כי בבוא מר אלחנן זה אל בגדד הלך אליו מר רב אסף ראש הסדר זכֹ לבֹ והראה כי הוא גורס לפניו התלמוד גירוס מנומר וזה מקצת דרכיו הנודעים. The fragment is evidently a copy of the original that was sent to Ḳairowān. Verso contains a letter from the Exilarch Ḥezeḳiah. The expression בשם אבות is shortened from בשם אבות בית דין. Thus Sherira in his Letter (ed. Neub., I, 41) writes וסמיכיניה להאיי בננו באבות בית דין; from אב evidently an abstract noun אָבוּת was formed to indicate the dignity. R. Asaph Rosh Hasseder is perhaps identical with ומֹר אסף נמי כך פסק מֹבֹ שיטין, mentioned in a Genizah fragment containing several decisions of Babylonian Geonim (*J. Q. R.*, IX, 689, top). An explanation of his is also mentioned together with one of Hai's by Abraham b. Solomon (*H. B.*, XX, 9). Kamenetzky's emendation כי לא יוכל להתערב [בעיבור וקידוש] is hardly satisfactory; [בדבר זה] seemed to be more likely. For the expression עמד על ראשו, cp. Ginzberg, *Geonica*, I, 25–6. The reference to גאון צבי makes it clear that Elḥanan came into conflict with the ‘Gaon of Palestine’ (ארץ הצבי = צבי). It disposes of the fanciful speculations of Kahana (*Haḳḳedem*, III, 1 ff.) that Elḥanan's antagonist was Samuel b. Ḥofni.

When Elḥanan died is obscure.[1] We only find Solomon b. Yehuda, when already Gaon, speaking disparagingly of him as well as of his son (עובר), as will be discussed in the third chapter. But so far the Genizah sheds no further light on the relations between these two scholars. Not even the name of Elḥanan's son has been preserved.[1]

III

(1) The last section of this chapter will be devoted to Palestinian affairs, more especially to the Gaonate. The province of Syria, conquered in 969 for the Fāṭimids by Jaʿfar b. Fellaḥ, was in a chronic state of revolt (see above, p. 21). On the accession of Aẓ-Ẓāhir in 1021, the authority of the Egyptian government was scarcely felt in this province (L.-P. 158–9). These insurrections, accompanied by the raids of the Karmāṭīs, must have left deep marks on the population. Palestine was swept into the maelstrom of fiercely contending factions. It became frequently the battle-ground of the Egyptian armies coming from the south and the northern invaders. On the whole, the power of the Fāṭimid Caliphs could assert itself more in Palestine, at least as far as Jerusalem, than in distant Damascus. The Palestinian Jews were materially in a bad plight and greatly dependent on the help they received from their Egyptian brethren. This will become evident in the following chapters. Three communities of importance existed in the Holy Land, Ramlāh, the

[1] He was no longer alive in 1026. T.-S. 18 J 2[16] contains a document, drawn up in Iyyar, 1337 Sel., concerning the appointment of a guardian (אפטרופוס) of orphans. Two of them were already of age, as had been proved some time ago before Elḥanam (נתאמ[תו] במושב מֹור אלחנן ראש הסדר נֿעֿ). Elḥanan is also mentioned in T.-S. 16. 304, but the fragment is so faded that very little substantial information can be culled from it. It is addressed to X. b. Aaron the Ḥaber. The preamble covers thirty lines (recto). A brother of a certain Daniel b. Sahl had been claimed at the Muslim court (apparently at Ramlāh) by a co-religionist as his slave. This Jew is to be protected from this preposterous demand, and influential people in Fusṭāṭ are asked to intervene on his behalf. There are mentioned the 'two congregations' (שתי הקהלות, verso, l. 5, i. e. Babylonian and Palestinian), אדוננו הסגן (l. 7), Ephraim השר (l. 9), probably identical with Ephraim Hakkohen, Dayyan in Cairo, see Ch. III) and ישיבת גאונינו שֿצֿ (l. 13, i. e. the Palestinian school). Margin, l. 1, reads ... מֹו[רֹ] אלחנן ראש הסדר נֿטֿ רֿחֿ עם דברים רבים.... Probably Elḥanan was also asked to intervene in this affair.

seat of the government for the province of Filastīn, Jerusalem, and Tyre. In addition there were minor congregations in Ashḳelon, ʿAkko, Ḥaifa, Tiberias, and several others. The data concerning these communities are discussed in the fourth chapter.

Jerusalem, though possessing relatively a small number of Jews, was distinguished as a spiritual centre. The Rabbinites had an academy there presided over by a Gaon. But the school frequently changed its place of residence. Owing to circumstances, we find it occasionally in Ramlāh, Ḥaifa, ʿAkko, and Tyre. The Ḳaraites also had an important settlement in the Holy City. Aided by the local Muslim authorities, they enjoyed on some occasions a privileged position as against their opponents. As a spiritual centre of Ḳaraism, Jerusalem was of great importance for the sect. There existed a Ḳaraite school of considerable standing. Several scholars of renown lived there who composed works on the Bible, Hebrew philology, legalism, theology, and philosophy.

(2) For the purpose of our inquiry it is necessary to go back about three centuries before our period, viz. to the conquest of Palestine by ʿOmar (636–40). The last years of the Byzantine rule (from 628), when the Emperor Heraclius reconquered the country from the Persians, were times of great distress for its Jewry. Terrible revenge was meted out to the Jews for their support of the Persian invaders (see Graetz, V^4, 31 ff.). The Jewish sources are very scanty and only a few details are known. Probably to these years of terror refers the report that the Jews of Palestine were forbidden to read the Shmaʿ or say their prayers, but were allowed only to assemble in the synagogues on Sabbath mornings to recite psalms and liturgical compositions.[1] The arrival of the Arabs was a great deliverance indeed for the Jews. The later Jewish writers do not fail to point out the radical change for the better in consequence of the new régime. The

[1] See *Geonica*, II, 150–51, and cp. *J. Q. R.*, N. S., VII, 437, note 17. The Shmaʿ was evidently forbidden because it emphasized the unity of God (as against the Trinity), while the expression ולא יתפללו probably denotes the Tefillah, the technical term for the eighteen Benedictions; the reference to the Christians (ולנצרים) in the twelfth Benediction, as the Palestinian text of the ʿAmidah retained it (see, e.g., *J. Q. R.*, X, 657), was no doubt the cause for the prohibition to recite the whole prayer. (See Addendum, *infra*, p. 280.)

stipulations of ʿOmar may have been harsh (see Graetz, V[4], 122–3), but, compared with the former Byzantine yoke, the burden imposed on all non-Muslims alike must have been regarded by the Jews as light. Since the time of Hadrian, Jerusalem was forbidden territory to the Jew.[1] Only once a year, on the 9th of Ab, was he permitted to visit the ruins of the Temple and shed tears while reciting the Lamentations. For the privilege of staying a little longer and weeping a little more, he had to bribe the Byzantine soldiers who were on guard, as Jerome, in the fourth century, graphically describes this sad annual visit of the Jews to their Holy City.[2] When the latter capitulated to the Arabs, the Christian population stipulated that no Jews should reside in the city. This condition is expressly mentioned in the treaty of surrender as given by aṭ-Ṭabari, the well-known Arab historian of the first half of the tenth century.[3] There are also the traditional

[1] Except during the short periods of the Emperor Julian's reign and the Persian invasion under Khusrau (614–28 C. E.).

[2] See Schürer, *Geschichte des jüd. Volkes*, I[4], 699, 703–4. Constantine the Great, on his conversion to Christianity, re-confirmed Hadrian's edict. However, in practice, the prohibition was not carried out literally. There are several references in the Talmudic literature to frequent visits of Jews to Jerusalem after the periods of Hadrian and Constantine. (See Frankel, *Mebo ha-Yerushalmi*, 6[b].) Cp. also the statement of the Palestinian author of ספר הוריית הקורא (see *infra*, p. 73, note 2): והקריאה הזאת אשר בארץ ישראל היא קריאת עזרא הסופר ולפי שעד עתה [לא] נפסקה עדת ישראל מהארץ רק מירושלים לבדה בזמן שמלך אדום על ישראל וישראל מלמדים את בניהם דור אחר דור זאת הקריאה. Sahl b. Maṣliaḥ in his introduction to his 'Book of Precepts' (printed by Harkavy in *Hammeliṣ*, 1879, p. 640, l. 26 ff.) writes: (i. e. Jerusalem) ואחרי עזבם למקום נשאר יתר מחמש (supply מאות) שנה לגלים מעון תנים ולא היה אחד מישראל יכול לבוא · והיו היהודים אשר במזרח באים אל מדינת מעזיה [טבריה] להתפלל שם · ואשר במערב היו באים אל מדינת עזה · ואשר בארץ הנגב היו באים אל מדינת צער · ובימי קרן זעירה פתח יי׳ לעמו שערי רחמיו ויביאם אל עיר קדשו וישבו בה ויבנו מקומות (*v. l.* בתים) בתורה לקרוא ולפתור ולהתפלל בכל עת ולהעמיד משמרות בלילות... A similar statement is found in a Ḳaraite commentary on Daniel (to be published by me in *J. Q. R.*, N. S.). Sahl states that 'more than 500 years' no Jew could 'enter' (i. e. reside in) Jerusalem, viz. from the Bar Kokhba revolution till a short time after the Arab conquest.

[3] The text of the treaty, together with an English translation, is given by Lane-Poole, *Proceedings of the Royal Irish Academy*, XXIV, sec. C, No. 13. For the translation see also Butler, *The Treaty of Miṣr in Ṭabari*, 1913, 35–6. See also, Bar-

Arabic accounts of how ʿOmar compelled the bishop Sophronius to show him the exact site of the ruined Temple, which in course of time became a heap of refuse.[1] There ʿOmar built the famous mosque known as al-Aḳsa, the Rock.[2]

Quite a different story do we read in a letter from the Rabbinites in Jerusalem, written during the Gaonate of Daniel b. ʿAzarya (1051–62). Among the Arab conquerors there were a number of Jews who showed them the exact spot of the Temple. The Jews seem to have given valuable aid to the new rulers and therefore obtained from them a number of concessions. In the first instance the Holy City became free to the Jews, who, add our informants, reside there since then up to the present day. The new residents undertook to see to it that the Temple site be kept in a clean state. They were given the permission to pray there without interference. They also bought Mount Olivet as public property of the Jewish community, whereon services were held, indeed, for centuries, on the festivals and especially during Hoshana Rabba, in the presence of numerous pilgrims from all over the Diaspora.[3]

Hebraeus, *Chronicon Syriacum*, ed. Bruns and Kirsch, 1780, Syr. part, 180, דלא שליט יודיא דנעמר באורשלם; cp. Graetz, V[4], 122.

[1] This was the work of the population of the town out of spite to the Jews who came on the 9th of Ab to recite the Lamentations before the Temple ruins (cp. Gr., V[4], 121, and Le Strange, *Palestine under the Moslems*, p. 139.

[2] See especially Le Strange, *l. c.*, pp. 138 ff. The traditional Arabic accounts are first given in a work composed in 1351.

[3] The letter is given in A. C. 11 (see *infra*, p. 164 f.). The corresponding lines are, ומאת אלהינו היתה זאת כי הטה עלינו חסד לפני מלכות ישמעאל בעת אשר פשטה ידם ולכדו את ארץ הצבי מיד אדום ובאו ירושלים היו עמהם אנשים מבני ישראל הראו להם מקום המקדש וישבו עמהם מאז ועד היום · והתנו עליהם תנאים כי הם יכבדו את בית המקדש מכל גיאול ויתפללו על שעריו ולא יהיה ממחה על ידיהם · וקנו הר הזיתים אשר עמדה השכינה עליו . . . Also the author of ‘Nistarot de R. Simon b. Yohai’ (in Jellinek, *Beth Hammidrash*, III, 79) calls the second Caliph ʿOmar ‘a friend of the Jews’ (המלך השני שיעמוד מישמעאל יהיה אוהב ישראל ויגדור פרצותיהם ופרצות ההיכל). Then follows the reference to his erection of the Mosque on Mount Moriah. See also the so-called Prayer of R. Simon b. Yoḥai, ibid., IV, 120, top. From Sahl b. Maṣliaḥ's words (cited above, p. 43, note 2) it also appears that ʿOmar made Jerusalem free for the Jews. This can also be gathered from the Ḳaraite commentary mentioned above.

We have here conflicting accounts. The clause in the treaty of surrender, prohibiting the Jews to reside in Jerusalem, is probably genuine since aṭ-Ṭabari, a reliable source, gives it. But it is likely that for some reason or other it was not carried out and the Holy City was again free for the Jew. As for the story of the discovery of the exact site of the Temple, the account given in the above letter, three centuries older than that of Arab writers, should be preferred. It is true the epistle dates more than four centuries after 'Omar's conquest. But there must have been an old tradition well known in the community, and there may have even existed written documents to this effect which have been lost.[1] Moreover, it stands to reason that the Jews knew the exact spot of the Temple since they visited the ruins annually on the 9th of Ab. During the Persian invasion (614–28) they could enter the city freely. Very likely after Heraclius had driven out the Persians, even the annual visit was prohibited. But during this short time till the arrival of the Arabs the site could have hardly become so disfigured as not to be recognized by them.

(3) Be it as it may, soon after the Arab conquest, Jerusalem attracted a number of Jews as permanent settlers, and much larger numbers of visitors and pilgrims.[2] The Ḳaraite Salman b. Yeruḥam (about 940–60) gives an interesting account of the vicissi-

[1] It should be borne in mind that the Crusaders, on entering Jerusalem in 1099, practically wiped out the whole Jewish community (see *infra*, p. 199 f.), and very likely destroyed all the Jewish records or manuscripts they could lay hold of.

[2] The earliest Hebrew source mentioning the Jews of Jerusalem in the Arab period is the fragment in *Geonica*, II (above, p. 42, note 1; see *J. Q. R.*, N. S., *l. c.*, 474, note 18). As will be shown elsewhere, its author was Ben Bāboi, a disciple of Raba the disciple of Yehudai Gaon (760), hence about 800 C. E. The Holy City had then a goodly number of Jews hailing from Babylon. The Coptic book of Daniel has a fourteenth vision wherein it is mentioned that the last 'Omeyyad Caliph, Merwān II (died 750), commanded *the Jews to return to Jerusalem* (see Becker, *Nachrichten der Königlichen Gesellschaft zu Göttingen*, *histor.-philos. Klasse*, 1916, pp. 33-4). But, as Becker points out, this is one of the features peculiar to all this class of apocalypse, and is not historical. See also *Oriens Christianus*, I, 1901, 305 ff., where the Katholikos Timoteos I (beginning of the ninth century) states in a letter that Jews, who received instruction in Christianity, told him of books found ten years previously (i. e. before the date of the letter) in the neighbourhood of Jericho. When the *Jews of Jerusalem* were informed, they betook themselves in large numbers to the spot, and found there books of the Old Testament and other writings in Hebrew script. (See Addendum, *infra*, p. 280.)

tudes of the Jewish community since the Arab conquest.[1] But the historicity of his statements is not beyond suspicion because he would, as befits a sectarian polemic, describe the Jewish residents, who prior to the influx of Ḳaraites to the Holy City (see *infra*, p. 59 ff.) were exclusively adherents of Rabbinic Judaism, as morally depraved. Salman tells us that during the reign of al-Rūm (Christian Byzantium) for '500 years and more' the Jews could not enter the Holy City under penalty of death. 'When, by the grace of God, al-Rūm was expelled and the reign of Ishmael (Arabs) became manifest', the Jews were granted the privilege of entering and residing in the city. The Arabs handed over to them 'the courtyards of the house of God where they prayed for a number of years'. (This agrees with the story in the above letter that the Jews undertook to keep the Temple site in a clean state.) When after some time the Caliph heard evil rumours about the Jews that they were guilty of vulgarities, quarrels, drink, and immorality, he commanded that they be confined to one quarter of the temple, where they could pray, but were not prevented from visiting the other quarters. This lasted for a certain period. As they continued in their sinful practices, they were expelled from that quarter too (?). 'Now the Christians endeavoured by force to drive us out from Jerusalem and entirely to separate us from it, but I trust in God that their wish be not fulfilled.' The last statement, which seems to deal with the condition in Salman's own time, is obscure.

[1] In his Commentary to Ps. 30. See the extract from a MS. Petrograd given by Neubauer, *Aus der Petersburger Bibliothek* (109, VII; cp. p. 12), unfortunately printed incorrectly: וכמא הו מעלום אן פי מלך אלרום מכת בית אלמקדס ת"ק סנה̈ וניף לא יכונוא ישראל יצלון אלי אלדכ̇ול אלי ירושלם ומן דכ̇ל ועלם בה קתל פלמא אנתקל (r. אלרום) מנהא דפצל (r. בפצ̇ל) אלהי ישראל וט̇הר מלכות ישמעאל אטלק לישראל אלדכ̇ול ואלסכני ודפע עליהם חצרות בית ה׳ פכאנוא פיה יצלון מדה̈ (supply סנין) ת̇ם רפע כ̇ברהם אלי מלך ישמעאל במא יפעלון מן אלקביח ואלערבדה̈ ושרב אלכ̇מר ואלם כד (r. ואלסכר) ואלקדף פאמר בטרדהם אלי דאב הן אדאב (באב מן אבואב) פכאנוא מדה̈ סנין עלי מת̇ל הדא פזאדוא מן (probably r. ען) פעל אלמעאצי פקאם עלינא מן טרדנא מן באב אלקדס (probably only from Temple site) ת̇ם אלאן אלערלים פי חיל יצבון (read perhaps ינצבון) עלינא ליכ̇רוג̇נא מן אלקדס ויפרקואביננא ובנה וארג̇ו בפצ̇ל אלהי ישראל לא יתם מראדהם ולא יסהל (r. יסאל) אמורהם.

The Christians in Jerusalem seem to have agitated then for the entire expulsion of the Jews from the Holy City. Of course, they would need the approval of the Arab authorities to bring this about. Neubauer (*loc. cit.*, p. 12), from whose rendering of Salman's account I have differed, connects this episode with the victories of the Byzantine Emperor Nicephorus Phocas over the Arabs in Northern Syria (968–9) which resulted in the capture of Antioch. But it is improbable that events in Northern Syria would have had such an effect as to make the Christians in Jerusalem dare openly to betray their longing for the restoration of the Byzantine dominion by threatening the Jews with expulsion as its sequel. It must have therefore been a local affair wherein the Christians endeavoured to obtain from the Arab rulers a concession for carrying out, about three centuries hence, the clause in 'Omar's treaty prohibiting the Jews from residing in the Holy City.

To return to our subject. Very little is known about the occupations of the new settlers. But a section which grew up in course of time, known as 'the mourners for Zion' (אבילי ציון), deserve special mention. They led a life of asceticism, spending their days in fasting and lamenting over the destruction of the Temple and in praying for its restoration, and the advent of the Messiah. The spirit of mysticism and 'practical Ḳabbalah' found a fruitful soil among this section.[1] Speculations would abound about the events before and after the coming of the Messiah, the calamities that would befall Israel and the subsequent deliverance. The Holy City became a congenial place for such kindred spirits to live together. Their circle would be increased by Jews from all over the Diaspora who were heartbroken, and who through adverse circumstances lost all interest in life.

The earliest reference to these 'mourners for Zion' is to be found in the Pesiḳta Rabbati (c. 34).[2] They are described as

[1] Cp. the famous responsum of Hai Gaon (in Aschkenazi, *Ṭa'am Zeḳenim*, 54 ff.), from which it appears that in his time Palestine was a fertile soil for 'practical Ḳabbalah', though the same was the case in Byzantine countries (ארץ אדום) too.

[2] *Pesiḳta*, ed. Friedmann, 158^b, reads: לבקרים אותם [שמשכימים] בכל בוקר ובוקר לבקש רחמים אף [ישועתנו בעת צרה] אלו אבלים שחמדו את הישועה

'ardently desiring the salvation evening, morning, and midday'. They were a minority and seem to have been ridiculed as unworldly dreamers. But the author warns Israel of an impending calamity owing to this ridicule of the 'mourners for Zion'. The redactor of the Pesiḳta was probably a native of Southern Italy. Several characteristics of this Midrash have indeed led a number of scholars to the opinion that it was composed in that country.[1] But a more probable solution is that the redactor was an Italian Agadist who settled in Jerusalem in the first half of the ninth century, where he 'joined the mourners for Zion'.[2] It is interesting to find another South Italian scholar, R. Aḥima'aṣ the elder (who lived in the time of the Byzantine Emperor Basileos I, 868 C. E.), visiting Jerusalem three times and giving donations

ערב ובוקר וצהרים · והיתה צרה גדולה [לישראל] שמבזין אותם ומלעיגים עליהן . . . כל רואיהם יכירום אילו אבילי ציון . . . והרואה אותם יושב ואומר לשוא שחקנו לשוא לעגנו על דבריהם . . . (159ª) . . . באבילים שנצטערו עמי על ביתי ההרב ועל היכלי השמם . . . אלו אבילי ציון שהשפילו את רוחם ושמעו את חרפתם ושתקו ולא החזיקו טובה לעצמם. . . .

[1] See Eppenstein, *Mtschr.*, LV, 1911, 626-8, for the latest discussion of the problem.

[2] Friedmann (Introd. 24) points out that chapters 34-7 are different in style from the rest of the book, and maintains that they are the earliest. But it is more likely that they were composed by the redactor of the Midrash, who lived in the first half of the ninth century. This is evident from ch. 1 (1ᵇ): מתי אבא [ואראה פני אלהים] אמרו לו ישראל רבש"ע אימתי אתה מחזיר לנו את הכבוד שהיינו עולין בג' פעמי רגלים ורואין פני השכינה (here Agadas by R. Joshu'a b. Levi are inserted) אמרו אימתי את מחזירנו לאותו הכבוד הרי כמה זמן שחרב בית חיינו הרי שבוע הרי יובל הרי שבע מאות ושבעים ושבע ועתה הוא כבר אלף ומאה וחמשים ואחד מתי אבוא ואראה פני האלהים. . . . As Friedmann already pointed out (note 16), the second date, ועתה . . . ואחד, is clearly an insertion by a copyist who lived 374 years later. Accordingly the editor of the Pesiḳta lived 777 years after the destruction of the Temple, about 845 C. E. He probably removed to Jerusalem, where he joined the 'mourners for Zion', in whose defence he writes. Another passage in ch. 1 (2ª) also points to his residence in the Holy Land: ובזכות מה ישראל זוכין לכל הכבוד הזה בזכות ישיבה של ארץ ישראל שהיו (r. שהם) יושבין ומצטערין בין האומות בעולם הזה. . . . Friedmann's interpretation (note 24) וכלו' שהם מצטערין בין האומות להיות זוכין לישיבת א"י is forced. It seems to me more natural to explain the passage, that in spite of altered circumstances and heavy taxation Israel persists in having a settlement in Palestine. The Patriarchs, too, the author argues, were very anxious to be at least buried in the Holy Land.

on each occasion '*to the mourners for His majestic habitation*'.[1] Soon after the conquest of Egypt in 969, the famous Palṭiel is also reported to have visited the Fusṭāṭ synagogue on the Day of Atonement and, on being called up to the reading of the Law, to have promised donations for the Palestinian Gaon and the academy, for '*the mourners for the everlasting house*' and for the Babylonian schools. Likewise his son Samuel gave large legacies to these 'mourners'.[2]

(4) We propose now to deal with the Palestinian Gaonate from

[1] *Aḥima'aṣ Chronicle* (in Neubauer, *Med. Jew. Chron.*, II, 113, l. 22 ff.), איש יהודי היה ביומו · ור׳ אחימעץ שמו בירושלם (r. לירושלם) עיר ההוללה ; פעמים שלש בנדרים עלה · ובכל פעם עלייתו · מאה זהובים הוליך אתו . . . להטיב לעוסקי בתורתו ולאבלי זבול תפארתו. Instead of the former usual visits three times yearly, it seems that a pious Jew made it his duty to visit the Holy Land and City at least three times during his lifetime. Hence the question of the redactor of the Pesiḳta (cited on p. 48, note 2), 'When wilt Thou, O God, restore the honour when we used to make pilgrimages three times yearly?' And he answers homiletically that in the future the pilgrimages will take place on every New Moon's Day and on every Sabbath (כשיגיע הקץ אני בונה אותו ואין אתם עולים ג״פ בשנה אלא כל חודש וחודש ובכל שבת [ושבת] אתם עתידים להיות עולים).

[2] Ibid., *l. c.*, 128, l. 21 ff.: והיה ביום הכיפורים נקרא ר׳ פלטיאל לקרוא בתורה . . . לאחר שהשלים קרייתו · נדב לאלהי תהלתו · חמשת אלפים דינרים . . . אלף לראש הישיבה ולחכמים · ואלף לאבילי בית העולמים · ואלף לבבל לישיבת הגאונים . . . וחילקום כמצות ר׳ פלטיאל · לישיבות ולכנסיות ולאבילי ציון . . . (p. 130, l. 8 ff.) והעלה (R. Samuel) אביו ואמו בירושלם (r. לירושלם) בארונות . . . והקדיש . . . מזהב עשרים אלף דרכמונים · לדלים ועגונים · לחכמים והדרשנים · אשר התורה משננים · ולמלמדי תינוקות וחזנים · ושמן למקדש בכותל מערבי למזבח שבפנים · ולבתי כנסיות לקהלות הרחוקים והשכינים · ולאבילי ההיכל המשכנים · הם העגומים על ציון ואבילים · ואל הישיבה לתלמידים ולתנאים · ולחכמי בבל לישיבת הנשיאים ·. There is no corresponding rhyme to ואבילים. No doubt in the preceding clause for המשכנים, which gives no sense, המשכילים should be read, 'and for the mourners for the temple, the learned ones'. There is no justification for the assumption that משכיל became a specifically Ḳaraite term in those times. We find Elḥanan b. Ḥushiel of Ḳairowān expressing the desire to be one of the משכילים (*J. Q. R.*, N. S., IX, 162, note 156). Very likely the Ḳaraites borrowed the term from the Rabbinites, just as they did with the expression אבלי ציון (see *infra*, p. 61). It is interesting that there existed then in Jerusalem 'synagogues belonging to distant congregations' and others to the 'residents' (השכינים). Probably the pilgrims from the various countries of the Diaspora met in their respective synagogues. It recalls conditions in Jerusalem in Temple times (see e. g. Acts 6[9]).

its inception to the time when Solomon b. Yehuda became president of the academy. Our inquiry must first extend to a particular function of the Gaonite in order to obtain a fixed date. The great past of the Holy Land bestowed upon it a certain tradition of learning. It retained or put forward claims for a number of privileges over the countries of the Diaspora, even when adverse circumstances reduced its Jewry to penury in numbers, material prosperity and intellectual activity. One of these privileges was the sole right of the principal and the members of the Palestinian academy to fix the calendar for each year. The discovery of the documents bearing on the dispute between Ben-Meir and Sa'adya about the calendar of the year 921/2 has thrown new light on this hitherto unknown prerogative of Palestine in the Gaonic period. Bornstein[1] re-edited all the texts available to him, devoting to them an exhaustive and thorough study. Since then supplementary material was published in *J. Q. R.*, N. S. (vol. V, 546 ff.).

Ben-Meir put forward the claim that the Babylonian Jew had always accepted the fixing of the calendar as proclaimed on Mount Olivet on behalf of the president and the members of the Palestinian academy.[2] And this claim is emphatically reiterated about 170 years later by the Gaon Ebyatar Hakkohen in his 'Scroll'. The calculation of the calendar was indeed laid down in the 'four chapters' (ארבעה שערים), but the actual proclamation of it was an exclusive right of the Palestinian Gaon.[3]

[1] מחלקת רב סעדיה גאון ובן מאיר, in Sokolow's ספר היובל, 1904, pp. 19–189. See also Malter, *J. Q. R.*, N. S., III, 500–9, on the *Documents on the Ben-Meir Controversy*. Cp. also Marx, *J. Q. R.*, N. S., I, 63 ff.

[2] He writes in his supposed second letter (full text in *J. Q. R.*, N. S., V, 553, l. 14 f.) כי אבותיכם נ״נ היו מקבלים הכרזת הר הזתים ומעולם לא שינו אבותיכם נ״נ זה המנהג ולא החליפו חוק. Also in his supposed first epistle we read (Bornstein, *l. c.* 65, ll. 2–3): ומכלל כל הדברים הללו יש הרשות לחבורת ארץ ישראל על חכמי בני הגולה · ואין לבני הגולה רשות על בני ארץ ישראל.

[3] *Megillat Ebyatar*, *J. Q. R.*, XIV, 472, l. 10 ff.: אבל סמיכת הכל שיקדש ראש הסנהדרין שהוא ראש ישיבה ויקבענה אחרי אותו החשבון אם מעוברת אם פשוטה · וכל העושין על אותו החשבון צריכין הן במצות התורה . . . לסמוך על גאון החבורה ואין להימין ולהשמאיל ממנו . . . וכל שהן עושין בכל שנה ושנה בכל גליות ישראל צריכין הן לחשוב כי . . . מפיו הם עושין ואם אינם עושין כן אינם יוצאין ידי חובתן. See also Bornstein, *l. c.* 50.

So far the one side. Let us hear what the scholars of Babylon had to say. Their case is fully developed in a letter from Babylon to Ben-Meir, probably emanating from the Exilarch, written quite at the beginning of the dispute when civilities were still exchanged between the parties.[1] The writer argues that as regards the fixing of a leap-year there is no longer any difference of opinion between Palestine and Babylon, because this is done by a traditional calculation generally accepted. It is only about the fixing of the months Marḥeshvan and Kislev, whether they be 'full', 'ordinary' or 'defective' (מלאים, כסדרן, חסרים), that a dispute may arise. Babylon was indeed formerly dependent on Palestine as regards the fixing of these months, because the scholars of the former country were not well versed in the calendar calculation. But 'many years' ago several scholars from Babylon visited the Holy Land, where they sought instruction in all the intricacies of the calendar. Since then the calendar is fixed independently in both countries. There has never yet arisen a difference of opinion, since the calculation is the same. Even the oldest members of the Babylonian schools cannot remember that the Palestinian authorities had to be consulted about the fixing of the calendar.[2]

[1] Printed by Bornstein, *l. c.*, 87 ff. (cp. also *J. Q. R.*, N. S., III, 500–2). The text is now supplemented in *J. Q. R.*, N. S., V, 546–7.

[2] *J. Q. R.*, N. S., V, 546, l. 17 ff.: וכבר אין בינינו וביניכם חילוף בעבור שנים
באדר ואדר מפני שהכל תפסו את המסורת בידם לחשבון . . . ולענין עיבור
וחשבון כבר הכל שווין ואין בינינו לביניכם שינוי בעיבור שנים אבל קביעת חדשים
לחשב מלאים וחסירין וכסדרן אינו מן העיבור שנה · ובודאי שרבותינו שבבבל
בדורות הראשנים היו שולחין ודורשין מרבותינו שלארץ ישר׳ קביעת חדשי שנה
בשנה לפי שלא היו בקיאין בסדר העיבור כמותן לפיכך היו כותבין אליהם
אבל מן שנים רבות כבר עלו כמה חכמים מבבל אל ארץ ישר׳ ודקדקו עם חכמי
ארץ ישר׳ בסוד העיבור ופשפשו וחיפשו בזו עד שנתבוננו בו יפה יפה וכבר הם
קובעים חדשים בבבל זה שנים רבות לבדם וגם חכמי ארץ ישראל מחשבים
וקובעים חדשים לבדם וכבר בכל השנים האלה עלה חשבונם אחד לא נמצא
ביניהם חילוף . . . ולא ראינו קילקול כזה (read בזה) ולא פירצה כזאת (read
בזאת) ובודאי (supply לוּ or אִלּוּ) אנחנו התחלנו לקבוע חדשים בבבל היה לו
לראש ישיבה (i. e. the then Gaon of Palestine) להוכיח אותנו ולאמר שניתם מנהג
ועברתם על דברי רבותיכם הנה נא יש בישיבות זקינים שהגיעו לגבורות וגם
הזקינו מאד וכולם אין אחד מהם זוכר שהוצרכו אנשי בבל לשאול עיבור שנים

Here we have a circumstantial historical account of interest. When did this visit of the Babylonian scholars to Palestine take place? Eppenstein (*Mtschr.*, LIV, 1910, p. 317) dates this event in the late Amoraic times, that is to say, when the Patriarch Hillel II is supposed to have laid down the rules for fixing the calendar. But with fine insight Bornstein (*loc. cit.* 44, note 1) infers from the style of the cited passage that it does not deal with an event about 600 years previously.

The Genizah fragment, given in A. A. 13, enables us to state definitely that in 835 C. E. Babylon was dependent on the fixing of the calendar by the president and the members of the Palestinian academy. The fragment is a part of a letter from the Babylonian Exilarch to some community. Unfortunately both beginning and conclusion of the epistle are missing. The question arose in 4595 A. M. whether Marḥeshvan and Kislev be both 'full', so that the ensuing Passover begin on a Thursday, or 'defective' and accordingly Passover to fall two days previously, on a Tuesday.[1] In Palestine the months were declared as 'defective'. The Exilarch writes (recto, l. 1 ff.) that, in order to preserve unity in Israel, 'our forefathers (i.e. the *Exilarchs*) *and the academies go by this custom* (i.e. *of accepting the fixing of the calendar by the Palestinian authorities*) *till now*, 1147 *Sel.* = 4595 A. M.'[2] In that year Marḥeshvan and Kislev had to be made 'defective' because the new moon of Nisan would be visible on Tuesday, 10 a.m. If these months be declared as 'full', Passover would fall on a Thursday and consequently Rosh Ḥodesh Nisan also on that day, while the new moon would be visible in the West already on Tuesday, hence a flagrant miscalculation

וקביעת חדשים מארץ ישר׳ אלא אתם מעברים כמנהגכם וגם אנחנו מנהג אבותינו
בידנו ואנחנו מעברים כדרכנו וחשבון אחד הוא.

[1] Mahler in his *Handbuch der jüd. Chronologie*, 1916, makes 4595 A. M. to have been a בשה-year, viz. both Marḥeshvan and Kislev 'full', and Passover to have commenced on Thursday (see Tables, pp. 610 and 614). But from our fragment we learn that it was fixed as a בחג-year (p. 615).

[2] Apparently the writer reckoned the Sel. year to have begun in 312 B.C. But almost in all documents drawn up in Egypt and in Palestine (as known to us from the Genizah) there is only a difference of one in the figures below ten of the corresponding Sel. and A. M., e.g. 1465 Sel. = 4914 A. M. (see e.g. A. D. 19a discussed, *infra*, p. 232). Accordingly 311 B.C. is taken as the beginning of the Sel. era. This point still needs clearing up.

(recto, ll. 7–13). The Exilarch therefore defends the fixing of the Palestinian authorities and continues (verso, l. 9 ff.) :—There is no question in this case which the head and members of the school (of Palestine) decided as 'defective', since there can be no alternative ('ordinary' or 'full'). But even when alternatives are possible '*we always rely on them* (i. e. the Palestinian authorities) in order that Israel be not divided into sections. '*And I, the heads of the schools, the scholars and all Israel rely on the calendar which has been dispatched* (*from*) *before the scholars* (*of Palestine*).'

Our identification of the writer of this epistle with the Exilarch is evident from the fact that he places himself in front of the Geonim (of Babylon), and also that he writes with an authority only applicable to the political head of the Babylonian Jewry. Probably the holder of this office in 835 C. E. was David b. Yehuda, who successfully maintained his claim to it against his opponent Daniel. In 1144 Sel. the Exilarch David appointed R. Isaac as Gaon of Sura (see Sherira's Letter, ed. Neubauer, p. 38). We may assume that he was still alive three years afterwards, in 1147 Sel. Be that as it may, the Exilarch unreservedly confirmed in 835 the Palestinian prerogative of fixing the calendar. When Ben-Meir, about 85 years subsequently, claimed for himself and his school this right, he based himself on an old genuine privilege and was by no means a usurper. But, for some unexplained reason, the Babylonian scholars found it necessary soon after 835 to acquire in Palestine a thorough knowledge of the calendar rules and thereby become independent. Perhaps it was the sequel of the question of the calendar of 835 which formed a subject of discussion in the above epistle. That the visit of Babylonian scholars to Palestine took place soon after 835 is evident from the fact that during the Ben-Meir controversy, about 85 years hence, even the oldest members of the Babylonian academies had no longer a recollection of Babylon being dependent on the Holy Land as regards the calendar.

It is noteworthy that so far the first Babylonian Gaon to occupy himself with the calendar problem was R. Naḥshon of Sura, 874–82 (see Bornstein, *loc. cit.* 155 ff.). Now his father R. Ṣadoḳ occupied the Gaonate from 823–5. R. Naḥshon was then a very young student. Who knows whether more than a decade subsequently, when after 835 the Babylonian scholars visited Palestine for the purpose of learning the calendar 'secret', R. Naḥshon was not a member of the party? And the literary evidence of his newly acquired knowledge we have in the 'cycle' that bears his name (עגול דרב נחשון גאון).

(5) The above letter from the Exilarch is of interest not only for the calendar problem but, to a still larger degree, for the question of the Gaonate in the Holy Land. As long as Ben-Meir was regarded to have put forward specious claims for Palestinian prerogatives, the Gaonate was taken to have been the sequel of his ambitions. Thus Poznański in his recent work [1] writes, 'Ihr (der Geonim) Auftreten steht *ohne Zweifel* mit dem Streit um den Kalender, der im Jahre 921 zwischen Palästina und Babylonien ausbrach und jetzt in allen seinen Details bekannt ist, im Zusammenhang.' We know now of the existence of the Palestinian school already in 835. Its head went by the same title, ראש החבורה, as Ben-Meir was styled.[2] The school in the Holy Land was very likely kept up during all the centuries of the Byzantine dominion. But since Jerusalem was forbidden ground

[1] *Babylonische Geonim im nachgäonischen Zeitalter*, 1914, p. 82.

[2] Sa'adya in his *Sepher Hamo'adim* (in Bornstein, *l. c.*, 76, l. 22) quotes an epistle from Babylon to Ben-Meir, beginning: שלום לראש החבורה ולבניך ולאחיך וכו׳. Likewise he is frequently styled ראש ישיבה, since he presided over a fully organized academy (see the beginning of Ben-Meir's letter, *l. c.*, 62, bottom). The Babylonian Geonim usually were addressed ריש מתיבתא, since Aramaic was the language of the scholars in Babylon, whereas Hebrew was that of the Palestinian scholars. Very seldom is the Palestinian Gaon styled ריש מתיבתא. As for ראש ישיבת גאון יעקב, shortened into the familiar title גאון, it was used alike by the presidents of the academies of Palestine and Babylon. Cp. also the titles ראש הסנהדרין and גאון החבורה in the Ebyatar scroll (above, p. 50, note 3). The members of the Palestinian school were usually styled חברים (חברייא), Ḥaberim; hence the expression חבורה for the whole college. These terms are frequently used with reference to the academies of the Holy Land, especially that of Tiberias, in the third and fourth centuries. (See in particular the instructive article by Bacher, *Mtschr.*, XLIII, 1899, 345–60, and cp. Chajes, ibid. 572.) Those disciples who had not yet the ordination (סמיכה) entitling them to go by the title 'Rabbi', were styled Ḥaberim (see *l. c.* 353). There were older Ḥaberim and younger ones (חברייא רברבייא, חברייא זעירייא, *l. c.* 352). This was the case in the Talmudic period. However, in our period, the Ḥaberim were the 'ordained' scholars of the academy, several of whom presided over the courts in various communities (see *infra*, pp. 264 ff., 272 f.). Those disciples that had not yet the authorization went by the name of תלמידים.

for the Jew, the academy continued in Tiberias from the times of R. Joḥanan. Soon after the Arab conquest of the country (about 640 C.E.) the gates of the Holy City were thrown open to the Jews, who were permitted to settle and reside there. Naturally the school of Tiberias found a more suitable home within the hallowed precincts of Jerusalem.[1] The activities of the academy since the country came under the sway of the Muslims are on the whole obscure. But one of its rights was the fixing of the calendar unreservedly accepted in Babylon still as late as 835 C.E.).[2]

Data found in the *Aḥima'aṣ Chronicle* as to the school of Jerusalem have been entirely ignored. It is true they were misconstrued by Kaufmann (*Mtschr.*, XL, 468 ff.) and thus were altogether disregarded. Only Marx (*J.Q.R.*, N.S., I, 67) makes use of some of them, without, however, pointing out Kaufmann's erroneous account. Aḥima'aṣ the elder came into personal touch with a 'head of the academy' presiding over a college of scholars (חבורה) in Jerusalem. As we heard above (p. 48 f.), he visited the Holy City three times and on each occasion brought donations from his native country, Italy, for the scholars and the 'mourners for Zion'.[3] Moreover, a scholar from Palestine once visited Venosa,

[1] That the Jerusalem academy was known to have been originally situated at Tiberias is also evident from the interesting fact that the Nasi and Gaon, Daniel b. 'Azarya, who succeeded Solomon b. Yehuda in 1051 C.E. (see *infra*, p. 178 ff.), is once styled '*Gaon of Tiberias and head of the school of Israel at Jerusalem*'. Thus a poetical letter of greeting (T.-S. 12. 358) begins: מרשות דגלי רזיא ושרי בשמיא ... וברשות נשיא וגאון טבריא ו[ריש] מתיבתא דישראל דבירושלם בית אל רבן דניא[ל] ורשיון אב בית דין די בקושטא ידין וקדמיה קמין . . . כהנא דבראשא וסיענא קשישא ואף עמא קדישא סבין. The person addressed in the epistle is named רב שמואל. Greeted are also his uncle Aaron, his son Yeshu'a, and son-in-law 'Āli.

[2] The literary productions of Palestinian scholarship during this period, the Midrashic literature, the Massorah, the Tiberian vowel-system and the piyyuṭim are known, and are outside the scope of our theme here. How far the members of the school participated in some branches of this work is discussed in A. A. 14.

[3] See the passage from the *Aḥima'aṣ Chronicle* on p. 49, note 1. In the continuation the 'dead' reader is supposed to relate to Abū Aaron his visit to the academy of Jerusalem in the company of Aḥima'aṣ: כשהיינו יושבים בסעודה מסובים עם ראש הישיבה · ותלמידי הרחבה · פצחו בפציחה . . . נתנו עיניהם בתלמידיהם · היושבים לפניהם · וראש הישיבה שלהם · הביט אליהם.

in Italy, where the local Rabbi, Silanus by name, slighted him (*loc. cit.*, 114, last line). On his return to Jerusalem, he related his grievance to the members of the school. As a result, R. Silanus was excommunicated. Now when Aḥima'aṣ came to the Holy City he was invited by the academy to conduct the service in the synagogue. On that occasion he recited a piyyuṭ by this R. Silanus which won general approbation because the Rabbinites were therein eulogized while the 'heretics' (i. e. the *Karaites*!) were denounced.[1] When the Gaon and his school heard that R. Silanus was the author of the piyyuṭ, they revoked the ban that had been imposed upon him.

Now Kaufmann (*loc. cit.*, p. 468) gave a wrong turn to these data by making the 'dead' reader, whom Abū Aaron is supposed to have discovered in Benevent, to have been a Palestinian. This was the cause of his misconstruing the whole account. But this 'medium' of Abū Aaron was clearly not a Palestinian but an Italian whom Aḥima'aṣ would take with him as companion on his pilgrimages to Jerusalem. Surely the reverse would not be the case that a Palestinian Jew should travel to Italy with donations (נדרים).[2] Hence the story wherein the 'head of the school' figures refers to the Holy City and not to Italy. Kaufmann (*loc. cit.*, p. 473) likewise misunderstood the Silanus affair. The slighted scholar from Palestine is taken to have had R. Silanus, the spiritual guide of the Venosa community, ex-

[1] Ibid., p. 115, l. 12 ff.: ועלה אל החבירים · אשר בישיבה סבורים · וסיפר להם הפגע רע · אשר אליו הוגע ואירע . . . ובירכו ר׳ סילנו הנבון ועמד בנידויו ימים ושנים מאוחרים · עד עלות שם (i. e. to Jerusalem) ר׳ אחימעץ עם הנדרים . . . כשעלה היו עשרת ימי תשובה · ופייסוהו החברים וראש הישיבה · לעמוד לפני התיבה . . . שאלוהו בשאלה מי היה פה המחבב . . . שאהב ועילה הרבנים · וריחק ותיעב המינים.

[2] *l. c.*, p. 113, l. 24 ff. ובפעם השלישית שעלה · (a technical expression for a pilgrimage) לאמי שאלני בשאלה · תנהו לי · להיות אצלי · לעלות עמי · להנאת עצמי. Thus relates the 'dead' reader to Abū Aaron, that Aḥima'aṣ took him as a companion for his travels to the Holy Land. There is no doubt that בירושלם (above, p. 49, note 1) has to be corrected into לירושלם. Only thus becomes the whole story intelligible. Cp. also the passage (above, p. 49, note 2) where it is related that Palṭiel's son, Samuel, brought the remains of his parents to Jerusalem. There, too, we read והעלה אביו ואמו בירושלם בארונות; obviously לירושלם is meant.

communicated at a supposed academy there. Aḥima'aṣ arrived there with donations while on his way to Jerusalem (!). Accordingly we obtain 'a head of the school', living in Venosa, whereas all this really refers to the school in Jerusalem. The Palestinian scholar, whom R. Silanus slighted, was very likely a representative of the academy (שליח) who travelled in Italy to collect donations for it. That the Italian Jewry in the second half of the ninth century supported the seat of learning in the Holy City is evident from the fact that Aḥima'aṣ during his pilgrimages brought with him donations from his native country.

The *Aḥima'aṣ Chronicle* is certainly a grotesque mixture of legends, mysticism, and superstition. Yet there is no reason for doubting the historicity of the persons and the institutions mentioned in the narrative. The references to the academy in Jerusalem find now full confirmation by the above epistle from the Exilarch in 835. Nor was the school a ne institution in the first half of the ninth century. Elsewhere I am giving new material as to the relations of R. Yehudai Gaon (760 C. E.) with the scholars of the Holy Land, by whom, most likely, the members of the academy are meant. In short, there is now sufficient justification for the statement that, just as in Babylon, we have in Palestine a *Gaonic period* following that of the Amoraim. Unfortunately we possess no 'Sherira's Letter' to give us a chronological list of the principals of the Palestinian school. Several names of these Geonim have been rescued from oblivion by the Genizah finds. Of Ben-Meir's predecessors, probably his father, Meir, and his grandfather, Moses, as well as an earlier ancestor, Mūsa by name, presided over the school. As such they came into conflict with the Ḳaraites, who had then an ascendancy in the Holy City.[1] We

[1] Ben-Meir in his letter to Babylon (see full text in *J. Q. R.*, N. S., V, 554, l. 16 ff.) describes the sufferings he and his forefathers had to undergo on the part of the Ḳaraites in Jerusalem: והזכרתם שניתן נפשינו על ישראל זו היא וסתינו ווסת אבותינו . . . וחמישית מר׳ מוסי שנהרג בעזרה מתחת יד זרע ענן ׳ ומאבותינו ר׳ מאיר ור׳ משה שבמה פעמים ביקשו השונאים (i. e. Ḳaraites) להרגן ועשה שדי למען שמו · וששית ממנו אנחנו אשר עבר עלינו צרות רבות ורעות וחבישת בית האסורים ועינוי הכבל ומ[לק]ות עד לצאת הנפש הכיפורים (?) ראשונה ושנייה מתחת יד בני ענן השונאים ׳ ובאנו אליכם להיעזר ביי׳ אלוהינו ובכם ועשיתם חסד ושכרם (read ושכרכם) מיי׳.

are able to reconstrue a list of the Palestinian Geonim from Ben-Meir till Ebyatar Hakkohen, in whose time the school perished amidst the ruin that overtook the Palestinian Jewry in consequence of the First Crusade.

The earliest period of the Gaonate is still shrouded in obscurity. About 520 C.E., Mar Zuṭra, the posthumous son of the executed Exilarch of Babylon Mar Zuṭra, was brought to Palestine. In course of time he seems to have become head of the Tiberias school (ראש סנהדרין).[1] Assuming that his descendants, whose names have been preserved, occupied the same position, as is likely, it is possible to draw up a list of presidents of the school for the next ten generations, viz. R. Gurya, Mar Zuṭra II, R. Jacob, R. Shemaya, R. Ḥanina (for רב נינא in the text, as suggested by Brüll), R. Megas, R. Misa (Moses?), R. Nehemiah, R. Abdimi, and R. Pinḥas. As Mar Zuṭra's period of activity as head of the academy falls in the middle of the sixth century, that of Pinḥas, the tenth generation after him, brings us to about 800 C.E. (10 × 25 years). The latter is probably identical with the Massorite and grammarian Pinḥas (ראש הישיבה). As shown in A. A. 14, he was a contemporary of Asher the elder and a group of Massorites whose time could be approximately fixed in the first quarter of the ninth century. Tiberias remained the centre for the study of the Bible and the Hebrew language. But not all the Massorites lived there. Only Aḥiyahu Hakkohen the Ḥaber is expressly mentioned as 'from מעזיה' (= Tiberias). Another scholar, Moses, was a native of Gaza. Our Pinḥas was 'head of the school', situated then at the Holy City. Who succeeded Pinḥas is obscure. We hear of a son of his called

[1] *Seder 'Olam Zuṭa* (in Neub., *Med. Jew. Chr.*, II, 73) mentions that Mar Zuṭra became a ריש פירקא (ועיילוה בריש פירקיה). But the Hebrew version (p. 76) states והכניסוהו לריש פירקיא (פרקין) ובשנת תנ״ב לחרבן הבית שנת ד׳ אלפים ור״פ עלה לא״י והיה ראש [ל]סנהדרין (i.e. of the academy, see above p. 54, note 2). Eppenstein (*Mtschr.*, 1908, 464, note 1) suggests that Mar Zuṭra first became Rosh Happereḳ, and subsequently head of the school. If so, עלה לא״י ought to precede והכניסוהו. See also Marx, *l.c.*, 68–9. Another version (in Neub., I, 178) states: ובימיו ברחו כל ישראל (!) מבבל לארץ ישראל ומשאר (read ולשאר) ארצות · ונעשות (read ונעשה) אחד ששמו מר זוטרא ראש ישיבה בא״י דהיא (*sic*!) בנו של בשתנא. The Hebrew version (p. 76) continues to enumerate Mar Zuṭra's descendants: ואחריו רב גוריא · ואחריו מר זוטרא בנו · ואחריו מר יעקב

חצוב, but a variant makes the latter to have been a son of Jacob, Pinḥas's brother. Whether Ben-Meir's family was related to that of Mar Zuṭra cannot as yet be ascertained. Both families descended from David. But whereas Ben-Meir traced his origin from Rabbi Yehuda Hannasi, Mar Zuṭra was an offspring of the Babylonian Exilarchs.[1] The gap between Pinḥas and Ben-Meir, separated by a century, can only tentatively be filled up by the names of the latter's ancestors, viz. Meir, Moses, and Mūsa. Also a certain Yehuda b. 'Alān (of Tiberias), '*head of the academy of Jerusalem*', may have flourished in the ninth century.[2]

(6) Here we may conveniently deal with the relations between the Rabbinites and the Ḳaraites in Jerusalem. As has been suggested above, the school was transferred from Tiberias to the Holy City not long after the Arab conquest of Palestine, about 640 C.E. It became the spiritual centre for the Jewries in the Holy Land as well as in the neighbouring countries, Syria and Egypt. Rabbinic Judaism was supreme till 'Anan started his schism in Babylon in the second half of the eighth century. 'Anan was unsuccessful in his candidature for the office of Exilarch, and his followers, for some generations after him, must have been hardly pressed by the Rabbinites who had political champions in the 'heads of the Diaspora' (Exilarchs) of 'Irāḳ (Babylon). This must have induced a number of Ḳaraites to leave Babylon and Persia and settle in Palestine, where the

בנו · ואחריו רב שמעיה בנו · ואחריו רב נינא בנו · ואחריו רב מיגס בנו · ואחריו רב מיסא בנו · ואחריו רב נחמיה בנו · ואחריו רב אבדימי בנו · ורב אבדימי הוליד את ר׳ יעקב ואת ר׳ פינחס · ור׳ יעקב הוליד את ר׳ חצוב. This is the most complete list of his descendants. For a discussion of the other defective texts see Brüll, *Jahrbücher*, V, 94-7. The addition at the end of *Seder 'Olam Zuṭa* (*l.c.*, p. 73) mentions three sons of R. אביי (an evident corruption of Abdimi), viz. Jacob, Pinḥas, and 'Azarya, and adds that חצוב was the son of Pinḥas (and not of Jacob). Brüll suggests that חצוב is identical with the Massorite חביב בירבי פיפים, and that Pinḥas went by a second name פיפים. But as shown in A. A. 14 there is no ground for thus connecting these two scholars.

[1] About the difference between R. Yehuda Hannasi and the contemporary Babylonian Exilarch Huna as regards their respective descent from David, see Yer. Kilaim 32b, ll. 37-8.

[2] Firkowicz (in Pinsker, *Likkuṭe*, Appendices 64) gives an extract from an Introduction of Levi Hallevi (the son of Jefet b. 'Āli) to Deut. wherein we read of an explanation of ודי זהב (Deut. I. I) by Yehuda b. 'Alan (of Tiberias) ראש ישיבת ירושלים (see also Bornstein, *l. c.*, 181, top). But nothing further is so far known about him.

authority of the Exilarch was not so sustaining as in ʿIrāḳ. Gradually Jerusalem became a very important centre of Ḳaraism. Poznański (in Luncz's *Jerusalem*, X, 83 ff.) has discussed the problem of the first settlement of these sectaries in Jerusalem.[1] He had not yet the full text of Ben-Meir's second letter before him and therefore he assigned the beginning of the tenth century, about 150 years after ʿAnan, as the earliest date of their presence in Palestine. But Ben-Meir tells us expressly that his immediate ancestors, Meir and Moses, were the victims of animosity on the part of the Ḳaraites; hence two generations before 920. Moreover, a still earlier ancestor of Ben-Meir, Mūsa, probably also a head of the academy, actually lost his life in the עזרה through the 'seed of ʿAnan'. By עזרה, originally the Temple court, seemingly Mount Olivet is meant, where public services were held and where on several occasions (see *infra*, 63, note 1) the issue was fought out between the Rabbinites and the Ḳaraites. It is also probable that ʿAnan's descendants settled in Jerusalem, where, as members of the Davidic family, they would be the spokesmen of their fellow-sectaries. Therefore Ben-Meir refers to these Ḳaraite Nesiim[2] as the 'seed' or the 'sons' of ʿAnan (בני ענן, זרע ענן). This fact induced the later Ḳaraites to invent the fable that ʿAnan himself emigrated to the Holy City (see Pozn., *loc. cit.*, 85 ff.). The presence of the Ḳaraites in Jerusalem in the time of Aḥimaʿaṣ the elder can also be gathered from the story how R. Silanus' piyyuṭ, denouncing the 'heretics' (i.e. Ḳaraites), found such favour in the eyes of the members of the academy. These sectaries made their presence felt in more than one way, and their antagonism was a problem that must have greatly concerned the academy.

Probably Ḳaraism found a foothold in Palestine quite at the beginning of the ninth century, as indeed Salman b. Yeruḥam reports that after Benjamin Nahawendi the Ḳaraites began to build up a centre in Jerusalem.[3] They occupied a special quarter

[1] See also Munk, *Notice sur Abou'l Walid*, 14, note 3.

[2] About the Ḳaraite Nesiim see especially *infra*, p. 176 ff.

[3] In Pinsker, ל"ק, 22, top: ואח"כ עמדו אנשים ממזרח וממערב והוסיפו החזקה בדת והשקידה בחכמה ושמו מגמת פניהם לשבת בירושלים ועזבו רכושם וביתם ומאסו בעוה"ז והם הנמצאים כעת בירושלים עד שתתגלה בסופם השארית ... ואלה הם השושנים. See also Pozn., *l. c.* 88–9.

which went by the name of that of 'the Easterns', since most of them hailed from Babylon and Persia (see *infra*, p. 275). The new section characteristically adopted the mode of life of the 'mourners for Zion', whom they found in the Holy City. It became, as it were, the *raison d'être* for their stay there. Those who spent their life in such religious pursuits in Jerusalem were given the name of 'Lilies', still prevalent in the time of Solomon b. Yehuda (see *infra*, p. 141). The Ḳaraite spokesmen, in their appeals to their fellow-sectaries in the Diaspora to come and help to build up and (later on) to sustain the settlement, urged each one to leave all worldly pursuits in exile and spend one's life in the Holy City in prayer for Israel's redemption. This is the key-note of the appeal in a tract by one of the earliest Ḳaraite settlers (to be published by me in *J. Q. R.*, N.S.) as well as in the epistle of Sahl b. Maṣliaḥ.[1] Sahl's letter, in addition to the one addressed to Jacob b. Samuel, a disciple of Sa'adya,[2] contains interesting information about the internal life of the Palestinian Jewry. According to Sahl, Rabbinite disciples in Jerusalem and Ramlah followed in many respects the doctrines of Ḳaraism.[3] If this be given credence, these sectaries must have carried on an active propaganda and succeeded in winning over adherents of tradition. Needless to say this was not conducive to peaceful relations between the two sections, and friction must have been acute and frequent.

From Ben-Meir's letter, discussed above, it is evident that in the second half of the ninth century the Ḳaraites in Jerusalem had a great ascendancy over the Rabbinites. He himself suffered twice from them, so that he had to go to Bagdād to induce influential Rabbinites to intervene at the Caliph's court. It is difficult to account politically for the favour shown by the authorities in Palestine to these sectaries. It is stated that the Ḳaraite way of fixing the calendar by lunar observation, as against the Rabbinite calculation, found favour in the eyes of

[1] Published by Harkavy, *Hammeliṣ*, 1879, 639–42. See also Pozn., *l. c.*, 97 ff.

[2] In Pinsker, ל״ק, Appendices 27–43.

[3] P. 33: ואם יאמר אדם כי הנה אחינו תלמידי הרבנים בהר הקודש ובכרמלה (r. וברמלה) רחוקים מן המעשים האלה חייב אתה לדעת באמת כי הם בדרכי תלמידי התורה וכמעשי בני מקרא עשו ומהם למדו וכו׳. About the relations between the two sects in the time of Sol. b. Yehuda, see *infra*, p. 134 ff.

the Muslims as being a concession to Islām.[1] This may have been one of the factors, but it does not yet explain the privileged position of Ḳaraism in the Holy Land more than in any other country under Muslim sway. The following may be a probable solution. Nominally Palestine was a dependency of the Abbasid Caliph of Bagdād till Aḥmad ibn Ṭūlūn became governor of Egypt in 868 C.E. This powerful ruler soon began to extend the boundaries of his province. Throwing off all semblance of obedience to the Caliph, he marched, in April 878, on Damascus and overran the whole of Syria. Since then, with short interruptions, the latter province was governed by Egypt till the second half of the eleventh century, when the Seljuḳs became its rulers. Aḥmad died in 884, but his descendants continued to hold both countries. In 905 the house of Ṭūlūn was overthrown by an army dispatched from Bagdād. For thirty years afterwards Egypt remained in an unsettled state, being ruled by governors appointed by the Abbasid Caliph (see L.-P., 61 ff.).

Ibn Ṭūlūn's break with the court of Bagdād probably induced the Ḳaraites to make political use of the new state of affairs in order to gain the ascendancy in the Holy Land. Aided by influential fellow sectaries in Fusṭāṭ, the descendants of ʿAnan, the Ḳaraite Nesiim in Jerusalem, may have drawn the attention of the authorities to the fact that the chief political champion of the Rabbinites was another member of the Davidic family, the Exilarch, accredited to the court of Bagdād. In this way, apart from the general attitude of the Ḳaraites to curry favour with the Muslims in power (e. g. their lunar observation, as mentioned above), they succeeded in having the better of their opponents. Naturally their antagonism would be felt above all by the spokesmen of Rabbinism in the Holy Land, the Gaon and his school. It seems as if the academy had to be transferred from

[1] Thus the author of the tract (referred to above, p. 61) writes: ולא יכלו דורשי תורה לפתוח פיהם במצות ײ מפחד רבנין כי היו . . . עד בוא מלכות ישמעאל כי הם עוזרים תמיד לקראין לשמור כתורת משה ועלינו לברך אותם . . . והם אוהבים לשומרי חודש בירח. An anonymous writer (in Pinsker, *l. c.*, Appendices, 95) states in the name of Saʿadya that ʿAnan, in order to curry favour with the ruling power of Islām, purposely adopted the lunar observation (עד שקמה מלכות ישמעאל וחדשו דת לבקש הירח ועמד ענן ראש הגולה בימיהם לבקש השררות ונעה אחריהם בעבור לעזרו).

Jerusalem to Ramlāh owing to the great local power of Ḳaraism in the Holy City.[1]

When the Ṭūlūnid dynasty was overthrown in 905 and both Egypt and Syria were again ruled by governors appointed by the 'Abbasid Caliph at Bagdād, the Rabbinites in Palestine probably began to appeal to influential Jews in the capital and particularly to the Exilarch to intervene on their behalf. Some time before 921, the Gaon Ben-Meir went in person to Bagdād to plead for the cause of Rabbinism. He writes distinctly in his letter to Babylon, 'And we came to you to be helped (first) by God and through you. You were kind to me. May God reward you.'[2] How far he was successful in his endeavour is not clear. Soon he was involved in severe conflict with Sa'adya about the calendar of 921/2. No doubt the Ḳaraites benefited by this dissension in the Rabbinite ranks to maintain their position in the Holy Land. Ben-Meir's own status as 'head of the school'

[1] Thus Sa'adya reports in his *Sepher Hammo'adim* (Bornstein, *l. c.* 74, bottom): וישלח את בנו בחדש הרביעי לשנת מאתים ושלשים ושלש ויבא ירושלם. From this it appears that Ben-Meir did not live in the Holy City. Now as Sahl b. Maṣliaḥ (above, p. 61, note 3) speaks of 'the disciples of the Rabbinites' in Jerusalem and in *Ramlāh*, it may be deduced that the Gaon and his school lived in this capital of the province of Filastin (Philistia), the seat of the governor. As we shall see farther on, other Geonim lived there (see also *J. Q. R.*, N. S., IX, 412). Jerusalem would be visited by them during the festivals, and especially on Hoshana Rabba, for the public services on Mount Olivet; also on special occasions, when public announcements were made by the Gaon or his representatives. Thus the fixing of the calendar would be proclaimed on Mount Olivet. Ben-Meir speaks of it as an old institution (see above, p. 50, note 2). The calendar of 921/2 was announced there. See *J. Q. R.*, N. S., V, 553, l. 11 ff.: והזכרתם כי ישבתם שומימין וקרא אתכם פחד ורעדה על הכרזת תלמידינו בהר הזתים סדרי מועדות (p. 555, l. 4 ff.); ובחזירתינו אל ארצנו (from Bagdād) הינינו שבחכם ובירכנו אתכם בהר הזתים מול היכל יי ובשער הכהן. See also the beginning of his first letter (Bornstein, *l. c.* 63): ותפילותינו עליכם תדירה ועל זקני יקר שלכם בהר הזיתים מול היכל ייי מקום הדום רגלי אלהינו ועל שערי מקדש ייי בקיבוץ כל ישׂ׳ לחג חג ייי חג הסכות.

[2] Above, p. 57, note 1. See also his supposed first letter to Babylon (Bornstein, *l. c.* 63, l. 10): וכשמוע כל ישראל שבחכם מפינו אז שמחו ועלצו . . . כי בהיותינו בבגדאד אצלכם לא נמנענו מלעזור אתכם בכל לבבנו ובכל נפשנו על הקושרים עליכם . . . Bornstein suggests that Ben-Meir sided in Bagdād with R. Mebasser and his following as against David b. Zakkai and Kohen Ṣedeḳ. But this point is still problematic.

was so well established that his antagonists in Babylon, the Exilarch and the heads of the schools, did not find it feasible to bring about Ben-Meir's removal from office by intervention at the Caliph's court.[1] The cause of Rabbinism in the Holy Land was probably greatly strengthened after the conquest of the Fāṭimids, when Palṭiel wielded great power in the state (see *infra*, p. 134, note 1).

(7) We have now arrived at a fixed date, viz. the year 921/2, when the calendar dispute between Ben-Meir and Sa'adya arose. Our chapter ends with the close of al-Ḥakim's reign in 1021. A century of the history of the Palestine Gaonate is to be considered here. Little is known of its internal affairs beyond what the documents about the calendar dispute disclose. Nor are responsa, emanating from the Jerusalem academy, preserved to any extent resembling those of the Babylonian schools. How far the authority of the Palestinian Geonim reached, and what amount of instruction they imparted to the Jewries all over the Diaspora, is very obscure. From the *Aḥima'aṣ Chronicle* we learn that Italian Jewry kept up connexions with these Geonim. In 960 'the people of the Rhine' (אנשי רינוס) sent to 'the scholars of Palestine' inquiries about the rumour of the advent of the Messiah, and about a legal difficulty (cp. *R. É. J.*, XLIV, 237 ff.). The Khazars also knew of the school at Jerusalem. Thus the Khagan Joseph, in his famous reply to Ḥasdai ibn Shapruṭ, writes about the date of the Messianic age, 'Our eyes are directed towards the Lord our God, and to the scholars of Israel in the academies of Jerusalem and of Babylon' (אנחנו עינינו אל ה׳ אלהינו ואל חכמי ישראל הישיבה שבירושלים ואל הישיבה שבבבל ואנו רחוקים מציון). We propose here, with the help of new material, to construe a few lists of families of Geonim from the time of Ben-Meir up to Joshiah. A few letters from the last Gaon will in conclusion furnish new information of interest concerning Palestinian affairs in general. Poznański (in *Babyl. Geon.*) summarizes all the data known to him about the Palestinian Gaonate (pp. 81–97). As a result of his construction of these data, we have the chronological list of the occupants of the dignity (p. 97). As will be

[1] Sa'adya in his *Sepher Hammo'adim* (*l. c.* 79) writes: ויניחו אותו ליום נקם ועברה השמור לכל מדיח ולא התעשתו לקחת אגרות מאת המלך להסירו.

shown here, this list is far from being complete, and several of his assumptions upon which it is based require modification.

(8) *Ben-Meir's Family.*

As pointed out above (p. 57), Ben-Meir's ancestors, Meir and Moses and Mūsa, were probably heads of the school. He himself presided over a fully constituted academy with an Ab-Bet-Dīn and other dignitaries.[1] Several times his sons are referred to, and once his brother (or brothers) are mentioned.[2] Perhaps Isaac Ab was his brother. One of his sons proclaimed on Mount Olivet the calendar for 921/2 which gave rise to the whole dispute between Palestine and Babylon. The school was probably situated then in Ramlāh, which was a flourishing commercial centre and must have been a more suitable place than Jerusalem. It is also probable that owing to the Ḳaraites possessing much power in the Holy City, the Rabbinites found it advisable to have their academy in Ramlāh. We have also found Sahl b. Maṣliaḥ, several decades later, referring to the 'disciples of the Rabbinites on the Holy Mount (i.e. Jerusalem) and in Ramlāh' (above, p. 61, note 3). Ben-Meir was succeeded by his son Meir, styled ראש ישיבת גאון יעקב (a title very likely borne by his predecessors). He probably took that active part in the calendar dispute which the documents report. His father remained in office even after the dispute. Though Palestine was then still under the suzerainty of the Bagdād Caliph, the Exilarch and the heads of the Babylonian schools did not endeavour to obtain, probably because of inability, from the government the deposition of their opponent Ben-Meir (above, p. 64). When he died is as yet unknown. Also his further activities are obscure. In A. A. 15 all the data about Ben-Meir's family are fully discussed. As a result, it has been established that this Gaon's name was Yehuda, and that his descendants were connected with the

[1] Bornstein, *l. c.* 62–3, see also *R. É. J.*, LXVII, 50 (Ben-Meir's letter): שאו שלום ממנו ומן יצחק אב בית דין שלנו ומן סנהדר׳ גדולה וסנהד׳ קטנה היושבת לפנינו ומן החכמים והמשנים ומפלהדרין ומן תלמידין ומן הזקנים והשפ׳ (=והשפטים) והסופ׳ (=והסופרים) והחז׳ (=והחזנים) ומן החורין והסגנ׳ (=והסגנים) ומכל עם ייי שארית ישראל הדרים במקדש ייי ובצבי ארצות. . . .

[2] Ibid. 64, l. 3: והיו חמודיי וכל סנהדרין שלנו בצאתם אל כל המקומות מודיעים וכו׳; see also above, p. 54, note 2.

Palestinian Gaonate till its close in the time of the Crusades The last Gaon from this family was Joshiah (*c.* 1015–20), but the last Ab, Ṣadoḳ, only attained this dignity after 1094. Severa members of this Gaonic family settled in Egypt.

About the individual Geonim from Moses Gaon, Ben-Meir's grandfather, to Joshiah Gaon very little is known. Ben-Mei and his son Meir became prominent on account of the calenda dispute in 921. Of the literary productions of all these heads of the academy almost nothing has remained. A few letters by Joshiah Gaon, whom we find in office in 1015, are discussed at the end of this chapter. It should only be added that his Ab was Ḥananya b. . . . Gaon, a priest, as will be shown there.

(9) *The priestly Geonim Joseph, Samuel and Yosé* (?).

We hear of a Gaon in Palestine in the second half of the tenth century, Joseph Hakkohen, about whose ancestors nothing furthe is known. In the damaged fragment (given in A. A. 16, I, no. 1), unfortunately undated, his signature is found together with that of his son Samuel Hakkohen the 'Third', who later on succeeded to the Gaonate. Whether the other signatory, Aaron Hakkohen the 'Fourth, and a descendant of Geonim', was another son of Joseph is not clear. But of an Abraham Hakkohen b. Joseph, 'head of the Palestine academy', we learn from MS. Adler 223 (discussed in A. A. 16, IV). He is no doubt a son of the above Gaon. The Memorial-list (no. 2) mentions, after Solomon b. Yehuda and his son, Samuel Hakkohen Gaon and his son Yosé Gaon. Evidently Samuel Hakkohen b. Joseph, who occupied the Gaonate towards the end of the tenth century, is meant, as we shall see presently. He ought therefore to have been mentioned before Solomon b. Yehuda. A Yosé Hakkohen Gaon occurs here for the first time. But while further evidence is lacking, it is doubtful whether he really presided over the school. Ibn Abitur, in his letter to Samuel Hakkohen (to be discussed presently), greets also his son, who would be identical with this Yosé. But under Joshiah Gaon we find a Ḥananya Hakkohen Ab b. X. Gaon, who, according to the chronology, should be a son of Samuel Hakkohen. Altogether the genealogy of this family is still obscure. Ibn Abitur also styles Samuel 'the descendant of Geonim' (נין גאונים). If נין be taken exactly in the meaning of grandson,[1] then Joseph's father was also president of the academy.

We shall now deal with the important MS. Adler 4009 (see my remarks in *J. Q. R.*, N. S., VII, 475–6). Since then I had occasion to make a copy of the whole fragment which is given in A. A. 16, II. It seems to be a part of a collection of letters received by the Gaon Samuel during his period of office. We have not before us the originals of these letters, but a copy of them arranged perhaps chronologically. Thus on leaf 1, r., ll. 1–12, we have the end of an epistle from Sherira and Hai, dated Ab 13th, 1300 Sel. = 989 C. E. Then we have לר' יוסף, the copyist's indication that the next letter emanates from R. Joseph (i. e. Joseph b. Isaac the Spaniard, Ibn Abitur). This letter extends from fol. 1, r., l. 13, till verso, last line. Between the leaves there is a gap. But the whole of the second leaf is the end of Joseph's letter to a Gaon, no doubt our Samuel. Very likely it is the same letter, the beginning of which we have on the first leaf. One or two leaves are therefore missing to complete the epistle.

The fragment tells us several details of interest. From the words of Sherira and Hai we learn that they were on intimate relations with the Palestinian Gaon. They refer at the beginning of the part preserved (ll. 1–2) to some person whom they greatly esteem. Samuel is requested to read the letter in public before the congregation, 'for thus has been done there to our fathers several times'. This shows that still earlier the Pumbedita Geonim kept up relations with the Palestinian Jewry.[2] The Gaon should report whether his correspondents' request has been fulfilled. If he has any demands to make from Sherira and Hai, they will be glad to comply with his wishes.

From Ibn Abitur's epistle we learn that he visited the Gaon and was well received by the school. He subsequently went to Egypt, whence the present letter was sent. There a certain person publicly insulted Ibn Abitur. He was evidently a partisan of the Spanish scholar's opponent, Ḥanok b. Moses. As is well known from Ibn Daud's account (ed. Neubauer, *Med. Jew.*

[1] See, however, A. C. 25, 1, where the Gaon Elijah Hakkohen b. Solomon is styled נין . . . שלמה.

[2] Cp. my remarks in *J. Q. R.*, N. S., VII, 474 ff.

Chron., I, 69–71), one of the foremost disciples of R. Moses, one of the famous 'four captives', was Joseph b. Isaac Ibn Saṭanas (known as Ibn Abitur), who translated the whole Talmud into Arabic for the King al-Ḥakam (961–75). After R. Moses' death, Ibn Abitur refused to accept the authority of his master's son and successor Ḥanok. Soon after Ḥasdai Ibn Shapruṭ's death, the Cordova community was split up into two opposing factions. Ḥanok's party had the upper hand, and Ibn Abitur, after having been excommunicated, left Spain and went as far as Hai's academy. But the Gaon did not receive him on account of his being under the ban. Finally Ibn Abitur left for Damascus, where he died.[1]

From our fragment we gather several other details not mentioned by Ibn Daud. Ibn Abitur stayed for a time with the Palestine Gaon, Samuel Hakkohen, whom he succeeded in winning over to his side. He afterwards went to Egypt (Fusṭāṭ), where a partisan of Ḥanok, whose identity is unknown, publicly insulted him. This person was excommunicated by the Spanish scholar and sentenced to undergo flagellation. He tried to escape his sentence by proposing to R. Shemarya (no doubt Shemarya b. Elḥanan, the head of the Fusṭāṭ court) to relieve him from the flogging on condition that he paid a fine to be distributed among the poor (fol. 2, r., 15 ff.). But Shemarya refused to absolve him from the ban. Ibn Abitur must have had followers in Fusṭāṭ and also authority to announce the ban on every Sabbath (verso, l. 1 ff.) against the abettors of the persons who insulted him. Even if this person leaves 'Egypt', i.e. Fusṭāṭ (l. 3), Ibn Abitur is to inform all the communities about him. The Gaon Samuel is requested to aid him in his cause. Samuel must have formerly written epistles to Ḥanok in a friendly and complimentary manner. These the partisan in Fusṭāṭ produced in the synagogue on a Sabbath to prove on whose side the Gaon was. But Ibn Abitur retorted on that occasion that these letters were written before the Gaon knew of 'the folly and weak-mindedness of that man' (i.e. Ḥanok). During his stay with the Gaon, he succeeded in winning him over to his side (ll. 11–16).

[1] ונכנס אבן שטנאש בספינה והלך עד ישיבתו של רב האיי גאון וכמדומה היה שיקבלנו רב האיי שהיה שונא לר׳ חנוך . . . ואעפ״כ שלח לו רב האיי שלא יבא לפניו שאם יבא אליו יחוש לנדיו הרב והלך אבן שטנאש לדמשק ומת שם.

The whole letter is written in a peremptory manner. Though styling himself 'the most insignificant of his disciples' (fol. 1, v., l. 4), Ibn Abitur shows little humility towards the Gaon and hints several times that the latter will be guilty of improprieties if he fail to support him fully by excommunicating all his opponents (see especially fol. 2, v., ll. 10–11). The Spanish scholar had a high opinion of himself, while those of the other side were not worth even 'the peeling of garlic' (fol. 2, r., l. 9). On the whole, his maxim was to convince those not agreeing with him by ruthless excommunication and punishment. In order to inspire the Gaon with the same attitude he writes (fol. 2, v., l. 19 ff.), 'Let his honour know that the grandfather of my grandfather (may God have mercy with them) had powerful authority in Spain. We cannot recount his (noble) qualities, both in religious and secular life. He had the right in Spain of resorting to the four kinds of capital punishment, which nobody else in the Diaspora could do. Because he was a rod for smiting the wicked, they named him "grievous scourge" (or "scourge of man", a second Attila!). This was praiseworthy before the Creator and (every) creature.' This report of Ibn Abitur is highly interesting. As is known from other sources, the Jewish ecclesiastical authorities in Spain seem to have had wide coercive powers, amounting even to capital punishment. Thus an informer used to be executed. Also on one occasion certain heretics (probably Ḳaraites) were flogged to death in Spain.[1]

From Egypt Ibn Abitur probably went to Bagdād to see Hai Gaon, but was not received. Ibn Daud tells us that he wrote from the East a letter to the Cordova community in praise of Ḥanok. This must have taken place some time after the above epistle, wherein he still shows animosity to his opponent. A. A. 16, III contains a poem by Ibn Abitur which he sent to the people of Andalusia after he left his native country. It is very damaged. Each strophe consists of three rhymed hemistichs,

[1] See my remarks in *J.Q.R.*, N.S., X, 129, note 192. Cp. further Ibn Daud (*l.c.* 79) עד שנתחזק הנשיא ר׳ יוסף . . . וגרשם (*sc.* the Ḳaraites) מכל מבצרי קשטילייא חוץ ממבצר אחד קטן שנתן להם מפני שלא רצה להרגם שאין דנים דיני נפשות בזמן הזה . . . It appears that had the Nasi wished so, he would have had the power to execute them.

while the fourth is from a Biblical verse ending in the Divine name. The poem shows clearly how incensed Ibn Abitur was against his countrymen who caused him to go into exile. God will punish them. Quoting Amos 8. 11, the banished scholar hints that one day the Andalusian Jews will recognize his superior knowledge and long to have him back in their midst (see l. 3). In a poem, modelled after the same pattern, a certain b. Ḳalima (?), evidently a follower of Ḥanok, retorts vigorously by accusing Ibn Abitur of serious misdeeds, especially of denouncing his co-religionists to the secular authorities. A grave charge indeed that of informing. It may be that after several years of wandering from one country to another, this hapless scholar discovered that his lot was the result of his own imperious temper, and became conscious also of the good qualities of his opponent Ḥanok.

(10) *The family of Ebyatar and Maṣliaḥ.*

A. A. 17 contains the data about this family of priestly Geonim. It had apparently no connexion with Joseph Hakkohen and his son Samuel (no. 9). The first of this family to hold office in the Palestinian school was apparently Yehoseph Hakkohen Bet-Dīn (probably = Ab-Bet-Dīn). He was descended from a family of Geonim who lived very likely in Sura. It has been established, moreover, that Yehoseph's son Solomon was Gaon in Palestine before Solomon b. Yehuda and probably after Joshiah. The genealogy of Solomon's descendants is outside the scope of this chapter. (It will be given farther on, Chapter IV.)

Reviewing the century dealt with here (921–1021), we find a number of Geonim belonging to three different families. The most represented one is that of Ben-Meir, who traced his descent from Hillel, hence Davidic origin. The members of the other two families were priests. We have thus obtained the following, to my thinking almost complete,[1] list of the Palestinian Geonim who held office during the above century. Wherever possible the name of the corresponding Ab is placed side by side. The dignity of Gaon was not hereditary. Hence the different families. Usually the Ab of the time became head of the school at the demise of its chief.

[1] It is possible that the father of Joseph Hakkohen (no. 7) was also a Gaon. A Yosé Hakkon Gaon b. Samuel Hakkohen (no. 9) is doubtful (see above, p. 66 f.).

Geonim.	'*Fathers*' (אבות).
1. [Mūsa, probably].	
2. [Moses, probably].	
3. [Meir I, probably].	
4. Yehuda = Ben Meir (921).	Isaac.
5. Meir II, ראש ישיבת גאון יעקב.	
6. Abraham.	
7. Joseph Hakkohen.	Joshiah.
8. Aaron.	Yehoseph Hakkohen.
9. Samuel Hakkohen.	Joseph (above, p. 37, note 1).
10. Joshiah (1015).	Ḥananya Hakkohen.
11. Solomon Hakkohen.	[Solomon b. Yehuda].
12. [Solomon b. Yehuda, died 1051].	

Of course, all these Geonim held previously the office of Ab. Of the 'Fathers', mentioned in the right-hand column, only Solomon b. Yehuda became afterwards Gaon.

(11) In conclusion, a few letters from Joshiah Gaon will be discussed. A. A. 18 is probably addressed to Egypt. In this epistle, full of invectives, a certain opponent of the Gaon is vilified. The community addressed, very likely Fusṭāṭ, is thanked for having deposed this hated person. He is accused of the knowledge of Ḳaraism (i. e. ʿAnan's views). The opponent of Joshiah was perhaps a member of the Exilarchic family, a descendant of Bustanai, who settled somewhere in Palestine or in Egypt, and as Nasi (perhaps of the Ḳaraites, see above, p. 60) came into conflict with the academy and its head (cp. the notes to the text). A. A. 19 is a letter sent by Joshiah to the congregation of Damietta. Its spiritual leaders are ʿAmram בית דין הממחה, evidently the head of the local Bet-Dīn, Elʿazar השופט, ʿAmram הדיין, and two other people, probably the Rosh Haḳḳahal and the Parnes. The Gaon asks for support as the Jews in Palestine are in great trouble and he suffers with them. He used to be *maintained by the government.* But since two years, when the Palestinian Jews were fined, he could not remind the authorities of the grant due to him. The Damietta community is requested to show their generosity to Joshiah as they did to the former Geonim (ll. 10–17). Above (p. 38 f.) we have seen that Elḥanan b. Shemarya also received grants from the Caliph. Probably with the persecutions of the Jews by

al-Ḥakim, which commenced in 1012, the Gaon Joshiah was deprived of the emoluments given to him by the government. It is obscure since when these grants date. Perhaps Menasse, when Wezīr of Damascus, or still earlier Palṭiel, were instrumental in inducing the Caliph and the court to support the central seats of Jewish learning in Egypt and in Palestine. About the deplorable conditions in the Holy Land during al-Ḥakim's persecutions, we are informed in A. A. 20. It is evidently a draft of letters by Joshiah which somehow found its way to Fusṭāṭ. Recto contains an epistle addressed to the congregation of Rafaḥ, a town on the frontier between Egypt and Palestine. On verso we have a copy of a letter, with beginning and end missing, which is clearly by our Joshiaḥ. It is to introduce Samuel b. Ṣemaḥ the Ḥazzan (b. Lamdaḳi), who probably went to Egypt to obtain support. The Gaon mentions that Samuel is a man of learning and the scribe of his school.[1] In fact this Samuel is one of the signatories of the document, dated 1015, drawn up at Ramlāh and signed by Joshiah (A. A. 15, 1). The Gaon mentions the destruction of the synagogues that is going on (l. 12 ff.). The Jews were probably expelled from Jerusalem. Hence the Gaon had to take refuge in Ramlāh (cp. ll. 18–19; right-hand side, l. 4). In a later epistle (A. A. 21), addressed to Netaneel, the banker, b. Aaron (probably of Fusṭāṭ), Joshiah mentions that the Palestinian Jews are still busy with the rebuilding of their synagogues (l. 13 f.). Evidently the persecutions were then at an end (about 1020). We thus find Joshiah Gaon still alive at the close of al-Ḥakim's reign. However, the school remained in a precarious state. Its upkeep was dependent on the donations from all over the Diaspora. The banker Netaneel is also appealed to for his contribution.

Al-Ḥakim's order to pull down the synagogues and the churches seems to have been conscientiously carried out even in the distant provinces. Thus the Jews of Tarābulus (Tripoli), on the Syrian coast of the Mediterranean, had their synagogue converted into a mosque. In addition, several of their houses were demolished, probably as a result of the persecutions. Subsequently government officials occupied their sites without paying any rent. When the persecutions ceased, the synagogues were

[1] סופר שער שלנו; שער stands for שער הישיבה.

in several places returned to the Jews (A. A. 22, l. 21). But in Tarābulus the former Jewish house of prayer, having been converted into a mosque, could not revert to its previous condition. The local Jews had to hire from the Muslims a rather unsuitable hall to serve them as a synagogue. They therefore appealed to Ḥesed b. Sahl, a brother of Abū Saʿad (both of whom were highly influential elders in Cairo-Fusṭāṭ from about 1025–48, see especially *infra*, p. 76 ff.), to obtain for them a government order entitling them to erect a synagogue on any of the sites whereon formerly their houses stood. In the letter it is also mentioned that the year before, the community of Jubail, also on the coast between Tarābulus and Bairūt, erected a new house of prayer and met with no opposition from the Muslim citizens.

Joshiah must have sent out appeals during the persecutions for support even to distant European countries. A. A. 23 furnishes interesting information. It is an epistle addressed to Ḥananya Ab-Bet-Dīn b. X. Hakkohen, the late Rosh Yeshiba, from Abū'l-Hayy b. Ḥakim. He acknowledges the receipt of the letter from Joshiah Rosh Yeshiba to the congregations 'that dwell in the cities of Sicily'. The epistle was duly read in the synagogue and the worshippers promised contributions for the school. But before these could be collected such a heavy impost was made by the government that many people became insolvent and some had even to flee the country. The elders of the community (probably of Palermo) do not like to reply to the Gaon without enclosing some money. Abū'l Ḥayy, probably the local scholar, therefore writes to Ḥananya, *the 'Father' of the academy*,[1] informing him of what had happened and promising to do his best for the school during the ensuing festivals. The letter is written on new-moon-day of Elul. It is not surprising to learn of the relations between Palestine and Italy, since already in the time of Aḥimaʿas the elder, as we have seen, donations were sent from the latter country to the Palestinian school.[2] This practice was probably kept up during the inter-

[1] See also my remarks in *J. Q. R.*, N. S., IX, 411–12.

[2] As a further example of the relations between the Jewries of Palestine and Italy we have the case of ספר הורית הקורא brought from Jerusalem to Bari. See *R. É. J.*, XXIII, 310–11: זה ספר הורית הקורא אשר הובא מירושלים לבאר

vening time. Our fragment appears to be the original. Whether it ever reached Ḥananya Ab or was retained for some unknown reason in Fusṭāṭ during the process of transmission cannot be ascertained. It may also have found its way back to Fusṭāṭ after its perusal by the 'Father' of the school.

בדרך קצרה והביאו יוסף בן חייא הסופר משם מתורגם בלשון ערבי כאשר העתיקו לשם ור׳ נתנאל בר׳ משלם (*v.l.* ר׳ משלם בן נתנאל) הפכו מלשון ערבי ללשון הקודש בעיר מיינצא. As Porges rightly suggests, for לבאר read לבארי. Accordingly the book was brought from Jerusalem to Bari by a short route. The bringer was Joseph b. Ḥiyya, the scribe, who copied the book, composed in Arabic, while Jacob b. Meshullam (or vice versa) translated it in Mayence into Hebrew.

CHAPTER II

The Period of Solomon ben Yehuda (died in 1051 C.E.)

OUR knowledge of the history of the Egyptian and the Palestinian Jewries, from the death of al-Ḥakim (1021) to the middle of the eleventh century, is greatly enriched by a considerable number of Genizah fragments. Only a few of them have hitherto been published, and on these several false constructions have been placed. The material incorporated here will render it possible to place persons and events in a proper historical setting, and to establish chronological order and sequence.

The period we are dealing with in this chapter may be called that of the Palestinian Gaon, Solomon b. Yehuda, who probably succeeded to the dignity in 1025. His death in 1051 is established by a Seliḥa composed by Ephraim b. Shemarya of Fusṭāṭ.[1] The material dependence of the Palestinian Jews on their Egyptian brethren becomes at this time more and more vital. The Gaon had to encounter much opposition within and to combat adverse circumstances without. A very prominent as well as energetic representative the Palestinian academy had in the above-mentioned Ephraim b. Shemarya, the spiritual guide of the Palestinian community of Fusṭāṭ. Solomon's letters are exceptionally numerous. Supplemented by other epistles, they tell us a good

[1] MS. Adler 2804 contains a loose leaf of a Seliḥa, beginning אבלה נבלה הארץ וכו'. The superscription reads as follows: (1) למא תופ[י] רבינו שלמה גאון (2) עמל אפ[ר]ים הדה אלסליחה (3) פי אלנצף אייר סנה אֹשֹסֹבֹ, 'When our master Solomon Gaon died, Ephraim composed this Seliḥa in the middle of Iyyar, 1362 Sel.' (= 1051 C. E.). There is hardly any doubt that by Ephraim the Fusṭāṭ Ḥaber is meant (see also *J. Q. R.*, N. S., IX, 412). Solomon's grandfather is called Berakya. Oxford MS. Heb., f. 29, fols. 69ᵃ–71 (cp. Bodl. 2729⁵), contains liturgical compositions by a contemporary of the Gaon: חיש זמן קץ לה בימי (69ᵃ, l. 7) אדונינו שלמה ראש הישיבה ביר̇ יהודה; (71ᵃ, l. 8) יוסף לקנות פעם שניה · יהיה ישראל שלישיה · בחיי אדוננו שלמה ברבי יהודה נין ברכיה.

deal of both the political and the internal affairs of several communities in Egypt and in Palestine.

We propose first to introduce here a number of prominent Egyptian Jews who on account of their influence, either direct or indirect, in the realm were appealed to by their co-religionists. Also the spiritual leaders of the Egyptian Jewry will pass under review. Some of these were already known. Yet their status and prominence were not fully appreciated. Subsequently the correspondence of Solomon b. Yehuda will be considered.

(1) Aẓ-Ẓāhir succeeded his father al-Ḥakim in the year 1021. The effects of that terrible quarter of a century of al-Ḥakim's rule could not be speedily undone. Nor was his son, sixteen years of age, the man for the crisis. The affairs of the state were for four years managed by his aunt, the Princess Royal. From 1025–7 the country suffered famine owing to a serious failure of the Nile inundation. During aẓ-Ẓāhir's reign the obnoxious restrictions of his father were cancelled and no further persecutions of Jews and Christians recurred. In 1036 the Caliph was the victim of a plague. He was followed by his seven-year-old son Maʿadd, heir to the throne already since the age of eight months. He now assumed the Caliphate under the name of al-Mustanṣir, 1036–94 (L.-P. 134–6).

We hear now of a Jew, Abū Saʿad, who began to exercise much power in the state. The following is Wüstenfeld's account (*l.c.*, Abt. III, 1 ff.). Two Jewish merchants became prominent in Cairo, namely, Abū Saʿad Ibrāhīm and his brother Abū Naṣr Hārūn, the sons of Sahl of Tustar (modern Shuster in Persia). The former was a dealer in very rare and precious things and made long journeys to acquire them. The latter was a banker with whom people deposited their savings. He acted also as a broker of goods from ʿIrāḳ and other countries. Both were widely known and popular. They acquired a huge fortune. The Caliph aẓ-Ẓāhir used to be a frequent customer of Abū Saʿad, from whom he bought antiques for his collections. Once he acquired from Abū Saʿad a beautiful Sūdānī slave-girl, who became afterwards the mother of Maʿadd, the future Caliph. When her seven-year-old son ascended the throne, the Wālīda managed the affairs of the state for him till he became of age. She had great influence in the court, and her former master,

Abū Saʿad, was in her confidence. As long as the old Wezīr al-Jarjarāi lived, viz. till 1044, Abū Saʿad kept in the background. In this year he made the Caliph's mother a present of a so-called silver ship provided with a tent. It is reported that the value of the silver amounted to 130,000 Dirhems (16 Dirhem = 1 Dīnār). In workmen's wages and in gilding the boat 2,400 Dīnārs were spent excluding the expenses of the ornamentation. If these figures are only approximately correct, Abū Saʿad's wealth was great indeed. The gold value of the Dīnār is 10*s*., but compared to the modern rate it was worth 30*s*.[1]

Ibn al-Anbāri was appointed in 1044 Wezīr, after al-Jarjarāi, on the recommendation of the Wālīda. He took objection to Abū Saʿad's influence in the court. The friction came to a head when once Abū Naṣr, Abū Saʿad's brother, was insulted by a servant of the Wezīr. Abū Naṣr thought that he had only to complain to the Wezīr in order to obtain satisfaction or at least an apology. But, on the contrary, he received from him still more insults. The Wezīr's hostile attitude towards these two brothers became manifest. The Wālīda was constantly incited against the chief minister of the state till he was deposed. On Abū Saʿad's recommendation, the next Wezīr was a renegade Jew, Abū Manṣur (or Abū Naṣr, Abu'l Fatḥ) Ṣadaḳa b. Yūsūf al-Fellāḥi. He was now entirely dependent on Abū Saʿad's goodwill. Meanwhile the latter continued his intrigues against his enemy, the ex-Wezīr Ibn al-Anbāri, with the result that he was executed in July, 1048. The new Wezīr, afraid lest the same fate should befall him, began to scheme against the life of the powerful Abū Saʿad. He bribed the Caliph's Turkish body-guard to assassinate the Wālīda's protégé. But she soon avenged her former master's death. Nine months later (still in 440 A. H.) the Wezīr met the same fate.[2]

The above account of Wüstenfeld is taken from Arabic sources. It is difficult to ascertain how far it agrees with the actual events, or more precisely, how far Abū Saʿad's tragic end was due to aggressive interference on his part or to the jealousy which a Jew in prominent position almost inevitably was bound to call forth.

[1] See Le Strange, *Palestine under the Moslems*, p. 44.

[2] See also Quatremère, *Mémoires géogr. et histor. sur l'Égypte*, II, 296 ff., and L.-P. 137.

The Persian traveller Naṣīr-ī-Khusrau, who visited Egypt in the years 1046–9, gives the following account, apparently that of an eye-witness, of Abū Saʿad's end.[1] There was a Jewish jeweller who had free access to the sovereign; he was very rich and the Caliph entirely trusted him with acquiring for him precious stones. One day the Caliph's soldiers fell upon him and massacred him. After having committed this murder, they feared the prince's anger. They mounted their horses, came together to the number of 20,000 on the site of Meidan, and gained the plain. This demonstration filled the population of the capital with terror. The soldiers remained on horseback till mid-day. A eunuch of the Caliph left the palace, and keeping close to the gate, shouted to them, 'The Caliph asks you whether you will obey him or not?' They all answered together, 'We are obedient servants, but we have committed a crime!' The eunuch spoke to them again, 'The Caliph orders you to retire'. They dispersed at once. The Jew that had been murdered was called Abū Saʿad. He had a son[2] and a brother. His riches were so considerable that God only can estimate them. It is reported that he had on the terrace of his house 300 vases of silver and in each of them a tree was planted. The great number of these trees, all laden with fruits, gave the terrace the appearance of a garden. Abū Saʿad's brother wrote a letter which he sent to the Caliph. Therein he promised, on account of the fear he had, to pay at once to the Exchequer the sum of 200,000 Dīnārs Magrebi. The Caliph did not accept the letter and had it torn up in public. Afterwards he sent word to Abū Saʿad's brother, 'Be without fear and return to your people. Nobody has any claim upon you. As for me, I have no need of the money you speak of.' He gave letters of surety to Abū Saʿad's brother and son.

So far Naṣir-ī-Khusrau. But this letter of surety availed Abū Saʿad's brother, Abū Naṣr, for a few hours only. From Genizah fragments discussed here it is evident that both brothers were killed on the same day. It is only natural that these two

[1] *Sefer Nameh, Relation du voyage de Nasir i Khosrau*, edited and translated by Charles Schefer, Paris, 1881, pp. 159–60.

[2] His name was Abū ʿAli al-Ḥasan. During 1063–4 he occupied twice the dignity of office of Wezīr (see Wüstenfeld, *l. c.*, III, 27). Whether he remained a Jew, and as such could be the first minister of the state, is not known.

Jews should have occupied a most prominent position within the Jewry of the Fāṭimid empire. Their names frequently recur in the Genizah fragments. The more powerful of the brothers was Abū Saʿad, but Abū Naṣr seems to have taken a more active part in the Jewish communal affairs. Abū Saʿad began to come to the forefront soon after 1025. His former slave-girl gave birth to Maʿadd on Jumada 16th, 420 A. H. (1029), who eight months afterwards was declared heir to the throne. Naturally the black Wālīda became then a very important person in the court, and through her Abū Saʿad became influential. His importance gradually increased after 1036, when Maʿadd ascended the throne and his mother was regent during his childhood. From 1044 Abū Saʿad's influence reached its zenith till he met his tragic end in 1048.

The full names of these two brothers were Abraham (Abū Saʿad) and Ḥesed (Abū Naṣr) b. Yashar (Sahl) of Tustār. In this city there existed a Ḳaraite sect, called Tustarians (Dastarians). We find also a Ḳaraite writer of the eleventh century called Sahl b. Faḍl (ישר בן חסד בן ישראל דסתרי).[1] But these brothers were undoubtedly Rabbinites. Their paternal uncle is probably a signatory of documents issued by the Rabbinite courts at Fusṭāṭ (see *infra*, pp. 122, note 1, and 150). As Babylonians they belonged to their native community in Fusṭāṭ. Accordingly we find Solomon b. Yehuda writing to Sahlān b. Abraham, the Alluf and Resh Kallah of this congregation, to acquaint Abū Saʿad with the Gaon's requests.

Firkowicz, who evidently knew something of Abū Saʿad's importance, has forged two colophons of Bible Codices relating to him. Strack and Baer, *Diḳduḳe ha-Ṭeʿamim* of Ben Asher (p. xxxiv, No. 12), printed the following colophon of a Pentateuch Codex from the Firkowicz Collection, זה ספר תורת יהוה תמימה עם

[1] Cp. Ibn al-Hītī's *Arabic Chronicle of Ḳaraite Doctors* (*J. Q. R.*, IX, 435), pp. 8 and 16; Pozn., *J. Q. R.*, XIX, 70–2. A copy of David b. Boʿaṣ's commentary on Num. 25. 10–30. 1 (פינחס) was presented to a Moses b. Ḥesed (Or. 2561, see Margoliouth, *Catalogue*, I, 227, col. 2: הקדיש אותו המשכיל עלי [בן] שלמה ז"ל על המשכיל משה (?) בן השר חסד ז"ל ועל דורות ב[ניו] אחריו בכל מקום שיהיו). Both ʿAli and Moses seem to have been Ḳaraites as they are each styled המשכיל. Moses' father, 'the dignitary Ḥesed', who presumably was also a fellow sectarian, should, however, not be identified with our Ḥesed (Abū Naṣr).

מסורת אבי מר ור׳ אשר המלמד הסופר הזקן הגדול נֹנ מכרתי אני נחמיה בנו
לכנֹק השר הגדול מר ור׳ אברהם אלתסתרי משנה למלך במצרים ומכרתי לידו
ביום ראשון יד׳ לראש חדשים ערב חג הפסח שנת תשכֹא לחרבן בית
קדשנו (= 790 C.E.) יבנה בימינו אמן יזכה להגות בו הוא וזרעו וזרע זרעו
ויקוים עליו הכֹ [1] לא ימושו מפיך ומפי זרעך וג׳ אמן.[2] In another colophon Abraham al-Tustari is supposed to have presented a Codex in 847 C.E. (ביום ד׳ טו׳ לחדש זיו כה לספירה שנת תשעה לחרבן שני) to the Ḳaraite synagogue of Fusṭāṭ (לכנסת בני מקרא בצען מצרים).

Strack and Baer pointed out that Firkowicz changed the dates in the originals. They could not then, of course, determine Abraham's exact date, and they even assumed that 'most probably' the first colophon was entirely Firkowicz's invention. Now that we know of Abū Saʿad's standing in the Fātimid empire, we may surmise that in the second colophon the date was most likely 1047, which Firkowicz changed into 847! And probably, in the first colophon too, the date was the same. Hence a year before his assassination. He was then in the height of his power. The flattering title 'second to the king in Egypt' is probably genuine.[3] We find the famous Nagid Meborak also styled likewise (see *infra*, p. 209). But, of course, Nehemiah, the son of Asher the elder, could not have been the actual seller of this Codex to Abū Saʿad. Very likely it was a Codex with Asher's Massora which a contemporary of Abū Saʿad, say Nehemiah the Ḥazzan, the son of Abraham b. Sahlān (see *infra*, p. 97), sold to him! The magic change this colophon underwent in Firkowicz's hands is thus made intelligible. The fact that Abū Saʿad presented a Codex to the Ḳaraite Synagogue in Fusṭāṭ (if Firkowicz is to be trusted) does not necessitate the assumption of his having been a follower of this sect. As a rich and powerful Jew he may have been generous to both Rabbinites and Ḳaraites.

A letter from a descendant of the famous Gaon Ben-Meir to Abū Saʿad (b. Sahl), 'the great dignitary' (השר הגדול) who is

[1] = הכתוב, Isa. 59. 21.

[2] The same colophon is printed by Ginsburg, *Massorah*, III, 294, end, where השר הגול׳ is an obvious mistake for השר הגדול.

[3] According to Ibn al-Ṭuweir, Abū Saʿīd al-Tustari was Wezīr under al-Mustanṣir before al-Jarjarāi (see Ḳalḳashandi's *Geographie u. Verwaltung von Ägypten*, tr. Wüstenfeld, *l. c.*, vol. 25, 188, top).

identical with the person described here, is given in A. A. 15, 9ª.[1] We have also seen that the Jews of Tarābulus wrote to his brother, Ḥesed (b. Sahl), 'the mighty dignitary' (השר האדיר), to obtain for them permission from the government to build a synagogue (above, p. 73). Appendix B (= A. B.) contains in the first instance a poem in honour of prominent Fusṭāṭ Jews (No. 1). Three 'pious men' (חסידים) are praised for their generosity and charity. They are the choice of the elders (סגולת הזקנים, r., col. 1, l. 7). The first and most important is Abū Yāshār (אבי ישר), the second is called Joseph, while the third is a scholar Saʿadya, an author of comments, legal decisions, and Bible explanations (ll. 10–15). In accordance with their great qualities, these elders have children of their type, viz. 'Ḥesed, whose kindnesses are as the heavenly dew', and 'Abraham, the chief of benefactors . . ., Abū Saʿad whom God in His grace supported and made rule everywhere. May He give him Palestine for an inheritance . . . and may the Rock protect him in the presence of nations, rulers, and enemies' (r., col. 2, 1 ff.). The whole poem is clearly in honour of our Abū Saʿad. The author requests support for some people, hungry and needy, whom, moreover, their former friends slandered. In conclusion, greetings are given to Abū Saʿad 'the lord of all the elders' and to his son (חמודך, cp. also the letter in A. A. 15, 9ª, l. 8). Indeed Naṣīr-ī-Khusrau mentions that he had one son who, as we have seen (p. 78, note 2), was for some time Wezīr. By way of introduction, the poet mentions Abū Saʿad's father Sahl (i.e. Yāshār; אבי ישר is for metre's sake), and also his brothers Joseph and Saʿadya (see *infra*, pp. 82, 122, note 1, and 150). The poet afterwards mentions only Yāshār's sons Ḥesed and Abū Saʿad, devoting the greater part of the composition to the latter.

The next fragment (A. B. 2) is an epistle from Solomon b. Yehuda to Ephraim b. Shemarya of Fusṭāṭ. The Gaon writes that a letter reached him in the name of 'the mighty elder' Abraham (Abū Saʿad) al-Tustari b. Sahl concerning a deposit in his trust. Several names of respected elders of the Fusṭāṭ community are mentioned, namely, Ṣadaḳa b. ʿEzra, Ḥalfon Hallevi, 'the official over the merchants (פקיד הסוחרים)' b. Yefet, Ḥalfon b. Moses (ibn אבוקרה), Yefet the Babylonian b. Mebasser

[1] See also *J. Q. R.*, N. S., IX, 410.

(אלתפלפל), Joshu'a b. Armand, and Yefet Hakkohen b. Joseph The title, 'official over the merchants', I have also found in thre other fragments (see A. B. 2, note 3). Muḥassan b. Ḥusair (אבן אונת שמעאן), mentioned in 1026 C.E., is probably identica with the 'official over the merchants' in a document issued b Shemarya b. Elḥanan's court (given in A. A. 7[a]). More dat about Abū Sa'ad and Abū Naṣr will be given in the course o this and the next chapters.

Three fragments (A. B., Nos. 3–5) inform us about the tragi end of these brothers. A. B. 3 has on verso the superscription 'Piyyūṭ for the two late brothers Abraham (Abū Sa'ad) and hi brother Ḥesed (Abū Naṣr) the sons of Sahl al-Tustari'. Rect contains only the beginning of a composition for 'the great lord Ḥesed b. Yāshār. Evidently the elegy was continued on th missing leaves, which contained also the Piyyūṭ for Abū Sa'ad. Th dirge begins, 'A letter came from the corner of Ṣo'an (= Fusṭāṭ) in the name of a man called Ḥesed, to his uncle Sa'adya wit greetings to the elders. . . . Sons of Zion, have ye seen a calamit like mine . . .' Sa'adya is evidently the scholar mentioned in th poem above (A. B. 1) in connexion with the brother's fathe Yāshār (אבי ישר). A. B. 4 is an extract of a letter from 'Āl המומחה b. Abraham to the elders David, X (?) and Meborak th sons of 'Amram. He writes that he is in monetary difficultie and had to flee from prison to Egypt. He hoped he would fin the elder Ḥesed. But 'God has done His will, and indeed th verse has been fulfilled, On that day will the glory of Jacob b brought low' (Isa. 17. 4). 'Āli relies now on the support of hi correspondents who 'remained as the beating of an olive tree an as the grape gleanings when the vintage is done' (cp. Isa. 24. 13) There is little doubt that our Ḥesed (Abū Naṣr) b. Sahl is mean here. From the discreet allusions it is evident that his death wa a political one. He must have also fallen victim on the da when the Turkish body-guard, at the instigation of the Wezi Ṣadaḳa, assassinated his brother Abū Sa'ad. The writer of th letter as well as his correspondents are unknown to me.

Highly interesting is A. B. 5. It is in Solomon b. Yehuda' handwriting. Of the signature only the name 'Solomon' ha been preserved. The Gaon writes to Sahlān Alluf b. Abraham the spiritual head of the Babylonian community of Fusṭāṭ, abou the death of the 'two righteous men' (שני הצדיקים, l. 8). He mentions that already the day before, when the terrible news reached him, he sent two letters of condolence, one to Sahlān and another to the משוש (= משוש הישיבה). The latter is probably Abraham Hakkohen b. Isaac, a very influential physician (see under 2, and cp. *infra*, p. 183). Solomon writes discreetly about them, and the whole style of the letter shows that they are meant. They were the upholders of religion. What a sad fate (מיתה משונה, l. 9) overtook them through slanderers and jealous enemies. They were no rebels to deserve such a death. May God avenge them and may He place them among the ten martyrs. The congregations of 'the land of the West' (i.e. Egypt, see above, p. 30, note 1) have suffered a great loss. Indeed, through the sin of our generation the glory of Jacob is brought low. Solomon is calling together the Jews of Jerusalem to hold a memorial service. In conclusion the Gaon solicits support for his academy, which is in great straits. The former sources of income have dried up. Solomon complains that he is weak and cannot go even to synagogue. He was then very old. We know now that he lived for another three years.

(2) It is evident that neither of the brothers occupied the position of Nagid, else they would have been mentioned as such in our fragments. A document of 1038 (published by Gottheil, *J. Q. R.*, XIX, 467 ff.) mentions the 'just Sheikh Abū al-ʿImrān Mūsa ibn Yaʿḳūb ibn Isḥāḳ, the Israelite, physician to the exalted Majesty and chief of the Jewish community (in Fusṭāṭ), Rabbinite, Ḳaraite, and Samaritan' (p. 485, l. 17). A disputed synagogue of the Rabbinites was in his possession for more than forty years, since the 'upkeep, the jurisdiction, and authority in respect to it devolved upon whomsoever should be chief of the Jewish communities' (p. 487 f., ll. 36–7). The physician was probably the son of al-Moʿizz's doctor, Yaʿḳūb b. Isḥāḳ b. Mūsa (b. al-Razzan, Elʿazar, see above, p. 18). That he was Nagid (as Gottheil, *J. E.*, V, 68, col. 2, states) is not mentioned in this document. He was only the head of the communities in Cairo-Fusṭāṭ, hence ראש הקהלות, a title found in several Genizah fragments. As will be shown farther on (Chap. VI), this dignity was different from that of the Nagid who was the political head of the whole of Jewry in Egypt and in Palestine. In addition,

each congregation in the capital was represented by a chief wh bore the title ראש הקהל. Thus Samuel b. Abṭalion, as we sha see later on, was then head of the Palestinian community i Fusṭāṭ. But the whole subject will be discussed in the chapte on the communal organization (Chap. VI).

Nothing more is known about this 'chief of the communities' Mūsa, from the Genizah finds. As the Caliph's doctor he mus have been a man of influence. Two other physicians of promi nence were Isaac Hakkohen b. Furāt and his son Abraham A number of fragments given here testify to their importanc in the community. Isaac is styled, in a letter from Solomon b Yehuda to him, 'the elder of the congregations' (see *infra* p. 133). He is thanked therein for the political assistance h gave to the Palestinian school. The whole letter will be discusse in the next chapter. Isaac's son, Abraham, bears the title, 'th lord of the community'. He seems to have been a very influentia physician and also an all-round scholar.

A. B. 6 is from Elijah Hakkohen ('the son of a late Gaon', the later Palestinian Gaon of *Megillat Ebyatar* fame. He write to Abraham Hakkohen שר העדה expressing his sympathy on hi father's death. It appears that they were cousins. Elijah addresse Abraham as 'the son of our uncle' and signs himself 'the so of thy uncle'. Accordingly Solomon Hakkohen Gaon (b. Yeho seph Ab) was a brother-in-law of Isaac Hakkohen (b. Furāt) It seems that Isaac met with an unnatural death. Elijah write discreetly that they were greatly grieved at the news of hi death. 'Woe to the generation whose prominent men becom less and are taken away. Woe to him in whose days such thing happen. These prominent elders were unto us a shield an protection and remembered us constantly with their donation and gifts. May God protect thee, our lord, and rescue the from the upheaval and save thy life' (ll. 14–19). All this clearl indicates that Isaac met with a political death. Elijah evidentl sends this letter from the Jerusalem academy, which used to be sup ported by the late physician as well as by other prominent elders What position Elijah then held in the school is not indicated. Solo mon b. Yehuda was then still alive. This is evident from A.B. 7 which is a letter from the Gaon to Abraham Hakkohen שר העדה b. Isaac נוחו עדן. The object of the epistle is on behalf of som of the Gaon's acquaintances. The governor of a certain place, Abū'l Futuḥ, is prosecuting a certain Ḳain b. ʿAbduel for misdeeds long ago committed but now repented of (probably political acts). A friend of Ḳain, Marja, one of the notabilities of the town wherein the Gaon was then living (probably Ramlāh), requested him to write to Abraham about the matter in order that he should induce the governor to stop the prosecution. These people were probably Muslims. It shows the friendly relations between the Gaon and respected Muhammedans. Further, it makes clear the authority yielded by Abraham. Very likely he was physician either to the Caliph or to the Wezīr. In the letter from Solomon b. Jehuda to his father Isaac (referred to above) it is mentioned that Abraham was then away on his duty of 'escorting'. The Gaon expresses the wish that he return safely. Abraham was then probably in attendance on high dignitaries of the state and possibly on the Caliph himself.

A. B. 8 contains an epistle of eulogy from Zakkai Hannasi b. Yedidyah Hannasi to Abraham Hakkohen, the physician, called סר העידה, b. Isaac Hakkohen, the physician (נֿעֿ). Our Abraham is highly praised for his excellent qualities. A benefactor, of noble family, the head of the congregation. God bestowed upon him 'the priesthood, a noble heart, and the diplomas of the schools' (מעלות הישיבות, the Palestinian and the Babylonian?). Besides the verse introduction, the letter itself contains nothing else but greetings and expressions of thanks. It is unknown who this Nasi was.[1] A. B. 9 contains another interesting eulogy in honour of our Abraham. The author is ʿĀli the Ḥaber b. ʿAmram. Abraham's praises are recorded at every assembly of the congregation on Sabbath and festivals in ʿĀli's synagogue which goes by the name of Daniel Hannasi and Gaon. As ʿĀli signs several documents in Fusṭāṭ (cp. Chap. V, beginning), he evidently held office in this city. Very likely he was the

[1] Perhaps he is identical with the father of the Ḳaraite Nasi Yedidyah mentioned in a formula of a Ḳaraite Ketuba of the year 1392 Sel. = 1081 C.E. (ed. Margoliouth, *British Museum Catalogue*, III, 558, col. 1). But it is rather strange that a Ḳaraite should compliment Abraham for his titles bestowed upon him by Rabbinite academies (מעלות הישיבות). Poznański's tentative identification (*Babyl. Geon.* 122, 2) with a member of the family of the Mossul Nesiim (in the second half of the twelfth century) is now out of question, since we know the time of Abraham Hakkohen b. Isaac. Abraham probably held the title משוש הישיבה (cp. *infra*, p. 183).

colleague, and subsequently the successor of Ephraim b. Shemarya as Ḥaber of the Palestinian community of Fusṭāṭ. Thus their synagogue was called after the contemporary Gaon of Jerusalem. Daniel Hannasi, so well known from the Ebyatar Megillah, occupied at that time the Gaonate. Hence the letter was written between 1051–62 (see *infra*, p. 180). Abraham probably lived in Cairo, where he carried on his duties of physician. He is addressed as the son of Furāt (פרת). But in reality his father was Isaac b. Furāt. Of the many compliments paid to him by ʿĀli, it should be pointed out that he is reputed to have been a scholar in Bible and Talmud (l. 18, לאדיר התורה גבור במקרא גדול בגמרא).

Of further interest is A. B. 10, 1, which is defective at beginning and end. Abraham is styled שר העדה הוד הזקנים פאר הכהנים. The writer points out that formerly our physician held only the first and the last titles. He has now added to them הוד הזקנים, an honorific name held many years ago by the Sheikh Abū ʿĀli b. Faḍlān at Bagdād, and has since then been bestowed upon no other person. He now gave Abraham this additional title and recited public prayers for him. 'May this be a good omen to augment his honour and continue his authority.' The author of the letter was evidently a man of communal standing, who bestowed titles upon worthy elders. He also knew of the inner life of the Bagdād Jewry. It seems to me that he is identical with Daniel b. ʿAzarya, Nasi and Gaon of Jerusalem. We know that he hailed from Babylon, probably from Bagdād (cp. *infra*, p. 178 ff.). It is only natural that he should have corresponded with such an important person as Abraham was in Cairo. Attention is also drawn to A. B. 10, 2, which is in the same handwriting. There Abraham is already addressed as הוד הזקנים. It is therefore of a later date. Finally in A. B. 11, 1, we have another poem in honour of our physician. The name of the author is not indicated. A few more letters from Solomon b. Yehuda to Abraham are indicated in A. B. 11, 2, which, when published, will supplement the data concerning the latter. The above details testify to the great importance of this elder in Egyptian Jewry. Altogether we have here a fine type of a Jewish doctor, a favourite of the court, a scholar in Jewish and secular knowledge, generous and charitable, and a pillar of strength to his brethren.

(3) Both the Fusṭāṭ and the Alexandrian communities of this period were fortunate in possessing other prominent members who also had the welfare of their co-religionists at heart. Opportunities for communal service abounded, especially towards the end of the twenties of the eleventh century, when the Egyptian ports used to be visited by Saracen pirates who brought ship-loads of captives from Byzantine countries. The Saracens infested then the eastern Mediterranean and were the terror of the Byzantine mercantile navy. Only in 1035 were two fleets of African and Sicilian Muslims destroyed by the Byzantines (see Hertzberg, *Geschichte der Byzantiner*, 225). Indeed, for a considerable time hence the Genizah fragments are silent about captives from Byzantium that were landed in Egypt. When piracy flourished, the boats that arrived in Egyptian harbours, chiefly in Alexandria, usually contained a goodly number of Jewish travellers and merchants who were captured at sea. Their Egyptian co-religionists spared no efforts to free them. This we learn from a number of fragments we are able to discuss here. At the same time we obtain information about contemporary Byzantine Jewry and especially about the congregation of Mastaura, near the river Meandros, hitherto entirely unknown.

A captive fetched a fixed price, viz. 33½ dīnārs. It is appropriate to cite here Muḳaddasi (born 946, as quoted by Le Strange, *Palestine under the Moslems*, 23–4). 'All along the sea-coast of Filastīn are the watch-stations, called Ribāt, where the levies assemble. The war-ships and the galleys of the Greeks also come into these ports, bringing aboard of them the captives taken from the Muslims; these they offer for ransom—three for the hundred dīnārs.' Thus the fixed ransom for a captive was 33⅓ dīnārs, about £16 in gold, equivalent however, in the currency of the present day, to nearly £50 (cp. loc. cit., p. 44). Muḳaddasi continues to describe how when the Greek ships arrive the people hurry out to meet them at the watch-station. 'Then the ransoming begins. Some will be able to ransom a prisoner, while others (less rich) will throw down silver dirhems, or signet-rings, or contribute some other valuables, until at length all the persons who are in the Greek ships have been ransomed.' Similar scenes must have taken place in Alexandria when Saracen pirates entered the port with captives from Byzantium. Christians and Jews alike would hurry to ascertain whether some of their co-religionists were aboard. The same price ($33\frac{1}{3}$ dīnārs) was paid for a Christian or a Jewish captive in the hands of Muslim captors. Of chief interest is a Bodleian Geniza letter (dated 1028 C. E.), published by Dr. Cowley in *J. Q. R.*, XIX, 250–4. The other fragments given here deal with the same subject and several names recur in them. The writer of the Bodleian epistle was Yeshuʿa Hakkohen b. Joseph Dayyan, who was evidently the Ḥaber of the Alexandrian community of the Palestinians. In this capacity he writes to Ephraim b. Shemarya, but in the name of both local congregations, Palestinian and Babylonian. Both of them seem to have been neither large in numbers nor prosperous. It is mentioned that 300 people stood surety for the ransom-money.[1] Probably these were the heads of families (בעלי בתים), and their number likely comprised the whole congregation. The constant arrival of prisoners taxed the resources of the local Jews to the utmost. Therefore other Egyptian communities were asked to share the 'duty of freeing captives'. In particular, the Jews in the capital, Cairo-Fusṭāṭ, had to make the chief contribution. An individual donor, much eulogized for his generosity, was David b. Isaac Hallevi, who evidently was a prominent elder. A benefactor in Alexandria of great influence was Netaneel b. Elʿazar Hakkohen. These persons recur in the letters of Solomon b. Yehuda. We shall now discuss the fragments *seriatim*.

The following is a *résumé* of the Bodleian letter. Its purpose is to thank Ephraim b. Shemarya and his congregation for their generosity in contributing so much for the ransom of the captives. These were released soon after their arrival in Alexandria on surety given by 300 local Jews. Before the amount of $200\frac{1}{2}$ dīnārs arrived from Ephraim, the Arab captors pressed these Jews for payment during the whole month of Tishri. Only 40 d. were collected in Alexandria. When the money from Fusṭāṭ arrived (viz. $200\frac{1}{2}$ d.), a sum of $217\frac{1}{3}$ d. was at hand to pay the pirates. One of them, יבקי בן אבי רזין, was paid 50 d., evidently

[1] In l. 23 supply ונעשיתם כמי ש[פדיתם] שלש מאות. In this connexion it should be added that in l. 12 בפרז נא אמון probably means 'in the open part of Alexandria' (cp. Esther 9. 19); in l. 24 supply ו[מודיעים אנחנו לכם] כי בטרם וכ'; in l. 48 for כפיו r. מפיו; in l. 54, אל=על.

the balance of an account for former captives, while Mukhtar received $166\frac{2}{3}$ d. for five prisoners, $33\frac{1}{3}$ d. per head. The rest of the money available (i. e. $23\frac{1}{3}$ d.) was hardly sufficient for the maintenance of these freed Jews as well as the expenses of their home journey. Six Jews before were sent back and arrived safely. But meanwhile a servant of the pirate יבקי בן אבי רזין brought another seven Jewish merchants from Anṭalia (Anatolia). The prisoners were marched to Netaneel's house, as he was the most prominent Jew in Alexandria. Four of them were Rabbanites and three Ḳaraites. We thus learn of the spread of Ḳaraism to Byzantium already in the first half of the eleventh century. The Arab demanded their full price, viz. 233^1 d. ($= 7 \times 33\frac{1}{3}$). But Netaneel pointed out that the poor Jews of Alexandria (l. 36, אילו העניים) were hardly able to maintain them, not to speak of ransoming them. Therefore ten more well-to-do co-religionists stood surety for the seven prisoners till their ransom be obtained from the other communities. The Alexandrian Jews had thus to maintain twelve prisoners. Netaneel undertook to pay for one captive $33\frac{1}{3}$ d., while for the remaining 200 d. he advised to send two letters to Fusṭāṭ to both Ḥaberim and their Rabbinite congregations (i. e. Palestinian and Babylonian) and one to the Ḳaraite community. Netaneel himself is to enclose letters to the elders requesting them to bestir themselves and collect the necessary amount. Epistles are also to be sent to Tīnnis, Damietta, and Ṣahragt, to both Ḳaraites and Rabbinites, to contribute to the ransom-money and also to the expenses of maintenance and home-journey of these captives. The Alexandrian Jews expressed their gratitude to the generous Netaneel, who was also very helpful in building the synagogue (probably of the Palestinians).[1] Ephraim b. Shemarya is requested to read the letter before the congregation and impress upon them the highly deserving case of the captives, who are respected people

[1] It is quite likely that the synagogue was demolished during al-Ḥakim's persecutions, and had to be rebuilt after 1020. A document (T.-S. 13 J 1^7), dated Tammuz, 4793 A. M. (= 1033 C. E.) at Alexandria, mentions that Joseph b. Khalaf sent through תאבת Hakkohen b. Tobias the Babylonian ten dīnārs לכנסת הגדולה הידועה שאמיין כדי לבנות בהם ההיכל. It cannot be ascertained whether this donation was for the Palestinian synagogue at Alexandria or at Fusṭāṭ. The latter was rebuilt in 1025 (above, p. 36, note 1), but its interior may not have been completed till 1033.

in their native country. Yeshu'a Hakkohen, the writer of the epistle, mentions that when Ephraim's letter, enclosing the former contribution of 200½ d., was read before the Alexandrian congregation, they all applauded its beautiful verses and diction. In all twenty people sign the letter we have discussed here. Netaneel Hakkohen concludes the list. Of communal officials there are only mentioned Yeshu'a Hakkohen b. Joseph השופט (= Dayyan), and Surri, the Teacher, b. Ḥayyim. The date is Kislev (1)340 Sel. = 1028 C.E. The number of prisoners spoken of in this epistle is eighteen.

A. B. 12 is defective at beginning and end. It cannot therefore be ascertained to whom it is addressed. But probably either Ephraim b. Shemarya, or the Ḥaber of the Babylonians at Fusṭāṭ, Abraham b. Sahlān, was the recipient of this letter. A pirate had two Jewish prisoners. One he sent to Netaneel Hakkohen as a present. In return, Netaneel sent a gift worth one and a half times the value of the captive. Thereupon the other captive is sent to him and the captor received his ransom, 33⅓ d. Netaneel incurs in addition the expense of sending the liberated Jews home. The community (of Alexandria) was not asked to share the outlay. As a token of gratitude, a special prayer is recited for him in the presence of the whole community. But already previously it was the practice to mention both Netaneel and David Hallevi b. Isaac on every Sabbath in 'both synagogues', in special prayers in their honour. These two elders are called 'luminaries in our town as well as in yours' (Fusṭāṭ). David is also styled 'the glory of both parties' (פאר שתי הפאות), probably the two sects, Rabbinites and Ḳaraites.

Not long afterwards report came that a boat belonging to Jabarah b. Mukhtar (the latter is mentioned in the Bodleian epistle) had aboard ship ten Jews from Anṭalia from whom much money had been taken away. The boat stopped at Ramada on the way to the West. The missing continuation of the fragment is probably an appeal for contributions to defray the ransom for these unfortunate Jews. There is little doubt that in the end they were freed by their Egyptian co-religionists. The number of prisoners mentioned in our fragment is twelve.

In A. B. 13 the same pirates, יבקי b. Abū Razīn, Mukhtar and his son Jabarah recur. The representative of the Jews who carries on negotiations with the captors is the elder Nathan Hakkohen. He is evidently not identical with Netaneel. Hence the letter, defective at beginning and end, probably emanates not from Alexandria but from some other Egyptian port, probably Damietta. But it is certainly addressed to Fusṭāṭ, appealing to the local Jews for the ransom of the prisoners. Some arguments arose between the pirate and the Jews negotiating for the liberation of their brethren. The pirate was a relative of יבקי בן אבי רזין. He demanded apparently 250 d. The prisoners were cruelly treated. Among them was a girl. Against exorbitant demands the Jews argued that they could not act against the Talmudic law (Giṭṭin 4[6]), which forbade paying for a captive more than his or her value. A letter arrived from Mukhtar announcing that his son Jabarah sent some Jewish prisoners to Barḳah. Perhaps our fragment describes the negotiations that took place in connexion with the liberation of the ten Jews from Anṭalia mentioned in A. B. 12 (see also my remarks in *J.Q.R.*, N.S., IX, 420–21).

A. B. 14 contains an incomplete letter from Alexandria to Ephraim b. Shemarya and the elders of his congregation. It deals again with prisoners from Edom (Byzantium). A Jewish woman was ransomed for 24 d., besides the government tax. The Fusṭāṭ Jews contributed 12 d., while the remainder was defrayed by the co-religionists in Alexandria. Soon afterwards the sailors brought two other prisoners, a fine young man possessing knowledge of the Torah, and a boy of ten years. As they were maltreated by their captors, the Alexandrian Jews obtained their freedom by standing surety for their ransom. But shortly afterwards another ship arrived from Byzantium with many prisoners. Among them there were a physician and his wife. The Alexandrian correspondents appeal to Ephraim for help, as they cannot afford the expenses; times are critical and the taxes heavy. Here the letter breaks off. Again, we may be sure that Ephraim did his best not to leave Jews as slaves in the hands of Muslims. In A. B. 15 we find the Alexandrian Jews writing to Ephraim to express their gratitude to him and other benefactors for sums of money undoubtedly assigned for captive co-religionists. Ephraim b. Shemarya, the elders, the Ḥazzānim, and the Parnasim are saluted. A letter reached them from a certain Abraham through his agent, Joseph b. Yeshuʿa, enclosing the amount of 50 d. Perhaps this Abraham is identical with Abū Saʿad b. Sahl. Other communal accounts are mentioned. At the synagogue (of Alexandria) the scrolls of the Law were taken out and the readers recited prayers for Ephraim, for David Hallevi b. Isaac, and for Abraham b. X. (either Sahl or Sahlān). Also Isaac Hakkohen (b. Furāt) and his son Abraham seem to have been included in the prayers (the latter is probably meant by משוש הישיבה, cp. *infra*, p. 183). In A. B. 16 we find again Yeshuʿa Hakkohen (b. Joseph Dayyan), who was the author of the Bodl. epistle (1028 C. E.), writing on behalf of a prisoner from Anṭalia, Sabbatai b. Netaneel. The other fellow sufferers have been liberated and sent back to their country. But Sabbatai wanted to visit Jerusalem and the Holy Land. Ephraim is requested to help Sabbatai to carry out his desire. He is versed in חזנות and is an able man. Greetings are sent to Joseph, Ephraim's son-in-law. As will be shown later on, this Joseph died in Ephraim's lifetime, in the year 1035. Ephraim seems to have had no son.

A. B. 17 is again from both the Alexandrian congregations, this time addressed to David (Hallevi) b. Isaac. The letter is dated Shevaṭ, 1030–1 C.E. It is written concerning prisoners from Edom (Byzantium), three of whom were sent by the captors to some place. David is asked to send 33⅓ d. for one captive. Owing to the defective state of the fragment it is difficult to gather definite information. Line 25 seems to mean that a captive came to the synagogue while the local Rabbi gave a discourse. Sometimes the Alexandrian Jews would send one of the captives, whom they redeemed, to his native land to collect a sum of money and return in order to free his other countrymen. This is evident from A. B. 18, which is unfortunately very damaged. The Jews of Alexandria wrote to Mastaura in the land of Yavan (Byzantium) about prisoners from this place. Owing to critical times, and many other troubles, they could not afford to ransom them. They thus sent one of them, Leo by name, to his native place to obtain from the prisoners' relatives the amount necessary for their freedom. But no doubt they would meanwhile enjoy restricted liberty in Alexandria and be maintained by their brethren, who would stand surety for them.

It is touching to read how the Jews of Egypt commiserate their co-religionists living under Byzantine rule. 'The holy congregation scattered in Edom, delivered into the hand of enemies, put under the yoke of foes, and suffering under the burden of hard task-masters.' Compared with the intolerance of Byzantium, the Jews felt themselves free men under Muslim rule. It should be pointed out that this letter from Alexandria to Mastaura is provided occasionally with Babylonian vowel-points. Either the scribe belonged to the Babylonian congregation, or more likely the people in Alexandria assumed that the Babylonian vowel-system was in practice in Mastaura. But we shall presently see that the Tiberian system was adopted by the Byzantine Jews. This epistle was found in the Genizah, as probably the bearer Leo brought it back with him when he returned from Mastaura to Alexandria with the ransom money, or it may be that a copy of the letter was sent from Alexandria to Fusṭāṭ.

We can gather from the above fragments that a considerable number of Jewish prisoners were landed in Egyptian ports. As each cost about £50 (according to the present scale) to ransom, in addition to the expenses of maintenance, and the home-journey, it can be estimated how heavily the resources of the Egyptian Jewry were taxed. We shall also see how much the Palestinian Jews and the academy were dependent on support from the country of the Nile. In most cases the captive Byzantine Jews returned to their country. But some of them must have settled in Egypt. Thus some of their documents found their way to the Cairo Genizah. A. B. 19 is a Ketuba drawn up at Mastaura, by the river Meandros, in the year 1022 C.E. It supplements our very scanty knowledge of Byzantine Jewry. The document, moreover, deserves publication on its own merits. The bridegroom is named נמר b. Elḳana. Other characteristic names are נבון and שלחיה. The latter is found in the list of Paiṭanim in *Maḥzor Romania*.[1] Leon (לאון) is to be compared with Leo (ליו) in A. B. 18. The bride is called Eudokia, a name held by a Byzantine Empress. The belongings of a Jewish bride in Byzantium, as enumerated in our Ketuba, are of interest for our knowledge of the social life of the people. Some of the

[1] Cp. *Oṣar Ṭob, Magazin*, 1883, 15 ff.: Ḥananya b. Shelaḥya and Shelaḥya b. Ḥananya. See also Zunz, *Ltgsch. synag. Poesie*, 381, 385.

Greek words are vocalized. We learn therefrom that Tiberian vowel-signs were in use in Mastaura.

(4) The correspondence of Solomon b. Yehuda contains a number of names of people who were the spiritual leaders of the Fusṭāṭ Jews. Of these the most prominent one was undoubtedly Ephraim b. Shemarya, a native of Gaza, the Ḥaber of the Palestinian congregation. Another man of prominence was Samuel Hakkohen b. Abṭalion, the president of this community. At the head of the Babylonian section stood Abraham b. Sahlān and his son Sahlān. In A. B. 20 data are collected about the communal leaders of both sections. Ephraim's tenure of office evidently commenced about 1020. We find him in Fusṭāṭ in 1016 as a resident of the city (see above, p. 36, and A. B. 20, I, 6). But then he seems to have held no office yet. However, in 1022 C.E. at a meeting of both congregations, he and Abraham b. Sahlān sign the minutes and head the list of signatories. From documents we could trace Ephraim till the year 1029. His name recurs again on documents of 1039, 1041, and 1050. On the death of Solomon b. Yehuda in 1051 he composed an elegy (above, p. 75, note 1). No documents drawn up at the Bet-Dīn of the Palestinians at Fusṭāṭ, dated between 1029–39, have come to my notice. But Ephraim undoubtedly retained his office of Ḥaber during the whole time, though he had to encounter much opposition.

No son of his is so far known. But he had a son-in-law, Joseph, who apparently managed Ephraim's business. For our Ḥaber seems to have been in private life a merchant, though he may also have received remuneration for his communal services. This Joseph died in 1035.[1] From a letter from Elijah Hakkohen (b. Solomon Gaon), when already Ab (A. B. 21), we learn that Ephraim reached the age of eighty. Daniel b. ʿAzarya also corresponded with the veteran Fusṭāṭ Ḥaber (*infra*, p. 181).

[1] *J. Q. R.*, XIX, 255–6: a letter, dated חצי אב שנת שמֹו לשטרות, to Ephr. b. Shem.: (3) . . . ומהש[מע] (4) באסיפת מֹ יוסף רוח [אפ]נו הכאיב לבי . . . כל שכן אתה (5) שהיה לך כבן ע[ומד] בכל צרכיך ומה יכולת לעשות . . . (23) . . . ומה שהיה לך ביד אבו סעיד לא נזדמן מכירתו (24) וכל הסחורות בזול והמשתכר משתכר בעונות אל צרור נקוב . . . The rest of the letter will be discussed below (pp. 123–4).

About this time his colleague was probably 'Āli b. 'Amram, who also succeeded him to the spiritual leadership of the Palestinian congregation in the capital. Ephraim departed from this life in about the year 1060. It is likely that the epistle (above, p. 85 f.), introduced by verses in honour of Abraham Hakkohen, was written on the occasion when 'Āli was confirmed in his office after the demise of Ephraim. He thus sends salutations to the prominent physician assuring him that his name is honourably mentioned on every Sabbath and festival in the synagogue, which goes by the name of the Nasi Daniel, then Gaon of Palestine (hence before his death in 1062). It seems that the Palestinians in the capital styled their house of prayer after the contemporary Gaon in the Holy Land. We know that the synagogue of the Babylonians in Fusṭāṭ was called after Hai's school (see *J. Q. R.*, N. S., VII, 478, note 22).

Ephraim's standing, and his manifold activities in the community, could be gathered already from the number of fragments that dealt with the release of the Byzantine captives. How he stood in esteem of the Gaon Solomon b. Yehuda will be seen from his correspondence to be discussed farther on. As is the lot of every prominent man, Ephraim was exposed to much criticism and opposition. The calls on his generosity were numerous, and the kindness he showed to needy travellers from every country that came to Fusṭāṭ was indeed great. A. B. 21–7 contain a number of epistles to Ephraim, which will be discussed presently.

The president of the Palestinian community of Fusṭāṭ was Samuel Hakkohen b. Abṭalion (shortened Ṭalion). Solomon b. Yehuda, in a letter to him (A. B. 28, see *infra*, p. 103), addresses him מוֹר שמואל הכהן המומחה . . . נין ח[ס]ידים וג[א]ונים.[1] We find him already in 1116 signing a document drawn up at Fusṭāṭ. As president of the community his name recurs on documents of 1027–8, while in 1041 he signs as Samuel Hakkohen the Ḥaber b. Abṭalion (A. B. 20, I, 2–5, 7). His relations with Ephraim were not of the very best. We shall see later on that

[1] The name Abṭalion (in the Middle Ages) we have in the Paiṭān : אבטליון ברבי שמואל מיוחס (see Zunz, *Ltgsch. synag. Poesie*, 386–7). Was he our Samuel's father, and does מיוחס refer to his noble descent from Geonim ? Zunz, however, points out that Meyuḥas (*εὐγενής*) is common among Byzantine Jews.

a section appointed him as Dayyān (שופט) in opposition to Ephraim. But the latter was undoubtedly superior to Samuel in many respects, as the numerous fragments clearly reveal. Worman (*J. Q. R.*, XVIII, 14) states that Samuel's son, Solomon, was Rosh Yeshiba of Fusṭāṭ (cp. also Pozn., *Babyl. Geonim.*, 100). This is clearly a mistake. The two fragments (T.-S. 13 J 9^2 and 11^5) adduced as evidence (note 7) contain nothing about a Solomon, a supposed son of Samuel b. Abṭalion (Ṭalion). The first fragment is given in A. B. 35. Of the other names mentioned in A. B. 20 I, Yefet Ḥazzan b. David recurs several times in the documents. He was the reader of the Palestinian synagogue. Solomon b. Sa'adya is also mentioned in the letters discussed later on. He was a respected elder. We find him still alive when 'Ali b. 'Amram was the Ḥaber of the community after Ephraim b. Shemarya's death. Besides a Rosh Hakkahal we have four Parnasin referred to in A. B. 20, I, 7. Of the three brothers, the sons of Mebasser, the most eminent Parnes was Abraham, styled 'the choice of the Fusṭāṭ community and its favourite' (סגולת קהל צוען ורצויו). His name recurs on documents of 1028 and 1041. Isaac Hakkohen b. Ḥaggai (A. B. 20, I, 7) as well as his brother Abraham seem to have been highly respected elders in Fusṭāṭ. But in their father's lifetime they apparently lived in some other Egyptian town (cp. A. B. 23 and 30, which will be discussed presently). Abraham b. Solomon Gaon (A. B. 20, I, 2) is probably Solomon b. Yehuda's son, who visited Egypt several times, as will be shown later on. We thus find him in 1027 in Fusṭāṭ.

(5) We now turn to deal with the Babylonian community. Its spiritual head was Abraham b. Sahlān, styled Ḥaber, Alluf and 'the chosen one of the academy' (A. B. 20, II, 1 and 5). This confirms my suggestion that Hai's epistle (*J. Q. R.*, N. S., VII, 478, note 22) was sent to our Abraham, since the same titles recur there. The first title is Palestinian, the second Babylonian, while the third may emanate from either academy. By profession a banker (צירפא) he was also a scholar and communal worker. His genealogy has been preserved for six generations, viz. Sahlān, Abraham, Sahlān, Abraham, Solomon, Sabbath (?, probably read Sabbatai) of Sunbāṭ.[1] From the important

[1] For סנכאט read סנבאטי. About the position of this town in Egypt, see Guest,

enealogy list (given in A. B. 20, II, 1) we learn that he had two ons, Sahlān Rosh Hasseder and Rosh Kallah and Nehemiah ריש פירק (i.e. Ḥazzan, see *infra*, p. 269). The former succeeded is father as head of the Babylonian community.[1] Several etters from Solomon b. Yehuda to him have been preserved. n a Ketuba of 1037 (*l.c.* II, 4) Sahlān is styled ריש סדרא האלוף סגן הישיבה חמדת הנשיאו. Nehemiah b. Abraham had a son Joshiah vho was a liturgical poet. Abraham b. Sahlān is referred to in 032 as already departed from this world.

The interesting letter (MS. Adler, commented upon in A. B. o, II, 3) is clearly not by Sahlān Alluf b. Abraham, the con-emporary of Solomon b. Yehuda, as Dr. Marmorstein (מדרש חסרות ויתירו, 1917, pp. 76–9) assumes.[2] From the signature ahlān המומחה b. Abraham המומחה it is evident that neither the vriter nor his father bore any honorary titles from the academies. 'robably this Sahlān is the grandfather of Sahlān Alluf. The ate of the epistle is therefore about 1000.[3] We give here an nalysis of this fragment. Sahlān seems to have been away rom Fusṭāṭ, where his anonymous correspondent, so highly ulogized, probably resided. They were in constant communi-ation. Sahlān was first asked about the reading of a Midrashic assage which he subjoins. The next item of the inquiry was bout the meaning of the word דעוקת occurring in a Piyyūṭ.[4]

ournal R. Asiat. Soc., 1912, 964. Cp. also Sambāri (in Neub., I, 119), who reports f a holy scroll in the Must'arab synagogue in Cairo that was brought from Sunbaṭ 1 1623 C. E.

[1] T.-S. 13 J 1[10] is a document, dated Nisan, 1155 Sel. (= 1044 C. E.), at Fusṭāṭ. It egins: חצרנא פי מושב בית דין נט' רח' פי כניסה אלעראקיין מר עלון בן שלמה ומרב צביאן הכהן בר ס[עדיה] נ. The former claimed from the latter Dinar. After the signatures of the witness there follows the testatum of the court, באמת יודעים אנו בית דין...., together with the signature ...... סהלא[ן], o doubt identical with our Sahlān b. Abraham. One of the parties, Ṣabyān b. a'adya, figures in the lawsuit described *infra*, p. 209 f.

[2] From the fragments concerning Sahlān Alluf and his father which we discuss here, t is established beyond doubt that they lived in Fusṭāṭ and not in Kairowān, as was vrongly assumed by some writers (see also *J. Q. R.*, N. S., IX, 161, 417, and cp. 'ozn., *Hakkedem*, II, Heb. part, p. 96, No. 4).

[3] Indeed a document (T.-S.) dated 987 C. E. at Fusṭāṭ, mentions Saḥlān b. Abraham . Sunbaṭ (i. e. of the family of Sabbatai of Sunbaṭ). Very likely the writer of the bove epistle is meant.

[4] For comments on Piyyuṭim, see *J. Q. R.*, N. S., III, 546, where a Genizah

He had already told his correspondent before (evidently in Fusṭāṭ) that, in his opinion, the word was really עוקת and the ד an Aramaic prefix. Now in the place where he was then, he asked a certain R. Abraham about its meaning as perhaps based on a Rabbinic saying. Sahlān argued that the ד was like the Hebrew ש (=אשר). As a parallel he quotes the *hapax legomenon* שעטת (Jer. 47. 3). He evidently takes it to be equal to אשר עטת. But the actual meaning he gives to the word is not clear owing to the defective state of the fragment. However, R. Abraham is of the opinion that דעקת stands for וַעֲקַת ('the cry of'), just as זהב is דהבא in Aramaic. Sahlān further states that he cannot leave his place soon since he has not the necessary means. A certain person, who supplied his needs, is now dangerously ill, and he must await his recovery. This person is sure to lend him the money for his return to Fusṭāṭ. Highly interesting is the mention of the 'Book of Precepts' by Ḥefes Alluf b. Yasliaḥ of Mosul, which Sahlān bought for 4d. = £6.[1] Inquiries are also made about his mother (אמא מרתא) and a certain Yaḥya b. Manṣur. The day before, Sahlān sent his correspondent three epistles with the request to transmit them to Solomon b. al-Aḥūl and also to receive from him a reply and send it on to our Sahlān.[2]

While the last scholar seems to have been in needy circumstances, his son Abraham evidently was successful in life and

fragment is cited containing an exposition of some words of the piyyuṭ את ערובת by Ezekiel b. 'Āli Hakkohen (see A.C. 25, 1). Likewise Sa'adya's Tokeḥah (edited by Brody, *J. Q. R.*, N. S., III, 83 ff.) had a whole commentary composed on it in Arabic (Or. 5554 B, fols. 23–4, contains a part of the introduction as well as the comments on letter Aleph of the liturgy; it is evidently a part of Bodl. 2847[1]. The author was Isaac the Spaniard).

[1] In the MS. only the letters . . . אר? can be read. Probably the word was originally [בעה]אר; there does not seem to be space enough for [בעים]אר. Dr. Halper (*J. Q. R.*, N. S., IV, 530) quotes the same statement, for which he is indebted to Prof. A. Marx. I presume that the latter scholar has cited it from a copy of MS. Adler, and not from an original Genizah letter at the Jewish Theological Seminary of America.

[2] T.-S. Box H 2 contains seven paper leaves of liturgical compositions. On fol. 2, verso, we read: מעריב לשבת ועשור לסהלאן המומחה זל · בלילי צום העשור וכו'. Very likely our Sahlān is the author. Fol. 3, verso, contains Sa'adya's composition for Purim: מעריב פורים לרבינו סעדיהו בן יוסף גאון זכר צדיק ל' . . . אנני ניתן לימיני במושיע וכו'.

became a banker. He and his son Sahlān Alluf, though belonging to the Babylonian section, were supporters of the Palestinian school as well as of the Jerusalem poor, as we shall see from the following fragments. Solomon b. Yehuda was on very friendly terms with them. Also Ephraim b. Shemarya had intimate relations with them. Abraham was a brother-in-law of Sa'adya b. Ephraim.[1] In the Dukran Ṭob (A. B. 20, II, 1) the last person is styled Ḥaber, and his three sons are called Sa'adya the Ḥaber, Palṭiel the Ḥazzan, and Revaḥ. Sa'adya is also styled Alluf (A. B. 29). His brother Palṭiel is perhaps identical with the signatory of the document, dated 1002, drawn up at Fusṭāṭ under Shemarya b. Elḥanan (*J. Q. R.*, XI, 646, note 2).[2] Of Revaḥ, the third son, nothing is so far known. Leaving the other names of the memorial-list for later consideration, mention should be made of Yehuda Hakkohen, styled 'the great Rabbi, Rosh Hasseder'. From the data collected in A. B. 20, II, 1, note 3, we see that he was a son of Joseph Ab, the brother of Elijah Gaon. Joseph died in 1053. Yehuda's activity in Egypt probably continued for several years subsequently. His cousin, a son of Elijah Hakkohen, the later Gaon, sends him greetings in a letter dated 1055 in Jerusalem (see *infra*, p. 101). Yehuda was the author of a commentary on Sepher Yeṣirah, and probably also on the Bible. Several of his responsa are also preserved. The president of the Babylonian community seems to have been Yefet Hallevi b. Tobias the Babylonian (cp. A. B. 20, I, 3, and *infra*, p. 137). As repeatedly mentioned before, all the titles held by communal dignitaries are discussed in the last chapter. Finally, attention is drawn to A. B. 20, III, which contains a list of 62 liturgical compositions by Sahlān Rās al-Kal (=Resh Kallah). Except No. 1, they all begin with ס or שׂ, being the first letter of the acrostic Sahlān. Only five of the poems are

[1] A document of evidence (Or. 5550, see *Catal.*, III, 564), dated Marḥeshwan, 1291 Sel. (979 C. E.) at Fusṭāṭ, is signed by אפרי]ם בר צדוק] (several letters beneath and above the signature cannot be deciphered). Perhaps our Ephraim is identical with this person. The parties mentioned in the deed are Sa'adūn b. Sa'id of Aleppo and Meborak b. Ḳiyām. Also the names Manṣur b. Wahb and Salāmah and Manṣur the sons of 'Amram occur.

[2] A colophon of a liturgical fragment (in T.-S., Arabic Box, Poetry and Liturgy) has the name פלטיאל בר' אפרים החבר זלה״ה, no doubt identical with the above person.

identical with those known from elsewhere (see Bodl. *s. v.* Sahlān b. Abraham and cp. also *J. Q. R.*, N. S., VIII, 27, from MS. Adler). We thus see what a prolific liturgical writer this Fusṭāṭ scholar was.

(6) We shall consider A. B. 21–31 in detail. No. 21 is from Elijah Hakkohen Ab b. Gaon (זֿל, i.e. Solomon) to Ephraim b. Shemarya, addressed as 'the excellent Ḥaber and distinguished president of the Bet-Dīn'. Elijah complains that Ephraim's letters are rare. Has he perhaps reversed his decision. If so, who was the cause of it. Let no evildoer mislead you, 'the sun of our generation'.[1] By God's favour you have reached the age of 80. We have suspected you of no enmity. The late 'Third' as well as all that knew you have testified to your pure intentions and acts. The allusions, rather obscure, are to the frictions in the academy (as described in the next chapter). In conclusion, Elijah mentions a certain 'Amram the teacher who thanks 'our brother Joseph'. 'Amram seems to have been on a visit to Fusṭāṭ and Ephraim is requested to help him to return home to Jerusalem, where his family awaits him. Greetings are sent to Ephraim, and also to his son-in-law, '*the son of our uncle*'. We have seen above (p. 94) that one son-in-law of Ephraim, Joseph, died in 1035. He cannot be meant here, since Elijah was certainly no Ab till after 1053, while in 1045 he was still 'Fourth' (as shown in A. A. 17). But we have also found that the celebrated court-physician Abraham Hakkohen b. Isaac (b. Furāt) was Elijah's cousin (above, p. 84). Hence it is very likely that Abraham was Ephraim's son-in-law referred to here.

[1] ושמשת דו[רנו] l. 14; שְׁמְשָׁה being a feminine of שֶׁמֶשׁ. But perhaps read ושמשת דו[דנו], and you have studied ('served') under our uncle, viz. under a Gaon who was our uncle. As we find Ephraim in Fusṭāṭ already in 1016, he probably received his diploma in Palestine prior to this date. Accordingly his master was either Joshiah Gaon or possibly Samuel Hakkohen b. Joseph, and hence one of these Geonim was Elijah's uncle. In A. B. 34, l. 9, Solomon b. Yehuda refers to 'the Geonim of Israel, both the late and the present, who gave him (Ephraim) the diploma' (סומכיו גאוני ישראל המתים והחיים). When Ephraim was ordained, Solomon b. Yehuda held of course a prominent position in the school, either 'Third' or 'Fourth'. Solomon Hakkohen (Elijah's father) was the latter's senior in rank, and therefore advanced to the Gaonate after Joshiah's death (about 1020). Solomon b. Yehuda then became Ab, and afterwards Gaon (about 1025). Cp. also *infra*, p. 108, where Ephraim b. Shemarya styles himself 'the disciple' of Solomon b. Yehuda. See further, A. A. 17, end.

He must have been of much political assistance to the Fusṭāṭ Ḥaber, enabling him to have the better of his opponents.

In A. B. 21, note 1, a part of a letter from Elijah's son Ṣadoḳ, dated 1055 at Jerusalem is given. Elijah's other sons Ebyatar and Solomon (the father of Maṣliaḥ Gaon) are known from *Megillat Ebyatar*. Ṣadoḳ signs (ירושלם=) קטון תלמידי שלם. He asks his friend (האח) in Fusṭāṭ to greet Yehudah Rosh Hasseder. A request follows in the name of Ṣadoḳ's son-in-law, Meborak, concerning a deal in spiced oil with an official (פקיד) Ben Sha'ya. The latter was probably an 'official over the merchants' (see above, p. 81 f.). Greetings are also sent in the names of Moses Dayyan and a certain Joseph.

The latter cannot be identical with his uncle, the brother of Elijah, since he was no longer alive then. Elijah also sends salutations. A. B. 22 is apparently from Elijah to Ephr. b. Shemarya. A certain Spanish Jew arrived at Jerusalem, via Fusṭāṭ, with a complaint concerning his wife. He evidently reviled Ephraim for not exerting himself in his case. But Elijah writes, 'I have done to him as a man of his type deserves and he became silent.' Probably he threatened to excommunicate him. The letter is written in a hurry before the feast of Tabernacles. Elijah is going to inform Ephraim of the happenings on Hoshana Rabba on Mount Olivet. Usually all communal problems were then settled, often by means of banning the opponents. This gave rise to disputes and sometimes to grave disturbances. The day was regarded by both parties as a trial of strength.

A. B. 23 is by a certain Joseph b. Elijah, who was travelling in Egypt. Writing to Ephraim, whom he styles 'the מומחה from the Great Bet Sin' (i. e. holding a diploma from the Jerusalem school), he describes how after leaving Fusṭāṭ he arrived at Ṣahragt by boat on Thursday. He came then across the Rosh Hasseder (probably Yehuda Hakkohen, mentioned above, p. 99), who met with some accidents at sea (בים). The Rosh Hasseder stayed with Solomon the judge. On the Sabbath he preached in the synagogue on the weekly portion כי תצא למלחמה. His text was appropriately, 'The Lord goeth forth like a warrior' (Isa. 42. 13). The writer would have repeated to Ephraim the whole sermon but for the fear of making his epistle too long. The preacher had donations in all 7 'Fourths' and 100 Zuz. The quarter dīnār was a common coin in the Fāṭimid period (see Houtsma's *Enc. of Islām*, I, 967, col. 1). The Zuz is probably equivalent to the Kirāt ($\frac{1}{24}$th d., see Le Strange, *l.c.* 56). Altogether the remuneration of the Rosh Hasseder amounted to nearly 6 d. On Sunday night he left for Damietta (חנס, see A.A. 19, note 1). Probably he was then on a pastoral tour. Joseph b. Elijah is also proceeding on his journey. He requests Ephraim to write to him of his desires, which he will endeavour to carry out faithfully. Through a certain Yaḥya he sent word to Ephraim. Perhaps it was the son of Solomon b. Yehuda (see *infra*, p. 107). The present epistle was evidently sent a week afterwards. For he mentions that he spent (in an unnamed place) the Sabbath קומי אורי (i.e. the Haphtarah of כי תבא) with Ḥaggai Hakkohen and his two sons (Abraham and Isaac, above, p. 96). But perhaps in that year the weekly portions כי תצא and כי תבא were joined. In this case, Ḥaggai lived in Ṣahragt. He and his sons are eulogized for their hospitality to all travellers, both scholars and merchants. Later on we find Ḥaggai's sons in Fusṭāṭ. Our letter is of interest as it gives us a glimpse of the inner life of the Egyptian Jews in the first half of the eleventh century.

Solomon b. Yehuda writes to Ephraim concerning a certain Samuel b. Sahl of Ḳairowān, who was the bearer of a letter from a merchant of Seville, Sa'adya b. Moses, on some matter. Unfortunately the fragment breaks off here (A.B. 24). We should have liked to know what a Spanish Jew had to write to Palestine through a Ḳairowān co-religionist. There is in this fragment a reference to the quarrels in the community, which will be considered in the next chapter. A.B. 25 is a letter from a certain Isaac, a friend of Ephr. b. Shemarya. Since we separated, he writes, I learned nothing of what you were doing for me. I am like a prisoner and am a burden on the people with whom I stay. Do with me as your practice is with many a scholar from Byzantium and Palestine. Time presses; if you can do anything for me as regards the tax-collector, let me know. I am afraid they will imprison me. Another letter is from a member of the Jerusalem school in the name of the Gaon (Solomon b. Yehuda), who was then unwell (A.B. 26). The epistle is damaged. This much can be inferred from it. A countryman of the Gaon (this shows that Solomon was no Palestinian), X. b. Moses, arrived at Jerusalem in straitened circumstances, and wanted to settle there. But times are critical and he wishes to return to his own country. He is going to Egypt to obtain support. It is mentioned that he would like to go to the Maghreb (מערב). Ephraim is requested to help this man either to return home or to Jerusalem. Ephraim's son-in-law, Joseph, is greeted. Thus the letter dates before 1035. A. B. 27 is much damaged. Who its writer was cannot be ascertained. But the Ḥaber addressed is most likely our Ephraim b. Shemarya, who is asked to interest himself in the bearer of the epistle. He was a respected and rich inhabitant of his place. But the governor of his town fined him so heavily that he had to flee. Having arrived at Damascus, he decided to continue his journey to Jerusalem. On the way he fell a victim to brigands, who despoiled him of all he possessed. Since in Jerusalem, where he at last arrived, no help could be found for him, he set out for Egypt (Fusṭāṭ) in the hope of obtaining enough to enable him to return home. Again Ephraim is solicited to collect from his congregation the means for this unfortunate Jew. Undoubtedly a member of the school sent this letter. Finally, attention is drawn to the data (given in A. B. 27) concerning letters from Ṣahragt and Milij to Ephraim. His fame must have spread far and wide. Hence all these appeals to him to use his influence and act in accordance with his good practice (כווסתו הטוב) in matters of charity and lovingkindness.

A. B. 28 is Solom. b. Yehuda's letter to Samuel Hakkohen b. Abṭalion, the president of the Fusṭāṭ Palestinian community. He thanks Samuel for his support of 'our elder' Yehuda b. Manṣūr, who had great troubles in a lawsuit about his house that had been mortgaged. The difficulty arose on account of the change in the mortgage-law in Ramlāh (probably at the Muhammedan court). Solomon mentions 'troubles, wars, and upheavals in Ramlāh, the like of which have not taken place before'. He concludes 'written (*sc.* the letter) in sorrow'. Probably he alludes here to the terrible events in connexion with the rebellion in the reign of aẓ-Ẓahir (from 1024–9), which will be discussed below (Chap. IV). Evidently Yehuda's lawsuit involved also people residing in Fusṭāṭ. Hence Samuel b. Abṭalion is asked to intervene.

A. B. 29 is a small epistle from an anonymous writer to Sahlān Resh Kallah, the friend of Solomon b. Yehuda. The correspondent mentions that he reached a certain place (in Egypt) and stays in the Hotel (?) אלקאיר. The day before he arrived at Ṣahragt, where Sahlān's letter reached him with the request to report his arrival in this town. But he had there no time to write. He does this therefore to-day. Greetings are sent to Sa'adya Alluf (as he is also styled in Solomon b. Yehuda's epistle, ibid., note 2), Sahlān's uncle, and other people. Evidently the writer was Sahlān's agent on some errand (either communal or business).

A. B. 30 is from Isaac the Ḥazzan al-Fāsi to Abraham Hakkohen b. Ḥaggai at Fusṭāṭ. The letter is written from Damascus. Abraham is highly eulogized for his love for scholars and pious people whom he supports. Already from Tyre Isaac wrote to our benefactor. On his arrival at Damascus he found there Meshullam b. Yefet and also 'Āli b. Yefet Hallevi (b. X.), who supported him. He further relates how this 'Āli rose up in the Damascus synagogue and said to Ḥazzanim, 'Take out the Scrolls of the Law and bless the name of Abraham Hakkohen b. Ḥaggai because he showed great kindness to my brother Mufarraj on his way from Byzantium, and supported him like a brother'. Abraham's name became famous. Also Sahlān Resh Kallah was greatly eulogized for his kindness to Mufarraj. His brother 'Āli Hallevi seems to have been a scholar and a man of standing in Damascus. He addressed the people and told them the good qualities of Abraham. Greetings are sent to his brother Isaac. The writer intends going after Passover to Jerusalem, and from there he may set out for Egypt. Another Ḥazzan, Ja'īsh b. Sahl of Nahrwān (in Babylon), also thanks Abraham for his kindness. Greetings are sent to his brother Isaac, to Abū 'Āli Ḥasan and his son Ephraim. Isaac b. Ḥaggai signs a deed, dated Fusṭāṭ, 1037, together with Ephraim b. Shemarya. These two brothers were undoubtedly men of renown in Fusṭāṭ for their charity and benevolence.

In conclusion, A. B. 31 contains a number of extracts from Solomon b. Yehuda's letters. The first (No. 1) forms the end of an epistle of greetings and eulogies to a certain elder who probably resided in Fusṭāṭ. He is thanked for his good deeds, probably towards the Jerusalem community. Of the several signatories only the Gaon and his son, Abraham the Ḥaber, are known. The latter evidently was 'Fourth' of the academy towards the close of his father's life (No. 2). Abraham b. Solomon הפקיד to whom the Gaon writes was apparently a respected elder (in Fusṭāṭ). His father was probably 'official over the merchants'. He is referred to in another epistle by the Gaon (see *infra*, p. 145). His son, Abraham, is commended for his generosity in the letters from Sahlān Rosh Hasseder to the Gaon. Sahlān is also mentioned in the epistle to Netaneel Hallevi b. Ḥalfon (No. 3). The Gaon also refers to the Alluf (=Resh Kallah, Rosh ha-Seder) in a letter he sent to the Alexandrian community (No. 4). The congregation is headed by Solomon Ḥazzan b. Moses. His name is not found in the letter of 1028 to Fusṭāṭ (above, p. 90). Probably he held then no communal office in Alexandria. The Ab-Bet-Dīn, referred to in the epistle, is probably the 'Father' of the Jerusalem school who, as we shall see in the next chapter, settled in Egypt, where he spent the last years of his life.

In the above pages a number of prominent Jews in Egypt, and chiefly in Fusṭāṭ, were introduced. Their names have been rescued from oblivion by the Genizah fragments that furnish the information about them. We can now realize what an important community the capital of the country possessed. Though we also hear of strife and dissension, yet the acts of benevolence and generosity exhibited by the local Jews atone for a good deal of the less creditable facts. But our object is not to apologize but to obtain information about Jewish life in the country of the Nile, and in the Holy Land, during the period treated here. Nothing ought to be suppressed. Both the bright and dark sides should be displayed. Petty and spiteful people exist in every age, and the personal ambitions and jealousies are common to every generation. The next chapter will reveal several unpleasant episodes in the history of these Jewries. Nevertheless, the record of the Fusṭāṭ community as regards fraternal feeling for a Jew, from whatever country he might hail, and for generosity and lovingkindness, is one that any modern congregation might well engrave in golden letters.

CHAPTER III

The Period of Solomon ben Yehuda (concluded).

(1) WE shall now deal with the Gaon's correspondence that has a bearing on the communal affairs in Egypt as well as on the conditions of the Palestinian Jewry, and particularly of the academy. So far one epistle only has been preserved from the time when Solomon was still 'Father' of the school. A. B. 32 is addressed to some prominent man in Egypt (Fusṭāṭ). Its beginning is missing. Solomon writes through his son on behalf of the Jerusalem Jews who were in such trouble, 'the like of which did not occur since the Jews returned' to the Holy City (i. e. since the Arab conquest, cp. above, p. 44 ff.). The majority of the inhabitants died from the plague that raged there. The remainder came to Solomon (אל מושבינו, l. 5, probably in Ramlāh, see also A. A. 20) and reminded him that he had promised to go to Egypt and intervene there on their behalf. But certain events happened which prevented him from going. His son should therefore make the journey instead. He was on his way to Aleppo, intending to travel as far as Mesopotamia. But, on hearing some report, he returned and is now setting out for Egypt in accordance with the people's request. He has with him letters from the congregations (of Palestine) to those of Fusṭāṭ and surrounding places. Solomon appeals to his correspondent to assist his son in successfully accomplishing the task he has undertaken.

Who the recipient of this epistle was, whether already Ephraim b. Shemarya, cannot be ascertained. We learn here of a serious plague in the Holy City. Yet, as-Suyūṭi in his treatise on the plagues[1] mentions none in Syria in the eleventh century prior to 1056. It is not clear what was the request of the Jerusalem

[1] See Kremer, 'Ueber die grossen Seuchen des Orients nach arabischen Quellen,' in *Sitzungsber. der Wiener Akad. d. Wissenschaften, philos.-histor. Klasse*, XCVI, 1880, p. 122.

community. It seems to have been more political than monetary aid for which they asked. Perhaps they solicited for a remission of the taxes. These were fixed and let to tax-farmers. As many people died from the plague, the remainder could not afford to pay the whole amount, and asked for relief. The bearer of this letter, Solomon's son, was either Abraham (whom we found in Egypt also in 1027, above, p. 96), or more likely Yaḥya. We find him later on in Bagdād studying under Hai (*infra*, p. 119, see also *J. Q. R.*, N.S., VIII, 348–9). Probably he was already at the time of this letter on his way to Hai's school. But he came back and undertook the mission of the Jerusalem community to Egypt. Subsequently he departed to Bagdād as originally intended.

A. B. 33 is an epistle addressed to Solomon b. Yehuda, evidently when already Gaon. So far there exists another letter to this Gaon, viz. MS. Erzherzog Rainer, which will be considered presently. It is only natural that the Fusṭāṭ Genizah should contain those letters sent by the Gaon from Jerusalem or Ramlāh to Egypt and beyond (in the latter case they were copied in Fusṭāṭ). For some reason or other a few epistles addressed to the Gaon found their way to the capital of Egypt. The anonymous writer requests Solomon to pray for him to recover from his illness. The letter seems to have been written on the eve of Passover. The following day, on the feast of unleavened bread, Solomon will recite prayers for the Jews of Palestine, Egypt, Damascus, Aleppo, and elsewhere. The sick correspondent of the Gaon requests that in these prayers his name should be expressly mentioned just as the elders of Jerusalem, Ramlāh, and Egypt enjoy this privilege. The latter know him well and hold him in respect. Probably he lived in a place near Jerusalem (very likely Ramlāh). Thus a letter written on the eve of Passover could reach the Gaon on the very same day. He wishes Solomon to behold his son Yaḥya back safe and sound. Very likely he was then away in Bagdād studying under Hai. We also learn that on Passover many elders went up to Mount Olivet to pray there. As we shall see farther on, Solomon had three sons, Yaḥya, Abraham, and Manṣūr. Of the last nothing further is known. Yaḥya studied in Bagdād. But whether he attained any scholarly standing is unknown. Abraham is often referred to in Solomon's letters. He held the dignity of 'Fourth' (above, p. 105). Yaḥya, who seems to have been a promising student, perhaps died when still young.

(2) A number of fragments inform us about dissensions within the Palestinian community of Fusṭāṭ. Ephraim b. Shemarya's position was much assailed by adversaries. A graphic account of local conditions is given in a fragment among the MSS. Rainer, published over twenty-five years ago.[1] There is very little doubt that it emanates from Fusṭāṭ, because the writer requests Solomon b. Yehuda to thank the 'dear and righteous elder Ḥesed, the respected dignitary' for the powerful aid he affords him (ll. 41–2). We know now who this Ḥesed was, viz. Abū Naṣr, the brother of Abū Sa'ad b. Sahl al-Tustari. A comparison of the handwriting of this letter with other fragments by Ephraim b. Shemarya, as well as internal evidence, make it most probable that he is its author. The many corrections show that we have before us a copy only and not the original which was sent to Palestine. It very likely emanates from the Cairo Genizah (cp. the editor's remarks, p. 127, and Epstein, *R. É. J.*, XXV, 272).

The writer of the letter calls himself the disciple of the Gaon (l. 10). The 'Sixth' of the school was then in Fusṭāṭ. Perhaps he is identical with Solomon's son, Abraham, whom we find there in 1027. (Later on Abraham advanced to the dignity of 'Fourth'.) Trouble arose in the synagogue on the arrival of a certain Reader, Solomon (Sabiḳ), with a letter of recommendation from the Gaon. He came to the synagogue to officiate and thus obtain some assistance from the congregants, but most of them objected to him as being under the ban. Witnesses gave evidence that a certain R. Joseph excommunicated this Reader. (Perhaps this Joseph is identical with Elijah Hakkohen's brother who died in 1053.) Moreover, the elders of Ramlāh wrote that this Sabiḳ was excluded from Jewish communion on account of his practice of magic. Against all this the writer, as the spiritual head of the synagogue, contended that the Gaon would not have given this Reader a letter of recommendation had he known anything of his excommunication. The result was a great quarrel. Had not

[1] Kaufmann and Müller in *Mitteilungen aus der Sammlung Erzherzog Rainer*, V, 128–9; cp. *R. É. J.*, XXV, 272–6.

the writer restrained the disputants, a good many would have fallen into the hands of the secular authorities and disgrace would have been brought on the community no less than on the school. For one of the other readers went so far as to suggest doing away with this new-comer. Finally, the writer undertook not to allow him to officiate until a letter arrived from the Gaon, with his own signature, accompanied by those of the Ab and the Third, to the effect that Sabiḳ's misdeed had been pardoned. Solomon b. Yehuda is asked to write this epistle himself and not merely to sign it, so as to have a greater effect on the congregation. The writer complains that strife is rampant in his community. Let the Gaon strongly reprove them and impress upon them the need for unity. He should also thank Ḥesed for his efforts to preserve peace. It is evident that we deal here with conditions in Fusṭāṭ. The Jerusalem Gaon would have great influence on the congregants of the synagogue, whose spiritual head the writer of this letter was. What else could it be but the Palestinian synagogue, and who else could the writer be but Ephraim b. Shemarya, the Ḥaber of this section in Fusṭāṭ? And we have here a graphic picture of the state of things with which Ephraim had to grapple.

The Gaon, Solomon b. Yehuda, indeed, faithfully stood by Ephraim throughout his career and endeavoured to silence his opponents. A. B. 34 is a letter from the Gaon to the congregation of חטאי.[1] Solomon writes that a letter reached him from Fusṭāṭ (מצרים) to the effect that a certain Abraham b. Aaron of Baṣra, a 'reader and preacher', quarrelled with Ephraim 'the superior Ḥaber, and abused him and the Geonim, both the late and the present, who gave him the diploma' (סומכיו, see above, p. 100, note 1). Abraham was therefore excommunicated at the academy on Ab 9th. The Gaon warns his correspondents not to have any intercourse with this person.

[1] The exact place in Egypt is unknown to me. Read, perhaps, תמאי, تمى, Tumai, a Ḳūrah in al-Ḥauf ash-Sharḳī, see Guest, *J. R. A. S.*, 1912, 974. The local Jewish community goes back to several centuries. About 622 a religious dispute between Christians and Jews is said to have resulted in about 375 Jews embracing Christianity (see Griveau, 'Histoire de la conversion des Juifs habitant la ville de Tomei en l'Égypte d'après d'anciens manuscrits arabes', in *Revue de l'Orient chrétien*, 1908, 298 ff.).

Of much more interest is A. B. 35.[1] It throws much light on the internal affairs of Ephraim's community. Solomon signs his letter to the Ḥaber by alluding to the anxious times they are having in Palestine on account of the Arabs (בני קדם), who laid waste the country and stopped all intercourse and travel. He is constantly praying that victory be vouchsafed to the Caliph's armies. This very likely refers to the grave rebellion of Arab chiefs in Palestine and Syria against az-Ẓahir in 1024–9, which will be discussed in the next chapter. We shall learn of the terrible sufferings of the Jews, especially those of Ramlāh, during these upheavals. But, moreover, Solomon is greatly perturbed by the letters that reach him from Fusṭāṭ ('Egypt') communities who are split up into fiercely opposing parties. Ephraim's adversaries wrote to the Gaon threatening him that the majority of the people wanted to complain to the government about him for giving authority as Ḥaber to an unworthy person (i.e. Ephraim). They even hint that because of Ephraim's presents and donations, Solomon writes epistles to Fusṭāṭ in Ephraim's favour. But all this, says the Gaon, is due to a certain 'suspect' (החשוד) who instigates people to write lampoons against the Ḥaber. For a while a state of peace reigned, and Solomon already wrote to commend and congratulate those that worked for the cause of peace. But a new quarrel broke out. A document with many signatures reached him to the effect that everybody agreed that Samuel Hakkohen b. Abṭalion should be the Dayyan (probably instead of Ephraim). The 'suspect' further goes about to the elders (זקנים) showing them a letter from Solomon wherein he spoke disparagingly of the former 'heads' (ראשים) of Fusṭāṭ. Such, we know, were Elḥanan (I), Shemarya, and Elḥanan (II). Now Solomon said that the former 'heads' were ready to shed each other's blood, and insulted R. Elḥanan (probably II) by saying, 'Look at his work and at that of his son' (העובר). The

[1] This fragment has already been printed in *R. É. J.*, LXVIII, 44–6; see also *J. Q. R.*, N. S., VIII, 17, note 17. But a comparison of the two texts will justify the reprint (see my remarks, *J. Q. R.*, N. S., VII, 481, note 25; IX, 413). There is, of course, not the slightest justification for making our Ephraim a son of the famous Shemarya b. Elḥanan (as is done in *R. É. J.*, *l. c.* 45, note 3). Ephraim's father was a native of Gaza (העזתי, אלגזי, see *R. É. J.*, XLVIII, 171, l. 10, and cp. p. 145, note 1; Bodl. 2873[28] = *J. Q. R.*, XIX, 250–4).

Gaon admits that he wrote in this strain but justifies his words.[1] Everybody knows of the previous grave discord in the community. Also the 'son' (העובר) had his mind set only on pleasure. Solomon bitterly complains of the conditions under which he has to labour. He admonishes the Ḥaber to try his best and give no further cause for complaints against him, though he is sure that the fault lies with his opponents, who prefer quarrel and strife. The Gaon intended first to excommunicate by name all those that slandered the Ḥaber, but he recognized the futility of his bans. Let them, he exclaims, appoint as ראש whomever they please. 'I remain in Jerusalem lamenting my lot and the (present) times.' These and similar sentiments expressed in this letter, as well as in the following epistles, are eloquent evidence of the Gaon's depressed state of mind. In conclusion, the Gaon mentions a letter he sent to the Sheikh Abū 'Āli Ḥasan ibn al-Ṭayyīb. He is perhaps identical with his namesake referred to in a letter to Abraham Hakkohen b. Ḥaggai (above, p. 104).

(3) Before proceeding with the description of the affairs in Fusṭāṭ, two fragments will be discussed which bear on the Nesiim. Hitherto it has been the general assumption that Daniel b. 'Azarya was the first Nasi who settled in Palestine, and thus revived the Patriarchate as a counterpart to the Exilarchate in Babylon (cp. especially Pozn., *Babyl. Geonim*, 111 ff.). We have seen above that there existed Nesiim already in the end of the tenth century, either in Palestine or in Syria (p. 24 f.). In the next chapter we collect other data concerning the holders of this dignity. Here it is intended to deal with a Nasi residing in Jerusalem when Solomon b. Yehuda occupied the Gaonate. He is mentioned anonymously several times by this Gaon. Sahlān b. Abraham, we have seen above (p. 97), had (in 1034 and 1037) the title חמדת הנשיאות, evidently on account of his services to the Nasi. It may be taken that in Jerusalem there lived a Nasi about this time. A. B. 36[2] contains a letter from Solomon b. Yehuda to some dignitary in Fusṭāṭ. The beginning is missing. He writes that he heard that X. (unfortunately the name is illegible) Hannasi was about to leave

[1] See also my remarks in *J. Q. R.*, N. S., VII, 481; IX, 413.
[2] Now printed by me in *J. Q. R.*, N. S., IX, 415.

Egypt for Palestine. This pleases him greatly, as there is none to be the (political) representative of the Palestinian Jewry. The Gaon mentions that he spoke 'to-day' (ביום הזה) 'to the highly respected elder' (in Jerusalem), Sa'adya b. Israel, requesting him to write to 'our prince and leader, the elder of the house of Israel and its glory', setting forth the Gaon's attachment to the Nasi and his desire of the Nasi settling in Jerusalem. Now the time is pressing because the festivals are at hand. Solomon would like the Nasi to come before New Year, and bring with him a letter from the government that his authority on dissenters be effective. 'My whole desire is that he (the Nasi) should act with a high hand and raised horn to break the jaws of the evildoer; for my heart is greatly grieved and I cannot write all that I feel. Our Nasi will tell him all details.' This shows that the Nasi was already for a short time in Jerusalem, and then left for Egypt to obtain recognition by the government. The Gaon continues, 'Let him (i.e. the high dignitary mentioned before) act in his kindness. May the Rock hear my prayer for him and for (his) brother, the lord, the glory of the house of Israel, their children and (their) whole family.' There is little doubt that the high personage who is to obtain from the government support for the Nasi is Abū Sa'ud b. Sahl al-Tustari, and that his brother is Abū Naṣr (Ḥesed). Hence the letter was written before 1048. In conclusion, Solomon greets his correspondent and his son. Very likely Sahlān b. Abraham received this letter. As head of the Babylonian community to which these influential brothers belonged, Sahlān could support the Gaon's plea. Solomon also wrote about this matter to the Ḥaber (l. 5, i.e. Ephraim b. Shemarya).[1]

Who this Nasi was is not certain. But A. B. 37 makes it probable that David, the son of Hezekiah, the Babylonian Exilarch, is meant here. The fragment is very badly preserved and the end is missing. This much is certain, that it has been written from Jerusalem and addressed to David the Nasi b. Ḥezekiah the Exilarch. The writer is very grieved at David's departure from Jerusalem, where the internal conditions of the community are very bad. In style the epistle consists of a skilful combination of Biblical verses. David's father is not

[1] See also my remarks in *J.Q.R.*, *l.c.*, 414–17.

alled Nasi, but ראש הגולה, which seems to indicate that he was xilarch in Babylon. But his son, having resided in Jerusalem, ould assume the title Patriarch. (The same difference of titles etween father and son we find in the memorial-list, A. B. o, II, 1.) As this epistle found its way to Fusṭāṭ (and it is vidently the original), it is clear that David left Jerusalem for gypt. His father, Ḥezeḳiah, was then still alive. He is known s the exilarch of Bagdād in the time of Hai. (A letter of his, ated 1020, has been printed in *R.É.J.*, LV, 51.) After Hai's eath (1038) he occupied the Gaonate for some time (for the atest discussion of this point, see Pozn., *Babyl. Geonim*, 1 ff.). t is quite likely that David is identical with the Nasi referred o in the previous letter from Solomon b. Yehuda. He went o Egypt to obtain letters patent from the government for his ffice. The two influential brothers Abū Sa'ad and Abū Naṣr, s Babylonians, naturally supported the son of the Bagdād xilarch. Of course, both his father and Hai Gaon must have ighly recommended him to the Babylonian section at Fusṭāṭ. lso Sahlān b. Abraham, as Alluf of this community, took much nterest in David becoming Nasi in Jerusalem and wielding olitical authority[1] side by side with the spiritual leadership of he Gaon. In short, the attempt was made to establish a dual eadership in Palestine, after the example of Babylon. And vidently the Gaon was willing to accept this new arrangement. ut it seems to have worked for a short time only. Solomon b. ehuda refers a few times to the Nasi in his letters. But nothing urther is heard of David. Perhaps A. B. 37 tells us of his final eparture from Jerusalem. Only after the Gaon's death (in 1051) aniel b. 'Azarya combined the Gaonate and the Patriarchate in he Holy City for about eleven years. After his death in 1062 lijah Hakkohen became Gaon, but the Patriarchate remained acant. Daniel's son, David, acted in Egypt as Nasi from about 080 till his deposal in 1094. This will be discussed more fully n the next chapter.

[1] On account of this David is styled (l. 3) 'the Nagid of God's people'. But the eal Nagid over the whole of Egyptian Jewry was then either Samuel, the son f the famous Palṭiel, or Yehoseph b. Samuel (see *infra*, p. 184). The other title, the pride of Jacob', is evidently complimentary, and does not denote that he ccupied the Gaonate.

(4) A group of fragments (A. B. 38–42) give us further in formation about the internal conditions in Fusṭāṭ and the par played by Solomon b. Yehuda. A. B. 38 is from the Gaon t Ephr. b. Shemarya, whom he addresses 'our friend and belove authorised in our academy . . . who is zealous for our cause an stands by us with help, who accepts our authority and steadfastl adheres to our love'. We learn of a Ḥaber from the Palestin school who in Fusṭāṭ accepted the title Alluf from the Babylonia school. Both Ephr. b. Shemarya and the Gaon are indignan though the latter is more lenient towards this scholar wh changed his allegiance. Solomon writes that after the festival he sent Ephr. letters in reply to his epistles. Therein Eph wrote about the man that 'despised the waters of Shiloa (i. e. Jerusalem) to drink the waters of the river (Euphrates, i. Babylon)'. He is the loser thereby, for he is satisfied wit the title Alluf instead of Ḥaber. In Solomon's opinion, o course, the former title is inferior to the latter. Though tha person disparaged his *alma mater* (הקל בכבוד אם), insinuating tha it had deteriorated (שכחה תורתה), and greatly commended th 'stepmother' (אשת אב, i.e. the Babylonian school as compare with the Palestinian), God will restore the prestige of the ancien seat of learning.[1] Solomon further recapitulates what he wrot in the preceding letter about the delay in the arrival of 19½ dīnā (from Fusṭāṭ). This is the remainder of a loan (by the Jerusalen community) for which '*our Nasi*' stood surety. The creditor i very urgent. Also a certain Aaron returned to somebody hi due. The Gaon reassures Ephraim to have no fear that th consignments of money from the Fusṭāṭ community would not b used for their proper purposes. Whomsoever the Nasi will orde to give the amount to, it will duly be handed over. We fin that there were frictions about the donations arriving from Egyp Sometimes the Gaon would keep a consignment (דיוקני) fo himself, to which the members of the school (בני החבורה) or th community at large would put forward claims. The conclusio of our fragment is somewhat obscure. Anyhow we find a Na in Jerusalem who evidently was at the head of the congregation he stood surety for their loans (to meet the taxes) and als supervised the distribution of the donations that arrived.

[1] See also my remarks in *J. Q. R.*, N. S., IX, 414.

A. B. 39 also deals with the acceptance of the Alluf-title by a Fusṭāṭ Ḥaber. Evidently he was at the head of a community which thus came under the jurisdiction of Babylon. This meant a loss of income to the school of Jerusalem. Hence there arose some friction between Solomon and Hai, though previously they seem to have been on very friendly terms, and the former even sent his son Yaḥya to study under the Great Bagdād Gaon. Highly interesting is therefore this fragment, unfortunately very badly preserved; beginning and end are missing, but the handwriting as well as the contents leave no doubt that the writer is Solom. b. Yehuda and the recipient Ephraim b. Shemarya. The Gaon begins by alluding to the loyalty the people of Juda showed to their king (David). Not that he is a king nor are the others (i. e. the Babylonian Gonim), but this by way of example. What fault have they found in him? Has he given undue trouble or praised one at the expense of the other? His whole desire is peace. He alludes to Babylonians in Palestine (but the text is here defective, ll. 6–7). The dissenters do not consider that by transferring a community from him to another Gaon (יושבי חוץ), the result will be that he will suffer want. But, on the other hand, he has no obligation on them. Whither they send their legal questions, they receive their responsa (as is well known the questions would be accompanied by donations). 'Why complain, my brother the Ḥaber?' By their forsaking the Palestine academy and accepting the authority of the school of the Diaspora (ישיבת חוץ), the burden of responsibility is eased from the man in authority (מהיושב בשבת, i.e. the Gaon). Solomon only wishes that his request be fulfilled and some worthy person relieve him from his office. He has constantly to contend with urgent creditors and slanderers (דרכי חצים). He thanks Ephraim and his confederates for the gift they have sent him. The Gaon further mentions that Ephraim in his letter spoke of epistles from R. Hai to Fusṭāṭ. Solomon uses here bitter remarks that they (i. e. the authorities of the Babylonian school) try to extend their influence, if it were possible, over the whole inhabitable world in order to augment their income. He, however, is satisfied with as little as possible. Evidently the Gaon reproaches here Hai and his academy for detaching a community that formerly belonged to the jurisdiction of the Palestine school. Unfortunately the fragment is much damaged.

A. B. 40 deals with the same person who exchanged the Palestinian diploma for a Babylonian one. Solomon writes again to Ephraim, whom he calls 'the choice of the Palestinian academy, active', and serving his people with all his might. The Gaon sent epistles from Jerusalem, and one of them in Arabic (הגרי). Further, from Ramlāh he wrote to him.[1] On the invitation of the elders Solomon went there, and was received in honour. The town has been corrupted by 'the congregation of law-breakers' (עדת פריצים). A fast was proclaimed, and a large assembly decided to excommunicate all evildoers. Who these people were is entirely obscure. Perhaps the followers of Malik ar-Ramli, the sectarian chief, are meant here.[2] From this city Solomon sent three epistles, one to Ephraim in Arabic (הגרי), as a reply to the dignitary (השר) Ephraim Hakkohen (who was a Dayyan in Cairo-Fusṭaṭ, cp. above, p. 41, note 1, and *infra*, p. 131), a second one to this Ephraim, whose brother is also referred to. As we shall see farther on, Ephraim's brother was Menasse, an uncle of Elijah and Joseph (b. Solomon Hakkohen Gaon), well known from *Megillat Ebyatar*. Solomon b. Yehuda seems to have had some altercation with this Ephraim. The third epistle was a long declaration, with the Gaon's signature, to be recited before the whole congregation (of the Palestinians at Fusṭāṭ), concerning the man that 'despised the name of Ḥaber and chose the name of Alluf. God knows that he is very dear to me. Two letters before have I torn up, for when writing, sharp expressions come into my mind, and I put them down. But afterwards I remember our former friendship, and say to myself, "It is not right to denounce benefactors and cast off friends." Though he started the dissension, his ambition carried him away because his desire was not fulfilled. . . . If he found it advisable to be honoured by outside Geonim (יושבי חוץ), he ought not to have mentioned anybody else. But this man went on to praise

[1] From that city the Gaon also dispatched three epistles to Abraham Hakkohen b. Ḥaggai, see about him above, pp. 96, 102, and 104.

[2] Towards the end of the eighth century Ramlāh had a prominent sectarian, Malik ar-Ramli, who seems to have had a following of his own (see Pozn., in Luncz's *Jerusalem*, X, 92–3). In Ḳirḳisani's time (i. e. that of Sa'adya and Ben-Meir) the sect was still in existence. But whether about a century later Malik's adherents were still to be found in Ramlāh or elsewhere in Palestine is so far unknown.

and eulogize those that honoured him by his new title.' He also found fault with Ephraim without justification. Yet the Gaon cannot utterly condemn him. 'Love sets at nought the line (of strict justice, אהבה מקלקלת את השורה).' With the present letter are enclosed two epistles, one to Samuel b. Abraham of Tahort (a correspondent of Hai Gaon, see *J. Q. R.*, N.S., VIII, 357), and another to Samuel Hakkohen b. Abṭalion, the well-known Rosh Haḳḳahal. In conclusion, Solomon thanks Ephraim for having restored peace, in a private affair, between father and son. The Gaon makes it his practice to repeat in his letters what he wrote in his former epistles. Probably he was afraid that some might be lost on the way. He therefore took the precaution of recapitulating his former words. The letter to Samuel b. Abraham of Tahort Ephraim would probably forward to Ifrikiyya. We obtain an inkling of how correspondence was transmitted from one country to another.

A. B. 41 clearly deals with the same topic. Beginning and end are missing; but the handwriting is that of Solomon (or of his secretary who wrote the former epistles). The correspondent is a Ḥaber, while from the tone of the epistle it appears that it was sent to Ephraim b. Shemarya. He evidently asked that the new Alluf (formerly Ḥaber) should be deprived of his title and deposed. Solomon opposes this strongly, and draws an interesting sketch of Ephraim and his opponent. It seems that the 'Gaon of the Diaspora' (l. 3), i. e. Hai, wrote a letter against Ephraim. Solomon explains that this was due to hasty anger. He ought to have only recommended the new Alluf, and not mentioned anybody else (i. e. his opponent). Now this Alluf should not be proceeded against. 'If he repents, discards the name of Alluf, and returns to the allegiance of the Palestine academy, far be it that he be deposed. You, our friend and Ḥaber (colleague), ought to thank God for having endowed you with patience, forbearance, and an anxious mind to serve the people in all their needs. These qualities your opponent possesses not. Your and his own friends will testify that each of you has certain qualities. The one is conciliatory (i. e. Ephraim), the other impatient; the first alert in all communal affairs, as in the case of imposition, gifts for officials, and calling upon them at their residences; he also knows how to arbitrate and restore peace in lawsuits. But the other is too impatient to be a proper Dayyan; he cannot also interview officials, katibs, and tax-collectors; on the other hand, he has other qualities for which he is cherished and respected by the people. Not everybody can command all qualities. Therefore he that possesses some of them ought to be grateful for them, and strive to preserve peace.' In this way, it must be conceded, diplomatic and skilful, the Gaon tried to restore peace between Ephraim and his opponent. The latter must have belonged to a highly respected family in Egypt, whereas Ephraim was a native of Gaza, and not a countryman of the people.

(5) The dissensions in the Fusṭāṭ community seem to have been chronic, lasting for several years with intervals of patched-up peace. But before proceeding with the discussion of the fragments that have a bearing on them, a few other letters from the Gaon and his school will be considered. A. B. 42 is from Solomon b. Yehuda to Abraham b. Sahlān and to his brother-in-law Sa'adya (b. Ephraim the Ḥaber). Abraham was no longer alive in 1032 (above, p. 97). The fragment is very damaged. Greetings are sent to Abraham's son (i. e. Sahlān). The Gaon refers to earthquakes (זועות) which they experienced. As will be shown in the next chapter, Palestine was visited by a great earthquake in 1033. But since Abraham was no longer alive then, the allusion is here to some earlier event. Solomon reports that he sent four letters. Subsequently, in Marḥeshvan, a young man from Tyre, Khalaf b. Moses, was the bearer of two epistles (from the Gaon) to certain elders. Two others were addressed to the elder Shemarya b. Yefet concerning a man, Isaac of Wādi'lḳura' [1] (in Arabia), who had left his family in 'Ammān (the capital of the Balḳa) already four years previously. Greetings are sent to Mebasser, and to Obadya and his son Joseph. On verso we read bitter remarks by the Gaon about the state of affairs in Jerusalem. He apparently fled from Jerusalem (to Ramlāh) because he suffered there much. 'You (Abraham) have visited me, and know all my doings.' Through Menasse Hakkohen a letter (from the Gaon) was sent to the dignitary Ephraim Hakkohen (his brother).

A. B. 43 is again from the Gaon, as the handwriting proves,

[1] About this Jewish community see *J. Q. R.*, N. S., VII, 489.

to X. b. Abraham, a great friend of his. The correspondent evidently came to Egypt to settle a lawsuit. Solomon learned with pleasure of his safe arrival at Ṣo'an (Fusṭāṭ). He advises him quickly to wind up his affair, and not stay long there (cp. ll. 11–31). Greetings are sent to him from Abraham and Manṣur. These are apparently the Gaon's sons. A letter also reached him, at the end of Marḥeshwan, from Yaḥya at Bagdād, saying that he was studying the Halakot Gedolot before Hai, who also enclosed an epistle. This must have been before Solomon's friction with Hai, as described above. Ephraim Hakkohen is again mentioned. Also greetings are sent to Abraham b. Sahlān, to Sa'adya (his brother-in-law), to Mebasser b. Ephraim the Ḥaber, and also to the sons of Israel (?). Perhaps the recipient of this letter was Samuel b. Abraham of Tahort. We have seen that the Gaon was in correspondence with him. We have also found him passing Ḳabes on his way from Tahort to Egypt (*J.Q.R.*, N.S., VIII, 357). In Fusṭāṭ Samuel had several friends and acquaintances. Perhaps when Solomon mentioned (above, p. 117) that he dispatched an epistle from Ramlāh to this Samuel, he referred to our fragment here.

A. B. 44 is again from the Gaon to Abraham b. Sahlān. The Gaon writes that in a previous epistle he thanked him for the donation of the Fusṭāṭ community that had been sent through the elder Solomon b. Sa'adya (see above, p. 96) to Levi b. Menaḥem (evidently a communal leader in Jerusalem). The purpose of the present letter is on behalf of a certain Ṣadaḳa b. Menaḥem (perhaps a brother of the above Levi). This person greatly eulogizes Abraham for his kindness. He repents his former misdeeds and relates that the 'mighty elder' (הזקן האדיר) promised him to write to some of his representatives to find him (Ṣadaḳa) some employment in Egypt. Abraham is requested by the Gaon to interest himself in this Ṣadaḳa. Greetings are sent to Abraham's two sons, i.e. Sahlān and Nehemiah (above, p. 97), and to his brother-in-law (i.e. Sa'adya). The 'mighty elder' is most likely Abū Sa'ad b. Sahl al-Tustari, who, as a man of great wealth, could give employment to several people on his estates and in other business concerns. In another small epistle (note 5) the Gaon mentions that he wrote to this 'mighty elder' to support a certain R. Simḥa. The above Ṣadaḳa was evidently a native of Jerusalem who was for some time in Egypt endeavouring to find there a living. A. B. 45 is a letter from a member of the Jerusalem school to David b. Aaron in Fusṭāṭ, with whom the Gaon also corresponded. The writer mentions that his epistles were delayed on account of the upheavals they experienced. This refers probably to the revolution in Palestine in 1024–29. 'Thank God, we are alive. Afterwards we went to Damascus and restored peace. The Gaon is very pleased with your letters. I wrote to you during the festivals; perhaps the letter will reach you. This week Ṣadaḳa b. Menaḥem arrived here. He greatly praises you for your kindness. Please continue to do so.' Here the letter breaks off. No doubt this Ṣadaḳa was about to return soon to Egypt.

(6) We come now to discuss further the internal affairs of the Palestinian community of Fusṭāṭ. A group of fragments inform us of the dissensions between Ephraim b. Shemarya and another Ḥaber. It is doubtful whether the latter is identical with the scholar who changed his title from Ḥaber to Alluf (as discussed under (4)). A son of Solomon b. Yehuda went to Egypt on behalf of certain prisoners in Jerusalem (probably the victims of heavy impositions), but his mission was unsuccessful owing to the communal strife in Fusṭāṭ. Several letters from the Gaon refer to this topic. A. B. 46 is by him, as the handwriting shows, though the signature is missing. Ephraim b. Shemarya is evidently the recipient of the letter. Greetings are sent also to his son-in-law. We have found above (p. 96) Abr. b. Solomon Gaon in Fusṭāṭ in 1027. Probably the fragments refer to events in that year. Solomon is very bitter in this epistle. He adjures his correspondent to send home at once his son. Let not the Jerusalem people say that he stops there for his own interest. 'For I have enough of shame. Between wolf and shepherd, the lamb is torn into pieces: between the two Ḥaberim the prisoners suffer.' He impresses upon Ephraim to keep pace with his opponent. Now, after receiving thanks for what he has done to his son before, let him earn more gratitude from the Gaon by providing his son with the means of returning home.

A. B. 47, an important letter in Solomon's handwriting (beginning and end missing), informs us about a serious charge levelled against Ephraim, who is evidently the Ḥaber meant here. It appears that he, together with other people, were imprisoned in consequence of the accusation. The Gaon denounces the slanderers and informers. How grieved he was when hearing what had happened 'to our Ḥaber, who had been ordained in our academy' (l. 6)! But news reached him of the 'salvation brought about by righteous and intelligent people' (ll. 9–10). The 'regent who is victorious in the realm' (l. 12) took care to examine himself the witness who brought forth the charges. The falseness of his evidence became clear, and he was dismissed in disgrace. The 'regent' reported the result to the Caliph, who forthwith ordered the release of the imprisoned. The Gaon describes how he publicly commended the Caliph for his gracious act, and also the viceroy (הסגן). The latter seems to be identical with the 'regent' (הגביר) who conducted the examination of the witness (see ll. 20–24). He seems to have been the commander-in-chief of the armies. Solomon recited prayers for them in the synagogue at Ramlāh on the Sabbath, ויצא יעקב. The letter is evidently written from this town. The Gaon is to order the people in Jerusalem also publicly to thank the Caliph and the viceroy for their gracious act. Several influential Jews in Fusṭāṭ worked in Ephraim's favour. These were also included in the public prayer recited by the Gaon. 'We also blessed our master, lord and leader' David Hallevi b. Isaac (whom we know from the former fragments above, p. 88 ff.), and also the 'respected elders' Shelah, Sa'adya, and Joseph, the sons of Israel (read בני for בן, l. 30), known as al-Dastura (דיאסתרה), i. e. nobles. Thanks were finally accorded to all the officials, Kātibs, and other elders (of both sections, i.e. Rabbinite and Ḳaraite, זקני שתי הפאות, l. 32), who helped to bring about the freedom of the prisoners. What the charges against them were is not stated. But the whole affair must have been the outcome of the conflict between Ephraim and a fellow-Ḥaber (who is unnamed, perhaps Samuel b. Abṭalion). The Gaon urges his correspondents to do away with strife and persist in maintaining peace. It behoves the Ḥaberim to join hands and work for the community's religious and moral welfare and settle their lawsuits. In this epistle the two brothers, Abū Sa'ad and Abū Naṣr, are not mentioned. Very likely this event took place before they attained such influence in the court.[1] This tends to strengthen our suggestion that it was in 1027 when Solomon's son Abraham was in Fusṭāṭ and, as we shall see presently, stayed there a whole year. Interesting is the fact that influential Ḳaraite elders in Fusṭāṭ took active part in the communal affairs of Rabbinite congregations.

A. B. 48, defective at the end, but clearly in Solomon b. Yehuda's handwriting, deals with conditions a few weeks later. It is addressed to Abraham b. Sahlān. A consignment of money for Solomon has been lost on the way. Thence to meet pressing needs, the Gaon had to use temporarily an amount of money presented to the Jerusalem people. As a result we hear of recrimination of the donor in Egypt. Solomon mentions that letters arrived from Abraham and his son, the Resh Kallah (i.e. Sahlān). Then there reached him an epistle from his own son about the loss of the dīnārs. He therefore decided to use the other money to tide over the critical time. But hardly had he began to do so when his son wrote him about the complaints of the donor. This letter reached him through a certain Abraham b. Isaac, to whom the Gaon gave 5 dīnārs as well as a new cloak (טלית) and a garment of his son's. Together this would

[1] Very likely the first of the 'noblemen', Shelah b. Israel (p. 121), is identical with their father Sahl. His brothers were Sa'adya and Joseph, the same people whom we found in A. B. 1 (see above, p. 81) as the uncles of Abū Sa'ad and Abū Naṣr. A signatory of a document of our period (see *infra*, p. 150), Joseph b. Israel al-Tustari is probably identical with our Joseph b. Israel. Cp. also above, p. 38, note 1. We thus learn that a Jew of Tustar, Israel, had three sons who settled in Fusṭāṭ, and attained there a high position. The first of these brothers, Shelah, was the father of the famous Abū Sa'ad and Abū Naṣr. His Arabic name was Sahl; indeed the similarity of the names is obvious. From A. B. 49 (see *infra*, p. 125) we gather that on some occasion Solomon b. Yehuda honoured our Sahl by giving him the flattering name ישר, upright! The Gaon states that he was guided by the etymology of Sahl (سهل) in Arabic being = מישור, a plain. Since then Sahl went also by the Hebrew name of Yashar, whereas his original name was Shelah. Our present epistle seems to have been written before he received this honorary name. Perhaps by the sons of Israel (?), above, p. 119, these three brothers are meant. Their full names are given in the address (verso) of an Arabic letter sent to them by Mūsa and Isaac the sons of Barhūn (T.-S. 12. 133): לשיכי וריסי וגלילי אביאלפצל ואבי יעקב ואבו סהל סהל ויוסף וסעיד בני ישראל אלתסתריין אטאל אללה בקאהם מן מוסי ויצחק בני ברהון נע. Thus Abū'l Faḍl Sahl was the father of Abū Sa'ad and Abū Naṣr, while his brothers went by the names Abū Ya'ḳūb Joseph and Abū Sahl Sa'īd (Sa'adya) respectively.

make 10 d. Abraham is to keep these garments as a pledge till Solomon repays the 19 d., and is to inform the people in Fusṭāṭ of this transaction. Also a certain R. Levi (perhaps identical with the elder Levi b. Menaḥem, above, p. 119) sent an epistle. And the Gaon thought that their letters reached their destination. But instead, epistle follows epistle from Egypt, enlarging upon the peremptory demand of the donor to return the money. On Ṭebet 10th there reached him epistles about this affair from Abraham b. Sahlān and from his own son. The Gaon is much pained and is afraid lest the strife in the Fusṭāṭ community, that had just been allayed, break out again. 'Since my son came to Fusṭāṭ all these evils befell me.' Solomon b. Sa'adya (cp. above, p. 96) is to be given permission to spend some dīnārs for a certain purpose.

Similar accusations against the Gaon we find in a letter, dated Ab 1035, from some person of Ḳairowān to Ephraim b. Shemarya (*J.Q.R.*, XIX, 255–6, cp. N.S., IX, 163).[1] The writer,

[1] A few lines have been cited above (p. 94, note 1). Here the remainder is given:
(1) ל[אהוב] . . . הנכבד במושבו הכקי בתעודה . . . (2) . . . [העוסק בדברי
תור]ה ומכבד לומדיה בלי לב ולב . . . (3) . . . הגיע [כתב]ך יקירי וששתי
בשלומך . . . (8) . . . וראיתי בכתב ידידי נוסח מה שקיבלו על עצמם השתי כיתות
הנה מה טוב ומה נעים (9) גדול שלום ושנואה המחלוקת וכתבתי לך כתב עם מוהוב
אשתקד המתחבר לבן ישעיה (10) . . . גם לא ראיתי כתב מרבינו ראש ישיבת
ארץ צבי המקום יאריך (11) ימיו ואילולי שהזכרת לי ששיגרת כתבי אליו הייתי
אומר בשביל שלא ראה ממני כתב ובתוך כת[ב] (12) זה כתב אחר משגרהו
(r. תשגרהו) בחסדך וסיפר לי שמואל אלברקי מקצת המודע התבוננתי [גם] (13)
מדבריך מקצת ואל תשם בדעתך כי לא כתב לך הנגיד יחי לעד . . . (14) [ש]מא
השליח לא עשה שליחותו ולא נעלם ממך דברי רבות לא כל הרוצה ל[יראה]
(r. ליקח) את השם . . . (16) . . . ואני שואל (17) ממך שתעביר על מידותיך . . .
והחזק במוסרך (18) כי הוא וסתך מעודך ואל תאמר אשלמה רע קוה לײ ויושע
לך והוגד לי כי באו כתבים (19) [מה]נגיד שׂצ̇ במהדיה מספרים כי שילח מי שבידו
הממון כמו ששים זהובים כדי שייהנו בה כל בני החבורה (20) ולקחם ראש ישיבה
לעצמו ונשארו הכל ריקנין חזרו מאצלו בפחי נפש ואם גוזר המקום (21) ואתועד
עם הנגיד אחרי בואו ממהדיה יודיעני אמיתת הדברים וחלילה חלילה מרבי[נו]
(22) אם יעירהו לבו לכך אבל היה ראוי לך תכתוב לי עיקרי הדברים כדי להשיב
(23) על המוציא ריבה (r. דבה) תשובה ניצחת . . . (24) . . . אל תחשוב עליו
(25) בחסד אל עליך שלא תפסיק כתביך בבל צרכיך ובריאות גופך כי היא

who seems to have been an intimate friend of Ephraim, mentions that he read in the Ḥaber's letter (to him) about the conditions which the two parties accepted. How greatly he is pleased with the peace that has been restored (in the Fusṭāṭ community). More about this we shall learn from the following fragments. 'I sent you a letter yesterday through Mauhub who travels together with Ben Isaiah. I have received no epistle from the Gaon of Palestine (i.e. Solomon b. Yehuda). Had you not mentioned (in your letter) that you had transmitted my letter to him, I should have thought his silence was due to his not having received one from me. I now enclose another letter to him. Please forward it. Samuel al-Barḳi told me some news, while the rest I gather from your writing. Be not upset that the Nagid (of Ḳairowān, i.e. Jacob b. 'Amram, who was in office about this time, see *J. Q. R.*, N.S., IX, 162–3) did not write to to you. Perhaps the messenger did not do his duty. Be not revengeful. I know your habit of forbearance. I have also been told that letters came from the Nagid in Mahdiya (near Ḳairowān) to the effect that a donor sent 60 d. for all the members of the school (of Jerusalem), but the Gaon kept them for himself. When the Nagid comes back from Mahdiya I shall discuss the whole matter with him. Far be it from the Gaon to do such a thing. But you had better write me the facts, so that I be able to refute the scandalmongers.' This is the drift of this letter. The writer is perhaps Samuel b. Abraham of Tahort, who on his travels visited Ḳairowān and during his stay in Fusṭāṭ became acquainted with Ephraim b. Shemarya. Some proof for our suggestion is the fact that the writer's son bore the name of Abraham, which would fit in with this Samuel whose father was also an Abraham (cp. also above, p. 119).

From the above letter of 1035 we learn that at last an agreement was entered upon by both parties (or sections). Probably then communal peace was finally restored in Fusṭāṭ. But we still have to discuss several fragments that are of a previous date. A. B. 49 (a long letter in the Gaon's handwriting, but unfortunately torn across its whole length so that the lines are

תאותי (26) ותקבל שלום רב מאברהם המזרי (חמודי .probably r) ומאַחַי ורעי
אלהי צורי אחסה בו (27) חצי אב שנת שׂמֹו לשטרות.

preserved in halves only, also beginning and end missing) deals with an interim settlement of the dispute between the two Ḥaberim. It seems that it was agreed upon that they should together serve on the Bet-Dīn, whereas formerly each administered justice in his own synagogue. Ephraim b. Shemarya obviously resented this infringement of his authority as spiritual head of the Palestinian community, and we shall see presently that the new régime did not work satisfactorily. We give here a *résumé* of A. B. 49 as far as it is possible from the part preserved. The Gaon probably writes to Ephraim. He mentions that he ordained several fasts at Ramlāh (cp. above, p. 116). Also the sects, Rabbinites and Ḳaraites, are referred to. 'They asked (Solomon?) to be one day with the former and another with the latter' (verso, l. 2 ff.). The two sects intermarry (l. 5). Apparently Ephraim complained to the Gaon that a letter of his to the congregation favoured his opponent. Solomon apologizes that he had only written for the sake of peace. 'I knew not that it would turn out so' (ll. 13–14). The Ḥaberim should be together on the Bet-Dīn that there be peace between them (l. 16). The Gaon also apparently changed a certain man's Arabic name into Hebrew, viz. from Sahl into Yāshār, because מישור in Hebrew = سَهْل, סהל in Arabic (ll. 26–7). Probably he refers here to Sahl al-Tustari the father of Abū Sa'ad and Abū Naṣr (cp. above, p. 122, note 1). The latter seems to have taken the part of Ephraim in this affair (we have seen above, p. 108 f., how he supported our Ḥaber), and had some resentment against the Gaon (see A. B. 50 and *infra*, p. 128 f.). Therefore the Gaon probably points out how he respected his father Sahl by bestowing upon him the name ישר 'upright'. The Gaon further mentions the Dayyan Ephraim Hakkohen, 'whose brother left (the maintenance of) his family to me' (ll. 32–5). We shall presently see that this Ephraim's brother, Menasse, had to go to Egypt. On recto Solomon seems to write about his son, who, after the hardships he encountered on his journey to Egypt, spent there more than a year for the sake of certain prisoners, but did not succeed in his mission. The people had to sell all they possessed to redeem themselves (l. 11 f.). Also Solomon b. Sa'adya is alluded to. The 19 dīnārs the Gaon promises to repay with God's help (ll. 17–18). The rest deals with a private affair. Only towards the end (l. 40)

Solomon again mentions his stay in Ramlāh. There is no doubt that this fragment dates from the time when Abraham, the son of the Gaon, went to Fusṭāṭ on behalf of certain Jerusalem Jews who were imprisoned, and when the consignment of 19 d. was lost, as described above. Abraham, however, seems to have already returned to Palestine.

It is very difficult to piece together a connected narrative from the letters at our disposal. Many links are still missing. Moreover, seldom is one of them dated, and by internal evidence only, as it appears to us, they are arranged in the Appendix. But this much can be gathered with certainty. The opponent of Ephraim was made Ḥaber by the Jerusalem school at the instigation of the Ab, who was about to leave for Egypt. The Gaon was against the appointment, but had to give way. In Fusṭāṭ a sort of agreement was made that both Ephraim and the new Ḥaber act together on the Bet-Dīn. But soon discord broke out again. The new Ḥaber wanted to usurp all power. In the long run he seems to have been defeated. Who this person was is very obscure. It is possible that he is identical with the Ḥaber who became Alluf. Solomon declared that he be not deposed if he renounced his new title. Assuming that he did not obey, he was removed from being a Ḥaber of the Palestinian school. Subsequently it may be that the Ab worked in his favour and carried through that he be reinstalled. The Ab then left for Egypt, where he must have stayed for some time and where he died, as we shall see farther on. This construction of the data will gain in probability as we proceed in the discussion of the following fragments. First, Saadyana XLII should be analysed as it has a bearing on our topic. Some erroneous constructions are placed upon it by Pozn. (*R. É. J.*, XLVIII, 158–9). I have re-examined the fragment, and the following new readings are given below.[1] In that letter Solomon

[1] L. 1–2 אפרים החבר ה[יקר סגולת] ישיבת צבי; l. 2 כנגזרת באין . . .; l. 5 for בגרובה r. בגדו בה; l. 8 for גֿעֿ r. גע (reached); for להסתפח r. להסתפ[ח]; l. 22 ועצה מחכ[ם]; l. 24 for למותו r. לבזותו; l. 30 החביר can also be read החסיד; l. 32 for מושיע (?) r. משוע, protesting; l. 41 for ולא יקש . . . r. ולא יכש[ר ה]דב[ר]; l. 42 for על שמו . . . r. על שמו זה; l. 45 for גנעתי r. יגעתי; l. 46 for לכל r. לבל; l. 47 the continuation of לעשות בו אשר is on the right-hand margin of תרצה חלף עבודתך;

addresses Ephraim as the 'choice of the Palestine academy that remain depressed as a barren woman and forsaken as a widow (נגזרת)' without (help and support). But formerly it was mistress issuing decisions about all kinds of law. 'All her friends dealt treacherously with her to bring every one of her disciples into disrepute.' But he (Ephraim) remained steadfast in his allegiance. Ephraim's letter to Solomon's son arrived after he had left on a journey aboard ship. Times are critical for the school and there is no support. Hence he had to make a journey because the Gaon could not travel himself; there was no way by land, therefore his son had to go by boat. He evidently did not go to Egypt because, firstly, he could have travelled by land; and, secondly, the Gaon does not mention that he would call on Ephraim. Hence we can only assume that the Gaon's son went to Italy and perhaps to Spain to appeal personally for the maintenance of the school. Solomon continues that he consulted the 'Third' about the contents of Ephraim's letter, and they were astonished at the proceedings in Fusṭāṭ. Solomon does not mention the Ab. We shall soon see that he was then in Egypt. Somebody was going to deprive Ephraim of a diocese which he obtained from the Gaon and his school. But first Solomon urges upon Ephraim to give no cause for dissension. The Gaon does it in a gentle manner and assures Ephraim that he is aware of his abilities and tact. Ephraim's letter reached him on Sivan 24, and on the following day, Monday, Sivan 25, they met in *a cave* in great assembly, took out Scrolls of the Law, and excommunicated those that stirred up strife and sent false letters about in the name of innocent people. For certain things were written as emanating from R. Nathan the Ḥaber (in Fusṭāṭ), but when the letter was sent to him for verification, he was greatly annoyed, since he never wrote it. He publicly disowned it and asked for a ban in order to free himself from the suspicion. We also, continues the Gaon, will excommunicate those that report untruths about innocent people to fan up strife and discord. It is not clear why the Gaon had to meet in a cave for the purpose of announcing the ban. But probably this was due to a general government order forbidding the ban to be

l. 49 הנשואה is correct. Verso: l. 1 ויקירנו כנק . . . החבר בסנ' גדולה; l. 2 [ברבי שמר[יהו נבע; l. 3 [ישע ר[ב; cp. also Worman, *J. Q. R.*, XIX, 727, top.

proclaimed on Mount Olivet, as will be discussed in the next paragraph (p. 138). Ephraim also mentioned in his letter the supervision of the markets (i. e. bazaars of butchers) and the people appointed for this task. Somebody appointed his son, and in this way upset the communal arrangement of affairs. The benefits from the supervision of the market were due to Ephraim as settled by the elders. 'Has that man', asks the Gaon, 'not enough, to deprive another communal servant (i.e. our Ephraim) of his due? This place is in my name (i. e. the Palestinian Gaon) and the other is in his name, the latter belonging to the Babylonians, the former to the Palestinians. Does he indeed desire to eradicate the rights of the Palestinian academy in Egypt? The result will be that he himself will lose thereby.' 'How I laboured when mentioning him on Hoshana Rabba till I declared him as Ḥaber. He ought to have helped you and not take away what belongs to you and give it to a suspect.' The allusions here are obscure. But it seems that the Ab in Fusṭāṭ acted against the interests of Ephraim, and that his protégé was the newly-appointed Ḥaber, who was a 'suspect', viz. that he had leanings towards the Babylonian school. Solomon emphasizes that this source of income (i. e. the supervision of the markets) was fully granted by him and the 'Third' to Ephraim to dispose of it as he pleases. In conclusion there is an allusion to a private matter. A letter is enclosed to R. Nathan, who was innocently accused, to appease him and assure him that the Gaon bears no longer any ill-will against him.

We learn already from this letter of the friction between Ephraim and the new Ḥaber. The Gaon sides with the former, whose cause was also upheld by Sahlān b. Abraham and other Fusṭāṭ dignitaries. A. B. 50 is from Solomon to Sahlān. He writes, 'Your letter reached me. I can see that your friendship is genuine (לשם שמים; a passing cloud must have obscured it for some time). Previous to this letter, I wrote you a few lines of consolation on the death of your dear father (i. e. Abraham b. Sahlān; we know that he was no longer alive in Tammuz 1032, above, p. 97). May God comfort you and all your relatives. As regards the "mighty elder" R. Ḥesed (i. e. our well-known Abū Naṣr b. Sahl al-Tustari), may God's favour be with him, his sons and his brother (i. e. Abū Sa'ad). I always mention him (in my prayers) favourably. As to what you write about the Ḥaber Ephraim (b. Shemarya), I made no person his colleague. God knows that before the Ab left (for Egypt), he asked that this man be made Ḥaber. But I did not like it because I remembered his misdeeds, though I never did him any wrong. (Evidently this man acted in Egypt against the interests of the Gaon.) You know that formerly the authority was divided, but now it is combined. A condition was made that nothing be innovated unless by the consent of four. (Probably the Gaon refers here to the Palestine school. Formerly the Nasi's authority was distinct from that of the Gaon; but subsequently they had to work in unison. A stipulation was made that any appointment made by the school should have the consent of *four*, viz. Gaon, Nasi, Ab, and Third.) Had you seen me that day (i. e. Hashana Rabba, when that man of Fusṭāṭ was proclaimed Ḥaber), you would have been surprised. Those that prohibited me to appoint (Ḥaberim), they themselves nominated. It thus became known to anybody with an insight that I have lost authority. "Time has come to depose, and also to appoint." Far be it from me to forget a friend (i. e. Ephraim), and remember him that has (formerly) despised (the school, probably by accepting the title Alluf from the Babylonian academy).' The letter is here defective. A certain משוש (i. e. one who held the honorary title משוש הישיבה 'the delight of the school', probably Abraham Hakkohen b. Isaac, cp. *infra*, p. 183, and also above, p. 92) wrote some epistles. Also 'our Nasi Hezekiah' is mentioned. (Is he identical with the Bagdād Exilarch, the father of David? He was then still alive, because our letter cannot date later than Tammuz, 1032, when we found Abraham b. Sahlān referred to as departed from this life. In note 1 a fragment mentions a 'son of a Nasi', Joseph b. Hezekiah, who composed הלכות שחיטה. Perhaps he is this Nasi's son.) Solomon continues, 'My sun is setting, and I am much perturbed by the death of my contemporary (בן גילי, i. e. Abraham b. Sahlān). My only prayer is to live through this year, that people say not, "Both died in the same year". I am like a shadow. "No authority is left to me except the name (of Gaon)." I am weak, and my handwriting is that of a child beginning to learn how to write. I am also concerned about the safety of my son, who went to Aleppo to fetch certain things he left there.' In conclusion, the Gaon thanks some donor for his grant, and also sends greetings to Sa'adya (Sahlān's uncle). Already then the Gaon felt very old, but we know that he lived at least another nineteen years (till 1051); he must have therefore reached a great age.

Another letter from the Gaon to Ephraim b. Shemarya deals with the same topic, but contains in addition several other details of interest (A. B. 51). It seems to have been written about four months after Sa'adyana XLII. The latter dates from the end of Sivan, when Solomon's son was away on a mission for the school. Our present epistle is written after Tabernacles (of probably this summer), when the Gaon's son was already back at Jerusalem. Solomon writes, 'Your letter reached me after the Festivals (החגו, i. e. Tabernacles), enclosing 10 d. sent by the elders (of Fusṭāṭ). The bearer was Faḍl b. Daniel. The Parness (of the Jerusalem community) received the money because I have nothing to do with the donation for the poor. I wrote him a receipt, but he (Faḍl b. Daniel) was not satisfied till I wrote another in the name of the (Jerusalem) elders, which they signed. (The donations evidently came from the rent of a house which did not yield enough for the needs of the poor, especially on the ensuing Passover. The donor was Tobias שר העדה, a worthy man. His representative in Bagdād was Raja b. 'Āli, who embezzled his money and left for Khurasān.) A letter also reached my son about the attitude taken up by the man who has been nominated (as Ḥaber) by the Ab. He ought to be modest and not stir up strife, of which we had enough in the past. I had already in mind to excommunicate him. But he has in him good qualities, and comes from a respected family. Now do not be deterred by this man's agitation. You are the "head" (of the Palestinian community). He is still an outsider. I do not want that there be two "heads" (ראשים) in the congregation.' (See also my remarks in *J. Q. R.*, N. S., IX, 412.)

'As regards my letter to Menasse Hakkohen, if he requests you to help him to recover a house that has been robbed from him, support him as much as you can.' The 'Third' was much interested in the matter, and asked the Gaon to write a postscript (verso) to Ephraim setting forth its details. The house went by the name of the late Gaon. But originally it belonged to thi

Ienasse and his sister, the Gaon's wife. After her death, her usband became her heir. Now "when Menasse was caught (for npositions) in the days of בן חבורה" (probably referring to the ase of the prisoners for whose sake Solomon's son travelled ɔ Egypt, above, p. 120), and could not pay his share, Khalaf . 'Alvan brought about his release. According to Khalaf's tatement, he paid for Menasse 100 d., and had his house ıortgaged through a non-Jewish court. After Khalaf's death, is wife inscribed this house as a dowry for her daughter. 'hereupon the "Third" and the "sons of his mother's sister" . e. his cousins) went to Ramlāh (the seat of the governor of 'ilastin) and protested against the transaction, since the house ent by the name of the Gaon and not by that of Menasse. ;phraim Hakkohen, Menasse's brother, ought to do something ı this matter, and not leave it to others to take the trouble. This Ephraim was Dayyan in Cairo-Fusṭāṭ, cp. above, p. 116.) 'he "Third" also sent a letter to Damascus through his cousin oseph, where the ban was announced (apparently against the ımily of Khalaf b. 'Alvan, who must have had some connexions ı the Syrian capital) on every Monday and Thursday (as was he custom then, see Additional Note to A. B. 51).'

It appears from this epistle that the late Gaon was Solomon Iakkohen, the father of Elijah and Joseph. (The latter went to)amascus.) Menasse Hakkohen was his brother-in-law, while he 'Third' was his nephew. When he died his sons were very 'oung. It is only in 1037 that Elijah was 'Sixth', while eight 'ears later he was 'Fourth' (as shown in A. A. 17). The 'Third' ıentioned here probably died as such. When Elijah, in a letter o Ephraim b. Shemarya, mentions רבינו השלישי ז״ל (above, p. 100), .e very likely refers to his cousin. In a note to A. B. 51 an extract ; given from Solomon b. Yehuda's letter to Ephraim b. Shemarya bout excommunication in a lawsuit. It was certainly written efore 1035, since Ephraim's son-in-law is greeted therein (see above, ›. 105). The reference to the terrifying rumours (ll. 5–7) probably lludes to the events in consequence of the revolution of 1024–9.

A. B. 52 and 53 probably bear on the same topic in connexion vith the discord between the two Ḥaberim in Fusṭāṭ. Unfortunately, in both fragments, the lines are only preserved in halves. \. B. 52 is clearly in the Gaon's handwriting. It seems to have been written to the Ab, who resided in Egypt. They were apparently not on good terms. Owing to the state of the manuscript, the following *résumé* must be regarded as only tentative. After referring to some people who were in trouble, and to a debt of 200 d., Solomon writes (l. 13 ff.): 'My letter is in reply to your second long epistle. Were we even alike in years, you ought to have shown therein more respect to me, as the Gaon of the Palestinian academy. The man whom you nominated as Ḥaber at once began to stir up strife. Because your son (in Egypt) was very friendly with this man, he impressed you in his favour. From your letters to your son (who seems to have been at the time of our epistle studying in Jerusalem) I can gather that you regard him as a great scholar. Listen to me on account of my age, if not because of my knowledge. If you give ear to the rebel (המורד), the end will be serious. Far be it from me to cause quarrel. I also wrote to the dignitary (השר) Ephraim Hakkohen, may God reinstate him in his dignity—(we have seen that he was Dayyan; it seems that he had then been temporarily deposed)—that I could not do anything before I met the Ab and the Third.' It appears that this Ḥaber was agitating in Fusṭāṭ both against Ephraim b. Shemarya and against his chief supporter Solomon b. Yehuda. A movement was gathering force to have a rival Gaon in the Holy City, as we shall see farther on.

In A. B. 53, a signed epistle from the Gaon to Ephraim, we hear more of rebels and dissenters. Ephraim is praised because he did not join them. Allusion is made to the משוש הישיבה (see above, p. 129). A certain man dealt treacherously with the congregation, but the Ḥaber risked his life and opposed him. The object of the epistle is to introduce a person whose grandfather the Gaon knew well. Ephraim should be kind to this man. His family was highly respected in Fez, and seems to have been the Gaon's benefactor. It appears that Solomon visited Fez some time previously. If our suggestion that 'al-Fasi' (*infra*, p. 150) refers to him be correct, then the Gaon hailed from distant Magreb. That he was no native of Palestine we have read above (p. 103). The countryman of the Gaon is mentioned here as intending to leave for the west. Possibly he was about to return to his native land. In conclusion of his letter Solomon states that Solomon b. Meir (a descendant of the Gaon Ben-Meir [1]) joined the 'conspirators' (against the Gaon and Ephraim).

More about this 'conspiracy' in the next but one paragraph. But as regards Ephraim's opponent, the nominee of the Ab, it appears that he was worsted. In A. B. 54 the Gaon thanks Isaac Hakkohen, the physician and 'elder of the congregations' (the father of Abraham שר העדה, above, p. 84 ff., who is also greeted in the letter), for his intervention on behalf of an innocent person to deliver him from a usurper appointed by 'one person' only (i. e. the Ab) without permission of his colleague (i. e. the Gaon). He ought to have shown humility and respect towards those that were greater than him in scholarship, and had a prior claim by their long service. There is little doubt that we deal here with this Ḥaber, the opponent of Ephraim. His attempt to gain the superiority over the latter was frustrated by the influence of Isaac Hakkohen, his son Abraham, and probably other men of standing in Fusṭāṭ. Abraham שר העדה was away at the time of this letter on his duty of escorting (see above, p. 85).

At last the two parties came to some sort of an agreement. We have found (above, p. 124) a reference to this in the letter of Ab, 1035, from Ḳairowān to Ephraim. A small fragment (A. B. 55) probably deals with the same subject. It is clearly in the Gaon's handwriting. He thanks therein God for the safety vouchsafed to him and his companions, though they are still excited and in fear. May God have mercy upon those that are afflicted and flee from their homes. May He repent of the evil. This is probably a reference to the sufferers from the earthquake in Ramlāh and Jerusalem in December, 1033, as will be seen in the next chapter. The Gaon continues to describe how greatly he was grieved about the 'dissension that was amongst you' (i.e. in Fusṭāṭ). God be praised that it has ceased. Solomon enlarges upon the importance and the merits of communal peace and unity. Probably this epistle dates from the beginning of 1034. It is indeed a great relief to find no more documents dealing with discord in the Fusṭāṭ Palestinian community during the remainder of the Gaon's life, viz. for the

[1] See A. A. 15.

following seventeen years (till 1051). Ephraim's position seems to have become at last firmly established. Elijah Hakkohen in his letter to him (above, p. 100) alludes to Ephraim having overcome two formidable opponents (המכה את שני אריאל). Their names cannot be ascertained with certainty. One of them was probably Samuel b. Abṭalion. Let us hope that further Genizah finds will solve the problem. Ephraim attained the age of eighty. In 1057 we find already his successor 'Āli b. Amram as the Ḥaber of the Palestinian Fusṭāṭ.

(7) Affairs in Jerusalem will now be discussed, chiefly those of the school, while more will be said about the internal conditions in the Holy Land in the next chapter. The Ḳaraites were numerous as well as influential in Egypt and in Palestine. In the time of Ben-Meir and his ancestors they had the upper hand in Jerusalem (above, pp. 61 ff.). Of a conflict between the two sections in the time of Solomon b. Yehuda we learn from a number of fragments. It seems that the Rabbinites had the supervision of the markets (bazaars) and the sale of 'ritual' meat (בשר כשר). The Ḳaraites did not accept the Rabbinic way of 'examination' (בדיקה), while they prohibited the slaughter of pregnant animals. They also differed from the Rabbinites in the fixing of the calendar and, hence, in the days on which the festivals fell. But the latter, having the control of the markets, could coerce the Ḳaraites to keep their shops closed on the Rabbinic Holy Days.[1] In the year 1024 an edict of religious tolerance and freedom of action was issued by the Caliph. This we learn from a highly interesting Genizah fragment (published by Gottheil, *Harkawy Festschrift*, 121–5). His translation is subjoined here. The beginning of the edict is missing.

'. . . . from following your custom and continuing in the traditions which you have learned in your religions, without any

[1] The Rabbinites clearly had then the upper hand over the Ḳaraites, whereas in Ben-Meir's time the reverse was the case. This radical change was probably the sequel of Palṭiel's great political influence in the Fāṭimid court at Cairo. It may also be that Menasse b. Abraham ibn Ḳzāz, when Wezīr in Damascus (see above, pp. 19 ff.), helped the Rabbinites to become supreme in the Holy Land. The Gaon and his school even received grants from the government till al-Ḥakim began his persecutions (see p. 71 f.). Whether these grants were resumed after 1021 is obscure. But the dominant position of Rabbinism in Palestine continued till the time of the edict discussed here.

hindrance being raised by the one party against the other or any harsh treatment being meted out by either of the two sections against the other; permitting the followers [of each party] to live up to their beliefs; enabling you and them [to prevent] any molestation [one from the other] in regard to that which is necessary *in the ordinary course of buying and selling as they either follow or neglect upon their festivals* [*such business*] according to their choice and free will, warning all of you against interfering or causing trouble, one to the other, or daring to trespass upon this decision in adding to it[s provisions] or in failing [to carry them out].

'Security is accorded both to you and to them so that you restrain any evildoer among you from disputing that which ought ordinarily to be avoided, and that you prevent ostentation and discussion which causes provocation of malice in regard to those [differences] between you. Notice is given to all that whosoever in his folly and presumption transgress this limitation so as to encourage [any one] to do the like of that which is not allowed him, such a one will be punished most severely and chastised in an exemplary manner, [thus] restraining him and deterring all those who in their folly go in his footsteps. At the same time [all] are prohibited from interfering *with the sect of the Ḳaraites* in their synagogue, which belongs to them to the exclusion of all others. Let this be known as the mandate and as the official act of the Commander of the Faithful. Let action be taken in consonance with it and let every one be brought to obey and to act accordingly. Let [then] the *Amīr al-Juyūsh*—may God help him, give him victory and good assistance—and all the heads of the various provinces take good care of the two divisions of the Jews, whom the covenant made with their sect protects, the righteous decision guards, the provinces of the kingdom shelter, keeping them away from evil and preserving them in the beaten track and causing them to do according to the decisions [contained] in the letters patent.

'Let [the governors] give order that they are protected and cared for; that they refrain from hurting and oppressing them. Let [this decree] be honoured by those to whom it is written, if so it please God.

'Written upon Wednesday the 11th day of Jamāda, the first, in the year Four Hundred and Fifteen. Copied in the Protocol Ministry . . . .'

The Commander-in-Chief (Amīr al-Juyūsh, in Hebrew נגיד המחנות) was at that time Anūshtegin ad-Dizbiri, whom aẓ-Ẓahir sent against the insurgents in Palestine and in Syria.[1] Ad-Dizbiri was charged by the Caliph to carry out the provisions of the above edict, Syria and Palestine. But from 1024–9 there were great upheavals in these countries during the formidable revolution of Arab chieftains (see next chapter). It is hardly likely that ad-Dizbiri had the leisure to enforce this edict. But after 1029, when order was restored, it began to take effect, as we learn from the fragments we discuss here. Members of the Jerusalem school seem to have acted against the decree in Ramlāh, and were imprisoned and taken to Damascus, where probably ad-Dizbiri resided then. This arrest caused much friction between the two sects.

A. B. 56 is a letter from Solomon b. Yehuda to Sahlān Resh Kallah b. Abraham (the latter no longer alive). He writes: 'Letters have been sent in reply to your epistles. We thank you and your synagogue for your support. Now I want you to intervene with the government and the Wezir (רוזן ?) on behalf of the prisoners. Messengers have been sent (to Damascus) and we hoped that they would obtain the release of these prisoners. But letters reached us from Damascus to the effect that they were still in prison, only their chains were removed. Yet the officials still punish them, and they are ill.' They were Ḥaberim of the Jerusalem academy. They would be released on the condition that they took an oath by God and the Caliph not to go any more by the name of Ḥaber nor to hold any communal office in Palestine. Evidently this would be their fine for having infringed the provisions of the edict. This condition was sent to them in the name of 'Adi b. Menasse, known as b. al-Ḳzāz (see above, p. 20). There is no need to assume that the son of the famous Wezīr was a Ḳaraite. Only, as an important Katib (secretary) in government employ, he was instructed by the governor to deal with this case.

[1] See Ibn Khallikan, *Biographical Dictionary*, tr. de Slane, I, 631. Cp. also Wüstenfeld, *l. c.*, II, 125, 'In Damascus, Ramlāh, and 'Ascalon, there were in 414 (1023) Egyptian troops that stood under the commander-in-chief of the Governor of Caesarea, Anūshtakīn ad-Dizbiri, who received the title of Mustaiḥab ad-Daula, the chosen one of the realm.'

The Gaon continues: 'The prisoners replied that they would like to hear the conditions, to be imposed upon them, orally from 'Adi. Letters were sent on behalf of these prisoners from Netaneel Hakkohen Abū'l Fakar (the respected elder of Alexandria, above, pp. 88 ff.) and from Meborak השר (evidently a dignitary in Fusṭāṭ) b. 'Āli Abū'l Faḍl.' The Gaon thought that they would have effect. They probably were addressed to 'Adi, who was in charge of this case. But now the people in Damascus demand Solomon to come personally. Being an old man, he cannot do it in the winter. He mentions the severe conditions imposed upon the Rabbinites, viz. that the ban be not used in the community (in Palestine?), that the Ḳaraites have a separate shop in the Jewish market to sell therein meat without Rabbinic 'examination' (בדיקה) and supervision, that they take no part in the slaughter of a pregnant sheep or cow, and that they open their shops on the Rabbinite Festivals. The prisoners should be forbidden to visit Jerusalem and Ramlāh. For all these stipulations the Gaon and the elders should be made responsible. He refuses to do this, and urges upon Sahlān to do his utmost and obtain influential Rabbinite support in Fusṭāṭ. Let the governors in Ramlāh and Damascus be instructed not to compel the Gaon and his colleagues to accept such conditions. Greetings are sent to Sahlān's uncle (i.e. Sa'adya). The Gaon is very depressed. He wrote concerning this affair to Jesse the Ḥaber, to Samuel (probably b. Abṭalion), to Ephraim Hakkohen, to Yefet (ראש הקהל) (of the Babylonians in Fusṭāṭ, see above, p. 99), to Jacob, and finally Netaneel (probably Hakkohen of Alexandria, or perhaps Hallevi b. Ḥalfon, above, p. 105). They should all use their influence.[1]

The imprisoned Ḥaberim must have remained in confinement for some time. Their cause was taken up by the whole Rabbinite community in Egypt and in Palestine. The above letter was written in winter. On the following Hoshana Rabba the dispute between the two sects was still very acute. (But perhaps the following fragment dates from Tabernacles before this winter.) Bodl. 2807[18] (printed in *R.É.J.*, XLVIII, 172–3) should be analysed here in the light of the new material. Solomon b. Yehuda writes to Ephraim b. Shemarya: 'My previous

[1] See also my remarks in *J.Q.R.*, N.S., IX, 417–20.

letter was to tell you that the misunderstanding between us had passed. Your statements I have found true. Be at your ease and endeavour to live in harmony with your colleagues. The common people (עמי הארץ) only rejoice at strife between the scholars.' Here the Gaon alludes to the communal dissensions in Fusṭāṭ, as described above under (6). We have seen that peace was restored in 1035. But evidently this letter is of an earlier date. The Gaon continues: 'You will hear all the details of what happened on the Festivals (very likely from pilgrims from Fusṭāṭ), I write to you in a general way. Most of the people arrived with the spirit of contention, and demanded clean separation from the other sect (i.e. the Ḳaraites).' This shows that in those times the cleavage was not so great. Indeed from some Ketubot (see *infra*, p. 176 f.) we see that intermarriage between the sects was not rare (cp. also above, p. 125). Even a Nasi and head of an academy, David b. Daniel of Megillat Ebyatar fame, did not shrink from marrying a Ḳaraite lady (*J. Q. R.*, XIII, 220–1). We shall also see that the Ḳaraites in Jerusalem had some share in the appointment of the local Geonim of the Rabbinites (*infra*, p. 143). Only in the time of Maimonides and his son Abraham did the separation between the two sects in Egypt become more pronounced.

To return to our letter. Solomon mentions that the pilgrims were incensed against anybody that did not favour the complete severance from the Ḳaraites. They accused such a person of having secret leanings towards these sectarians. And it seems that the Gaon did not join the extremists. The governor of Ramlāh received orders from the Caliph and the Amīr-al-Juyūsh (נגיד המחנות) that no announcement of the ban be allowed on Hoshana Rabba on Mount Olivet. (We have seen above (p. 137) that one of the conditions of the Ḳaraites in Damascus was that the Ḥerem be not used in the community. The interpretation given to the edict of tolerance was evidently that no coercion be brought to bear on dissenters by means of excommunication. We therefore find that when Solomon b. Yehuda and his school banned all those who in Fusṭāṭ wrote unauthorized lampoons in the name of other people, they had to do it in a cave in secrecy (above, p. 127). To do it openly they would have been liable to prosecution.) The Ramlāh governor thereupon sent instructions to the prefect to be present on that day on Mount Olivet in order to see that the ban be not announced. (Probably the Ḳaraites in Egypt instigated these orders to be issued by the central government.) Solomon therefore decided to abandon the procession to the Mount because he did not want to be hampered in his actions. Not to announce the Ḥerem against those that deserved it would mean to change an old custom. The people were much upset and accused the Gaon of lack of courage. Against the demand of proclaiming utter separation from the Ḳaraites, the Gaon argued that there was no need to do it because before the 'ordained ones' (i.e. Ḥaberim) left (for Damascus) as prisoners (בטרם לכת הסמוכים אסורים), the people of חולה (probably Ramlāh)[1] carried out this separation since the Ḳaraites eat meat without Rabbinic examination (בדיקה). Solomon also refused to send a circular letter to the communities to this effect.

As far as can be gathered from the fragments, we see that the Ḳaraites in Palestine, in Ramlāh and Jerusalem, had then the upper hand. The edict of 1024 gave them a weapon to strike at their opponents. A letter from Solomon b. Yehuda to Egypt, which no doubt dates from this time, reveals the fears of the Rabbinites in the Holy City (A. B. 57). The letter, defective in the beginning, evidently was sent to Egypt (Fusṭāṭ). The Gaon writes: 'My son is afraid that there is no more hope. Wherever we turn we find closed doors. Has indeed the time come to be driven out from the Holy City? How many letters did I write for them (i.e. the imprisoned Ḥaberim) both in my name and on behalf of the academy. Why had they no effect?' He now urges upon his correspondent to take his former epistles, read them in public and arouse the people to hasten for help. Let them induce the elders, called al-Dastura ('the noblemen', see above, p. 121), to intervene. 'You ought to know that if *the Rabbanite sect* has no help from you, they can have no existence in Jerusalem.' Eventually the Gaon's appeals had effect. A representative of the Nagid and other influential merchants undertook the long journey to Damascus, and by their intervention the prisoners were released.

This we learn from a highly interesting letter (A. B. 58),

[1] Raml in Arabic = חול 'sand', see Pozn., *R. É. J.*, *l. c.*, 173, note 1.

defective at the beginning, from Solomon b. Yehuda to Egypt. He recapitulates the arguments of the Ḳaraites which were probably used during the dispute. They accused the Rabbinites of allowing impermissible things and changing most of the commandments; most of them desecrated the Sabbath and the Festivals, invoked the Muslim courts in lawsuits, practised witchcraft in which the Ḳaraites included the Rabbinic prohibition of eating meat with milk. (Similar charges against the Rabbinites in Palestine are found in Sahl b. Maṣliaḥ's polemical letter in Pinsker, *Likḳuṭe*, Appendix 32.) The Gaon, on the other hand, argued that there were worse offences committed in the community than the refraining from eating meat with milk. It is evident that he wielded no proper weapon for defending Rabbinism against the attacks of the Ḳaraites. A Sa'adya would have acted differently. Solomon continues that the dissension was great and the government had to intervene. Lives would have been lost had not the faithful messenger of the 'Nagid of the Diaspora' arrived, who probably on his way to Damascus passed Ramlāh and Jerusalem and influenced the governor and the prefect, respectively, in favour of the Rabbinites. The Gaon thanks this representative of the Nagid as well as the important merchants who assisted him. May they return safely home. All this trouble was caused by 'our brethren who compose false edicts'. 'The whole community here (in Jerusalem) is desirous of peace. May God grant it to them.' In conclusion Solomon mentions the arrival of a donation of 25 d. He assures his correspondent that now it will certainly be spent for no other purpose than for the payment of a communal debt.

The Nagid was probably Yehoseph b. Samuel, whom we find holding the dignity during the Gaonate of Daniel b. 'Azarya (1051–62). His father Samuel was also Nagid and very likely is identical with Samuel b. Palṭiel mentioned in the *Aḥima'aṣ Chronicle* (see above, p. 49, and *infra*, p. 184). Abū Sa'ad and Abū Naṣr, the two influential brothers, are so far not introduced in this affair. But their father and uncles seem to have been appealed to for aiding the Rabbinites (above, p. 139). The names of the influential Ḳaraites in Cairo-Fusṭāṭ are not given (see, however, *infra*, p. 176 f.). That they were numerous can be seen from the few lines extracted from a long letter, given below, which bears on our subject.[1] Finally, A. B. 59 contains a letter from an anonymous Ḳaraite to his community, asking for the announcement of the ban against certain people who suspect him of stealing. The date of the epistle cannot be ascertained. I have appended it here as an interesting detail of the communal organization of the sect with whom the preceding fragments dealt.

(8) The last section of this chapter deals with the internal affairs of the Palestine academy. A group of fragments, we are able to discuss here, give a sad picture of bickerings and intrigues in the academy for personal advancement and benefit. But, as stated before, it is not the object of history to hide facts which may be disagreeable. The dark side of things has to be depicted too. At the same time these fragments give us many details of interest as regards the organization of the school. Let us first set forth our construction of the data, which will be verified as the material is discussed in detail in the following pages. A member of the school, Nathan b. Abraham, settled in Egypt. He was probably a disciple of Samuel the 'Third'

[1] T.-S. 13 J 19[16], r. and v., beginning and end missing. The handwriting is that of Solomon b. Yehuda. A part of it is also found in T.-S. 13 J 16[15], in different handwriting. (*sc.* the Ḳaraites) ואוגיב אלי דאלך פלם יקבל[ו בל] קאלו (r., l. 2)
קד חצל לנא אלוקת אך זה היום | שקוינוהו מצאנו ראינו . . . כהנים ותלמידי חכ׳
מצׄרובין | מחמולין ויש (= וישראל) בוכים צועקים והם שמחים . . . ואדא גרא בינהם
ובין אלרבנין כלאם | אתפקו כולהם כלאם ואחדה להכרית את שמם מן הארץ
ויקולו נפלה לא תוסיף קום גביו אלקום קול אלחכים והאים יבקש את נרדף . . .
ואני כל מא אפכר פי מא גרא אעתגב כיף כאן הדא אל | מועגז אקול מאת יי׳
היתה זאת וג׳ ואשכר אללה ברוך יי׳ אינו (= אלהינו) אשר נתן כזאת | בלב
אדוננו המלך לעולם יחיה ובלב אדוננו המשנה יצליחהו האים (= האלהים) לדבר
בשלומנו ולדרוש | טובתינו יתרומם שמו לעדי עד מי שמע כזאת מי ראה כאלה
וג׳ אמדו לאים מה | נורא מעשיך הם בטחו בשריהם ובסופריהם ועשיריהם והקרובים
אל המלכות ואנחנו בשם יי׳ אינו נזכיר מה נשיב ליי׳ כל תגמולוהי עלינו יא שיכי
פי קבלי אש יוקדת מן קום תגׄאיאו פי הלאכנא יגעלו אנפסהם אלשושנים וגירהם
אלקוצים יגעלו משכילים והם גיר מותפקין אי מנהם אלמשכיל ? . . . The caustic reference to the 'Lilies' alludes to the title given to the early Ḳaraite settlers in Jerusalem (see above, p. 61).

b. Hoshana, who introduced him to Shemarya b. Elḥanan (already before 1012, above, p. 27 f.). This Nathan was evidently a scholar of high standing. His uncle was the Ab who also resided in Egypt. When the Ab died in that country, the ordinary course would have been for the 'Third' (the cousin of Elijah and Joseph the priests) to advance to the dignity of 'Father'. But his scholarship was not such as to command general recognition. A party of elders came from Fusṭāṭ to Jerusalem together with this nephew of the late Ab, Nathan b. Abraham, and succeeded in carrying through his appointment as Ab. Nathan evidently had many followers in the principal community of Egypt, whose generosity was of great importance for the Palestine school, and also in Jerusalem. Soon afterwards the new Ab began to undermine the Gaon's authority, and finally declared himself as 'head of the school'. We find him bearing this title in 1039. After several years of discord between the parties of the two rival Geonim, some settlement was agreed upon between them in 1042. Nathan must have died soon afterwards as nothing more is heard of him. Solomon survived him till 1051. In the same year we hear already of the new Gaon, Daniel b. ʿAzarya the Nasi.

A. B. 60 is from Solomon b. Yehuda to an Alluf (no doubt Sahlān b. Abraham). The Gaon writes: 'I shall inform you in short how the peace came about. When the people here heard that this man (Nathan b. Abraham) was to come, they decided that he be called neither Rosh nor Gaon in the school. Soon afterwards the news of the death of the Ab reached us and a memorial service was held for him. I maintained that the "Third" be his successor. But when Nathan arrived at the Holy City he brought with him the dignitary Meborak b. ʿĀli b. ʿEzra (probably identical with Meborak b. ʿĀli Abū'l Faḍl, above, p. 137). Some people had already advised the "Third" not to accept the new office because he was inexperienced to pray for the people and to preach. Also the elders from Egypt would be against his advancement.' This actually happened. Meborak b. ʿAli asked the 'Third' publicly to consent to remain in his position and give preference to the new-comer; thereby the dissensions would come to an end. The 'Third' assented, but during the whole proceedings the Gaon kept silent. He remarks how human settlements are of no avail. Because the late Ab came to an agreement with this 'Third' that, after the demise of the Gaon (Solomon b. Yehuda), the latter would be the former's second (i.e. Ab). But now it turned out that this Ab was gathered to his fathers and the new-comer became his substitute, while the 'Third' had no advancement at all. The Gaon is apparently pleased with the new Ab. 'His heart is better than it has been described to me.' In conclusion Solomon writes about a donation of 10 d. that reached him and for which he bought corn for his household. This 'Third' is probably the cousin of Elijah Hakkohen, mentioned in the former letters. We have seen that he died as such (above, p. 131).

A short time after the new Ab's arrival Solomon had reason to change his opinion about him. In a letter to Ephraim b. Shemarya (A. B. 61) he uses very strong invectives against him. Ephraim is styled 'our beloved and Ḥaber, who keeps our appointment and obeys our authority. Letters preceded informing you of the work of ראש הפעור, may God rebuke him,' &c. He is ungrateful and acts as is his evil report. He rides about the whole day on his ass, visiting people to curry their favour. He follows the ways of his (maternal) uncle the (late) Ab, and seeks the support of the Ḳaraites, who only rejoice when the leaders of the Rabbinites are without religion. 'And I have fallen between the two, the one too righteous (i. e. the "Third" who gave up his legitimate claim to the dignity of Ab), the other too wicked (i. e. the new Ab), and I am between.' This new-comer calls together low people, makes them elders, feasts them, and imposes upon them the oath 'to love his friends and hate his enemies', i. e. become his partisans. Solomon declares himself unable to adopt such methods. Many of 'the other sect' (i. e. Ḳaraites) help him secretly though outwardly they pretend to side with the Gaon. 'Since his uncle died there was some peace. But since his arrival the quarrel broke out again.' The Gaon requests Ephraim to give the original of the letter he sent to the Fusṭāṭ community to the משוש (= משוש הישיבה, probably Abraham Hakkohen, *infra*, p. 183) to send it on to the 'West' (Magreb, very likely to Ḳairowān). Probably therein the Gaon set forth the doings of his rival. That the latter on his part sent lampoons to the contrary is only natural. Solomon accuses him of spreading broadcast false letters and pamphlets (l. 16). In this way this unpleasant correspondence grew. In conclusion of this epistle the Gaon requests Ephraim to send him a copy of his own letter written 'at the time of the donation', as he possesses none for reference. 'I have written a long letter to the whole community. You will read it.' Evidently this epistle was to be forwarded by the משוש to the West.

In another letter to Ephraim (A. B. 62) Solomon again refers to 'him that lies in wait like a beast of prey, and opposes in rebellion' (l. 7). But the Ḥaber staunchly adhered to the Gaon who thus styles him 'he that keeps the appointment of truth and righteousness, scatters the conspirators and removes the traitors' (ll. 1–2). It seems that Ḥesed (= Abū Naṣr) with other elders were on the Gaon's side (ll. 15–19). But he is not to adopt the method of the 'rebel' to appeal to his influential friends for help. He relies on God's protection. 'If it pleases Him to preserve my name (as Gaon), it is well. But if He says thus, I do not desire thee, I am ready. Let Him do to me accordingly' (ll. 23–5). He אבי הששונות (probably = משוש הישיבה) reported what happened to the Ḳairowān community. Their enemies had almost the better over them, had not some help come through the Nagid R. Jacob (b. 'Amram, see *J. Q. R.*, N.S., IX, 162–3, and above, p. 124). In conclusion the Gaon mentions the arrival of a certain Isaac and also of a letter from Shemarya.

A. B. 63 deals with the same topic. Both epistles (I and II) are in Solomon's handwriting. Their recipient was most likely Sahlān b. Abraham because, in the first instance, greetings are sent to Sa'adya (i.e. Sahlān's uncle), but chiefly since in II the Gaon writes, 'I have already explained to (you my) friend how the peace came about' (ll. 2–3). This evidently refers to A. B. 60. The Gaon writes in a bitter spirit. In I he confesses that his letters are a burden on his friends. For unlike business-letters, they mostly allude to his private needs; therefore he endeavours to be short and not always remind his friends of the relief he requires. He tries to be satisfied with as little as possible. In this epistle the Gaon requests Sahlān to inquire whether two books, containing the commentary of Ḳohelet by the late Nasi, have arrived in Egypt.

.et him consult about them Solomon the official (הפקיד, probably official of the merchants', above, p. 105). They have been acked in a bale addressed to him from a certain Israel. Who he author of this commentary was is quite unknown.[1] In II he Gaon writes, 'Your synagogue had some altercation with our late father (i.e. Abraham b. Sahlān), who thought that had written to the traitor (הבוגד). Far be it from me to have nything to do with him. I have written to you already about he peace. I had nothing to say in the matter. When the Ab ied, he (the new-comer) came and succeeded him. And when e came the sun arose and also set' (a caustic allusion to Kohel. 1^5).[2] The epistle is on the whole obscure. It is unnown what friction there was between the late Abraham b. ahlān and his congregation, and also who this בוגד המעולה was see, however, *infra*, p. 182, note 1). But the succession in the ignity of Ab, as we have seen above, is clearly referred to in he epistle.

A further document bearing on this topic we have in A. B. 64, which is clearly in the Gaon's handwriting. Unfortunately beinning and end are missing, while the lines are only partly reserved. He is greatly grieved with the discord in the school, nd his constant prayer is for peace. 'Let no people say that in is days much strife was rampant and through him a house of rayer was closed.' Evidently the government had to intervene s on former occasions. Solomon b. Yehuda seems to have had he better of his opponent. The governor of Ramlāh and the ommander of Jerusalem, acting on instructions from Egypt, ecided in his favour. This we learn from Solomon's letter to ome dignitary in Fusṭāṭ (A. B. 65). He writes (l. 7 ff.), 'It surasses my ability to tell you the wonder which God did to me. Blessed be He who wondrously was kind to his servant in fortified city so that my enemy and violent foes rejoiced not ver me." From my son's letter you will learn all the details.' he commander of Jerusalem and other local dignitaries helped

[1] It is hardly likely that Solomon meant a commentary by the Ḳaraite Nasi David Bo'aṣ (see Pozn., *Babyl. Geon.*, 129, 5, where the whole literature is given). ut it may be that the commentary *belonged* to the late Nasi (אשר לנשיא נג). We hall thus have a Nasi who died in Jerusalem in the Gaon's period.

[2] Cp. also Gen. R., ch. 58, and parallels.

the Gaon. They were instructed by the governor in Ramlāh who had orders from the Caliph and the Wezīr ('the mighty viceroy'). All these people are thanked as well as 'the pleasant dignitary, the lord of rest', also Mauhub b. Yefet and all those that helped to 'quench the flaring fire (of dissension)'. Probably השר הנאה שר מנוחה is some influential Jew who held some government office, but his identity is unknown to me.[1] The Gaon suffered enough from his opponents who were instigated by that 'wicked man who stirred up the strife . . . Every evil blemish belong to him.' It is clear that the Gaon refers here to his rival, the new Ab. In conclusion greetings are sent to Samuel Hakkohen (b. Abṭalion), the head of the congregation, and to Abraham (probably the Parnes, b. Mebasser, above, p. 96).

That the rival of Solomon b. Yehuda assumed the title of Gaon and was called Nathan b. Abraham is evident from the following fragments. We learn of the existence (in 1039) of Nathan ראש ישיבת גאון יעקב b. Abraham. A. B. 66 is a letter from him to Netaneel, styled 'help of the school' (עזר הישיבה), b. Revaḥ Hallevi of Fusṭāṭ. This Gaon sends greetings to him in his own name and in the name of the whole school (ומכל בני ישיבתנו). He is greatly desirous of seeing this Netaneel, with whom he must have been well acquainted. The letter is dated Tammuz 1350 Sel. A peculiar ending of his epistles is ישע יקרב. (Solomon b. Yehuda usually concluded with ישע רב, while Daniel b. 'Azarya chose the word ישועה, cp. *infra*, p. 179.) Also this Gaon placed his name in front of the letter, as was the practice of Joshia Gaon and Elḥanan b. Shemarya (see A. A. 10, 11, 18–21). (Solomon b. Yehuda generally concluded his epistles with his signature.) In the same handwriting is A.B. 67, also dated Tammuz, 1350 Sel. and again with the ending ישע יקרב. The same phrase of greeting (ll. 3–4) recurs (cp. A. B. 66, ll. 10–12). There is no doubt that our Nathan Gaon is its author. The beginning is missing, so that neither his own signature nor his correspondent's name is preserved. Nathan uses here Babylonian vowel-points as he does in another letter of his to be considered presently. The recipient of the epistle must have been at the head of a community (probably somewhere in Egypt, l. 7). Meborak the 'head of the

[1] Perhaps David Hallevi b. Isaac is meant here, since he is styled in A. B. 4 ll. 28-9, השר הנאה. Cp. further about this title, *infra*, p. 260 f.

communities' (not to be confused with the later Nagid Meborak) wrote to Nathan commending this correspondent for his attachment to the Gaon. He is therefore mentioned in the prayers recited on every Sabbath and festival in the presence of the Gaon. Greetings are sent to him and to his son. We see thus that the 'head of the congregations' (probably in Fusṭāṭ) was on the side of Nathan. Perhaps he is identical with the dignitary Meborak b. 'Āli (b. 'Ezra) whom we found above (p. 142) in Jerusalem proposing the appointment of the new-comer (i.e. this very Nathan) as Ab. Some years subsequently Meborak held this high communal office in Fusṭāṭ, and was one of the chief supporters of his protégé, who assumed the Gaonate.

That this Nathan lived previously in Egypt, where he passed through many vicissitudes, is evident from A. B. 68, in the same handwriting as the previous fragments and also with the conclusion ישע יקרב. It is written to 'our disciple' Netaneel b. Revaḥ of Fusṭāṭ. There is no doubt that he is identical with the recipient of A. B. 66, who was in 1039 'the help of the school'. (Cp. the similarity of the addresses.) Our fragment was written before Nathan was Gaon. He writes, 'My separation from you caused me great grief, especially when bearing in mind what had happened to me. Weary of the long business journeys I had to make, I thought to invest my money in other people's enterprises so that I might be able to study the Torah. But misfortune befell me, and I lost everything. It seems that Nathan had to leave Fusṭāṭ bereft of his wife and children. He was even afraid to summon his partners to court. He gives certain directions to his disciple with the request to inform him of what is going on in the community, and also about the dealings of his father-in-law with a certain Christian (probably in a business affair). Nathan reports that the people (of the place from where the letter came) received him cheerfully. He stayed with Ḥasan b. 'Alān. On the Sabbath he was asked to go to the synagogue (probably to preach), but could not owing to his indisposition. The letter seems to have been written on a Sunday. On the following day he was leaving for Damietta (חנס, see A. A. 19, note 1). It seems that while in Fusṭāṭ Nathan had a sort of a school. One of his favourite disciples was Netaneel b. Revaḥ. For a time a business man, our Nathan subsequently settled in Fusṭāṭ, while other people traded with his money. The result we have just learned. Where he went from Damietta is not mentioned. But after some time we find him in 1039 bearing the title ראש ישיבת גאון יעקב.

A. B. 69, of which the beginning is missing, is most likely also by him. The handwriting is almost the same as that of the preceding fragments. Who the recipient of this epistle was is unknown. He bore the title 'the friend of the school'. We learn about the struggle in consequence of Nathan becoming the rival of Solomon b. Yehuda. He writes (l. 2 ff.), 'I inform you that I have written to you several times. The delay of (your) replies perturbed me till I ascertained that "the congregation of the hypocrite" (עדת חנף, i. e. his opponent's followers) took them away (i.e. Nathan's letters). A ban was announced against those that were guilty of this offence. I know that you would have replied at once, had you received my letter. With the present epistle I enclose others to "our elder, the trusted person of the school and the head of the congregations, Mebasser b. Jesse". From your letter I can see how all of you respect Abraham the Ḥaber b. Shelah, who received his diploma in my academy. He should be encouraged and assisted because every congregation that has no proper spiritual leader has its affairs neglected. Now the Feast of Tabernacles is near and many people "will go up" (to Jerusalem on a pilgrimage). I want your community to come in full numbers since you are my friends.' (In this way Nathan's party will be the stronger. This clearly shows that he resided in the Holy City.)

He continues, 'The elders of Ramlāh had to-day an audience of the governor and said, "If you hear our complaint and administer justice, it will be well. But if not, we shall call together all the people and make a demonstration before the viceroy's (המשנה, probably the commander-in-chief) residence. Why should Revaḥ and his relatives force us to accept the authority of a Gaon (ראש) whom we do not want. We shall swear by God not to obey him. If you want to force us, you may (just as well) compel us to become Muslims." These elders did not leave the governor till they separated from the other party. They took possession of the *synagogue of the Palestinians* (כנסת אלשאמיין, presupposing the existence of a Babylonian house of prayer in Ramlāh!), where

I should be recognized as Gaon. They also installed a person authorized by me in the bazaar (to supervise the ritual slaughter of animals).' The 'Sixth' entered the synagogue where he probably preached. (In 1037 Elijah Hakkohen was the holder of this dignity. Whether he accepted the authority of the new Gaon is not known.) In conclusion the writer mentions that 'everybody forgets Revaḥ and his relatives'. Probably these people (unknown from elsewhere) were the leading partisans of the rival Gaon (i.e. Solomon b. Yehuda) in Ramlāh.

Of course, we have here a one-sided account only. According to this report the 'elders' of Ramlāh forced the governor to give way to their demand. But we can see that he was siding with the other party. Indeed, above (p. 145), we have read that Solomon b. Yehuda had the support of the authorities in Jerusalem and Ramlāh. Probably the 'synagogue of the Palestinians' in the latter place was closed for a time. Solomon b. Yehuda lamented that through him a house of prayer would be barred to its worshippers (above, p. 145). Very likely he referred to this Ramlāh synagogue. When its members recognized the new Gaon, the governor ordered that it should be closed. But subsequently he had to yield to public opinion and reopen it. The place of destination of the above epistle cannot be ascertained. The 'head of the congregations' there is no longer Meborak, but a certain Mebasser b. Jesse. The local community appointed not long before a new Ḥaber, Abraham b. Shelah, who was authorized by the new Gaon and his school. On the whole, it must be conceded that he uses no offensive language against his rival, a fact that is creditable to him. It may be that Solomon b. Yehuda had every reason for being greatly incensed against the new-comer, who was a usurper. But the invective he uses in A. B. 61, coming as it does from a Gaon, does not redound to his dignity.

A. B. 70 is from Nathan Gaon to his disciple Beraka b. Revaḥ, probably a brother of the above Netaneel, in reply to his epistle. Therein Beraka mentioned that he had forwarded to the Gaon letter after letter which the רצוי הישיבה ('the favourite of the school') sent to him. This dignitary is to write to the 'West' (Magreb) against the 'boy' Ben-Meir (probably the son of the Rosh Hasseder, see A. A. 15), who has been excommunicated in

Fusṭāṭ, ʿAkko, and Ramlāh, and this too by his own father. His offence was that he wrote an epistle in Fusṭāṭ, probably against the Gaon and his party. Then follows a description how on Taʿanit Esther the people of Damascus voted for Nathan as head of the school. In the evening there was a great assembly to whom the Megillah was recited from 30 copies. The hall was illuminated, non-Jews were present and also about 200 Ḳaraites. Nobody visited the Babylonian synagogue, while that of the Palestinians had about 20 worshippers, and with 'the man of Fez' were about ten people. Who the latter was is not clear. (Perhaps Solomon b. Yehuda is meant (see above, p. 132). In that case he was then personally in Damascus). There was great rejoicing on this Purim, the like of which people had not celebrated since the days of al-Ḳzāz (i.e. Menasse b. Ibrāhīm, the Jewish Governor of Damascus, towards the end of the tenth century, above, p. 20 f.). Through Nathan's action the strife between the parties, most probably Rabbinite and Ḳaraite, was ended. It must have continued for some time since the arrest of the Palestine Ḥaberim (as described under 7). Nathan seems to have adopted a tolerant attitude towards the sectaries. We have read before (p. 143) that the followers of ʿAnan in Jerusalem were siding with him soon after his arrival there. They must have had a grudge against the old Gaon Solomon b. Yehuda. In conclusion Nathan mentions that he is going to write to Peraḥ Rosh Happereḳ.

This dignitary is no doubt identical with Peraḥya b. Mumal Rosh Happereḳ in Fusṭāṭ, to whom the beginning of a letter from Nathan has been preserved (A. B. 71). He seems to have been a scholar, Ḥazzan and physician, and also a supporter of the Gaon. We find him heading the signatories to a statement of evidence which has been sent to the 'head of the school', very likely our Nathan b. Abraham. Herein he signs פרח בר מומל. Probably he was president of the Bet-Dīn established in the synagogue, where he officiated as reader. One of the signatories Joseph b. Israel of Tustar is probably identical with Joseph, the uncle of the famous Abū Saʿad b. Sahl al-Tustari (above, p. 81; A. B. 1; p. 122, note 1). In 1018 Peraḥ signs a document at Fusṭāṭ together with Jacob b. Joseph Ab-Bet-Dīn, whom we found afterwards in Aleppo (above, p. 37).

After several years of strife between the two rival Geonim peace was at last restored. A. B. 72 is the end of a letter from Nathan, dated Marḥeshvan, (1)354 Sel. = 1042 C. E. The handwriting as well as the ending ישע יקרב leave little doubt as to the authorship of the epistle. It is very likely sent to Fusṭāṭ. The correspondent is called גדולינו, probably he held the title גדול הישיבה. Greetings are sent in the name of Nathan's son Abraham, whose son, Nathan, in his turn was probably Ab of the school under Ebyatar, as will be shown farther on (p. 193 ff.). The Gaon writes in a cheerful tone. He and his family are very desirous of visiting their good friends (in Egypt). 'You have received already (the account) of how the peace came about and what we did for the sake of peace in Israel.' Here most probably allusion is made to his agreement with his rival Solomon b. Yehuda. Nothing more is heard of Nathan. Probably he was not long afterwards gathered to his fathers. In 1046 there was only one Gaon in Jerusalem, viz. Solomon b. Yehuda,[1] who, as we have seen (above, p. 130), died in 1051 at a very advanced age.

We have reviewed about a century and a half of the history of the Palestinian Gaonate. So far no literary work of standing, produced by the school in the Holy Land, has been preserved. The number of responsa is also remarkably small. Within that period Sura can lay claim to a Sa'adya and a Samuel b. Ḥofni, and Pumbedita (Bagdād) to a Sherira and a Hai, scholars of prominence who have enriched Jewish literature. In contrast to them the Palestinian Geonim really can advance poor claims only for eminence. And by the paucity of their responsa, as compared with those of the Babylonian Geonim, it is evident that the communities in the Diaspora did not fail to notice this difference in quality. The best criterion can be found in the fact that the highly intellectual Ḳairowān scholars sent very numerous questions to Sherira and Hai, but hardly any to Solomon b. Yehuda, though the latter, as we have seen, was in correspondence with this community and received from it

[1] Neub., *Med. Jew. Chron.*, I, 178: ורבי שלמה בר יהודה ראש ישיבת ירושלים ·עיר הקודש . . . והוא ראש ישיבה עתה בשנת ד׳ אלפים ותת״ז (r. ותת״ו) ליצירה . . . See Bacher, *J. Q. R.*, XV, 80, note 1, and Pozn., *Babyl. Geonim*, 1.

donations for his school. No doubt conditions in the Holy City were very unfavourable. But in addition to the distressing material circumstances, we have a sad picture of internal bickerings which were naturally adverse to serious study and literary work. Solomon b. Yehuda could write a good and fluent Hebrew, as his numerous letters clearly show. But posterity would have been more grateful had he employed his command of Hebrew to a better purpose.

CHAPTER IV

Conditions in Palestine and in Syria. Nesiim and Geonim.

THE former chapters contained a good deal of information concerning the communities in Palestine and in Syria. This material is supplemented here by a number of fragments that throw much light on political and internal conditions in several communities of these countries. The data cover a considerable number of years, from the period of Solomon b. Yehuda till about the first Crusade (1099 C.E.). They are of course incomplete, and do not as yet render possible a connected and detailed account of the vicissitudes of these Jewries. But where till now there was almost a blank page of Jewish history, every additional line, every new word, as it were, that help to cover up this blank are of importance.

The first part of this chapter deals with a number of Palestinian congregations, e.g. Ramlāh, Jerusalem, Tiberias, Ashḳelon, and others. Subsequently, data concerning the Nesiim are collected and discussed. Though most of them resided outside Palestine, the Patriarchate as an office had its origin in the Holy Land. After Solomon b. Yehuda's death in 1051 a member of the Davidic family, Daniel b. ʿAzarya, successfully usurped the Gaonate at Jerusalem. The vicissitudes of the Palestinian academy up to the first Crusade form the subject of the third part of this chapter, which is concluded by furnishing some information about conditions in Ṣyrian congregations in the eleventh century, while the later period is reserved for the next chapter.

I

(1) Appendix C (=A.C.) 1 contains a letter to Fusṭāṭ; beginning and end are missing. The epistle evidently emanates from a community within the Fāṭimid realm. The local Jews, in order

to obtain redress of their complaints against their governor, sent a messenger to Cairo-Fusṭāṭ for letters patent from the government. Very likely they lived in a Palestinian town, though the exact locality cannot be ascertained. The appearance of the MS. makes it probable that it belongs to the eleventh century. Here and there Babylonian vowel-points occur.

The local Jews had much to suffer from hostile Arabs. They write, 'Through our sins the Arabs have the upper hand'. Led by the Ḳāḍi Ibn Aktabū'l-Syād, the elders of the town stopped the water-supply for the Jews. 'How should Arabs drink the same water as Jews?' was their argument. Whenever the Jews protested to the governor, the townspeople would assemble and oppose them. Now there came to the town a new governor Ḥaidara, bearing the title 'Renown of the State', who wielded authority over the people. The Jews thereupon sent a messenger to Egypt (Cairo-Fusṭāṭ) to obtain letters patent for permission (1) to open up the water-supply as before, (2) to slaughter animals in the Shuḳ (bazaar) according to Jewish rite (which the local Arabs prevented them from doing), (3) that the taxes be collected from them within the corresponding Muslim year and not before the year began. When the messenger came back with the documents, they were presented to the governor. The Jews had also letters of recommendation from a high dignitary called 'The eminent of power' and other great officials. But the governor paid no heed to these documents till he and his entourage received heavy bribes. The money had to be collected even from the poor, orphans, and widows in the community. Then at last he opened the aqueduct to the Jews. When the Arabs protested, the governor silenced them by referring to the Caliph's decrees. In addition a certain elder testified that the Jews enjoyed formerly the water-supply. The Ḳāḍi was also instructed to issue orders permitting the Jews to practise their ritual slaughter of animals. If the community thought on that day that their troubles were over, the next day soon undeceived them. A number of soldiers arrived and the governor, in order to maintain them, sent to the Jews for the taxes due for next year five months in advance. A sum of 250 d. (about £375 in current value) was his claim, promising the Jews to be free from taxes for the whole of next year. Here the fragment breaks off.

Very likely the promise was soon broken, and the community is appealing to the Fusṭāṭ Jews to intervene on their behalf. We have here a characteristic example of the plight of the Jews in a distant place. The central government was favourable to the Jews, but its authority in Palestine and Syria was not sustaining enough. It depended a great deal on the local governors, who often acted arbitrarily. To put an end to the excesses of Jew-haters, bribery would have in many cases induced these governors to exert themselves to a degree which no patent letters from the central government could ever accomplish.

(2) Ramlāh was the capital of the province of Filastīn including Jerusalem. The town was no less important on account of its commerce. Muḳaddasi describes it as 'a fine city and well built; its water is good and plentiful, its fruits are abundant. Commerce is prosperous and means of livelihood easy.' It was founded by the Caliph Sulaiman. The inhabitants of Ludd (Lydda), the former capital, were removed thither and Lydda fell into decay (Le Strange, *l.c.* 303). Hence the town is designated in Genizah fragments רמלה הסמוכה ללוד (cp. A. A. 5 and 15).[1] In the time of Muḳaddasi it was 'the emporium for Egypt and an excellent commercial station for two seas' (Le Strange, *l.c.* 306). The importance of the Jewish community in Ramlāh could be gathered from the preceding pages. It was of much help to the Jerusalem Jews. We have found the Geonim of the Holy City residing there on several occasions.

Towards the end of the year 1033 Ramlāh and the whole of Palestine were visited by a great earthquake. The Persian traveller Naṣīr-i-Khusrau, who visited the city in 1047, writes, 'Over one of its porches (i. e. of the Ramlāh mosque) there is an inscription stating that on Muḥarram 15th of the year 425 (Dec. 10th, 1033 C. E.) there was an earthquake of great violence which threw down a large number of buildings, but that no single person sustained any injury' (Le Strange, *l.c.* 306–7). On the other hand, the Arab chroniclers state that one third of the town was destroyed and many persons were killed under the

[1] Cp. also the formula of a Ḳaraite Bill of Divorce (in Margoliouth, *Catalogue*, III, 520, col. 1, top): ואן כאן פי אלרמלה תקול בשנת כן וכן . . . במדינת רמלה אשר בשרון הסמוכה ללוד בארץ ישראל. In Bodl. 2806[34] read רמלה הסמוכה לל[וד].

ruins. Thus Ibn al-Athīr (see *l.c.* 101) reports that Syria was visited by destructive earthquakes in 407 A. H. (1016) and in 425 A. H. (1033). 'In 407 the great Dome fell upon the Rock (as-Sakhrah) in Jerusalem. In 425 earthquakes were frequent both in Egypt and Syria. The most destructive was that felt at ar-Ramlāh. The people abandoned their houses for many days; a third of the town was thrown down and many people were killed under the ruins.' As-Suyūṭi (see Sprenger, *Journal of the Asiatic Society of Bengal*, XII, 744) *s.a.* 425 A. H. reports that many earthquakes took place in Egypt and in Syria; one-third of Ramlāh was destroyed; the walls of Jerusalem fell down, and many villages were swallowed up by the ground.[1]

An account of an eye-witness in Ramlāh we have in A. C. 2. The beginning is missing, while the signature of the writer is not preserved. But the handwriting is that of Solomon b. Yehuda, and there is little doubt that the Gaon, who stayed there in 1033, described his experiences in this letter sent to one of his friends in Egypt (Fusṭāṭ), either to Ephraim b. Shemarya or Sahlān b. Abraham. The earthquake happened on Thursday, Ṭebet 12th, which fits in exactly with 4794 A. M., when Ṭebet 12th fell on a Thursday = Dec. 5th, 1033. The Muhammedan sources give the date Muḥarram 15th, 425 A. H.

The writer describes graphically how people left their houses because they saw them collapse; many died under the ruins. This agrees with Ibn al-Athir's account. We give here a translation of this interesting description. '. . . . they went out from their houses into the streets because they saw the walls bending and yet intact, and the beams become separated from the walls and then revert to their former position. The strong buildings collapsed and the new houses were pulled down. Many died under the ruins, for they could not escape. All went out from their dwellings, leaving everything behind. Wherever they turned they beheld God's powerful deeds. The walls wrangled together and collapsed. Those that remained are shaky and rent. Nobody resided in them, for their owners feared lest they tumble down over them yet before daybreak.

[1] As-Suyūṭi (*l. c.* 745) reports another earthquake in Palestine in A. H. 460 (1067 C. E.) when Ramlāh was entirely destroyed, and only two houses remained; 25,000 people were killed.

To describe a part of the happenings, the hand would weary. Also the mind is distraught from what the eye saw and the ear heard. The verse has been fulfilled, "Behold the Lord empties out the land and lays it waste, distorts its face and scatters its inhabitants". He that is prudent will understand. For all were alike, like people like priest, like servant like his master, when they left their places and sought refuge for their lives. Many resigned themselves to the (Divine) judgment, reciting several verses (from Jer. 10. 10, Ps. 104. 32, Job 9. 6, Amos 9. 5, Hos. 4. 3, Nah. 1. 6). This event took place on Thursday, Ṭebet 12th, suddenly before sunset, alike in Ramlāh, in the whole of Filastīn, from fortified city to open village, in all fortresses of Egypt (i.e. Fāṭimid ruler), from the sea to Fort Dan (Baniyās), in all cities of the south (Negeb) and the Mount to Jerusalem (and surrounding places), to Sheḥem and her villages, Tiberias and her villages, the Galilean mountains and the whole of Palestine.'

'Those that travelled on the high roads relate the mighty acts of the living God. They say, "We have seen the mountains shake, leap like stags, their stones broken into pieces, the hillocks swaying to and fro, and the trees bending down." In some places the waters in the cisterns reached the brim. The tongue is inadequate for the tale. Were it not for God's mercy that it happened before the day was gone, when people could see and warn each other, and had it been in the night when everybody was asleep, only a few would have been saved. But His mercies are many and His kindnesses numerous. Though He decreed, He will not utterly destroy. He, moreover, in His goodness brought out thick clouds and heavy rain-drops fell. Two great rainbows appeared. One of them split up into halves and fire was visible from the south-west. Thereupon the earthquake took place, the like of which was not since early times. On that night (the earth) shook again. All were in the streets, men, women, and children, imploring God, the Lord of the spirits, to quieten the earth and set it at rest and save both man and animal. On Friday, as well as on the following night, the quakes recurred. All were terrified and fear-stricken. Earth and its inhabitants were molten (for fear). They all wept and cried with a loud voice, O merciful One, have mercy and retract from the intended punishment. Do not enter upon judgment. In anger remember to be merciful and pay no heed to (our) former sins. All are trembling, sitting on the ground, startled every moment, shaking and swaying to and fro. Since eight days the mind is not satisfied and the soul is not at rest.'

'What could the writer (of this letter) do (but to) address the people to declare a fast, summon a solemn assembly, go out to the field, the cemetery, in fasting, weeping and lamentation, and recite, "Tear your hearts, and not your garments, and return to the Lord your God, &c. Come, let us return to God, &c. And let us ask for mercy. Who knows, (perhaps) He will retract and repent, &c. Perhaps He will go back from His fierce anger, so that we perish not." (God) magnified the miracle that all the days, which the people spent in the streets and in the open, no rain fell. Also the governor of the city, with the men in the Caliph's employ, pitched tents for themselves outside the town, and are still there. May the Lord, the God of the universe, look down mercifully upon his world, have pity on (His) creatures, save man and animal, and have compassion with babes and sucklings and those that know not (to distinguish) between right and left, so that we perish not. May He deliver you from this and the like, protect from all harsh decrees, hide you in His tabernacle on the day of evil, and shelter you in the protection of His wings. May He exalt you and may your good acts, kindnesses, and righteous deeds stand you in good stead. May He make you dwell securely and at ease from evil fear, and you be at peace, your houses and all that belong to you at peace. Receive ye peace from the Lord of Peace.'

(3) Conditions in Palestine and Syria were in a chronic state of unrest owing to the constant rebellions and insurrections. Both Ramlāh and Jerusalem suffered terribly in particular during the revolt of 1024–9 in the reign of aẓ-Ẓāhīr. Becker (*Beiträge zur Geschichte Ägyptens unter dem Islam*, I, 32 ff.) gives a connected account of the rule and policy of this Caliph about 415 A.H., according to Mussabiḥī. What interests us here is the description of conditions in Palestine (p. 44 ff.). Three chieftains combined against the Caliph. Ḥasan of the Banū Jarraḥ was to conquer the country from Ramlāh to the Egyptian frontier, Saliḥ of the Banū Kilāb was to hold the territory from Ḥaleb (Aleppo) to

'Anā, while the third conspirator, Sinān b. 'Alyān, was to take Damascus. In Rabi' II of 415 H. the officials of Ramlāh were still appointed from Cairo. During the following two months Ḥasan's rebellion must have broken out. In Rajab he plundered Ramlāh and extorted everywhere, including Jerusalem, great sums (*loc. cit.*, p. 45). Sinān could not take Damascus but Saliḳ succeeded in 417 H. to enter Ḥaleb. Ḥasan burned Ramlāh after he had plundered from it 400 loads of goods and men. Only then did the prefect of Caesarea, ad-Dizbiri, having received the title Amīr al-Umarā, prince of princes (see also above, p. 136), open a campaign against the conspirators, and after hostilities lasting several years succeeded in defeating Saliḥ and Ḥasan (cp. also L.-P. 159–60; Wüst. II, 125, 128–9).

How the Jews fared during the crisis we learn from A. C. 3 and 4, which will be discussed presently. Above (p. 110) we have found Solomon b. Yehuda referring in a letter to the campaign in Palestine against the rebellious Arabs (בני קדם). Also in a letter to Samuel b. Abṭalion the Gaon mentions 'troubles, wars, and upheavals, the like of which have not taken place before' in Ramlāh (above, p. 103). The extortions and excesses which the rebels committed were unbearable. We have read before (p. 131) how Menasse Hakkohen had to pay in Ramlāh 100 d. (= £150 in present currency) in order to obtain his release. The communities in Ramlāh and Jerusalem suffered terribly. This we learn from their pitiful appeals to their brethren in Egypt. A letter from Ramlāh to Fusṭāṭ (undoubtedly written during these upheavals) begins, 'Be gracious unto us, our brethren, the house of Israel, for (God's) punishment has afflicted us'.[1] A letter from the community of Tyre, dated 1028, to that of Aleppo also refers to the deplorable conditions in Jerusalem. The Holy City has been grievously stricken.[2]

[1] *J.Q.R.*, XIX, 733, No. XXXIX, הנונו חנונו אתם אחינו בית יש׳ כי יד נגעה בנו. The address reads:

לאחינו בית יש׳ אשר במצרים   אחיהם הכת העלובה ברמלה
ישמרם אינו ויצר׳ (r. וינצר׳) צורינו   ירא אי׳ אבותינו ויוכח׳

(cp. Gen. 31. 42). For another letter from the Rabbinites in Ramlāh to Fusṭāṭ, see *l. c.* 743, No. XCI.

[2] Wertheimer, גנזי ירושלם, III, 15^b, l. 16 ff. (cp. above, p. 37, note 1): שאו שלום גדול ממנו אנו אחיכם אוהביכם חביביכם הקהלות השרוים במדינת צור ·

A. C. 3 is a letter from the Jerusalem Rabbinites to Ephraim b. Shemarya. They tell a pitiful tale of their sad plight. The annual tax hitherto was heavy enough. It amounted to 100 d. (=£150), which for the greater part was obtained from the rent of shops in Ramlāh (probably being legacies for the benefit of the Jerusalem community). But now most of the Ramlāh people are gone, and only a few paupers remained. The congregation is now faced with heavy impositions. It seems that out of an amount of 10,000 d., the Jews of Jerusalem had to pay 6,000 d.; the Rabbinites to give 3,000 d., and their 'brethren' (אחינו, probably the Ḳaraites) the other half. We can imagine what it meant for the poverty-stricken Rabbinites to pay 3,000 d. (£4,500). After the greatest exertions they could only bring together 2,500 d. They had to mortgage or even sell their houses, and some pawned their household things. On account of the shortage of 500 d. several Jews were tortured and many died under the punishment. The letter is defective at the end. No doubt Ephraim is appealed to to help the congregation in their dire need.

More details we obtain from A. C. 4; beginning and end missing. It establishes the fact that we deal here with the events in connexion with Ḥasan's rebellion. In order to pay the impositions people had to sell out their goods at any price. Precious silks and linen fetched a quarter of their value. The distress was general, including Muslims (גוים) and Christians (ערלים). Men and women died, some from torture, others from fright. The elders (of the Jewish community) borrowed money on interest (about 600 d.?) till they made up the required sum. Then a second tax was exacted (probably the annual one of 100 d.). The correspondents write that there remained (in Jerusalem) only about 50 men (probably heads of families).

הרעודים בפחודים (r. הפחודים) הנאנחים על מכת השפלה העיר ההוללה · הנאוקים למחלותיה · ועוצם מכותיה · אשר צרותיה נכפלו · והוותיה נקהלו · ואל צור נשוע ונחנן · ונגדיל עתר ורנן · להקל מעליהם · ולהחיש רחמיו עליהם · וכן יעש · ויסיר הכעס. Jerusalem is clearly meant by העיר ההוללה and not Tyre, as Wertheimer, Introd. 7, assumes. Moreover, had the correspondents meant conditions in their own city they would have written in the first person, and **not** in the third (להקל מעליהם . . . רחמיו עליהם).

They made a living mostly from the Ramlāh officials and merchants who were their customers. But Ramlāh has been ruined. The whole of Palestine is in the throes of civil war. Since the Arab conquest no such upheavals occurred there. The writer of this fragment describes how various Bedouin tribes assembled and broke into Ramlāh in Rabi' (1025). They committed there unspeakable barbarities and killed a large number of people. The remainder of the inhabitants went into exile. As we know, the town was sacked. But after Dizbiri's campaign it was soon rebuilt. In 1033, during the earthquake, we find there already Jews, and the town seems to have been already fairly inhabited (as described above under 2).

As dating from this time we have to place here A. C. 5, being a letter from a student of the Jerusalem academy, Ṣadoḳ Hallevi b. Levi, to Ephraim b. Shemarya. The writer was some time later Ab of the school (note 9). Ṣadoḳ seems to have been on intimate terms with the Fusṭāṭ Haber. In a previous letter Ephraim complained that his patience was taxed by disobedient people who refused to accept his ruling and decisions. Ṣadoḳ remarks, 'The like we have many in our place. Again and again God's punishment overtakes them. But they take no heed.' Ṣadoḳ writes the letter to introduce its bearer Revaḥ Hakkohen (a Ḥazzan) b. Pinḥas, a Babylonian. He made a pilgrimage to Jerusalem in the previous year. 'But he was caught in the net of the Arabs and robbed of everything he possessed.' Now he intends going to Fusṭāṭ to obtain there means for returning to Babylon. 'For in the whole of Palestine there remained no community, except Tyre, which could be of help to him.' During the rebellion in 1024–9 Tyre was evidently spared through the protection afforded to it by Dizbiri, the governor of Caesarea and commander-in-chief. Revaḥ spent there the whole winter, and was kept by the local Jews. Ṣadoḳ recommends Revaḥ's case to Ephraim as very deserving. The Ḥazzan had with him sufficient means for his journey. His object was to visit Jerusalem and other places in the Holy Land. On his way he passed Damascus, where he officiated voluntarily. This he did also in Tyre. 'But while he was in Jerusalem, the visitation (גזירה) came upon Philistia (Filastin) and he was caught, with us, and had everything taken away from him.' Here we have a typical example of the hardships a Jewish pilgrim underwent in the Holy Land. The letter to Ṣadoḳ, when already Ab (note 9), comes probably from Fusṭāṭ, informing him of a scene between two people in the local synagogue of the Palestinians. Another correspondent of Ṣadoḳ is Solomon b. Netaneel, the banker. He is perhaps the son of the banker to whom Joshiah Gaon wrote an epistle (above, p. 72).

(4) A number of fragments (A. C. 6–11) inform us about the economic conditions in Jerusalem. They supplement what could be gathered from the preceding pages. The Rabbinites in the Holy City were constantly dependent on outside support. Probably a considerable number of them followed no other pursuit in life than that of a pious 'mourner for Zion', spending their days in prayer and study. A. C. 6 is a letter from Jerusalem. The handwriting is early. The Ramlāh people, as well as other Jews, used to support their brethren in the Holy City. But now, owing to critical times, all help stopped. A certain Samuel b. X. used to be a great benefactor of the Jerusalem poor. In winter he looked after their needs, and when the taxes had to be paid, he would make up the deficiency, that the community be not harassed. He evidently was no longer alive. The recipient of the letter is claimed to be his substitute in acts of charity. He sent several consignments of money. In the letters from the eleventh century the dinār (זהוב) is the usual coin mentioned. But here the correspondents speak of drachmae or dirhems (דרכמונים, also דרכמונים כונבייא). A certain Sahl b. Aaron and his son Abū Ṭayyīb 'Alvan b. Sahl are also mentioned as benefactors.[1]

[1] Perhaps the above letter is from the Ḳaraite community in Jerusalem, because the expression דרכמונים is found in their Ketubot. See A. C. 21, 5; Lucz's *Jerusalem*, VI, 237–9, where a Genizah Ketuba is printed, dated 26 Shevaṭ, 1339 Sel. (= 1027/8 C. E.). Interesting is the conclusion (p. 238, bottom): והתנו ביניהם שאם חס ושלום ותצא (r. תצא) סרוה זאת מן העולם בלא ילד ממנו ישוב כל שהביאה עמה אל יורשיה ממשפחותיה ולא יהיה ליורשיה על חזקיה זה מן המוהר המאוחר מאומה · ועל מנת שישמר מועדי יי בראית הירח ובהמצא אביב בארץ ישׂ ובלי לאכול בשר בקר וצאן בירושלים עד יתכן מזבח יי ושלא יצא אל משפטי הגוים להחליף משפטי התורה. Ten people sign the document, among them Solomon b. David Hakkohen, the teacher, Joshu'a b. 'Ali Hakkohen b. Zuṭa, Nathan b. Nisan Hallevi, the teacher.

A. C. 7 is from the Rabbinite community in Jerusalem to Sahlān, Alluf and Rosh Kallah, b. Abraham. Solomon b. Yehuda, who also signs the letter, probably wrote it in the name of the congregation. Sahlān is thanked for his efforts on their behalf. As their representative informed them, Sahlān preached to his congregation (in Fusṭāṭ) on the duty of supporting time after time their brethren in the Holy City, because of their heavy burden of taxation. Only if the taxes are paid, do the authorities refrain from molesting the Jewish pilgrims who visit Jerusalem, and allow them to go up to Mount Olivet in a procession, and to pray there facing the Temple ruins. There is a fixed amount of taxes which the Jerusalem community, owing to its smallness, cannot afford to pay. They have annually to borrow money on interest to complete the sum in order that the pilgrims be not constrained to do it. Hence the duty is incumbent upon all Israel to keep up the Rabbinite settlement in Jerusalem.

A. C. 8 is another letter from the Holy City to Sahlān. Again an appeal is made for support of the congregation. The taxes and impositions increase every year, but the donations become less. A source of income were the pilgrims, who would benefit the poor settlers in the Holy City. But in this year, the correspondents write, those pilgrims were few owing to civil war and the dangers of the roads. 'Palestine suffers from famine, plague, and terror. The only place we can appeal to is Egypt, though the people there are also in constant fear, but their lot is a little better than ours. We have sent our representative, Joseph the Ḥazzan b. Yefet the teacher, with our credentials. We appeal to you to induce your congregation to help us.' Sahlān's uncle (i. e. Sa'adya) is saluted. A similar letter was also sent on that occasion to Ephr. b. Shemarya, as is only natural (*J. Q. R.*, XIX, 107–8 = גנזי ירושלם, II, 17–18). 'The Rabbinite section persist in keeping up the settlement in the Holy City in spite of the "yoke of the Gentiles". In this year the pilgrims were few and their donations were not enough for the taxes. A loan had to be made to cover the balance. In addition we have a famine here. We sent Joseph the Ḥazzan b. Yefet with letters to the elders of Fusṭāṭ and surrounding places.' Ephraim is asked to see to it that Joseph's mission be successful. 'For you are the essential person' (כי אתה העיקר). The consignments of money are to be addressed to the Gaon (i. e. Solomon b. Yehuda). Perhaps the preceding letter (A. C. 7) is of a later date, and Sahlān is thanked for his assistance.

A. C. 9 is again from the Rabbinite sect in Jerusalem to Ephraim. The letter is written and signed by Solomon b. Yehuda. It has evidently been written after Tabernacles. Among the pilgrims was the elder Mebasser b. Levi, the dignitary, who brought a consignment of money from Ephraim's community amounting to 29⅛ d. From this sum 20 d. were spent in payment of a debt. Ephraim and his congregation were gratefully mentioned in the prayers on Hoshana Rabba (on Mount Olivet). There is an allusion to a foolish attitude taken up by most of that year's pilgrims (רובם לוקחים זה דרכם כסל למו). This must have been due to dissensions in the academy and the parties that were formed among the pilgrims on this account (see also above, p. 138 f.).

A. C. 10 is another appeal from Jerusalem to a certain Bishr b. Jalab (evidently an elder of Fusṭāṭ). The correspondents mention the amount of 120 d. due for taxes. On that year the arrears were 30 d. A loan had to be made and 'sacred things' of the synagogue (כלי הקדש) had to be pawned for the amount. The creditors are now urging and threaten to sell the pledges. The community persuaded their Parnās, Jacob Hakkohen, to go to Fusṭāṭ and obtain monetary help from the elders. Bishr is appealed to to be generous to this representative. The date of this epistle cannot be ascertained.

A. C. 11 is evidently not of the year 1187–8. We know now that there existed then in the Holy City no academy with a Nasi at its head. The only time when a Nasi presided over the school was in the years 1051–62, when Daniel b. 'Azarya became Gaon. Moreover, the whole style of the epistle is so similar to the former appeals of the eleventh century, that it is clear that it describes conditions in the Holy City prior to the Crusades, and even before the occupation by the Seljuḳs in 1071. There is a distinct reference to the raids of the latter invaders who laid the country waste (בני קדם). We hear the same story that the taxes were fixed, whether the members of the community be numerous or few. Should these not be paid, the pilgrims who came especially for Hoshana Rabba would be constrained to pay the balance. Therefore appeals had to be made frequently to the Jews of the Diaspora to help the local community to pay the annual taxes. Whereas the former letters were addressed solely to Fusṭāṭ, the present appeal is general to all the Jewries of the exile. The representative Jonah b. Yehuda, the Spaniard, probably made long journeys on behalf of the Rabbinites of Jerusalem. We read also interesting details about the first settlement of the Jews when the Holy City was occupied by the Arabs (see above, p. 44 f.).

In conclusion, A.C. 12, 1 will be of interest as an example of the hold Jerusalem had on Jews far and wide. It is a circular letter from probably a Spanish community to Egypt concerning Reuben b. Isaac, the bearer of the letter. He was a man of Rhodez in France, very rich and an estate-owner. One day his only son went with his servants to the field, and they were all murdered by Christian brigands. The governor of the town, when appealed to by the unfortunate father, took this occasion for confiscating Reuben's whole fortune for himself. The poor Jew left his home and travelled from place to place till he arrived at the town wherefrom the letter is written. Up to there he could make himself understood, though with difficulty (בלעג לשוני, probably speaking only French). Now he wants to go to Palestine and Jerusalem to die there, for life is to him of no further use. He asked for this letter to be written to the 'congregations on the other side of the sea' (i. e. Egypt), which he would pass on his journey, since he was ignorant of their language (i. e. Arabic). Probably such a Jew, when he arrived safely in the Holy City, joined the 'mourners for Zion'. Their mode of life was quite suitable for such a heart-broken person.

A. C. 12, 2 is a copy of a letter from Salonica to the communities in the diaspora having a similar purpose as the previous fragment, viz. to serve as an introduction for a Jew travelling to Jerusalem. Unfortunately the copyist left out the actual names of the persons mentioned. A Jew from Russia arrived at Salonica, where he met his relative who had recently returned from the Holy City and had with him an epistle from some prominent man (perhaps from the Gaon or another important member of the school). Now this Russian Jew, after having heard an account of the beauty of Palestine, is desirous to visit it. He knows neither Hebrew, Greek, nor Arabic, but only his native tongue Russian.[1] The letter is thus to be his mouthpiece and introduction, to make himself understood on his travels from Salonica to the Holy Land. We hear again of the Salonica community during the first Crusade, when a Messianic movement was set afoot within the Byzantine Jewry.[2]

(5) A. C. 13 contains a number of data about Tiberias. From the times of R. Joḥanan (died 280) to the Arab conquest the town was the centre of the Palestinian Jewry. When in Muhammedan times Jerusalem was opened for the Jews, Tiberias lost its importance as the leading Jewish community. The academy was transferred to the Holy City (see above, p. 55). Since then for several centuries the Jews of Tiberias are seldom mentioned. The town itself, Ṭabariyyah, was an important place as the capital of the province of al-Urdunn (Jordan). But it was especially famous in the Arabic period (just as centuries before) for its hot-springs, affording cure to people stricken with skin-diseases. Muḳaddasi (end of tenth century) reports, 'Within this district are other hot springs, as at a place called al-Ḥammah (the Thermal Waters). Those who suffer from the scab, or ulcers, or sores, and other such-like diseases come to bathe here during three days, and afterwards they dip in the water of another spring which is cold, whereupon—if Allah vouchsafe it to them—they become cured.'[3]

Many Jews visited these hot springs, and the needy among them required support. Hence several appeals (usually stereotyped formulae of begging-letters) from them are preserved in the Genizah finds. These patients would send representatives

[1] שפת כנען, as is well known, in the Middle Ages meant a Slav language. See Harkavy, *Die Juden und die slawischen Sprachen*, 1867, 20 ff.

[2] *J. Q. R.*, IX, 26–9, see Kaufmann, X, 139–51, and also Krauss, *Studien zur byz.-jüd. Gesch.* 47 ff.

[3] Le Strange, *l. c.*, 39, 335–6; see also the accounts of Idrīsi in 1154, and Yaḳūt in 1225 C. E. The latter reports that there are at Tiberias twelve sources, from each of which a special disease is healed. Isaac b. Samuel the Spaniard (Dayyan in Fusṭāṭ, first quarter of twelfth century, *infra*, p. 192) in his commentary to 2 Sam. 5.6, writes: וכאן רסם כל עור ופסח יקצד אל ירושלם כמא יקצד פי זמאננא הדא טבריה [אל] אלמבתלאין (*J. Q. R.*, X, 400). So also in his commentary to 2 Kings 15. 16 (*H. B.*, XX, 63).

to Fusṭāṭ and other places to collect money for their maintenance while taking the cure at Tiberias. We find such a messenger, by name Khalaf b. Yeshu'a, making his last will in Fusṭāṭ in the year 1345 Sel. = 1034 C.E. (A. C. 13, 1). Ephraim b. Shemarya would, of course, be appealed to (A. C. 13, 2). In these circulars the suffering of the patients are described in rather a crude way, no doubt to touch the would-be benefactors and evoke generous responses. A. C. 13, 3 is addressed to X. b. Jacob, 'Alluf of both academies'. Very likely Joseph b. Jacob b. 'Aubal is meant here. As shown elsewhere (*J. Q. R.*, N. S., VIII, 357–8), this Jacob was a pillar of strength in Fusṭāṭ to both the Sura and the Pumbedita (Bagdād) schools, and his son Joseph followed his example. Father and son held the title of Alluf (= Resh Kalla), probably granted to them by both these seats of learning. Joseph is now requested by the Tiberias sick to be generous to their representative, who is about to call upon him.

A. C. 13, 4 is addressed to the Ḥaber 'Āli b. ('Amram). He was probably, as we have seen above (p. 85 f.), the colleague and successor of Ephraim b. Shemarya in Fusṭāṭ. The letter is written on behalf of the Tiberias sufferers by the local Ḥaber, Nathan Hakkohen b. Isaiah. He evidently did not remember the name of 'Āli's father. Hence space was left in the fragment for the bearer to fill out in Fusṭāṭ. Salutations are sent from 'both sections that live in Tiberias' (שני הצדדים, probably Palestinians and Babylonians, perhaps Rabbinites and Ḳaraites). Nathan crudely describes the sufferings of the patients who visit Tiberias hoping to be cured by the water and the air. A representative, Karim b. Nathan, has been sent to Egypt. 'Āli is requested to give him 2 d. and to let the elders of the Tiberias congregation know the amount Karim collected in Fusṭāṭ. In Tiberias all the donations that come from various places are distributed by trustworthy persons to the sufferers in accordance with their standing and needs. That 'Āli and his congregants helped these unfortunate Jews is only natural.

A. C. 13, 5 is a letter from Samuel b. Moses, the Ḥaber, to our 'Āli. The writer was probably identical with the second signatory (שמואל ברבי משה החבר נע) of the letter from Tyre to Aleppo, dated 1028 C.E., referred to above (pp. 37 and 159). The leading Ḥaber of the town then seems to have been the last signatory,

Joseph Hakkohen the Ḥaber b. Baruk. We find our Samuel in 1037 in Fusṭāṭ, where he probably signed a deed. Several years later (in the time of 'Āli b. 'Amram) he holds office in Tyre as local Ḥaber. (Whereas in 1028 he does not style *himself* but only his father החבר, in 1037 he is already the holder of this title. He has therefore in the meantime received his diploma at the Palestine school.) In this capacity he acknowledges 'Āli's letter, which enclosed 13$\frac{1}{4}\frac{1}{12}$ d., being the donations of Solomon b. Sa'adya (b. Ṣajīr), who is known from above (p. 96). Solomon was then a 'mourner' (אבל, cp. l. 15). The amount was addressed to Samuel Hallevi b. Shemarya (b. Ri'akub), evidently an elder in Tyre. A trustworthy man is to forward the money to Tiberias, where it will be distributed by the elders among the needy sick. By the by, Samuel informs 'Āli that his full name is Samuel הנקדים b. צורת האדים, but he goes by the name of Mauhub. His family bears double names, viz. Hebrew and Arabic ones.[1] Salutations are sent to the benefactor, Solomon b. Sa'adya. We see thus how money was transmitted from Egypt to Tiberias. Sometimes through Tyre, when a person happened to go by boat. On other occasions usually the transmission would be via Ramlāh. The route from Damascus to Fusṭāṭ in 'Abbasid times (and essentially the same in the Fāṭimid period) was Damascus-Ṭabariyya-ar-Ramlāh-Gazza-Rafaḥ-Jurjīr-Bilbais-al-Fusṭāṭ (see Hartmann, *Z.D.M.G.*, LXIV, 665 ff.).

A few more data are collected in A. C. 13, 6–9. No. 6 is the usual appeal to a certain Samuel b. X. (there is here a blank in the MS., as the correspondents did not remember the father's name). Two representatives of the Tiberias patients, Khalaf and 'Obadya, have been sent to Egypt. In addition to their illness, these poor people were suffering from famine. Several cities in Palestine were ruined. Perhaps the letter was written during the invasion of the Seljuḳs in 1071 (cp. L.-P. 160–61). Another appeal is A. C. 13, 7. On verso the Ḥazzan Abū'l Ṭayyīb is mentioned. No. 8 is addressed to two rich brothers, one of them by name Mukhtar.

[1] Samuel b. Yaḥyā al-Magribi, who became a Muslim in Nov. 1163, writes (see Schreiner, *Mtschr.*, XLII, 124), 'My father, R. Yehuda b. Abūn of Fās, was called in Arab society Abū'l-Baḳa b. 'Abbās al-Magribi. Most of the prominent men among the Jews have Arabic names, which are either derived or different from their Hebrew ones.'

R. Nathan Hakkohen, alluded to, is probably identical with the Tiberias Ḥaber mentioned before. Also a Merwān Hakkohen occurs in the letter.

(6) The next Palestinian town to be considered is Ashḳelon ('Asḳalān). We hear of Jewish residents already in the time of the governor al-Ikhshīd (935–46). The Jews are reported to have helped the Muslims in 'Asḳalan in the destruction and sacking of the 'Green Church' (Wüstenfeld, *Maḳrizi's Geschichte der Copten*, 63). No doubt Jews lived there centuries before. A. C. 14–16 give us information about the community in the Fāṭimid period. It seems that both Rabbinites and Ḳaraites resided here. A. C. 14 is a letter from the Ashḳelon congregation to 'both communities' of Fusṭāṭ. The object of the epistle is to inform the 'Ḥaberim, Ḥazzānim, and elders' that the new governor of the town Abū Ḥaru' is very good to the local Jews and bestows upon them favours. In this he is assisted by the 'elder of the town' (probably the mayor) Abū Ḥarīz. The Fusṭāṭ Jews are requested to recommend these officials to 'our elders, the elders of the *Ḳaraites*' (l. 19). Thereby these officials will be highly pleased and continue to favour the local Jews. Evidently these elders must have been very influential in the capital, and could do a good turn even to Muslim governors and officials. We have read above (p. 140 f.) that the Ḳaraites had powerful advocates in Cairo, high officials and Katibs who were fellow-sectaries. The writing of the fragment as well as the style and spelling confirm me in the belief that the letter was written by Ḳaraites, though in the name of the whole community of Ashḳelon, which seems to have united the followers of both sections. It was sent to the Rabbinite congregations in Fusṭāṭ. No doubt a similar epistle was dispatched to the Ḳaraite community in the capital.

A. C. 15 is a private letter to the well-known Nagid Meborak. His brother, the former Nagid Yehuda, was no longer alive (ll. 5–6). Accordingly the epistle was certainly written after 1077 (see *infra*, p. 207 f.). Its date is most likely to be placed during the first Crusade. The writer, Joshu'a the Ḥaber b. 'Āli the Ḥaber, who resides in Ḥaṣor, asks the Nagid to write to the Ḳāḍi of Ḥaṣor and request him to give Joshu'a a letter of introduction to the governor of Ashḳelon in case the Ḥaber will have to take shelter in this town, which is fortified and offers more protection.[1] Probably Joshu'a, anxious about the approach of the Crusaders, takes the precaution of obtaining a permit to take refuge in the fortress of Ashḳelon when the need arises. Indeed, throughout the battles with the Franks in the first half of the twelfth century this town remained in the hands of the Muslims (cp. L.-P. 164–5).

By the by, Joshu'a informs the Nagid that the Ḥaṣor congregation, whose Ḥaber he is, is not congenial, and he is unhappy with them. The exact locality of Ḥaṣor is not known to me, though it must have been in the neighbourhood of Ashḳelon. Ḥarīzi seems to have visited it (see A. C. 16, 1). Our Joshu'a was a descendant of Hoshana, the father of Samuel the 'Third' and friend of Shemarya b. Elḥanan (above, p. 28). In 1096 we find him in Ramlāh, where he signs a document. Later on he became Ḥaber of Ḥaṣor. Whether he obtained the permission to go to Ashḳelon as well as his further vicissitudes are unknown. He was no longer alive in 1131 C. E.

A few data are collected in A. C. 16, 2 bearing on Ashḳelon Jewry. It is of interest to learn (A. C. 16, 3) that in 1112 the local Dayyanim were in communication with the erewhile Jerusalem Academy, then situated at Ḥadrak (near Damascus) and presided over by Solomon Hakkohen, Maṣliaḥ's father (*infra*, p. 196 f.). A member of the school was Elijah Hakkohen b. Ebyatar Gaon (no longer alive), to whom Nathan Hakkohen b. Meborak and Yeshu'a b. Yefet write from Ashḳelon. Unfortunately only a few lines of the epistle are preserved. Elijah never succeeded to the Gaonate, but died when still 'Fourth' (as shown in A. A. 17). These Dayyanim are the signatories of documents, drawn up at Ashḳelon and dated 1136 and 1142. Three years later (1145) they were no longer alive. Their successors were their sons Meborak and Yefet.

In 1153, Ashḳelon, the last hold of the Fāṭimids on Palestine, fell into the hands of the Crusaders. Saladin reconquered it in September, 1187 (see L.-P. 173, 208). But the Jewish community evidently continued to exist during the Christian occupation of the town. Benjamin of Tudela, whose visit falls within this

[1] The town was rebuilt and fortified by 'Abd-al-Malik (685–705 C.E.). Muḳaddasi in 985 found it strongly garrisoned (see Le Strange, *l. c.* 400 ff.).

period, found there about 200 Rabbinites, represented by R. Ṣemaḥ, R. Aaron, and R. Solomon, and also 40 Ḳaraites and 300 Samaritans (*Itinerary*, ed. Adler 29; see also *infra*, p. 240, note 1).

The *Megillat Ebyatar*, which will be discussed farther on, mentions several Jewish communities in Northern Palestine (Galilee). We have heard above of congregations in Jerusalem, Ramlāh, Tiberias, Tyre, Ashḳelon, Ḥaṣor, 'Akko, and 'Ammān. No doubt there were many Jewish settlements in villages where the people occupied themselves with farming or with other trades. A number of data about other communities are collected in A. C. 17. Banīyas (Fort Dan) had two congregations, probably Palestinian and Babylonian (no. 1). The fragment clearly dates from the beginning of the twelfth century since Moses Nagid, the son of Meborak, is mentioned therein (see *infra*, p. 212 f.). That Palestine had a considerable number of Babylonian Jews already in the eighth century can be gathered from an interesting Halakic fragment in *Geonica* II (see *J.Q.R.*, N.S., VII, 474). We have also seen above (p. 148) that Ramlāh possessed a כנסת אלשאמיין, presupposing a 'synagogue of the Babylonians'. Also Tiberias probably had two such congregations and likewise Damascus (above, pp. 150, 167).

Ḥaifa (no. 2) will be dealt with farther on. From nos. 3 and 5 we learn of Jews hailing from Ḥebron. But the community seems to have been small (see also *infra*, p. 248; A. D. 33, 5). No. 4 is in late handwriting, probably of the thirteenth century. The fragment is probably the end of a letter to a Nagid. We learn from it the names of several communal officials in Safed, Biriat, Gischala (al-Jūsh), al-'Aluya, and 'Alme, all places in upper Galilee. Though outside our period, we have inserted this fragment here to add to our knowledge of Palestinian congregations which probably existed earlier in the Fāṭimid era.

II

(1) The exilarchs of Babylon had rivals in Palestine, Syria, and Egypt. We find Nesiim in Fusṭāṭ, Jerusalem, Damascus, and elsewhere. Their history is very obscure. What authority they wielded over the communities by reason of their Davidic origin

will be discussed farther on (Chap. VI). The latest summary of all the known data is given by Poznański, *Babylon. Geon.*, 111 ff. He admits that they are scanty and allow no connected account. According to him the attempt to establish the Exilarchate outside Babylon is to be dated after the close of the Babylonian Gaonate (1038). Yet he admits the possibility of the Genizah furnishing surprises on this point (*l.c.*, p. 111). Now these actually happened. We have learned above of Nesiim, either in Syria or in Egypt, at the end of the tenth century. By name are known Semaḥ and a 'son of 'Aubal' (pp. 24–5). We have, moreover, seen that in the period of Solomon b. Yehuda there resided in the Holy City a Nasi who visited Cairo-Fusṭāṭ with the special purpose of obtaining letters patent from the government confirming his authority. David Hannasi b. Ḥezekiah, the exilarch of Bagdād, we have also found for a time in Jerusalem (above, 111 ff.). Yedidyah Hannasi b. Zakkai was a correspondent of Abraham Hakkohen b. Isaac the physician (above, p. 85). About Daniel b. 'Azarya and his sons more will be said in the next section of this chapter. We discuss here a number of new data which unfortunately furnish only scraps of information. Let us hope that more will be forthcoming in the course of time.

An interesting account of the doings of a bogus-Nasi, by name Shem Ṭob, we have in A. C. 18; beginning and end missing. After a general introduction, the drift of which cannot be ascertained owing to the defectiveness of the MS., the writers of this letter state that now in exile when a Jew claims to be a priest or a Levite, his statements have to be borne out by people of his native place who know his family. But if a priest comes to a distant place and no such verification can be effected, he may still act as such and need not produce a pedigree. It is of interest that the priest is mentioned to take tithes, Ḥallah, and other gifts pertaining to his dignity (see note 11). From l. 20 we have the following story, which is given here in translation. 'You, our brethren, are not unaware of the great things done in your congregation and in ours, and also in Jerusalem and the whole of Palestine, by that man, called Nasi and going by the name of Shem Ṭob. He had with him a pedigree. He acted as judge, appointed communal officers and officials (?), dispatched messengers, took 'tithes', and wielded authority (*lit.* 'made the burden heavy'). Travelling from place to place, he administered justice to Israel. In your city there were authorized scholars (סנהדרין וחברים), learned men and disciples, who were authorities in the Torah more than anybody else. Yet they accepted his rule, honoured and cherished him, and did not inquire after his origin. They ardently imbibed his words, eulogized and praised him before the Gentiles, and recommended him to the king and princes. In no place which he visited, from Fusṭāṭ to Kalnē (= Raḳḳah), did any scholar, head (of a community), or disciple object to him. His decisions made an impression upon everybody. After two years it became known that he was no Nasi, and his pedigree was proved to be false. Yet the people did not put him to shame nor pay him less respect, for they recognized that he was a wise man who by his personality could enforce the carrying out of his decisions. The people sent him away from Tiberias to Byzantium, and on the way he died. The purpose of our letter to you, our brethren, is to inform you in short about the man who passed by our place, since you have asked us (about him) through R. Jacob the Ḥaber. At the beginning there came suddenly to us a non-Jew, of the retinue of the governor over the district of the Euphrates valley (שעל שפת הנהר). He had with him a large document signed with the seal of a Nasi. We asked him whose letter it was and he said, "I am sent . . ."' Unfortunately the fragment breaks off here. By appearance it seems to be of the eleventh century. It is evidently a letter from a community in Northern Syria, not far from the Euphrates. From the use of Greek words (l. 22) it appears that the district was near the Byzantium (Rūm) frontier, where Greek words were still known. Especially the boundary between Rūm and Muhammedan Syria and Mesopotamia was in those times in a constant flux. Towns often changed rulers. Probably the letter was sent from Raḳḳah (= כלנה) to Aleppo. We have seen above (p. 37, note 1) that the Ḥaber of the town was Jacob b. Joseph in 1028. From the letter, printed by Schechter, it is evident that in Aleppo there were 'people of Torah and knowledge' (בעלי תורה וחכמה). If our assumption is correct, the fragment discussed here belongs to the first half of the eleventh century. We obtain an insight into conditions in Oriental communities. It shows the great respect which Jews everywhere paid to a descendant of David. A clever impostor could for two years wield much authority in several communities of Egypt, Palestine, and Syria.

(2) A. C. 19 is so far of interest here as preserving a pedigree issued to a person who successfully proved his Davidic origin. The persons concerned lived in the fourteenth century, thus outside our period. But the fragment fully deserves publication in this connexion. No doubt the earlier Nesiim had similar documents issued to them. Sar Shalom Nasi b. Pinḥas proved before the Bagdād congregation his Davidic origin, and his claim to the title of Nasi was verified in our fragment. The scribe was himself a Nasi, by name 'Azarya b. Yehalelel b. 'Azarya. We find this 'Azarya in Bagdād in 1341. Column 1 contains a poem in honour of Sar Shalom. No doubt 'Azarya is its author. Bagdād (עדינה,[1] l. 12) is to rejoice at the dignity acquired by this noble man, the fame of whose generosity reaches Egypt (l. 5). 'His sons, the Nesiim' (l. 8) are also referred to in the poem. In the genealogy list (printed in A. C. 19, end) one of his sons is mentioned by name, Joshiah. Seven generations of Sar Shalom's ancestors are enumerated. These are Pinḥas, Hodaya, Joshiah, Yehuda, Solomon, 'Uzziah, Joshiah. A Bible codex, written in 1312, belonged to our Sar Shalom (cp. Pozn., *Babyl. Geon.*, 124, 3, and the passages cited there). His genealogy mentioned therein is to be rectified by our list. Sar Shalom's four sons are mentioned, viz. Malki Ṣedeḳ, Pinḥas, Ḥezeḳiah, and Joshiah. The last occurs in our fragment. Sar Shalom is reported in that Bible codex to have had authorization from a Solomon Nasi (הסמוך אפי אדונינו ר' שלמה הנשיא ראש גליות ישראל המכונא מולא נפים אלדולא ואלדין). He is, perhaps, identical with the Nasi Solomon b. Jesse whom we find in Egypt in 1244 (cp. *infra*, p. 175). Thus Sar Shalom apparently left Egypt and settled in Bagdād.[2]

[1] Babylon is personified as such in Isa. 47. 8. Hence Bagdād (בבל) is often referred to as עדינה. See Ḥarīzi, תחכמוני (ed. Kaminka), p. 126 (ויגשו בראשונה וראיתי משוררי בבל . אשר שם היו גאוני תבל . . . וכל שרי עדינה), 190 (ומשם נסעתי לעדינה . היא פאר כל מדינה . ושם היו מעולם משוררי עדינה), 368 (ותען בבל ותאמר: אני עדינה [וחכמיה] גאוני תבל), 375 (ותען בבל ותאמר: אני עדינה), 406, 446. Likewise El'azar b. Jacob Habbabli in his Diwān speaks of Bagdād as עדינה (see Pozn., *Babyl. Geon.*, 64, no. 9, l. 30; 77, l. 38). Cp. also Bacher, *J. Q. R.*, XIV, 741.

[2] The Bible codex, which Safir brought from Yemen (אבן ספיר, I, 18^b; II, 175),

In A. C. 20 a number of data about other Nesiim are given. A document, dated 1114–15 at Damascus, mentions that the Bet-Dīn is under the authority of Ḥasdai Nasi (no. 1). Probably he resided in this city. He was perhaps the son of Samuel Hannasi b. Daniel b. 'Azarya who held the title 'Third' and presided over the Bet-Dīn of Damascus in 1085 (see *infra*, p. 185).

A Zakkai b. 'Azarya Nasi writes to the elders of Damascus (no. 2). He is evidently the fifth (or sixth) ancestor of the Nasi David b. Daniel of Mosul who in 1288 issued a ban against Solomon b. Samuel Petit in 'Akko on account of the latter's agitation against Maimonides' writings (see Pozn., *loc. cit.*, 121–2). Probably the epistle here was sent from Mosul to Damascus, Zakkai lived about a century previously, in the second half of the twelfth century. 'Azarya, his father, is styled נשיא גליות כל ישראל.

A Nasi Daniel we find in Fusṭāṭ in 1164–5. Documents of the Bet-Dīn are issued in his name (no. 3). He may have been the son or the grandson of David b. Daniel, who was deposed in 1094 after his well-known conflict with Ebyatar Gaon and Meborak Nagid.

In the time of Maimonides we find in Egypt a Yehuda Nasi b. Joshiah. A few data are given in no. 4. They show us that the Patriarchate in Egypt continued even after David b. Daniel's deposition, though it is as yet impossible to draw up a complete list of the holders of this dignity. Finally, we have in the middle of the thirteenth century a Solomon b. Jesse who seems to have been a recognized authority (no. 5). This Solomon was perhaps the brother of Hodaya b. Jesse Hannasi, who came into conflict with an Alexandrian Dayyan, Joseph b. Gershon. The latter's correspondence with Abraham Maimuni on this subject contains much interesting material about the social life of the Egyptian Jewry.[1] Hodaya was no native of Egypt, but probably hailed

and which has the same colophon as the one of 1312, originates from Egypt. It was brought to Yemen by Aaron 'Iraḳi, the banker of Sultan Selim, who settled there (see *Halebanon*, 1863, p. 32, col 1, where for ערקאי r. עראקי). Who knows whether this Aaron, a native of Babylon, did not obtain it in Bagdād? The date 1023 is impossible; more likely 1323 C. E.

[1] See *Ḳobeṣ*, I, nos. 250–51, and Simonsen, *Guttmann-Festschrift*, 217–24.

from Damascus. Ḥarīzi found there a Nasi Joshiah b. Jesse 'the great Nasi'.[1] Joseph b. Gershon, in the above correspondence, also gives Hodaya's father this title. We may perhaps assume that Jesse had three sons, Solomon, Hodaya, and Joshiah. The first settled in Fusṭāṭ, where he was much esteemed, while Hodaya spent there a few years only. In no. 6 we have a ban, dated 1235 C. E., by Joshiah b. Jesse, evidently from Damascus. Solomon b. Jesse is also mentioned. It is doubtful whether Hodaya b. Jesse is meant in the legal question (no. 7), as he had no such standing as to merit so many eulogies. More likely this Hodaya was the father of the Babylonian Nasi David, who signed a ban in favour of Samuel Schlettstadt (about 1376, see Pozn., *loc. cit.*, 119–20). Probably Hodaya also acted as Nasi in Bagdād.

(3) The Ḳaraites had also Nesiim, who adopted the rather pompous title 'prince of the whole (!) diaspora of Israel'. Most of them derived their origin from 'Anān, the founder of Ḳaraism. Poznański (*Babyl. Geon.*, 125 ff.) collected and discussed all the data known to him. We are able to supplement them here with new information. A. C. 21, 1 contains an important memorial list of Nesiim and communal leaders of the Ḳaraite congregation of Fusṭāṭ. First are mentioned Yefet Hannasi, Ṣemaḥ Hannasi, and a lady from this family. A draft of a Ḳaraite Ketuba, dated 1036 C. E. at Fusṭāṭ, introduces Ṣemaḥ Nasi b. Asa Nasi (no. 2). Both father and son were hitherto entirely unknown. They probably resided in the capital. Ṣemaḥ, mentioned in the memorial list, is very likely identical with Ṣemaḥ b. Asa. Perhaps Yefet was his brother. Their genealogy from 'Anan is not preserved. Another formula of a Ḳaraite Ketuba, dated 1081 C. E. (no. 3), mentions a Yedidya Nasi, who was perhaps a son of either Ṣemaḥ or Yefet.[2] As the spiritual heads of the Fusṭāṭ community they figure in the documents. However, in 1062 C. E. we find a Ḳaraite Nasi in Fusṭāṭ from another branch of 'Anan's family, as will be shown presently.

To return to the memorial list (no. 1). The second item is in memory of the members of a priestly family. Mentioned by name are Aaron and Moses, each of them styled 'the important

[1] *Taḥkemoni*, ed. Kaminka, 24; cp. Pozn., *l. c.*, 123.

[2] See also above, p. 85, note 1.

dignitary, mighty and noble'. Now a Ketuba, dated 1082 at Fusṭāṭ, tells us that David b. Daniel married the daughter of the influential Ḳaraite, Moses Hakkohen b. Aaron, styled 'the banner of the Jews, their stronghold and the joy of their pride'. In *Megillat Ebyatar* this Moses is alluded to as 'the lord of the (present) time' (see *infra*, pp. 187, note 1, and 188). He is no doubt meant here in the memorial list. His father Aaron was no longer alive in 1082. He probably belonged to that group of prominent Ḳaraites whom we found wielding so much influence in Fusṭāṭ during the period of Solomon b. Yehuda. Other dignitaries enumerated in the list are 'Amram, Shelah, and Abraham, perhaps being father and son in the order mentioned. Condolences are offered to their descendants, 'Amram, Solomon, 'Obadya, and Yefet. Whether these four were brothers, the sons of Abraham, cannot be ascertained. They evidently were men of standing in the community.

A Ketuba, dated 1062 C.E. at Fusṭāṭ, mentions Hezekiah Nasi b. Solomon (no. 4), who evidently is identical with the seventh lineal descendant of 'Anan. His son Ḥasdai figures in another Ketuba, dated 1109 at Fusṭāṭ (no. 5). The important memorial list (no. 8) gives us a list of 19 direct descendants of this Ḥasdai. We are thereby able to trace 27 generations from 'Anan. The list construed by Pozn. is to be corrected in accordance with the genealogy given in no. 9. It is unknown when exactly 'Anan's descendants left Babylon and settled in Egypt. But as soon as a Ḳaraite centre was founded in the Holy City very likely a member of 'Anan's family took up his residence there. The story that the founder of Ḳaraism himself left his native country, Babylon, for the Holy City, where he built a synagogue for his followers, is no doubt apocryphal (see Pozn., Luncz's *Jerusalem*, X, 85–91). But a few generations afterwards the sectaries had a centre in Jerusalem, and probably invited a descendant of 'Anan to be at the head of affairs (see above, p. 60 ff.). With the spread of the movement to Egypt, more scope was available for these Nesiim. In the capital of this country they found a wider field of activity than in the poverty-stricken Jerusalem. Thus Fusṭāṭ became the place of residence for the Ḳaraite Nesiim. Probably all the generations of Nesiim from Hezeḳiah (1064) and onwards lived there.[1] Perhaps already Hezeḳiah's grandfather, David b. Boʿaṣ, a prominent Ḳaraite Bible commentator and author, should be sought in Fusṭāṭ. However, in the beginning of the eleventh century we have there Asa Nasi, and afterwards (1036) his son Ṣemaḥ, who no doubt had their origin from ʿAnan. Perhaps Asa was a son of either this David (his other son was Solomon I) or of Boʿaṣ.

III

(1) We propose now to deal with the Palestine Gaonate, from the death of Solomon b. Yehuda in 1051 till the first Crusade. In the same year (1051) we find already Daniel b. ʿAzarya in Jerusalem, as will be shown presently. Ebyatar in his well-known *Megillah* writes, 'And after all these words and this vision, in the days of Joseph Hakkohen and Elijah Hakkohen, both Geonim, Daniel b. ʿAzarya of Babylon came (to Jerusalem in opposition to) them.' He had the support of the Ḳaraites (כת צלע, cp. especially *infra*, p. 274 f.; we have found them above (p. 143) taking part in the quarrels of the school) and other people, and also of the government. In Ḥanukah, 1365 Sel. (December, 1053 C. E.), Joseph Hakkohen died. Elijah, his brother, made peace with Daniel, the latter being Gaon, and the former Ab (1057). In Elul 1062, the Gaon died, and the Ab succeeded him

[1] To the Nesiim in Cairo-Fusṭāṭ Menaḥem גיצני refers in his letter from Alexandria (Pinsker, *Liḳḳuṭe*, Appendices, 51, bottom): עוד ממה שזכה (אלהים *sc.*) ארצכם (אנשי קהרא *sc.*) בחברת הנשיאים · אשר מכל יקר שכל הם מלאים . . . והמה ידועים זרע דוד המלך עה ידיד האל וכו׳. However, from the well-known colophon of the so-called Ben-Asher Bible Codex at Aleppo (printed in *Halebanon*, 1863, p. 23; Eben Sappir, I, 12^b–13^a), it appears that Hezeḳiah and his brother Joshiah lived in Jerusalem, because a dignitary, Israel b. Simḥah of Baṣra, presented the Codex to the Ḳaraite community at Jerusalem: על מנת שלא יצא מתחת ידי שני הנשיאים הגדולים כנק הוד הדור הנשיא יאשיהו והנשיא יחזקיהו בני כנק הנשיא שלמה בן הנשיא דוד בן הנשיא בעז תנצבה בגע תחת עץ החיים כדי שיוציאוהו אל המושבות והקהלות שבעהק בג׳ רגלים וכו׳. Also from the story dealt with *infra*, p. 199 f., it can be gathered that in 1106 the Ḳaraites of the Holy City were represented by a Nasi Solomon, perhaps a son of Hezeḳiah. This problem still needs elucidation, which only new material can render possible. In case these Nesiim resided in Jerusalem, the sectaries in Egypt inserted in their Ketubas and other documents the names of the respective Nesiim of the Holy Land.

to the dignity (see *Saadyana*, 86, 113–14). Hence Daniel's activity in Jerusalem lasted eleven years (1151–62).

A. C. 22 and 23 are letters from our Daniel. They are both in the same handwriting and contain the same ending ישועה 'salvation' (Solomon b. Yehuda used to conclude his epistles with ישע רב 'much salvation', while his rival Nathan b. Abraham chose the motto ישע יקרב 'May He (God) bring near salvation', above, p. 146). The second fragment is signed by the Nasi-Gaon. There is no doubt that the first also emanates from him. It is dated Ṭebet, 1363 Sel. (=1051–2 C. E.).[1] Daniel must have met with some opposition against his claims as Nasi and Gaon. It is well known, he writes, that our ancestors, the Exilarchs had authority over the people and were their leaders. This example should be followed. The authority of the house of David is the true one ordained in the Bible. Far be it from 'our Western brethren' to act contrarily to Divine command. It is clear that Daniel writes about a community in Magreb (or perhaps in Egypt, see above, pp. 30, note 1, 83) who refused him recognition. He then describes his experiences in Jerusalem. 'Since we came to this holy place we guide Israel, with God's help, in the whole of Palestine and Syria, and administer justice even to those in distant places. In all towns and settlements prayers are recited for us. The Ḥaberim and judges in every place are authorized by us. Nobody else has any influence even over a small town. You have no doubt received (my letter) after the festivals (i. e. Tabernacles). No cross word was exchanged between two Jews. But the pilgrims arrived in song, prayed and returned home cheerfully.' This was no doubt Daniel's first Tabernacles in Jerusalem. During this festival, especially on Hoshana Rabbā, the issue would be decided in times of controversy as to which part was to have the upper hand. Daniel reports that everything passed off smoothly, and he was generally recognized. He thus asks his correspondent to 'open the eyes' of his friends. 'Know that you will thereby have no loss, but there is reward for your work!' A gentle hint that Daniel will compensate those working (in Egypt and elsewhere) for him. In conclusion he seemingly asks his correspondent to let him know what 'our sisters' do. Probably they were related. This

[1] Only the last five days of Ṭebet, 4812 A. M., fell in January, 1052 C. E.

letter shows that in the summer of 1051, soon after Solomon's death, Daniel was already in the Holy City. Indeed in a fragment, cited in A. C. 23, note 4 end, we find apparently Daniel writing to some friend of his in Tammuz, 1050. It may be that he then resided already in Jerusalem. As Solomon b. Yehuda was very old and the question as to his would-be successor became actual, Daniel found it advisable to settle at the seat of the school and work in the interests of his candidature.

He had the support of the authorities in Jerusalem, who no doubt acted in accordance with the recommendations from the central government in Cairo. Most likely Daniel stayed there for some time on his arrival from Babylon. He succeeded in obtaining influential partisans, and supported by the hereditary prestige of a descendant of David, he obtained the Gaonate after the demise of Solomon b. Yehuda, though the sons of Solomon Hakkohen Gaon, Joseph and Elijah, had prior claims. Joseph was probably then Ab, while his brother was 'Third' (in 1045 he was 'Fourth'). What attitude the Palestinian community in Fusṭāṭ took up in this affair is unknown. Probably both parties had their followers. The influential physician Abraham b. Isaac Hakkohen was a cousin of Joseph and Elijah (above, p. 84). It may therefore be assumed that he sided with them. Ephraim b. Shemarya outlived the Gaon a few years. Elijah Hakkohen corresponded with him when already Ab (pp. 94–5). This dignity he most likely attained after his brother's death, towards the end of 1053 (Ḥanukah, 1365 Sel.). Ephraim was then already 80 years old. From Elijah's epistle it appears that some temporary misunderstanding existed between himself and the Fusṭāṭ Ḥaber. It may have been caused by Daniel's Gaonate. But in Marḥeshvan, 1057, we find the Gaon already at peace with his Ab, and the former was generally recognized. He corresponded with Ephraim (see *infra*) and seems to have won over the influential physician Abraham b. Isaac, bestowing upon him the title 'the lustre of the elders' (above, p. 86). Likewise 'Ali b. 'Amram, Ephraim's colleague and successor, informs Abraham that public prayers are recited for him in the (Palestinian) synagogue at Fusṭāṭ, which goes by the name of Daniel Nasi and Gaon (above, p. 85 f.).

A. C. 23 is probably addressed to this 'Ali b. 'Amram since

the title 'the superior Ḥaber' (l. 4) recurs in his signatures (see A. D. 1). Daniel assures him that he will stand by him and that his trouble will be rewarded; for every copper coin a silver one, and for every silver coin a much greater multiple. Let him only have patience. If the Ḥaber be afraid lest his authority within his community diminish, Daniel will write to the congregation on his behalf, while his opponents will be sharply reprimanded (l. 14 f. נשלח בו חצים שנונים). Here again we find the Nasi writing gently and with restraint, but also alluding to his purse. As Nasi, Daniel bestowed titles in connexion with the Nesiut (A. C. 23, note 4). In the small epistle cited there, greetings are sent to Ḥalfon Rosh Haḳḳahal, probably president of a congregation in Fusṭāṭ.

A. C. 23 a shows how Daniel was cherished by the Palestinian community in Fusṭāṭ after his Gaonate was well established, and a compromise concluded with Elijah Hakkohen Ab. That Daniel is meant in the epistle, of which beginning and end are missing, is evident from the titles '*our Nasi, our Gaon*' (l. 15). The correspondents also mention that they are well, 'though troubles passed over us during the *years of famine*, from all of them our God rescued us' (l. 5). In the year 444 H. (1052–3 C. E.) the Nile failed to irrigate the country, and in consequence the price of food rose enormously. Privation and misery were in force still in the following years, while the year 448 H. (1056–7) brought in addition a plague. But already in the following year (449 H., 1057–8) Egypt recovered when the usual overflow of the Nile took place (see Wüst., *l. c.*, III, 24; cp. L.-P. 142–3). It is clear that our letter was written about this time. The correspondents assure Daniel of their loyalty to him, 'rejoicing in thy kingdom (a reference to his descent from King David) and taking pride in thy epistle' (l. 2). Daniel sent a letter to Ephraim the Ḥaber (no doubt b. Shemarya) enclosing also an epistle to the community, evidently enjoining therein that concord reign between the two Ḥaberim (of the Palestinians in the capital, i. e. Ephraim and his partner, cp. above, p. 120 ff.). On the Sabbath ויגש at a full assembly in the synagogue the Gaon's epistle was discussed and applauded. Both the Ḥaberim were present and also the communal leader ('the important dignitary' השר הנכבד) Ephraim Hakkohen b. Abraham (probably identical with Ephraim

Hakkohen often referred to in Solomon b. Yehuda's correspondence, p. 116 ff.). In the fragment (verso) is also mentioned Samuel of Tahort (known to us from above, pp. 117, 119). Ephraim's colleague was probably 'Ali b. 'Amram, whose name we find on documents dated 1057 and onwards (see A. D. 1). As pointed out above (pp. 85 f., 95), he survived Ephraim b. Shemarya and became the recognized spiritual leader of the Palestinian congregation. Since when he acted in the capacity of Ḥaber is not known. It is also obscure whether he is identical with any of the persons who for some time belonged to the opponents of Ephraim. 'Ali styles himself 'the superior Ḥaber' (החבר המעולה). He evidently held a diploma from the Palestine school, and probably studied under Solomon b. Yehuda. The relations between master and disciple are obscure.[1]

To return to Daniel b. 'Azarya and his three sons, about whom a number of data are collected in A. C. 24. A document, the date of which is missing, is signed by Daniel and by the Ḥaber Yehuda b. Ḥuṣpit. From the names of the witnesses it is evident that the document originates from Jerusalem (no. 1). Joseph b. Yefet the teacher we found above (p. 163) as the representative of the Jerusalem community on a mission to Fusṭāṭ. We know that he was a Reader. Ṣemaḥ b. El'azar is a co-signatory of a Geṭ, dated Jerusalem 1057, together with Daniel (no. 3). Of interest is the signature Joshiah Hakkohen b. 'Azarya, *Gaon of Sura*. He is clearly identical with the supporter of David b. Daniel mentioned in the *Megillat Ebyatar* (*J. Q. R.*, XIV, 460, l. 6: (ורב יאשיהו בן דודתו בן רבינו עזריהו ראש ישיבה של גולה זל). We learn now that 'Azarya was no Gaon of Egypt, but of Sura. That his son held this dignity in the land of the Nile is mentioned nowhere. The first attempt to establish the Gaonate in Egypt was made by David b. Daniel and not before (as will be seen farther on). Joshiah was David's cousin (בן דודתו). Hence their fathers were brothers-in-law. As shown elsewhere (to be printed in *J. Q. R.*, N. S.), 'Azarya was probably the son of Israel Gaon,

[1] Perhaps Solomon b. Yehuda (in a letter to Sahlān, above, p. 145) refers to 'Ali by styling him הבוגד המעולה, a caustic allusion to the title החבר המעולה. If this be correct, then 'Ali is the rival of Ephraim, as described above (Chap. III). But nothing definite can be ventured before the recovery of several missing links will enable us fully to reconstruct the sequence of the actual happenings.

who died in 1034, and a grandson of Samuel b. Ḥofni (died 1013). The Sura Gaonate continued its precarious existence till about 1050. Probably about this time, Joshiah Hakkohen left Babylon together with his uncle Daniel b. 'Azarya, a member of the Exilarch's family. The reason of their departure, whether political or because of want of scope, is obscure. After staying for a short time in Egypt, Daniel became Gaon in Jerusalem in 1051, and his nephew Joshiah accompanied him to his new sphere of activity. Thus we find Joshiah signing the above document. After Daniel's demise in 1062, Joshiah apparently returned to Egypt and settled in Fusṭāṭ, where he must have been highly respected. But he held there no office of Gaon. Subsequently he helped his cousin David to be installed as Nasi there, as will be discussed presently.

Another document, dated 1053 at Ramlāh, is ratified by the Gaon-Nasi (no. 2). Its date Marḥeshvan 6, 1365 Sel., is of interest, as it is a few weeks before the death of Joseph Hakkohen, Elijah's brother (in Ḥanukah of the same year). It shows that David was then recognized as Gaon. The local Ḥaber of Ramlāh seems to have been Solomon b. Ḥayyim the 'Seventh' (השביעי). Interesting is the fragment of a letter (no. 4) from Fusṭāṭ, informing the Nasi-Gaon of the approaching visit to the Holy City of the banker Nathan, together with his son and company. They are Daniel's partisans and have plenty of money. Daniel should give them a hearty welcome. He would no doubt benefit by them. Probably these people were pilgrims to the Holy City. Abū Isḥāḳ Abraham המשוש (= משוש הישיבה), mentioned in another epistle addressed to our Nasi-Gaon, is probably identical with Abraham Hakkohen b. Isaac, the physician, whom Solomon b. Yehuda very likely honoured with this title (see the references to the משוש above, pp. 83, 92, 129, 132, 144).

Altogether the impression of Daniel as the usurper of the Gaonate, which the Ebyatar Megillat imparts, is proved to be wrong by the great respect he was held in and by the relations he kept up with several men of standing in Egypt and elsewhere. If there was a grudge against him, it seems to have been nourished chiefly by the descendants of Solomon Hakkohen Gaon, who thought that they had prior claims to the Gaonate, and regarded him as an intruder from Babylon. A. C. 24 a is of importance as it introduces for the first time a descendant of the famous Palṭiel. A certain scholar (evidently a Ḥaber in some community) writes to Yehoseph Nagid b. Samuel Nagid. Both are lavishly eulogized. The title 'Nagid of the Diaspora' is given to each of them. The writer, who was the recipient of the Nagid's bounty, states that wherever he recites prayers (in the synagogue in the presence of his congregation) for '*our lord Daniel Nasi and Gaon*', he does not fail to do the same honour to the Nagid. Daniel is styled 'the son of the world's light, may he live for ever'. It is not clear whether the last expression refers to Daniel or to his father ('Azarya). If the latter alternative be correct, then 'Azarya, acting as Nasi somewhere in Babylon, was still alive when his son was Gaon in Jerusalem. Yehoseph is very likely identical with the 'Nagid of the Diaspora' mentioned by Solomon b. Yehuda as having sent his representative to Damascus to settle the dispute between the Ḳaraites and the Rabbanites (above, p. 140). His father Samuel Nagid was Palṭiel's son. In 1054, when the *Aḥima'aṣ Chronicle* was written, Samuel was no longer alive. Yet no mention is made of his descendants.[1] We now learn that his son Yehoseph was also his successor as Nagid. Thus the dignity remained in this family for three generations. As will be shown farther on (Chap. VI), already in the lifetime of Yehoseph, Yehuda b. Sa'adya, the brother of Meborak, was designated as Nagid, and sometime after Daniel b. Azarya's death, when Elijah Hakkohen was already Gaon (1062 and onwards), entered upon this office. Of Yehoseph's descendants very little is so far known.[2]

Daniel had three sons (A. C. 24, no. 4). The best known of them is David (see the additional data collected in no. 5). A

[1] *Aḥima'aṣ Chronicle* (in Neub., II, 130): ויקם ר׳ שמואל בנו תחתיו · איש גדול ונכבד בדורותיו · ממלא היה מקום אבותיו . . . זכרו יהא לברכה וכו׳.

[2] A document (T.-S. 13 J 4[16]), dated 1493 Sel. = 1182 C. E. in Cairo, mentions X. b. Yeshu'a b. כבגק מרור . . . יוסף הנגיד זל. It may be that between X. and Yeshu'a one generation is missing. As Yehoseph died some time after 1062 C. E., the persons mentioned in this document probably were his descendants. No other Joseph Nagid is so far known. In 1055 Joseph succeeded his great father, Samuel Hallevi ibn Nagdela, as Nagid in Spain. It is not likely that he is meant in the above epistle, since the writer would have styled him or his father 'Hallevi'.

second son, hitherto unknown, was Samuel the 'Third' (no. 6). He settled in Damascus, where he presided over the Bet-Dīn (Tishri, 1084). A son of his was perhaps Ḥasdai Nasi, whom we found in Damascus in 1114–15 (above, p. 175). Daniel's third son was probably called Isaiah (no. 7). But nothing further is known about him. Daniel must have died comparatively young. This we gather from the fact that his son David was then only four or five years old. Ebyatar tells us in his *Megillah* that three years before he was designated as Gaon (i. e. two years before Elijah Gaon's death + 3 = 1083–5 = 1078 C.E., *J. Q. R.*, XIV, 458, l. 16 ff., 459, l. 27 ff.)[1] David left Palestine for Egypt, being about twenty years old. As his father died in 1062, David was then about four or five years old. We thus understand how Elijah Hakkohen the Ab could occupy the Gaonate without any opposition on the part of the late Gaon's children. These were then of a tender age. The struggle therefore began nineteen years afterwards, when Elijah declared his son Ebyatar as his successor. David was brought up in Jerusalem and probably studied in the academy. As he left it when only about twenty years old, he could not have attained a scholarly standing there. (His brother Samuel seems to have stayed on and advanced to the dignity of 'Third'.) Ebyatar was no doubt his superior in knowledge. During his early stay in Egypt, while Elijah Gaon was still alive (1078–83), David studied for some time with a Ḥaber Abraham (*loc. cit.*, 460, ll. 2–3).

(2) Before discussing the conflict between Ebyatar and David, let us turn to the period of Elijah's Gaonate (1062–83). About forty years passed since the death of the Gaon Solomon Hakkohen till one of his sons, Elijah, succeeded him. Probably at his death his children were still very young. Elijah's career in the academy has been traced in A. A. 17. 'Sixth' in 1038 and 'Fourth' in 1045, he was 'Third' at Solomon b. Yehudah's death in 1051. From 1053–62 he was Ab, while the Gaonate he occupied for twenty-one years (1083).[2] His Ab was probably

[1] ומרם זה בשלש שנים ירד דוד וכו׳ refers to the meeting at Tyre two years previous to Elijah's death. This removes the difficulty of the dates without altering שלש into שש, as Marx, *J. Q. R.*, N. S., I, 75, does. See also next note.

[2] Ebyatar in his *Megillah* writes that his father was Gaon twenty-three years. But from Elul, 1062 (when Daniel died), till Elijah's demise in Kislev, 1395 Sel.

Ṣadoḳ Hallevi b. Levi (above, p. 161). During the period of the preceding three Geonim, viz. Solomon Hakkohen, Solomon b. Yehuda and Daniel, we hear of several Abot who never attained the dignity of Gaon. These are the son of Joshiah Gaon, Aaron Ab, and the latter's son Joshiah Ab. Whether one of these was the Ab who died in Egypt (above, 142 ff.) is obscure. A nephew of this Ab, undoubtedly Nathan b. Abraham, was his successor and subsequently assumed the title Gaon (1039). The 'Third', who gave up his claim to the dignity of Ab, probably died as such. He was the cousin of Elijah Hakkohen and Joseph Hakkohen. We may safely assume that at Solomon b. Yehuda's death the latter was Ab, his brother Elijah 'Third', and Ṣadoḳ Hallevi 'Fourth'.[1] Joseph Hakkohen never attained the dignity, though styled Gaon for compliment's sake. Though having a prior claim, he was defeated by the Nasi Daniel b. 'Azarya. After Joseph's death (Ḥanukah 1053), his brother Elijah became Ab and Ṣadoḳ Hallevi 'Third'. When in 1062 Elijah at last occupied the presidency of the school, Ṣadoḳ became Ab. The 'Third's' name is not mentioned. The Gaon's son, Ebyatar, was 'Fourth' as he is styled in a letter addressed to him by 'Ali Hakkohen b. Ezekiel (A. C. 25, 1). The epistle was probably written during the Seljūḳ invasion of Palestine, culminating in the capture of Jerusalem in 1071 (see L.-P., 160–1). In this capacity Ebyatar signs behind his father the responsum sent to Meshullam b. Moses of Mayence (see Epstein, *Mtschr.*, XLVII, 343–5, and Pozn., *Babyl. Geon.*, 93, 5, and 136). Epstein cites Bodl. 2667[16], from which a copyist could transcribe for him a few lines only. He was right in suggesting that the fragment contained answers on the other questions, too, besides that about והשיאנו. A few lines excerpted by me from this very damaged fragment are given in A. C. 25, 2. In the course of Elijah's period of office, Ebyatar advanced to the dignity of Ab, his brother Solomon became 'Third', while Ṣadoḳ b. Joshiah Ab

(= October–November, 1083 C. E.), there are really only twenty-one years. Probably Ebyatar included the last two years of Daniel's life, when the latter was constantly ill, while his father was *de facto* head of the school. So also Porges, *J. Q. R.*, XX, 197, note 1.

[1] We are entirely in the dark as to the vicissitudes of Abraham the 'Fourth', Solomon b. Yehuda's son.

was 'Fourth'. Two years before Elijah's death, Ebyatar was declared Gaon, and accordingly Solomon Hakkohen advanced to be Ab and Ṣadoḳ 'Third'.[1]

The family of Joseph Hakkohen, Elijah's brother, was entirely eliminated from holding any office in the academy. He had two sons, Solomon and Yehuda, both of whom emigrated to Egypt. The first composed, in 1077, a poem on the occasion of the Turkoman defeat before Cairo (to be discussed in the next chapter). He was also a member of the Bet-Dīn in Fusṭāṭ.[2] The second son, Yehudah, we have found in Egypt in 1055 (two years after his father's death) occupying the position of ראש הסדר (above, p. 99).

(3) Elijah had three sons, Ebyatar, Solomon, and Ṣadoḳ (above, p. 101). Nothing more is known of the latter's activities. Ebyatar and Solomon were soon after their father's death involved in a severe struggle with David b. Daniel. The following is the account given in the *Megillat Ebyatar*, which naturally represents one side of the picture. About 1078 (as we have seen above, p. 185) David left Palestine for Egypt at the age of about twenty years. He arrived at Damiga (Damira?) without any means and in bad health. There an elder, Maṣliaḥ b. Yefet (b. זובעה), a native of Damascus, befriended him, maintained him for two years (1080) and obtained for him a teacher, Abraham the Ḥaber. David betrothed Maṣliaḥ's daughter, and his father-in-law equipped him with the means of entering Fusṭāṭ in a ceremonious way as befitted a member of the Davidic family.

[1] See the Ḳaddish edited by Schechter (in *Kaufmann-Gedenkbuch*, Hebrew part, 53). The fragment is probably identical with the one having now the class-mark T.-S. 6 H. 6[6], fol. 4[a]. Cp. also Pozn., *l. c.* 94, note 2.

[2] As such he signs among others the marriage document, dated 1082 at Fusṭāṭ, between David b. Daniel and the daughter of the influential Ḳaraite Moses Hakkohen, styled דגל [היה]ודים ומעזם ומשוש תפארתם (*J. Q. R.*, XIII, 220–1). Among the signatories we find [שלמה הכהן ביר׳ יוסף א]ב בית דין של כל ישר׳ נין שלמה גאון זצ״ל and Hodaya b. Joshiah Ab (probably a brother of Sadoḳ b. Joshiah Ab). Likewise a testatum from David's *Bet-Dīn*, dated 1092, is signed by him (*Sa'adyana*, 81, note 2, bottom). T.-S. 13 J 2[4], a document dated 1094 at Fusṭāṭ, is also signed by Solomon Hakkohen b. Joseph Ab. Likewise Or. 5542[2], end of a document, contains his signature. For a document of 1102 see A. C. 28, 1. A son of Solomon was El'azar Hakkohen (see A. A. 17), who is perhaps the signatory of the Ketuba, Bodl. 2873[36].

There the Nagid Meborak and Joshiah Hakkohen b. 'Azarya Gaon were his patrons. David married Maṣliaḥ's daughter, but soon divorced her and was ungrateful to her father, his former benefactor. Joshiah still worked for him and brought about his marriage with 'the daughter of the lord of the time' (בת רוזן הזמן), undoubtedly the influential Ḳaraite Moses b. Aaron mentioned before. This was in 1082. David showed his ingratitude to his cousin and benefactor, Joshiah, by denouncing him publicly and excommunicating him. He also plotted against the Nagid Meborak. By his instigation a certain בן אליביר, a proselyte, denounced the Nagid to the government, and he nearly lost his life. Meborak suffered exile to the Fayyūm, where he stayed a whole year, and to Alexandria. But afterwards 'the lord' (האדון, no doubt the famous Wezīr Badr al-Jamali, 1073–94, the real ruler of Egypt) found out the falseness of the charges against Meborak, who was restored to his dignity of Nagid and to his position of court-physician (either to the Caliph or to Badr).

During Meborak's absence David must have been supreme in the Egyptian Jewry. He had the support of influential Jews, viz. his father-in-law and this בן אליביר. Meanwhile Elijah died in Kislev, 1083, and his successor Ebyatar, as well as the other members of the academy, were soon to feel David's power. Unlike his father, who successfully obtained the Gaonate in Jerusalem, David endeavoured to set up a rival school in Fusṭāṭ, and, by reason of his being a Nasi, to make it supreme also in Palestine. Hence the struggle began whether Palestine was in the first instance to accept the authority of an Exilarch and a school of a country of the diaspora. In *Megillat Ebyatar* we read how David tried to extend his sphere of activity. He acted in a high-handed way in Fusṭāṭ, Alexandria, and Damietta.[1] He also dispatched representatives to Palestine, viz. to that part of the country unoccupied by the Seljūḳs. The coast-cities remained under the sway of the Fāṭimids. Thus the communities of Ashḳelon, Caesarea, Ḥaifa, Bairūt, and Gabal came under David's rule. Everywhere he imposed heavy taxes. But the chief struggle was fought out in Tyre. Owing to the Seljūḳ

[1] אי חנס ואי כפתור are both expressions for Damietta, see A. A. 19; *Megillat Ebyatar* (*J. Q. R.*, XIV, 461, l. 17).

occupation of Jerusalem in 1071, the school seems to have moved to Tyre. Elijah Hakkohen ordained there in 1081 his son Ebyatar as his successor, in the presence of a great assembly of Jews from all over Galilee. In 1083 the Gaon visited Ḥaifa, where he 'sanctified' the year and re-affirmed the settlement of the succession of the Gaonate in favour of his son.

On the arrival of David's representative in Tyre, called אבירם הסוכן בן דתן (being of course a nickname), the new Gaon Ebyatar had to leave the town (*l. c.* 461, l. 20 ff. וידחה את הר הישיבה ממנה; הר is a poetic synonym for ראש). The Ab, Solomon Hakkohen, and his family had to bear the brunt of the struggle. This Abiram was worsted for a time. But in 1093 another representative of David, a certain Hillel b. אלגסום, arrived at Tyre, whereupon the Ab had to flee to the North (*l. c.*, l. 28: וישם פניו אל נחלת השר (r. אָשֵׁר) בחוסר כושר · וקהל נפתלי המתאשר). We find him in Ḥadrak (near Damascus), where he opened a school of his own, as will be seen farther on. There remained in Tyre only the 'Third', i.e. Ṣadoḳ b. Joshiah, who had to continue the opposition against David's claim. The unscrupulous Abiram again visited this city. Evidently he made a tour from one community to another proclaiming anew everywhere David's appointment as Exilarch. He passed Alexandria, Maḥalla, and then proceeded along the coast of Palestine to 'Akko and Tyre. On the eve of the New Year (probably 4854 A. M. = 1093–4) he announced to the congregation of Tyre that certain dignitaries (in Fusṭāṭ) proclaimed David as Exilarch, having authority over Egypt and Palestine. They were the Sheikh Abū Sa'ad (for אלשיק r. אלשיך, for אבן r. אבו) אלווזאק and Abū Naṣr b. שעוב. They must have been influential at the court, though their identification is as yet obscure. Meborak no doubt was opposed to David, but, having for a time been in disgrace, had not yet the power to put a stop to David's new designs. Ṣadoḳ the 'Third' pointed out to the people in Tyre the untenability of the Exilarch's claims. Besides the fact that the people in Palestine were opposed to his appointment, three arguments were put forward by the 'Third'. (1) Fusṭāṭ could not be called גולה (Diaspora). That name applied only to Babylon, where there existed a Rosh Golah. (2) Even the Babylonian Exilarch had no authority over Palestine. (3) The Holy Land was not included under Golah to have a

Rosh Gola. At last the conflict was brought to an end in 1094, when the Nagid Meborak succeeded in deposing his rival David.

(4) The other side of the picture is presented in the interesting fragment (*Saadyana*, XLI, *J. Q. R.*, XIV, 477 ff.) emanating from David b. Daniel.[1] The Nasi writes that since several years he studies daily and has several times gone through the 'four divisions' of the Talmud (ארבעה סדרים; the last two sections קדשים and טהרות were not studied, as their contents had no practical interest). This to meet the charges of his opponents, that he was unfit to be the head of a school. He refers to his troubles and impoverishment. Hatred and strife is rampant in Israel (בקרב עדת איומה, leaf 1, v., l. 8 f.). But David is supported by the Caliph to carry out his designs and keep up the glorious academy which he had established (leaf 2, r., l. 12, בהדרת הישיבה המעולה אשר הצבנוה). 'He that led (the people) astray (i.e. Ebyatar) will experience God's punishment. Let him that lives in Palestine (leaf 2, v., l. 7, אשר ארש לו את נאות יעקב) not boast. Our origin is from King David, and the academy's authority extends to Palestine and Syria. In the times of the early Exilarchs (i. e. David's forefathers) the Palestinian school had no rights over the Jewry of Egypt, since this country is in the same status as Babylon. But when Daniel combined in himself both dignities of Gaon and Nasi, the Egyptian communities accepted his authority. But now the Exilarch (i. e. himself) has again claims on these congregations.' The Palestinian school is therefore putting forward specious demands. Here we have David's point of view. It is also the first clash between the schools of Egypt and Palestine. Previously there were no Geonim in Egypt. The local schools (such as that of Shemarya b. Elḥanan) accepted the authority either of Babylon or of Palestine. When David

[1] I give here the following corrections after having re-examined the fragment: Leaf 1, r., l. 12, for מבריו r. דבריו; l. 13, r. חד[ריו]; l. 15, for הים (?) החקוקים r. חוקים החֹ[ק]וקים; l. 16, r. ודרכיה ד[ר]כי [נוע]ם; leaf 1, v., l. 2, r. הוד והדר וכ[בוד]; l. 5, for נשאל r. נשאר; l. 6 לא (read לנו); l. 9, for עדתנו יומה r. עדת איומה; l. 12 אלמאמייה . . . אלמ[ק]דסה (cp. Goldziher, *J. Q. R.*, XV, 73); leaf 2, r., l. 7, for (?) והוא r. ויי׳ (i. e. God); l. 10, for לין r. תלין; leaf 3, v., between ll. 6–7 one line is omitted, [דעה] והשכל החולה לרפאות והנכשלת לאמץ [והנשברת]; leaf 4, r., l. 5, for חנר ומזח r. חגרו מזח.

writes that before his father Daniel no Palestinian Gaon had any rights in Egypt, the facts, as we know them from the preceding pages, all refute his argument. But now an innovation was started by David. As Exilarch he also placed himself at the head of a school in Fusṭāṭ and endeavoured to make Egyptian Jewry independent of Palestine. The country of the Nile is חוצה לארץ. Jacob and his sons dwelled there, and Moses was born there. Therefore it fully deserves to be the seat of an academy. Here David appealed to local patriotism, and thereby gained some followers. He was, however, deposed in 1094, and the first attempt to establish a Gaonate in Egypt failed. It is characteristic that he is never styled Gaon, but only Nasi. But the way was paved for Maṣliaḥ Hakkohen not long afterwards to preside in Fusṭāṭ over a Yeshiba going by the name 'Geon Ya'ḳob'.[1]

We have read how David claimed authority in Egypt as Exilarch in the Diaspora (חוצה לארץ). In order to make this claim apply also to the coastal cities of Palestine, the argument was advanced that these really did not belong to the 'land of Israel' (ארץ ישראל)! This we learn from the interesting letter given in A. C. 26. There is no doubt that it dates from the time of the conflict between David and Ebyatar. Shelah, the 'Sixth' of the school, b. Nāḥum writes to a certain Ephraim (Abū Kheir) regarding the rumour that reached him that certain people maintained that Ashḳelon was to be regarded as outside Palestine. Shelah mentioned this to the Gaon (i. e. Ebyatar), who gave a scathing refutation. Anybody that read the Book of Judges, he argued, could not have made such a statement. If Ashḳelon was to be excluded from Palestine because Joshu'a did not capture it, but the tribe of Judah later on, by the same argument Jerusalem, first occupied by King David, and likewise several other cities should not be regarded as belonging to Palestine. In conclusion of the long epistle, Shelah writes, 'before he (i. e. David) came to Ashḳelon, we were there'. Also in Ḥaifa the authority of the academy has been accepted. We have here an interesting example of how the followers of David

[1] Nothing more is heard of David, and it is unknown where and how long he lived after his deposal in 1094. He was probably the author of several liturgical compositions (see A. C. 25[a]).

attempted to bring these coastal communities under the authority of an Exilarch that resided in Egypt.

(5) Scanty information is at hand about the activities of Ebyatar and his school. A. C. 26[a] gives us in the first instance the end of a letter, issued from the academy in Tammuz, 1091 C. E., and addressed to a respected scholar Isaac. No doubt the beginning of the epistle contained Ebyatar's signature (just as the following fragment does). Probably it was sent from Tyre, which, however, the Gaon had soon to leave owing to David's persecution. Isaac, the recipient of the letter, is also styled be Rabbanan (= Resh be Rabbanan), no doubt identical with Isaac b. Samuel the Spaniard, a Dayyan in Fusṭāṭ (see A. C. 28). He is appealed to to help the Parnās of the Jerusalem community, 'all that returned to the city of our God', who undertook the risky journey to Egypt in order to obtain success for his fellow-citizens. When the Seljūḳs conquered Jerusalem in 1071, probably most of the Jewish inhabitants fled. Palestine, except the coast-cities, suffered terribly during the invasions and constant warfare lasting for several years. Subsequently a number of Jews returned and endeavoured to rebuild the former settlement. We find thus Ebyatar in 1091 pleading their cause to the Fusṭāṭ Jewry.[1] Greetings are sent in this epistle to a certain Parnās Abū'l-Ridha (?) and to the Ḥazzan Abū'l-Muʿamr.

[1] A document (T.-S. 13 J 5[1]), dated Adar II, 4845 A. M. (= 1085 C. E.) at Fusṭāṭ, tells us of a collection of 20 d. on behalf of the Rabbinite Jews who remained at Jerusalem. Solomon b. Ḥayyim 'the Seventh' (the latter signs a document dated 1053 C. E. at Ramlāh, above, p. 183) makes a declaration that he received from the Parnās ʿAli Hakkohen b. Yaḥya the above sum for the remainder of the Rabbinites in the Holy City, which amount he forwarded to them. This is certified by David Hannasi b. Daniel Gaon, Yakin b. Netaneel, and Joseph b. Samuel. בשמ̇ רח̇ יקול שלמה בן כנק מרנ ור̇ חיים השביעי בחבורה אנקבצ̇ת מן מר̇ ור̇ עלי הכהן הפרנס הנאמן ביר̇ יחיה נ̇ע עשרין דינארא . . . אחאלני בהא עלי אלבאקון מן ישראל אלרבונין פי ירושלם עיר הקדש . . . וקבצ̇תהא וצארת אלי' (= אליהם) ולם יבק לי ענד אלכ̇ץ(??) אחאלו בהא בני ישראל אלרבונין שיא . . . וכתבת כדלך בטי הדא ליכון עלי חגה̇ ללמד̇כורין . . . The signatures are:

יכין בר נתנאל ס̇ט̇ יוסף ביר̇ שמואל

דויד הנשיא בן דניאל הנשיא גאון

The Parnās ʿAli Hakkohen is one of the parties mentioned in a contract, dated 1085 C. E., at Alexandria (Bodl. 2876[11]). He is probably identical with the signatory

states, is mentioned nowhere. He most probably died in Ḥadrak, and was succeeded by his son Maṣliaḥ. A letter dated Adar, 1127, at Ḥadrak, wherein several times 'our lord the Gaon' is referred to (*l. c.* 102, n. 2; the publication mentioned there is inaccessible to me), probably speaks of the local Gaon Maṣliaḥ. But in the same year we find him already in Fusṭāṭ (see *infra*, p. 220 ff.). Very likely conditions were not favourable in Ḥadrak. Certainly the Gaon had more scope in the capital of Egypt. A poem in his honour (printed by Mittwoch, *Hoffmann-Festschrift*, 227–33) may have been composed on the occasion of his arrival at Fusṭāṭ. 'The dawn looked out in the days of our Gaon Maṣliaḥ, Thy light has arrived to shine upon thee, oh daughter of So'an.'[1] With Maṣliaḥ begins the period of the Egyptian Gaonate, which will be dealt with in the next chapter.

The list of the Geonim and the 'Fathers' of the Palestine academy (above, p. 71) can here be concluded as follows. Those 'Fathers' that became subsequently Geonim are marked with an asterisk.

Geonim.	*Abot.*
(1) Solomon b. Yehuda (from *c.* 1025–51).	(1) Aaron b. Joshiah Gaon.
	(2) X. died in Egypt, perhaps identical with no. 1.
	*(3) Nathan b. Abraham (before 1039).
(2) [Nathan b. Abraham (*c.* 1039–42)].	(4) Joshiah b. Aaron Ab.
	(5) Joseph Hakkohen (died 1053).
(3) Daniel b. 'Azarya (1051–62).	*(6) Elijah Hakkohen (1053–62).
(4) Elijah Hakkohen (1062–83).	(7) Ṣadoḳ Hallevi b. Levi.
	*(8) Ebyatar Hakkohen (before 1081).
(5) Ebyatar Hakkohen (1083–*c.* 1105).	*(9) Solomon Hakkohen (1081–93).
	(10) Ṣadoḳ b. Joshiah Ab (*c.* 1094–95).
	(11) Nathan b. Abraham (*c.* 1095–1100).
(6) [Solomon Hakkohen, in Ḥadrak, 1116].	

[1] שחר השגיח · בימי גאוננו מצליח · בא אורך אורי הבת [צוע]ן עדיך לנהור.
For ן[צוע] Mittwoch prints ציון. But in the facsimile only ן is clear, while the

The history of the Palestinian school during the second half of the eleventh century can by no means be called a golden period. In addition to the adverse political and economic circumstances, internal strife and contention there were enough and to spare. We obtain the same picture as the review of the earlier activities of the academy gave us (above, p. 151 f.). We are again impressed by the same paucity of literary production. There remains very little indeed of the venerable halo which we after several centuries should like to perceive around an academy bearing the grand title 'the pride of Jacob'. One would almost regret that the Genizah documents were unearthed from obscurity. But historical truth, it should be reiterated, ceases to be so if the attempt is made to paint the picture in exaggerated light colours. Nor need an apology be made when the dark side is too glaring. The facts have to be stated as they are. We have only another illustration of the well-known truism that, like every other human institution, the school of Palestine fell to a considerable degree short of what in the ideal it ought to have been as the spiritual centre of the Rabbinites in the Holy Land.

(6) Of the vicissitudes of the Jerusalem community since the Seljūḳ occupation (1071) till the capture of the town by the Crusaders (July, 1099) very little is known. We have read above (p. 192) of the collection made at Fusṭāṭ on behalf of the Rabbinites of the Holy City (1085). Moreover, Ebyatar Gaon appealed to the Fusṭāṭ co-religionists to help those residents that returned to their former homes (1091). They sent their Parnes to the capital of Egypt to plead on their behalf. It may be taken for granted that his mission was not in vain. A. C. 31 furnishes us with some information about the conditions a few years later (1094). The leading Rabbi of the congregation seems to have been a certain Baruk b. Isaac. A circular letter from him on behalf of a proselyte 'Obayda is published in Wertheimer's גנזי ירושלם, II. His date can now be fixed by the epistle written in Iyyar, 1094 C. E., which is given in A. C. 31. His correspondent is Joseph b. Samuel, who seems to have taken up a communal position in Egypt. Joseph wrote to Baruk during the previous Adar informing him of his welfare and his successful study of the

rest is faint. Zion is quite inappropriate here, since there were hardly any Jews then in Jerusalem. Supply [צוען] = Fusṭāṭ.

Torah. He requested his friend not to lose himself entirely in communal work, but to have a fixed time for study. Baruk now reassures his friend on this point, and states that his Bet-Hammidrash is not kept closed. Whenever he is busy with communal affairs, his son Joseph acts as his substitute in the house of study. Greetings are sent to Joseph b. Samuel in the name of the whole congregation (of Jerusalem). He must have been known there. Probably he left the Holy City for Egypt to find some scope for his learning, either in Fusṭāṭ or the surrounding places. In this epistle Baruk states that they are at peace, and things are normal. The flood of destruction which was to overwhelm the Palestinian Jewry with the arrival of the Crusaders was not yet in motion. The paiṭanic introduction to the letter in גנזי ירושלם seems, however, to refer already to the warriors of the Cross. Our Baruk evidently managed to leave Jerusalem before it fell into their hands in July, 1099.[1]

It is reported that the Crusaders drove the Jerusalem Jews into a synagogue and set it on fire, so that they perished in the flames.[2] No Jewish report of this terrible event is accessible. Very likely most of the Jews managed to escape before the siege began. But a Ḳaraite source tells us that the head of the sectaries in the Holy City, Solomon Hannasi, won favour in the eyes of Baldwin, the first king of the so-called Latin kingdom of Jerusalem, and succeeded in recovering the holy scrolls that were taken away from them. This is said to have taken place in the summer of 1106 C. E. How much reliance can be placed on this report is difficult to estimate. It is true this report did not pass through the hands of Firkowicz. However he seems to have had an inkling of it, and thus, in his usual way, was not

[1] P. 16b: נבהלו אנשי המדע במנת מדיך · איך נגעלו יושבי הטבור . . .
לותרם (?) (r. למסרם) אל עם לועז שפת לא ידעו תמול שלשום להשמיעם ·
ובתימו ה[נם] לשוסיהם . . . תקפה זרוע גיותנית והאיצה במטאטיה השמד וגירשה
את כל מיחדי שם מכל גבול עפרות קודש בלי לחוננה ולא להתרצות עוד באבניה
עם לועז The reference to · על כן נאנחה בשברון מתנים כי אנשו מכותיה is clearly to the Franks, whose language was entirely unknown to the Jews speaking Arabic.

[2] See Graetz, VI[4], 95. Where Graetz found that both Rabbanites and Ḳaraites were burned to death is inexplicable to me. The sources he cites (note 1) mention only Jews. (For *Bibliothèque des croisades*, IV, 92, read 12.)

sparing in historical fables.[1] But a substance of reality may be the basis of all these accounts. It is likely that the Ḳaraites made representations to the leaders of the Crusaders pointing out to them the antiquity of their sect as dating from centuries before the current era. In this manner they may have impressed the new rulers with the contention that their ancestors had no share in the death of Jesus, and that they should therefore be spared and also permitted to continue to reside in the Holy City. That historical fictions of this kind may have succeeded in their purpose is not beyond possibility.

In conclusion a letter from a Ḥaber in a Syrian city to a Gaon, probably of Jerusalem (A. C. 32), should be considered; beginning and end are missing. It gives us an insight into conditions in the communities of those times. From the defective commencement of the epistle it appears that the Gaon's reply to the writer's letter was lost, together with R. Ṣadoḳ's letter. This

[1] Harkavy prints in *Haṣṣefirah*, 1875, 47–8, the following colophon of a Scroll in the possession of a Ḳaraite: בשם אל רחמן לא נכחד מבנינו אחרינו להיותם מספרים תהילות יוי כמונו אשר נתן את אדונינו שלמה הנשיא לחן ולחסד ולרחמים בעיני האדון באלדואין אשר מלך תחת אחיו ויתן לו את חפצו ויצו לאנשי חילו אחינו בני עשו וישובו לנו את כל ספרי קדשינו וספר התורה הזה עמהם וזה חצי נחמה על כן אנחנו נקהלנו לכניסת רבינו ענן נשיאינו ומברכים את המלך יחי לעולם היום יום ששי צום עשרה באב ראש שנת תתרלז לחרבן שני אתיז לשטרות אמן כן ברחמיו ימהר יחישה מעשהו לנחמנו בקיום הבשורה שבשר כהיום ראש השנה לחרבן הראשון יחזקאל הנביא עה (Ezek. 40. 1 ff.) ושם העיר מיום (r. ביום) יוי ישועה אמן אמן כן יהי רצון במהרה בימינו נצח סלה אמן. There is nothing in the style of this colophon to arouse our suspicion. The 'synagogue of 'Anan' need not have been built by the founder of the sect. But the later Ḳaraite settlers named it after him, just as in Fusṭāṭ the Babylonian synagogue for some time went by the name of Hai, and that of the Palestinians in the name of Daniel b. 'Azarya (see above, pp. 85–6). The Nasi Solomon may have been a son of Hezekiah whom we found in 1062 (above, p. 177). On the other hand, the extract from Firkowicz's diary (given by Harkavy, ibid.) is evidently quite unhistorical. To mention one point only, the Nasi David b. Ḥasdai (b. Hezekiah) is reported to have left the fortress of David together with his son Solomon and the communal leaders in order to greet Geoffrey of Bouillon and his army when Jerusalem fell into their hands (1099). Firkowicz evidently thought that David's father Ḥasdai was then no longer alive, else he would have figured in the procession. We know, however, that he was still alive in 1109 C. E. (above, p. 177). See also the other fictitious accounts of the relations between the Crusaders and the Ḳaraites as given by Deinard (ibid., 112, 247).

R. Ṣadoḳ is perhaps identical with Ṣadoḳ b. Joshiah who is mentioned in *Megillat Ebyatar*. Accordingly the Gaon would be either Elijah Hakkohen or his son Ebyatar. The writer is displeased with the community he is serving. Also he was slandered to the Gaon and his school. Why should he take so much trouble with communal affairs and be so unjustly treated? 'You know', he writes to the Gaon, 'that my townspeople once before slandered me to the late Gaon and you sent me a reprimand. But afterwards my innocence was proved.' Now they slandered him again, after the community confirmed his appointment, and made him bring over his family. 'I am sorry that I did it, for you listen to the informers. Had not my family come such a distance, I should have left and gone to your place or to Egypt.' R. Ṣadoḳ will send the Gaon his full defence and, please God, he may yet personally prove his innocence. The Ḥaber mentions that he already called four times on the governor, who was pleased to receive him. He is leaving the following day for Kalneh (Raḳḳah) to settle there a communal dispute. The local Dayyan died recently, and a certain Babylonian wishes to become his successor. The Ḥaber concludes, that if he leave his own congregation there is sure to break out strife, for he is the peace-maker. Whenever there is a fast, the people plan something to his detriment. Let, therefore, the Gaon inform him whether he should remain in his post or leave and visit him. At least let the Gaon write to his community respectfully about him.

CHAPTER V

Egyptian Affairs from about 1050 C. E. *to the period of Maimonides* (*died in December*, 1204 C. E.).

A PERIOD of more than a century and a half is covered in this chapter. Not that such a large span of time can adequately be comprised in one chapter. But our remarks are chiefly based on new material. They have therefore to be accommodated to the information which the data at our disposal furnish.

I

(1) It is unknown when Sahlān b. Abraham, the spiritual head of the Babylonian section in Fusṭāṭ, died. Nothing is heard of him during the last years of Solomon b. Yehuda. He probably died before the Gaon, though he was still alive when Abū Sa'ad b. Sahl al-Tustari was assassinated in 1048 C. E. (above, p. 82 f.). Ephraim b. Shemarya we found in correspondence with both Daniel b. 'Azarya and Elijah Hakkohen Ab. The veteran Ḥaber probably departed this world about 1060 C. E. His colleague was for some time 'Ali b. 'Amram, who subsequently became the spiritual head of the Palestinian community in Fusṭāṭ. In Tishri, 1057 C. E., we find him signing a document, probably as head of the Bet-Dīn. He is indeed styled 'the superior Ḥaber, the delight of the academy, (and head of) the court established in Fusṭāṭ' (Appendix D=A. D. 1, 2). His father 'Amram is called 'the representative' (השליח), probably of the Palestinian school, on whose behalf he visited various congregations for the purpose of collecting donations for it.

An interesting epistle, coming probably from Alexandria, we have in A. D. 1. The writer's name is not preserved. But very likely he was the local scholar. The object of his letter is to introduce a Jew, Moses b. Joseph the Spaniard, who was the companion of the ambassador of the Sicilian king Ṣamṣām ad-Daula. He arrived at Alexandria (by which אל ארצנו, l. 4, is probably meant) before New Year and stayed on board ship. On the writer's invitation, he was his guest during the festival. Moses is praised as an accomplished scholar, both in Jewish and in secular knowledge; he is in addition pious and modest. Whenever consulted in Bible, Mishnah, Talmud, and secular knowledge, he was ready with competent information. Moses is going to Fusṭāṭ and 'Ali is requested to be hospitable to him in accordance with his standing. He is well-to-do and requires no monetary support.

Here we have a fine type of a cultured Jew. Probably his master, the ambassador, was on a political mission to Cairo. The mention of the king Ṣamṣām fixes also the date of our epistle. Affairs in Sicily were then chaotic. In 1035 there commenced a civil war which was the beginning of the end of Muslim rule in that country. The heavy taxes which the Amīr Aḥmad imposed upon the population drove the natives to arms (cp. also the letter from Sicily to Joshiah Gaon, above, p. 73). The ruler appealed to Byzantium for help against the rebels, who were led by his brother. The Zīrīdes were called in to the latter's assistance. After several years of internecine strife both Byzantines and Zīrīdes had to leave the isle (1042). The country was left to settle its affairs alone without foreign interference. A brother of the Amīr Aḥmad was called out as ruler, who assumed the pompous title Ṣamṣām ad-Daula, 'sword of the realm'. But the sword was blunt. During the civil war individual minor magnates and also municipalities learned how to look after their own interests by themselves. The country thus emerged no longer as an undivided state, but as a conglomerate of petty principalities and civic authorities. The homage they rendered to the new Amīr was only formal. Ultimately the Palermians expelled Ṣamṣām and declared a republic. The constant feuds between the opposing parties resulted in the defeated leader of the Arabs, Ibn Thimma, calling in the Normans in 1061. With their coming Sicily was lost for ever to the Muslims.[1]

Our letter probably dates from before 1061. When Ṣamṣām was driven out from Palermo he probably appealed to the court of Cairo for help. We find, therefore, his ambassador landing at

[1] See Müller, *Der Islam im Morgen- u. Abendland*, II, 625–6.

Alexandria and proceeding to Cairo in the company of a learned Jew of Spanish origin. How the Jews of Sicily fared during these upheavals is unknown. Altogether the history of this Jewry during our period is very obscure. We have seen above (p. 73) that they had relations with the Palestinian Geonim. Maṣliaḥ b. al-Baṣaḳ, a Dayyan of Sicily, visited Bagdād and came into personal contact with Hai Gaon (see Steinschneider, *Arab. Lit.*, § 85). A letter from the community of Sicily (i. e. Palermo) to Elḥanan b. Ḥushiel of Ḳairowān, probably written between 1030–35, has been published by me (*J. Q. R.*, N. S., IX, 162 ff.). Very likely during the civil war the Sicilian Jews were anxious for the country to remain under Muslim rule.[1] They must have dreaded the establishment of an intolerant Christian power. It may be that Moses accompanied Ṣamṣām's ambassador to Cairo with the special purpose of inducing the influential Jews of the capital to see to it that help be given to the new Amīr to consolidate his rule.

(2) How long 'Ali remained Ḥaber in Fusṭāṭ is not reported. The leading scholar of the Babylonian congregation after Sahlān b. Abraham seems to have been Nahrai b. Nissim. In A. D. 3 data are collected concerning him and his son Nissim. But first A. D. 2 is to be discussed. It is an epistle from Yeshu'a Hakkohen the Ḥaber b. Joseph '(head of the) Bet-Dīn'. He is no doubt identical with the Alexandrian Ḥaber whom we have found above (p. 88 ff.) writing in 1028 to Fusṭāṭ concerning the ransom of Byzantine captive Jews brought into the port by Saracen pirates. This letter also deals with the same topic. But no longer is the noble benefactor Netaneel Hakkohen b. El'azar mentioned. Probably he was then no longer alive. Conditions in the Alexandrian community seem to have been critical. A year of poverty, dearth, and distress, due also to heavy impositions, closed with the arrival of three captives who were

[1] Two centuries later the Sicilian Jews still spoke Arabic. This we learn from the statement of Abraham Abulufia in his אוצר עדן גנוז (Bodl. 1580, cited by Neubauer, *R. É. J.*, IX, 149): ואמנם הפלא הגדול הוא מה שקרה ליהודים בכל איסקיליאה שהם אינם מדברים בלשון לעז ובלשון יון לבד כלשונות הלועזים והיונים שדרים עמהם אבל שמרו לשון ערבי שלמדוהו מימים קדמונים בעת היות הישמעאלים דרים שם.

taken off a boat plundered by Byzantine soldiers. These Jews were despoiled of all they possessed and were nearly killed. Evidently Arabs ('the king's merchants', l. 18) ransomed them and brought them to their co-religionists, demanding compensation for their outlay. The Alexandrian Jews kept these unfortunate Jews for a month, and, owing to their poverty, could only collect 10 d. whereas 50 d. were required for their freedom. It appears that the Arabs, out of consideration, did not charge the usual rate of 33⅓ d. per captive, but only as much as they paid for these Jews. Nahrai is requested to obtain the missing 40 d. from the Fusṭāṭ co-religionists.

Another epistle from the same Yeshuʿa b. Joseph to Nahrai has been preserved (given in A. D. 2[a]). It shows us that Nahrai was recognized as a scholar. Yet when this epistle was written he must have still been young. His correspondent thus wishes him to become 'the Parnās of his generation and its guide'. Nahrai wrote to Yeshuʿa concerning a legal question that had been sent apparently from Alexandria to Fusṭāṭ. The latter replies that the text of the question, as cited by Nahrai, is not his but that of the Ḥaber (probably Yeshuʿa's colleague in Alexandria). He thereupon discusses the decision of the case in question as given by a certain scholar ('our lord the Rabbi', recto, l. 11 ff.). Nahrai is requested to refer again the case to him (v., l. 12 ff.). This Rabbi was evidently the chief authority in Cairo-Fusṭāṭ, whose decision would be accepted by the Ḥabrim and the Bet-Dīn in Alexandria. Perhaps Elḥanan b. Shemarya, who was Rosh Hasseder in the capital, is meant. The lawsuit concerned a widow whose husband died without issue. The eldest brother, upon whom the duty of marrying her devolved, had already a wife and children, while there were other brothers still bachelors. The widow now refuses to become the second wife of the eldest brother. The Bet-Dīn considered the matter, and in the synagogue both parties undertook to abide by the court's decision. Abraham b. Peraḥ and other four elders were delegated by the court to negotiate with the widow. They pointed out to her the duty of marrying the eldest brother of her husband. But she absolutely refused and threatened to commit acts of impropriety if she be forced to become a rival to another woman. She demanded that one of the other brothers who were single should fulfil the duty of levirate. On the other hand, the eldest brother took an oath not to release her by Ḥaliṣah. In this way the court was defied. Yeshuʿa complains about the loss of prestige of the Bet-Dīn, and states that several people in the community, who pretend to know the laws, incite the parties not to yield. The Rabbi in Fusṭāṭ is now requested to give his decision as to who should be compelled in this case to give way. Here we have a typical example of internal conditions in the communities. It illustrates how necessary was R. Gershon's Ḥerem abolishing the levirate altogether. In conclusion, Yeshuʿa promises Nahrai to send him pens made from reeds that grow by the Lake Maryūṭ (near Alexandria). This proves beyond doubt that the writer lived in Alexandria, and that the address of the epistle, as reconstrued by us in A. D. 2[a], is correct.

Nahrai and his son Nissim are mentioned in the Memorial List emanating from the Babylonian community (see A. B. 20, II). Nahrai is styled 'the great Rabbi, the great one of the Yeshiba'. He evidently was a scholar of renown. His signature is found on a document dated 1050 C. E. at Fusṭāṭ (A. D. 3, 1). Among the other signatories we find Yehuda b. Saʿadya the physician, who subsequently became Nagid, as will be shown presently. Probably R. Nahrai, who heads the first communal list (A. D. 3, 2), is identical with our scholar. The two lists (given there) contain several names which show how the Fusṭāṭ Jewry were recruited from districts far and wide. Bagdād, Damascus, Byzantium, ʿOkbara, ʿAkko, Giscala, France, Tyre, Andalusia, Aleppo, and others—these are the places of provenance of the local Jews. Nahrai was no longer alive in 1098 C. E. when his son Nissim signed a document at Fusṭāṭ, together with two other Dayyanim, Isaac b. Samuel the Spaniard and Abraham b. Shemaʿya the Ḥaber (both are dealt with in A. C. 28). It seems that Nissim was the chief Dayyan (probably residing at Cairo). He was no longer alive in 1147. His grandfather Nissim (I) seems to have been a native of Jerusalem (A. D. 3, 3). An exceptionally large number of letters to and from Nahrai and his son Nissim, nearly all in Jewish Arabic, are preserved among the Genizah finds. They fully deserve publication, as they throw light on contemporary conditions both in Egypt and elsewhere. A monograph on Nahrai b. Nissim and his connexions would be an historical contribution of value.

(3) The general affairs in the country of the Nile during the reigns of the Caliphs al-Mustanṣīr (1036–94), al-Musta'li (1094–1101), and al-Amīr (1101–31) are concisely narrated by Lane-Poole (*l. c.*, 136–57, 161–8). The first Caliph was a weak ruler. After a change of wezīrs, al-Yazūri was chief minister of the state for eight years (1050–58). During this time the Fāṭimid dominion was reduced to little more than Egypt itself. After Yazūri wezīrs came and went incessantly. In 1062 disorders broke out between the Turkish troops and the Sūdānī battalions, the favourites of the black Queen-mother. From 1066 to 1072 a great famine raged in Fusṭāṭ and in the whole country. Things were chaotic till the arrival in 1074 of the Armenian Badr al-Jamali, governor of 'Akko. Appointed commander-in-chief, he *de facto* was ruler of the country. Combining firmness with justice, he restored order in the land of the Nile. The last twenty years of Mustanṣīr's reign saw peace and plenty. But in Syria there was constant warfare with the Seljūḳs. When Badr died at the age of eighty, he was succeeded by his son Abū'l-Kāsim Shahanshah, better known by his title al-Afḍal, who wielded absolute power in the realm till his death in 1121. These two great Armenians were indeed from 1074 to 1121, in all but name, the sovereigns of Egypt, and to their mild and just rule, as much as to their energy and firm control, the country owed half a century of internal quiet and prosperity (L.-P., 162).

Several Jews held high office under these great Wezīrs, and, as a whole, Egyptian Jewry benefited by their auspicious rule. In the first instance we have to mention three Negidim who were the political heads of this Jewry during this period, viz. Yehuda b. Sa'adya, his famous brother Meborak, and the latter's son Moses. A. D. 4–8 contain our data concerning these Negidim. As shown in A. D. 4, 4, Yehudah probably became Nagid about 1065 (cp. also *infra*, p. 254 f.). Following his father's profession, he was a highly placed physician, very likely in attendance to the Caliph himself. When Badr became the most powerful person in Egypt (in 1074), Yehuda retained his dignity of Nagid and seems to have enjoyed the confidence of the Wezīr. This we learn from a poem composed in 1077 by Solomon Hakkohen

b. Joseph Ab (see above, p. 187) on the occasion of the Turkoman defeat before Cairo.[1] The editor did not fully grasp who the exalted persons eulogized in the poem were. Firstly, the Caliph al-Mustanṣīr is mentioned (p. 18, l. 5 ff.), then the commander-in-chief[2] the victor over the Turkomans. The poet continues (l. 18 ff.), 'May our God set him on high and for ever strengthen him (Badr), his servants and all his attendants . . . and at their head (i. e. the first of the Wezīr's subordinates) the glorious and honoured elder in unison with (בסיומים, in completion of, in supplement to) the faithful friend, like twin brothers'. Now Greenstone (in his translation and notes) makes these two persons, the 'elder' and the 'faithful friend' to have been the Caliph and his Wezīr. But these have already been referred to before (ll. 10–11 וגם עבדיו (i.e. Mustanṣīr's) האוהבים . . . ובראשם קצין צבאות). Accordingly in ll. 19–20 ושמשיו וכל עבדיו . . . ובראשם זקן ההוד, Badr's subordinates are meant. First among them is the 'glorious and respected' elder to whom evidently our poem is dedicated. 'May it please you, our lord, the choice of the people which is the head of all the nations (i.e. Israel!), Accept as a gift and repose many blessings and much peace, And give (you) thanks (קידה, 'bowing') from your soul (יחידה is a usual poetic synonym for נפש, see A. B. 9, note 8) in well-couched language (ברוב חידה והגיונים) to God who helped, preserved . . . and made rejoice the children of the living God (i.e. the Jews) who fasted, gave charity, and prayed for weeks by day and by night' (l. 23 ff.; ll. 23, 25 are incorrectly translated by Greenstone). There is little doubt that by זקן ההוד the Nagid is meant. To him, as a Jew understanding Hebrew, the poem is dedicated. Yehuda, as court-physician, was Badr's subordinate but highly respected together with 'the beloved friend (i. e. the poet's friend) like *twin brothers*'. Here clearly the Nagid's brother Meborak is meant. He no doubt was then already an influential doctor in the court. In 1080 we find him already installed as Nagid in succession to his brother (above, p. 187 f.). The author of the poem is no doubt Solomon Hakkohen b. Joseph (the brother of Elijah Gaon).[3]

[1] Published by Greenstone in *American Journal of Semitic Languages and Literatures*, Jan., 1906. It is cited here according to the pages of the reprint.

[2] קצין צבאות, l. 11 = Amir al-Juyūsh, see Ibn Khallikān's *Biographical Dictionary*, trans. De Slane, I, 612.

[3] Cp. also Pozn., *Babylon. Geon.*, 92. Solomon styles himself בן יהוסף נין

We have described above how Meborak, on the instigation of ıvid b. Daniel, fell in disgrace for some time and was banished Fayyūm and Alexandria. But he soon regained his office, d in 1094, the year of Badr's death, succeeded in deposing his emy David. Under al-Afḍal he was a great favourite in the ırt, as we learn from an important Genizah fragment (*J. Q. R.*, ., 29–36), to be discussed presently. He is greatly eulogized in epistles sent to him. He seems to have also been a scholar repute. He is styled אלוף הבינות, Ṛosh Hasseder 'the scholar the academy' (חכם הישיבה) and סנהדרא רבא (i.e. holding a diploma Ḥaber). These titles were probably bestowed upon him by Palestinian school. His brother Yehuda was styled Resh ıllah (=Alluf), which was a Babylonian title. It is quite likely ıt he was thus honoured either by Hai Gaon and Hezekiah Exilarch of Bagdād, or by the Sura Geonim Israel Hakkohen d 'Azarya. Meborak's first title אלוף הבינות may also have ginated from Babylon. This Nagid is also flatteringly addressed 'second to the king' (of Egypt, i.e. al-Afḍal, who assumed the me of 'al-Malik al-Afḍal, 'the excellent prince', see Ibn-ıallikan, *l. c.*, I, 612 ff.).

Before describing the events after Meborak's death, A. D. 5–7[a], ıich bear on him as well as on his brother Yehuda, should be cussed here. The first fragment contains the minutes of the ıṣṭāṭ Bet-Dīn, dated Kislev, 1355 Sel. = 1043, concerning a libel se. The name of Yehuda b. Sa'adya (both father and son ysicians) occurs therein as one of the witnesses. The interest the fragment lies in the sidelight it throws on the social life of community. Joseph b. Peraḥya is libelled by his kinsman byān b. Sa'adya as being a descendant of slaves. He forthwith ıds his garments (as a mourner) and takes an oath not to rtake of food till justice be done for him. The court thus has expedite the matter since this man is afflicting his soul by ıtinual fasting. The offender Ṣabyān is excommunicated and sentenced to spend three days at his house, from Friday to nday, in the status of a mourner. He had also to ask the intiff for pardon. After having complied with his sentence,

נאו. His father was usually called יוסף, but יהוסף is written here for metre's e (but see also A. A. 17).

Ṣabyān is freed from the ban and a prayer is recited for him the Bet-Dīn.

In A. D. 6, 1 we have a fragment of a letter of greetings eith to Meborak or to his brother Yehuda Nagid. The writer Ṣadaḳa, the Ḥaber who holds the title יסוד הישיבה. A. D. 6, 2 an epistle to 'Alvan, the Parnes, b. Ḥiyya (probably in Fusṭā A certain Shemarya b. Meshullam, who caused strife against t writer, is about to visit Egypt (Fusṭāṭ). Let the Parnes rememl this person's disgraceful behaviour and pay him back according. Let also Yehuda Resh Kallah and his brother the Alluf informed what type of man this Meshullam is. Yehuda is r yet called Nagid. But he was already the holder of the tit Resh Kalla and המעולה בחבורה. The first one was no dou bestowed by the Babylonian school, and the second by t Gaon of Palestine. The same also applies to his brother Mebor who is called Alluf הבינות and המעולה בחבורה. Both academ honoured these two learned and influential brothers who were hold the chief political position in the community. A. D. 7 a letter from a certain Joseph to Joseph b. Joshiah.[1] The wri was promised a donation from the latter, who has, however, n changed his mind. The Nagid and Resh-Kallah, as well as brother, the Ḥaber (i.e. Yehuda and Meborak), are reported have been surprised at this act. The writer evidently lived Cairo-Fusṭāṭ, but the place of residence of his correspondent not indicated.

Finally, A. D. 7[a] contains an elegy, composed by Ṣadaḳaḥ Yehuda (very likely identical with the writer of A. D. 6, 1), the death of Meborak's wife. The lady is eulogized as assuagi the king's wrath by her wisdom (l. 9). Probably she gave husband wise counsel when during his official career he met w disfavour from his superiors. It may also be that when Mebor fell in disgrace and was banished for some time, his wife succeed in restoring him to his office. In the poem condolences offered to the Nagid and to his two sons, Moses and Netaneel.

(4) After Meborak's death dangerous times began for t

[1] The latter is also referred to as Joseph אבן דהבי (l. 17). He is proba identical with the person mentioned in an inventory, dated 1091 Sel. (1080 C. E.) Fusṭāṭ (*J. Q. R.*, XX, 459, ll. 21–2): חף תורה לטיף הקדישתו בנת יוסף אל דהבי.

Egyptian Jewry through a Christian official who became al-Afḍal's favourite. This we learn from an important letter, unfortunately defective at the end, to the congregation of Constantinople (printed by Neubauer, *J. Q. R.*, IX, 29–36). The historical part of the epistle (pp. 35–6) has been discussed and translated by Kaufmann (*Z. D. M. G.*, LI, 444–7), who, however, failed rightly to elucidate two important details. The writer was formerly the chief steward of al-Afḍal's estates and possessions. Though slandered several times, he retained his master's confidence. At last his enemies succeeded; he was heavily fined and lost the whole of his fortune. Yet he remained in the Wezīr's employ, probably in a minor capacity. In this letter al-Afḍal is styled 'the king' (המלך). This is exact, because he bore the title 'al-Malik al-Afḍal', the excellent prince (above, p. 209). The writer continues to relate how subsequently a Christian, *Yuḥanna*,[1] the brother of the Patriarch (?), became the Wezīr's favourite. The year before he was the companion of the ambassador that was sent from Egypt to Constantinople. Having attained such great influence with al-Afḍal, Yuḥanna set about to remove all the Jews who held government offices. As long as Meborak lived he managed to counteract Yuḥanna's endeavours, since al-Afḍal held the Nagid in great honour. But when he died the enemies of the Jews could have the upper hand. The Egyptian Jewry began to experience grievous oppression. Four prominent Jews tried by a stratagem to do away with Yuḥanna. A letter of his, of harmless contents, was altered in such a way as to be a treasonable epistle to the *Franks*[2] in Palestine and in Jerusalem.

[1] איש ערל והנא אחי נוּפַּטְרִיאַרְכִי. Kaufmann suggests to alter the overlined word into either והוא or יהנא = John. But the Arabic form no doubt was יוחנא, and, as is shown in the text, a very probable identification of this official is suggested.

[2] For האפרגין in the MS., Kaufmann suggests האפרכין 'governors', and thereby he is misled to assume that the epistle was written in 1098–9, before Jerusalem fell into the hands of the Crusaders. But there is no doubt that the correct reading should be האפרנגין (افرنجين), Franks! Thus the accusation against the Christian official, which should prove to be his undoing, becomes evident. By the by, the phrase ושמו כי הוא כתבהו (*J. Q. R.*, *l. c.*, 36, l. 22), 'and they put (into it, i. e. altered it) that he wrote it to the Franks', &c., Kaufmann translated (*Z. D. M. G.*, *l. c.*, 447, top), 'Es war ihnen zu Ohren gekommen' (*sic*), as if the text read ושמעו!

The Christian official was thereby accused of having entered into dangerous relations with the enemies of the state he was serving. The forged letter was cast into the house of the Ḳaḍi at Damietta. Here our fragment breaks off. We have here a picture of the unscrupulous tactics employed in the struggle between the two factions of state officials and other dignitaries. Both the Christians and the Jews belonged to ' the people of tribute ' and were legally only tolerated by the ruling religion. Yet their common interest did not refrain them from waging bitter war against each other.

Under al-Afḍal we hear of the Christian officials Abū'l Faḍl ibn al-Uskuf, the Wezīr's Katib, and Abu'l Yāman Wazīr, head (' metwali ') of the Diwān of the Delta. But his favourite, mentioned before, is very likely identical with the Katib Abū Barakāt *Yuḥanna* ibn Abū'l Laith who was head of the treasury (metwali of the Diwān at-taḥḳīḳ, the board which regulated the expenses of the government). We find him in office already in 501 A. H. (1107–8). A church in Alexandria was restored by him and his brother Abū'l Faḍail. Yuḥanna survived his master for thirteen years, holding his high rank the whole time. In 1134 C. E. he was put to death.[1] The embassy to Constantinople very likely dates from 1104 to 1107, when the famous Crusader Prince Bohemund of Antioch, assembled in Italy an army with the intention of leading it against the Byzantine Emperor Alexius. Probably al-Afḍal made then a diplomatic move to conclude an alliance with Alexius against the growing power of the Crusaders in Syria and in Palestine. For this purpose he employed his favourite Katib Yuḥanna, the Christian.

How long this struggle between Yuḥanna and the Jewish officials lasted is unknown. Nor do we hear of its sequel. But another enemy of Egyptian Jewry is introduced in A. D. 8 and 9. His name was שיפ׳. But his identity I could not trace with certainty. A. D. 8 is an interesting letter from Abraham b. Sabbatai, the Ḥaber of Minyat Zifta, to the Nagid Moses, the son of Meborak Nagid, congratulating him after שיפ׳ has been overthrown. God is praised for having brought down ' an imperious and evil king from his throne ' (l. 3) who intended to

---

[1] See Abū Saliḥ, *Churches and Monasteries of Egypt*, tr. Evetts, pp. 115, 137, 150-1, 197 ; cp. especially p. 150, note 2.

[2] See Kugler, *Geschichte der Kreuzzüge*, 84 ff.

.o away 'with every respected man and elder, to rob, spoil, and ake vengeance'. But God did not grant his desire and baulked the plan of שיפין the wicked who crushed and scattered many. 3ut the Lord God crushed and pounded him', and all his followers eft him. 'For he lifted up his hand against the king; therefore God handed him over into the hand of his master.' Abraham vrites that he and his whole congregation praise God for the miracles' done to the Nagid and to Israel by the sudden verthrow of this foe, who is compared to Haman and whose fate .e met. Evidently this person was a high state dignitary, robably chief Wezīr (hence he is called king, malik = מלך, l. 3). 3ut his master, the Caliph, is the real king (l. 10). This שיפין eems to have started a rebellion and led an army (l. 9), who, owever, deserted him when the issue was fought out. Moses robably became Nagid as successor to his father Meborak about 1110). In 1141 we find already Samuel b. Ḥananya as he head of the Egyptian Jewry. The event, described here, ook place between 1110–40. Perhaps the Wezīr Ibn al-Baṭaïḥi s meant here who succeeded al-Afḍal in 1121 (see Wüst., III, 5 ff.). In a few years he made himself generally hated. A plan f his to assassinate the Caliph and put his brother on the throne vas discovered in 1125 and he was thrown into prison together vith his brother and thirty other persons of their entourage. n 1127 al-Baṭaïḥi and his five brothers were executed.

The same episode forms the subject of A. D. 9, containing oems in honour of Yakin b. Netaneel, who held the dignity of ראש הקהלו, 'head of the congregations' (probably of Cairo-Fusṭāṭ). He seems to have taken an active part in exposing the reachery of this 'Haman'. We find him signing a document, lated 1085, at Fusṭāṭ, together with the Nasi David b. Daniel see above, p. 192, note 1).[1] Whether Yakin was then already

[1] T.-S. 13 J 18^{17} contains also a letter, with a long introduction, to לכבוד (9) גדולת קדושת [השר ה]נכבד האדיר המיוקר יכין ראש הקהילות (10) [העושה כמה חסדים וכמה טובות החכם והנבון . . . (12) . . . ויחיה חמודיו השרי חנכבדים. . . Yakin's sons are also referred to in the poems. Bodl. 2873^{11} seems o be a poem in honour of Yakin. The author was in great distress: ונהפכו (l. 26) רננותי יגונות || ושמחותי לתוגותי תמורים | ברב יכין יסודן התלאות || והצרות אש המה זכורים (31) אשר שם (sc. God) לו תבונה בנבונים || וגם דעת במשכילי ומורים | שבחיו הם בפי הכל סדורים || נכונים כעשרת הדברים (34) ועתה הו

'president of the congregations' (a dignity different from that of Nagid, the head of the whole Jewry of Egypt and Palestine) is not indicated. But when this conflict with שיפין took place, he seems to have been a highly influential person in the court. Israel is asked to praise God 'who beheld from His dwelling the indignity of His poor, and destroyed His opposer in His anger and wrath'. The enemy 'rose up like the Agagite (Haman) to destroy' Israel ('God's memorial'). 'He played the traitor to his master who made him a prince.' But 'his Creator destroyed him together with his brother (or brothers) and his son'. 'My king in his palace, on hearing the noise of his uproar was zealous for the zealous God in order to bring low his nest from on high, put his trust in the might of God who had established him and revealed his secret to our faithful Yakin. Waiting for his day of calamity, he (Yakin) did with him as he liked. He caught him in his sin, evil, and arrogance. If he arose like Haman, behold Mordecai is here, viz. Yakin the strength of my head, the right-hand pillar' (Poem II).

Poem III tells us more about this Jew-hater's orders while still in power. God be praised for having 'rescued the scattered sheep (i.e. Israel) from a lion's mouth. Hear, over whom did not his evil pass. His decree was issued about the tombs of the dead, to pull down every monument and sepulchre, the bier to be taken out before daybreak. As for the living, to take away all their fortune with wrath, and to rob all their money so that there remain no coin. He also forbade the (ritual) slaughtering of meat for the storm-tossed nation (i.e. Israel). Said he, Your slaughtering is repugnant to us. . . . Blessed be God who cast him in the pit he dug, and blessed be He who, from the height of the pellucid sky, made the heart of the king of all the children of Hagar and Ḳeṭurah be inclined favourably to the glorious head of the congregations', Yakin b. Netaneel. The king clothed him in honourable garments, which he was to wear on festivals and days of celebration. Likewise his wife received expensive

כמו שר באמונים || ועל ראשם ככותרת פארים | לכן נקרא [ב]ראש המקהלות || קראוהו גאוני עם ושרים. (The double strokes indicate the hemistichs. The metre is — — ∪ — — — ∪ — — — ∪). T.-S. 12. 57 contains a fragment of a letter to מרנא ורבנא יכין השר הנכבד ראש הקהלות.

robes. Yakin also received from the king the palace which his foe built for himself by the Nile. In Poem IV Yakin is further eulogized as the saviour appointed by God. 'For when the foe arose, you too arose like Mordecai. If he was like a bereaved bear, you acted as a lion.' Yakin's two sons are mentioned by name, Mebasser and Netaneel. It is clear that the chief merit in ridding Egyptian Jewry of a vindictive enemy was due to Yakin. The Nagid Moses undoubtedly had a share. But the former may have been more capable and active.

(5) The Nagid Moses and Yakin were not the only Jews of influence in the court of Cairo. A great Jewish official under al-Afḍal was Abū'l Munajja b. Sha'ya, who was head of the Board of Agriculture. He gained fame through the digging of a Nile Canal, which was opened, after many years of work, in 1112. By thus extending the irrigation of the Delta-region he did a great service to the agriculture of this district. When the Canal was opened, al-Afḍal called it officially by his own name. But the people persisted in speaking of it as Bahr Abū'l Munajja. It is regarded as his last official work. On account of the great sums spent on this Canal, the Wezīr brought him to Alexandria and threw him into prison. After some years of suffering, Abū'l Munajja obtained his freedom by a bold act. He succeeded in writing in prison a Ḳurān, which he concluded with the colophon 'written by the Jew Abū'l Munajja', and sent to the market of Alexandria. This caused a scandal. When brought to trial before the Caliph, the ex-official declared that he did it in order to be released from prison by sure death.[1] Kalḳashandi[2] also relates the digging of the Canal by Abū'l Munajja (the administrator of the Eastern Delta-districts), and only adds that al-Afḍal, resenting the calling of the Canal after his subordinate, persecuted him and banished him to Alexandria. No more is known about the vicissitudes of this high state dignitary.

A. D. 10 contains poems in honour of the 'renowned Sheikh' Abū'l Munajja, who bore the title 'the exalted one of the state'

[1] See Goldziher, *J. Q. R.*, XV, 74, according to Ibn Duḳmaḳ, *Description de l'Égypte*.

[2] In his *Geographie u. Verwaltung von Ägypten*, tr. Wüstenfeld in *Abhandlungen der Göttinger Gesellschaft der Wissenschaften*, vol. 25, pp. 27–8.

(סני אלדולה). There is little doubt that the above official (b. Sha'ya) is eulogized in these poems. We learn from them that, sharing the fate of every Jew in exalted position, he had to experience slander and intrigues directed against him. Poem I is written after a victory Abū'l Munajja obtained over his enemies in the Caliph's Diwān. He is greatly eulogized and is styled 'the greatest dignitary of Israel' (שר שרי ישורון). Usually the Nagid held this title of שר השרים, and the holder of this dignity was then Moses b. Meborak. But here Abū'l Munajja is styled thus by compliment. He is the protector of Israel, 'the glory of Jacob and the pride of Yeshurun'. In his wisdom he is like Solomon (whose namesake he was), and by his excellence of speech he overcame all his enemies in argument in the presence of the king. And 'Thy king said, This is the truth, he exalted thee above them all and appointed thee'.

There is a gap between the leaves. From the change of metre we see that leaf 2 contains another poem (II), which is defective at the beginning since the superscription is missing. The occasion of the poem is thus not indicated. But it appears that the hero received a new honour from the Caliph, and a dress appertaining to the dignity was sent to him. The author addresses him, 'You are Solomon, the grandson of Jesse'. His Jewish name was Solomon, and perhaps his descent was reputed to be from David. From the eulogies bestowed upon him we learn that in his high position Abū'l Munajja was a tower of strength to his people and was distinguished by his charitable acts. 'Ṣo'an greatly rejoiced, . . . because the light of her sun truly shone. May God be his help and may he remain the lord of all that subsists in the world which through him is at ease.' The title of שר יקום תבל or שר כל היקום is probably a poetical expression for Abū'l Munajja's office of administrator of the eastern Delta-province. The poet concludes 'The song which I have composed for the lord of the whole existence, and which has been sent to Egypt (i. e. Fusṭāṭ)'. It is entirely unknown who the writer of the poems was. Of Poem III only the first two lines remain. Abū'l Munajja lost a child and the author consoled him.

No. IV contains an epistle, with a poetic introduction, to our dignitary. The style of the poem suggests that the writer was also the author of the preceding poems. We learn therefrom that Abū'l Munajja's Hebrew name was Solomon, and that his titles were 'the exalted one of the state and its trusted one'[1] (ll. 26–7). He did a great favour to the writer, saving his life thereby (l. 21). He is again requested to help him and deliver him from a certain eunuch and his retinue (l. 22). In conclusion, the writer wishes his patron every honour and success in his official capacity. We have read before how he was thrown into prison by al-Afḍal and how he succeeded in regaining his liberty. It may be that after the assassination of his enemy in 1121, Abū'l Munajja again entered the service of the state and also held a high position in the Jewish community. A document, dated 1450 Sel. (1139 C. E.) and drawn up at Fusṭāṭ, states that the Bet-Dīn is under the authority of 'our lord and leader of our generation . . . Solomon, the exalted dignitary, great in Israel and Judah'.[2] One is inclined to identify this Solomon with Abū'l Munajja b. Sha'ya. But nothing definite can as yet be stated. It is also possible that a different official is meant, viz. the chief Dayyan of Egypt, the so-called Dayyan al-Yahūd, as will be shown in the next chapter.

(6) Another prominent Jew in Cairo-Fusṭāṭ during al-Afḍal's period (1094–1121) was Joshu'a b. Dosa, who apparently presided over a school. In A. D. 11 we have discussed the data about him. He is probably identical with the great dignitary and scholar whom Yehuda Hallevi eulogized in a poem composed during his stay in Egypt while on his way to Palestine. Joshu'a was then in disgrace and imprisoned. He probably came into prominence during the last years of al-Afḍal and continued to hold an important position in the community till about 1145. A document, dated 1143–4 at Fusṭāṭ, mentions the Bet-Dīn as under his authority, which was probably granted to him by the

[1] סני אלדולה ואמינהא. In a book-list, dated Oct. 1244 (*Z. f. H. B.*, XII, 123, bottom), there is mentioned a person Amīn ad-Daulah Abū . . . . His identity cannot be ascertained. Cp. also *infra*, p. 227, note 1.

[2] T.-S. 13 J 2[14] (cp. also 13 J 8[2]) begins: מעשה שהיה לפנינו אנו בתי דינים הממונים מבית דין הגדול של שרנו ומנ[היג] דורנו כבוד גדולת קדושת מרנו ורבנו שלמה השר הנעלה הגדול בישראל ויהודה. Bodl. 2876[28] contains a letter, apparently dated Marḥeshwan, 1462 Sel. = 1150 C. E., to Zakkai the Dayyan and the great dignitary Solomon. Perhaps the same person is meant.

well-known Nagid Samuel b. Ḥananya. From the data collected in A. D. 17, 3 we learn that Samuel was already in office in 1142. We find that though the Nagid was the chief political representative of the Egyptian Jewry, and as such is mentioned in the documents, other prominent scholars and readers were also granted the privilege of having their names inserted in the deeds issued by the courts over which they had authority. In the first half of the twelfth century we have Maṣliaḥ, the Gaon of Egypt (1027–38), Solomon (1139), and Joshuʿa b. Dosa in 1143–4 referred to in the documents of the Bet-Dīn, though other people occupied the dignity of Nagid. This point will be discussed more fully in the next chapter.

To return to our Joshuʿa. He belonged to an influential family, and his father Dosa is styled 'the mighty lord in Israel'. The members of this family were probably among the state dignitaries that sprang up from the Fusṭāṭ Jewry. In A. D. 12 we have an interesting epistle from Isaac b. Benveniste to our Joshuʿa. The writer styles himself Joshuʿa's disciple. He is evidently identical with the scholar of Narbonne mentioned in the interesting treatise about the ritual slaughtering of animals by Samuel b. Jacob ibn Jamaʿ.[1] In our epistle Isaac refers to the hardships he experienced during his wanderings. In Fusṭāṭ Joshuʿa befriended this scholar. The letter is written from Damietta. Isaac, intent on his wanderings, is about to leave Egypt. He requests his patron to obtain from al-Afḍal a letter addressed to the Ḳāḍi of Damietta, wherein it should be stated that Isaac is a respectable man though poor. Facilities should be granted to him when he desires to journey to either Tarabulus, Jubail, Byzantium, or Turkey. The Ḳāḍi is to instruct the sailors not to molest this scholar, but to hold him in respect. We must bear in mind that it was during the Crusades, when the feelings of the Muslims against anybody from France must have been very hostile. As a Jew from Narbonne, Isaac was liable to be maltreated and suspected.

[1] Described by Steinschneider, Geiger's *Jüd. Zeitschrift*, I–IV; see *Arab. Liter.*, § 105. See, further, the same author's Addenda to the *ʿArukh* (printed by Buber, *Graetz Jubelschrift*, Heb. part, pp. 37, 38, 45; cp. also *H. B.*, XX, 41 = XXI, 87–8): זאת היתה לרבינו יצחק הרב בן רבנו בנבנשתי הרב נרבוני ואמר יש לשאול כך והתשובה שמעתי מחכם אחד ר׳ יוסף הדרשן שמו . . . שמעתי מפי ר׳ יצחק נרבוני.

In this letter al-Afḍal is praised for his benevolence towards Jews. 'Since Ben Asverus (i. e. Antoninus, the friend of Rabbi Yehuda Hannasi) no such pious ruler has been known.' The favourable position of the Jews in Egypt must have greatly impressed a co-religionist who hailed from France, where his brethren not long before passed through the terrors of the first Crusade. Joshu'a is also eulogized for his scholarship and influence in the court. What kind of school (ישיבה, l. 24) Joshu'a presided over is not clear. Perhaps it was the academy founded by David b. Daniel before 1094. A few years later Maṣliaḥ Hakkohen was invited to take charge of it, as will be discussed in the next section.

(7) In conclusion of this section another Jewish official in Egypt should be introduced. A civil servant, imprisoned for some offence, is the author of the epistle A. D. 13, defective in the beginning and end. The handwriting is certainly of the twelfth century, if not earlier. The writer insists on his innocence. He has done nothing to deserve his confinement in the pit. On the contrary his favours both to Rabbinites and Ḳaraites are well known. He accepted government service only in order to gain a livelihood and also to be able at the same time to do good to his co-religionists. His father was also an official in Alexandria. For fifteen years he was in charge of the port authority. All merchants from Byzantium and from other countries had to apply to him.[1] Here unfortunately the letter, written in fluent Hebrew, breaks off. Very likely the prisoner sent it to some

[1] A vivid description of the trade of Alexandria is given by Benjamin of Tudela in his *Itinerary* (ed. Adler, 67–9; cp. translation, p. 76). Merchants came thither from all the Christian kingdoms, from Venetia, Lombardy, Tuscany, Apulia, Amalfi, Sicilia, Calabria, Romania (Byzantium), Khazaria, Patzinakia, Hungaria, Bulgaria, Bakuvia (Ragusa ?), Croatia, Slavonia, Russia, Alamania (Germany), Saxony, Denmark, Courland (?), Ireland (?), Norway (Norge ?), Frisia, Scotia, England, Wales, Flanders, Hainault (?), Normandy, France, Poitiers, Anjou, Burgundy, Murienne (Savoy and the Maritime Alps), Provence, Genoa, Pisa, Gascony, Aragon, and Navarre. Likewise traders from the Muhammedan countries of the West visited Alexandria, viz. from Andalusia, Algarve, Africa, and also from the land of the Arabs. Thither came also merchants from India, Zawilah, Abyssinia, Lybia, Yemen, Shin'ar ('Irāḳ), Syria; also from Yavan (Greece) and Turkey. The merchants of India would bring all kinds of spices which the traders from Edom (Christian countries) would buy. Every nation had in Alexandria an inn (Khān) of its own.

influential co-religionists whom he requested to intervene on his behalf and obtain his release.

All the above fragments, in addition to those discussed in the former chapters, illustrate what a great rôle the Jews of Egypt played in the state.[1] It is a repetition of the same phenomenon which we find in Muslim Spain. Compared with conditions in Byzantium or any other Christian country, the Fāṭimid rule over the country of the Nile was on the whole, except for a short time of al-Ḥakim's persecutions, a golden period for the Jewish people. The breath of tolerance that swept over the land instilled civic duty and activity into the 'people of tribute'. Both Christians and Jews could serve the state to the best of their abilities and thereby benefit their fellow-countrymen.

II

(1) We have seen before that some sort of a school was kept up in Fusṭāṭ after David b. Daniel and that its head was Joshuʿa b. Dosa. From 1027–38 we find there Maṣliaḥ Hakkohen styling himself ראש ישיבת גאון יעקב (see Worman, *J. Q. R.*, XVIII, 14, note 14, and Pozn., *Babyl. Geon.*, 102). Now Maṣliaḥ's genealogy in the 'Memorial List' (A. D. 11, 1, and A. A. 15, col. A) is headed בית בן דוסא and in fact follows that of our Joshuʿa b. Dosa. We infer therefore that Maṣliaḥ was related

[1] We hear also of several Jews who were prominent in the realm in the period succeeding al-Afḍal's death. Besides the famous Nagid Samuel b. Ḥananya and his brother Abraham (see *infra*, p. 230), an important official must have been Isaac b. Joseph the Ḥaber going by the title ʿAmīd ad-Daula, 'the stay of the realm'. A document (T.-S. 10 J 23[2]), dated Kislev, 1454 Sel. (1142 C. E.), at Fusṭāṭ, under authority of the above Nagid, and signed by Moses b. Benjamin the Spaniard, begins: שהדותא דהות באנפנא אנן שהדי דח[תימין לתתא] . . . חצׄר אלינא אביאלכׄיר בר כבוד מרנא נאגי הפרנס ס[ט] וקאל לנא כא[ן] אלשיךׄ אלגׄליל כגׄק מרנא יצחק השר הנכבד סׄטׄ דידיע עמיד אלדולה בר כגׄק מׄור יוסף החבר המשכיל נׄעׄ וכו'. From the indication סׄטׄ (=סופו טוב) after Isaac's name it is evident that he was no longer alive in 1142. Abūl-Khair b. נאגי the Parnes is evidently identical with Solomon b. נאגי הפרנס who is mentioned in a document dated 1145 C. E. at Fusṭāṭ (Bodl. 2878[11]). In the second half of the twelfth century we have the Dayyan Yehoseph b. Nathan styled Amīn al-Mulk, 'the faithful one of the kingdom' (*infra*, p. 227, note 1), the important Katib Abū'l Barakāt Yehuda Hakkohen b. Elʿazar and his son Elʿazar. The latter went by the name Saʿad al-Mulk, 'the happiness of the kingdom' (*infra*, p. 250).

to the influential scholar Joshu'a; perhaps he was his son-in-law. This may have induced the Gaon to leave Ḥadrak, where his father continued to keep up the Palestinian school, as we have seen before (p. 197), and settle in Fusṭāṭ, where he no doubt found more scope. Be that as it may, Maṣliaḥ is the first Gaon in Egypt going by the name of ראש ישיבת גאון יעקב. A number of data about him are collected in A. D. 14. He was generally recognized and seems to have been popular. Two sons of his, still very young, are mentioned (שני חמודיו הפרחים, no. 1). Their names are unknown. When Maṣliaḥ died is not exactly known. But so far he is only mentioned in documents till 1038, and his demise probably took place about this time. None of his sons succeeded him as Gaon.

As head of the former Palestinian school Maṣliaḥ officiated in the synagogue of the Palestinians at Fusṭāṭ (A. D. 14, 3). It is of interest to cite here Bodl. 2834^{22}, which contains a copy of an official recognition of the rite of this house of prayer. The document was drawn up in Adar, 1522, Sel. (1211 C. E.), but the names of the signatories are not preserved. This proves that the fragment is not the original but a copy. The last two lines (in different handwriting) are by X. Hakkohen b. Sa'adya. In the document it is set forth that the signatories accept the traditional order of the prayers on week-days and New Moons; further, the prayer אלשיר (probably the corresponding psalm of the day, שיר של יום, see Tamid 7^4, R. Hash. 31^a; Seder R. 'Amram, I, 14^a) accompanied by the taking out of a scroll, called ספר אלשיר, from the Ark and carrying it to the Almemar, whereupon the Ten Commandments were recited and the scroll carried back without having opened it; this took place also during the services on Sabbaths and Festivals. The Triennial Cycle was used in this synagogue (as Benjamin of Tudela reports in his *Itinerary*, ed. Adler, 63).[1] Thus on every Sabbath the corresponding Seder (סדר, not פרשה!) was read from the scroll followed by the suitable

[1] Likewise Abraham Maimani in his *Kifayah* (cited by Dr. Büchler, *J. Q. R.*, V, 421) mentions that in Miṣr (Cairo-Fusṭāṭ) the whole Parashah is read in the Babylonian synagogue while in that of the Palestinians only a Seder (יקרי פי הדה פי ספר תורה פרשה ופי הדה סדר). See also Sambari in Neub. I, 118: ואנשי א"י אינם נוהגין כן אבל עושין מכל פרשה שלשה סדרים ומסיימין את התורה לסוף ג' שנים.

Hafṭarah. But, as a compromise with the Babylonian custom, the פרשה of the week was also read in the synagogue from ordinary copies of the Pentateuch! This seems to have preceded the reading of the Law. These rites, as well as those pertaining to every Festival, have been in practice for several generations till the time of Sa'adya, and subsequently continued throughout the periods of the Raīs Abū'l Faḍl (Meborak Nagid) and his court, Maṣliaḥ Gaon and his Bet-Dīn, Samuel Hannagid (al-Raīs Abū Manṣūr), R. Ḥiyya, R. Ephraim, R. Jacob Hakkohen,[1] Maimonides and their respective courts. The last authorities mentioned are Solomon (perhaps identical with the scholar mentioned above, p. 217, note 2), Isaac (Dayyan b. Sason) and X. Dayyan. Very likely one of the signatories of this document was the Nagid Abraham Maimuni.[2] It is of interest

[1] R. Ḥiyya is probably identical with the signatory of a document dated 1129 C.E. (Bodl. 2821[1i]). R. Ephraim (b. Meshullam) is mentioned in documents dated 1153 and 1156 C.E. (Bodl. 2806[4], 2836[22]), the first one drawn up in Fusṭāṭ by authority of Samuel Hannagid. Jacob Hakkohen (b. Joseph) signs a document at Fusṭāṭ, dated 1162 C. E., together with Meborak b. Nathan (Bodl. 2878[77]; see also 2855[15]). These three scholars were evidently the Ḥaberim of the Palestinian congregation.

[2] We give here the following lines from Bodl. 2834[22]: (1) . . . [נח]ן אלואצֿעון
כֿטוטנא באכֿ[ר] הדא אלמסטור אננא ראצֿיון במא ארתֿצֿוה אבאנא . . .
(2) . . . מן תיקון ומנהג אלכניסהֿ אלמערופֿה בכנסהֿ אלשאמיין (3) במצר אלהים
יכוננֿיה עד עולם סלה בתֿרתֿיב צלואתֿהא פֿי אלחול ורווס אלשהור וצלאה אלשיר
(4) וזפֿאף ספר תורה אלמערוף בספר אלשיר מן אלהיכל אלי אלאנבול וקראהֿ
עשר הדברות ורדה אלי אלהיכל (5) בגֿיר פתח ולאקראה בואגֿבה אלמֿרתֿב פי
אלסבות ואלאעיאד וקראהֿ אלפרשה פי אלמצחאף בואגֿב (6) כֿל סבתֿ ואן יֿקרא
פי ספר תורה אלסדר אלדי ואפֿק דֿלך אלסבת ואפֿטארתה . . . (7) . . . ועניני
אלאעיאד כל עיד ועיד כמנהגה וכתקונה אלדי אנמא בֿנית (8) מן אגֿלה עלי מה
ראוֿ מן תרתיבה עֿלמא דֿלך לגֿיל וקרֿרוה זֿל ולאגֿיל אלתי מן בעדהם ואממו
(9) עליה ואסתֿחסנוה וקבלוה ועמלו בה אלי זמאן אדוננו גאונינו סעדיה ראש
ישיבת גאון יעקב זֿל (10) וגֿירה מן אלגאונים ואלרבנים ואלחכמים זֿל אלי זמאן
אלרייס אבי אלפצֿל אדוננו נגידנו מבורך שר השרים (11) נגיד הנגידים סנהדרא
רבא צורבא מרבנן נר הגולה · תפארת חצי גרן עגולה · ובית דינו זֿל אלי זמאן
(12) אדונינו גאונינו מצליח הכהן ראש ישיבת גאון יעקב ובית דינו זֿל אלי זמאן
אדונינו שמואל הנגיד הגדול (13) שר השרים ונגיד הנגידים גביר הגבירים ימין
המלוכה והו אלרייס אבו מנצור זֿל ורבינו חייא ורבינו (14) אפרים ורבֿי יעקב
הכהן הרב הגדול זֿל [אל]י זמאן מרֿי ורבֿ אדונינו משה הרב הגדול המובהק

to learn that the Ten Commandments were recited daily in the Palestinian synagogue of Fusṭāṭ, and that the custom goes back to several generations before Saʿadya. It may be assumed the Palestinians in Fusṭāṭ followed herein the rite in use in the Holy Land. As is well known, this daily recitation of the Ten Commandments took place in the Temple by the priests (Tamid 5^1, Ber. 11^b, 12^a). After the destruction of the Sanctuary the intention was to introduce it in the synagogues (this seems to be the meaning of אף בגבולין בקשו לקרות כן, Ber. 12^a) but it was abandoned since the heretics (Gnostics ?) made use of it in their arguments (see also Yer. Ber. 3^c, l. 31 ff.). Attempts during the Amoraic period to revive the custom in Babylon (Sura and Nehardea) were not successful. Thus it remained in abeyance throughout the Gaonic period.[1] But it is remarkable that in Palestine the Ten Commandments were reinstated in the daily ritual, probably some time after the Arab conquest. Hence the Palestinians in Fusṭāṭ recited them in their synagogue.

הפטיש (15) החזק נר המערבי דגל הרבנים יחיד [הדור] או[ת] העולם ופל[א]ו ·
ממזרח שמש עד מבואו · (16) מרדכי הזמן צורבא מרבנן זֹצֹל ובתי דינם חקדוש
ומרֹי ורבֹי שלמה הרב הגדו[ל בישראל] זֹל (17) ומרֹי ורבֹי אדונינו יצחק הרב
הגדול בישראל דגל הרבנים זֹל וכבוד מרֹי ורבֹי אדונינו . . . . . (18) הדיין המשכיל
המופלא הרב הגדול המעולה נזר המשכילים זֹל ונחן באקיו עלי חפט (???) . . . . . .
(19) תרתיבהא ורסומהא אלי אלאן ואלי אלאבד ולא סביל לאחר אן יֹגיר מנהא
שי . . . . (20) . . . . ובהדא כתבנא כֹטוטנא פי אלעשר אלאול מחדש אד[ר]
(21) שנת אֹתקֹכֹב לשטרות מי שעשה עם אבותינו בו נסים ונפלאות יעשה עמנו
ועם כל ישֹ וכן יהי [רצון].

[1] In האשכול, II, 1, we read the following responsum of R. Hai: נשאל הגאון למה לא קרינן בשבת בסת֯ מוסף דשבת? והשיב גם אתם מקנתרין מה שתקנו קדמונים! בכך יאריך הדבר זה יאמר למה ערבו (r. עזבו) קריאת י׳ דברות שאמרו בכל יום במקדש זה (r. וזה) יאמר למה עזבו מ׳ (r. פ׳) בראשית שאמרו בכל יום במעמדות זה (r. וזה) יאמר למה אין קורין בכל יום בס״ת ולמה אין קורין בב׳ וה׳ פ׳ התמיד · ועלינו להתנהג כפי מה שתקנו גדולי הדורות בחכמה ובמנין ואין לשנות כדאיתא בעדיות עב״ל. This shows that in Babylon they adhered to the abolition of reading the Ten Commandments. Indeed there is no mention of it in ʿAmram's *Siddur*. Frumkin, in his edition, prints (I, 322 ff.) סדר מעמדות לרב עמרם גאון wherein עשרת הדברות בכל יום ויום are prescribed. But the whole rite is only for individuals and not for the congregation (see p. 325, bottom, זה המנהג הנכון לנהג היחידים אנשי מעשה והצבור אין נוהגין שלא יבטל איש ממלאכתו). Moreover, the authorship of R. ʿAmram is not yet established beyond question.

After Maṣliaḥ we hear of an Abraham ראש ישיבת גאון יעקב (b. Mazhir). Poznański (*Babyl. Geon.*, 11) thinks that he was the first principal of the reconstituted academy of Bagdād, because his name appears in a collection of poems by Isaac b. Abraham ibn ʿEzra who visited Bagdād in 1143. But the new material given here tends to show that he became in course of time head of the Fusṭāṭ school in succession to Maṣliaḥ. But in Marḥeshvan 1141 C. E. he did not reside yet in the Egyptian capital, but somewhere else. He then already held the title Gaon. Perhaps he was Gaon at Ḥadrak (Damascus) and subsequently removed to Fusṭāṭ, just as it was the case with Maṣliaḥ. There seem to have existed close relations between these two seats of learning since the time of Solomon Hakkohen, the father of Maṣliaḥ (see above, p. 196 f.). But lack of further information renders this point still obscure.

T.-S. 13 J 9[6] contains a letter in heavy Paiṭanic style from [Nathan] b. Samuel the Ḥaber to Abraham Gaon b. Mazhir.[1]

[1] The address, verso, reads: [אל הדרת יקרת הגאון] הגדול אדוננו צעיר משרתיה וקטון שמ[שיה][a] [נתן] ביר שמואל החבר זל. The full name of the Gaon is given on recto: (13) מרנו ורבנו אברהם ראש ישיבת גאון יעקב נטרוהי מן שמיא . . . (16) . . . ואדירי (17) ישיבתו הקדושה שרי ישראל סנסני התורה פחות הממשלה המשולה[b] (18) . . . בן אדונינו מזהיר הצדק (19) שרו שלעולם וגביר כל בית ישראל זקל. The whole epistle contains eulogies and praises merely. But of interest is the right-hand margin whereon the writer thanks God: אשר הגדיל עלי חסדיו ויעמידני במצבי כאשר בימי אדוני רכב ישראל ופר[שיו] . . . ובחסדי אלהים קהלות הקדש אותי אוהבים ושירותי רצונם (r. רצויים) וחסדם גדל עלי שבח למקום אשר עלי הטה חסד לפניהם וישימוני אתם למשמרת ונגידי בי חפץ ואני מוכלל בחסדיו ולא נעלם ממנה[a] אודות רבנו יהודה הלוי הצדיק החסיד זקל אשר עליו באמת ניבאו נביאי האמת . . . . ההיה גבור ביראת אלהים ובתומתו . . . . ומעידים צדקו . . . . למנחות . . . . מן אלהים · מרחשון אתנג. The name Mazhir occurs in Ḥarizi's *Taḥkemoni* (50th Makame, see Dr. Hirschfeld's *Catal. of Montefiore Library*, p. 106, bottom): ואלה עשיתי לשם ר׳ שמואל בן הראש ר׳ נסים בספרד · וחיברתים על שמו · ועל שם ר׳ מזהיר בנו · יהי אלהיו עמו ·; cp. also ed. *Kaminka*, p. 438, l. 8, שמו יקראו מזהיר. A Paiṭan Mazhir is also mentioned in an Eastern Maḥzor (see Halberstamm, in קבץ על יד, 1899, p. 1). R. Yehuda Hallevi, to whom Nathan refers in his letter as no longer alive, should not be identified with the

[a] The feminine suffixes refer to הדרת.

[b] Alluding to the Talmudic saying מאן מלכים מלכי רבנן.

It is dated Marḥeshvan, 1143 Sel. = 1141 C. E. The writer lived then in the Egyptian capital, as will become evident presently. He is glad to inform the Gaon that he is holding the same position as under 'my lord, the chariot of Israel and its horsemen', and that he is popular with the congregations as well as with the Nagid. The office of this correspondent fits in exactly with that held by Nathan b. Samuel, secretary of the Nagid Samuel b. Ḥananya. Yehuda Hallevi, who met this Nathan in Egypt, greatly eulogized him in a poem and also in a letter which he sent him.[1] Nathan is also styled 'secretary of the school'. He probably served already under Maṣliaḥ, as he is a signatory of some documents drawn up in Fusṭāṭ during the period of this Gaon.[2] Probably this is meant when he writes to Abraham Gaon in 1141 that he is retaining his old position as 'in the days of my lord, the chariot of Israel and its horsemen', viz. the late Gaon Maṣliaḥ.

After a vacancy of a few years the school of Egypt seems to have acquired the Gaon Abraham b. Mazhir for its head. A. D. 15, in the same handwriting and style as the preceding epistle, and accordingly having our Nathan b. Samuel as its author, is evidently written by order of Abraham. After eulogizing the Gaon, whose father Mazhir is styled 'the great dignitary, the foundation of the school' (recto, l. 14 f.), and after alluding to

famous poet, however the eulogistic expressions employed would tempt one to do so. As pointed out (*infra*, p. 229 f.), Yehudah Hallevi the Spaniard visited Egypt probably after 1141.

[1] *Diwān*, ed. Brody, I, no. 78, composed in Damietta in honour of our Nathan. It probably formed the introduction of the epistle (ibid., 214–16). Brody's heading is בדמיאטה · תשובה למכתב ר׳ נתן בר שמואל החבר סופר הישיבה בעיר מצרים, but in Bodl. 1970, I, no. 63 (in Neub., p. 645, top), we read וכתב אלי כאתב אלנגיד אלמדכור (i. e. Samuel b. Ḥananya, no. 62) רבי נתן ברבי שמואל החבר ז״ל גואבא ען כתאבה אליה. The heading of the epistle in Bodl. 1971, III, No. 9 (*l. c.*, p. 659), is נזר ; רסאלה גואבא ללנזר סופר הישיבה ערף באבן אלחאכיה stands for the title נזר החברים, held by our Nathan (see letter, l. 28). He is also given this title in a document (T.-S. 13 J 22[2]), beginning: דכלת יום אלסבת אל כאמס עשר פי סיון מע אלנזר ר׳ נתן בר׳ שמואל החבר נ״ע ומע רבי יהודה הכהן נזר הכהנים ומעוזם חדות הנשיאות בר׳ יעקב הדיין . . . Farther on we read expressly רבנו נתן נזר החברים.

[2] See Bodl. 2821^{1i}, 2873^{40b}, 2878^{7}; cp. 2878^{109}.

Ṣoʿan and Ḥadrak (l. 4), the writer informs his correspondent that his name is given a prominent place in the benedictions recited on every Sabbath and Festival, in the presence of the Gaon, for all the benefactors of the school. This person was evidently a generous patron of the academy, in whose records his good services were set forth (verso, l. 7). Also the writer does not miss an occasion of pointing out what the school owes to him. The real object of the epistle is to have his opinion and advice about the will of the late Gaon Maṣliaḥ, which seems to have been submitted to the Gaon Abraham in consequence of a lawsuit it entailed. Among the witnesses of this will were the Dayyan Nathan (b. Solomon Hakkohen),[1] who heard it dictated by the late Gaon, and Isaiah Hallevi b. Mishael (the author of a philosophical treatise on the soul, see *J. Q. R.*, XVII, 67–8). The latter was a brother-in-law of the influential Joshuʿa b. Dosa and was himself a member of a learned family (see A. D. 11). It is not indicated where the correspondent, to whom this letter was sent, lived. Perhaps he resided in Ḥadrak, where Maṣliaḥ might have had some property which he disposed of in his will.

How long Abraham b. Mazhir presided over the Egyptian school is unknown. Nor is it clear who became his direct successor. There is a problematic possibility that this was Moses Hallevi Gaon b. Netaneel the 'Sixth', whose acquaintance Yehudah Hallevi made during his stay in Egypt (*infra*, p. 234, note 3). But Moses' sons certainly presided over the Egyptian academy bearing the title Geonim. These were Netaneel Hallevi, styled Rosh Yeshiba of the Diaspora (שלגולה) and his brother Sar Shalom Hallevi, who again went by the same title of ראש ישיבת גאון יעקב as that of Maṣliaḥ and Abraham b. Mazhir. The activities of these two brothers, as shown farther on, extended from 1160 till about 1189 C. E.

(2) Before dealing with the period of Samuel b. Ḥananya and his successors, another epistle from Nathan b. Samuel (A. D. 16), as the style and handwriting clearly show, should be discussed here. It is again dated Ṣoʿan (= Fusṭāṭ) Marḥeshvan, 11453 Sel.

[1] This Dayyan is a signatory of several documents drawn up in Fusṭāṭ under Maṣliaḥ Gaon (Bodl. 2821^{1i}, $2873^{8.40b}$, and 2878^{7}). He was still alive in 1148 C. E., as is evident from Bodl. 2876^{7}. See also Bodl. 2834^{31} and 2878^{141}.

(1141 C. E.) and is addressed to Petaḥya Hakkohen the Ḥaber b. ʿObadya. The latter was Nathan's teacher, while Petaḥya was his junior school friend (cp. l. 28). Nathan complains that Petaḥya so seldom writes to him. Already some years passed since the demise of the Gaon (l. 30, no doubt referring to Maṣliaḥ Hakkohen), and no letter of his reached Nathan, who relied upon him for all the information about the happenings in his place of residence. Petaḥya's epistle to the Nagid (certainly Samuel b. Ḥananya) reached him through a certain dignitary named Baruk. Nathan read it before the Nagid about three times, in order to impress him with his friend's excellent lines. It seems that he now advises Petaḥya to come over to Egypt, where the Nagid will befriend him (verso, ll. 1–3). Nathan further inquires about his friends, and wonders why they do not reply to his epistles. These are Elʿazar 'the beloved of the school and its friend', going by the Arabic name Ibn Manṣūr Ghalib, and Menasse b. X. the Ḥaber. He would further like to know what his mother, sister, and a certain high dignitary (probably her husband), 'the mighty lord, lord of the house of Israel', are doing. Since two years he has been without any knowledge about them. Finally, greetings are sent from the writer's three sons Meborak, Saʿadya, and Yehoseph.[1] It seems that he was

[1] The eldest son, Meborah, was probably Dayyan of Fusṭāṭ after his father's death. Bodl. 2874^{34} contains a document, by authority of the Nagid Samuel, dated 1157 C. E. at Fusṭāṭ, and signed מבורך בר נתן החבר ז״ל; likewise another document dated 1162 C. E., by authority of Netaneel Hallevi (Bodl. 2878^{77}). See further, Bodl. 2855^{15}, 2876^{18}, $2878^{32.76}$. More important was the third son Yehoseph. T.-S. 13 J 13^{4} contains a letter to כגק מרנו ורבנו יהוסף השר האדיר בישראל החכם המופלא הדיין המעולה נזר השרים . . . ביר׳ כגק מרנו ורבנו נתן החבר המעולה הדיין המופלא. The address on verso reads: חצרה אלמולא אלגליל אלנזר אמין אלמלך רבנו יהוסף שצ׳ || עבדה יהודה הכהן בר׳ טוביהו החבר נע. The first title on the address אלנזר evidently stands for נזר השרים, while the second one, Amīn al-Mulk, 'the faithful one of the realm', was probably bestowed upon him by the government (cp. also above, p. 220, note 1). For a similar title, cp. Amīn ad-Daula, 'warden of the realm', held, e. g., by Ibn-Ammar, commander-in-chief under al-Ḥakim (see L.-P. 124, note 1). It is likely that the influential Joshuʿa b. Dosa (above, p. 217 ff.) also went by this title of Amīn-al-Mulk. The superscription of Yehuda Hallevi's poem in his honour reads in Bodl. 1971, III, no. 10: וכתב אלי אלאמין; אלשיך אלאמין אבי סעד בן דוסא אלמערוף באבן קרקה ז״ל probably stands for אמין אלמלך just as אלנזר for נזר השרים. Bodl. 2876^{38} is probably

a native of Damascus[1] and was acquainted with several prominent Jews there. His brother-in-law apparently held there a high official position. For some unknown reason he settled in Fusṭāṭ and became the Nagid's secretary. Perhaps he came over together with Maṣliaḥ Gaon, who installed him as secretary of the school. Subsequently he held the same position under Abraham b. Mazhir. This letter is of interest as showing us the connexions that were kept up between the two important Jewish communities, Fusṭāṭ and Damascus.

(3) We shall now deal with the period of Samuel Hannagid b. Ḥananya and his successors. A few words should be said in advance concerning the political conditions in Egypt. After al-Afḍal's death in 1121 Ibn al-Baṭaïḥi became chief minister of the state for four years only. In 1125 he was imprisoned and afterwards crucified. The Caliph al-Āmir became thereupon his own minister with the assistance of only two heads of the Diwān, Ja'far b. 'Abd al-Mun'im and a Samaritan Abū Ya'ḳub Ibrāhīm. Another secretary of the state under al-Āmir was Ibn Abū'l Damm al-Yahudi,[2] evidently either a Jew himself or of Jewish extraction. But nothing further is known about him.

The Caliph was assassinated in 1131 and was succeeded by his cousin al-Ḥāfiẓ (1131–49). Soon after the beginning of his rule, his sons quarrelled about the succession to the throne, and civil war broke out in the army, with the result that the unfortunate Caliph was compelled to do away with his son Ḥasan. Two court physicians, the Jew Abū Manṣūr and the Christian Ibn Kirfa, were summoned to prepare a deadly draught. The former came first before his sovereign, and when called upon

also addressed to Yehoseph; it is a letter from Samuel b. Moses to Yehoseph השר הנכבד, styled on verso Abū'l-Hajaj Yusuf . . . Dayyan al-Yahūd, i. e. chief Dayyan (see especially *infra*, p. 266 f.). Finally, our Yehoseph is likely identical with the person mentioned in the Memorial List (*J. Q. R.*, N.S., I, 51, top margin): וכנ̄ק מרנא ורבנא יהוסף השר האדיר בישראל נזר [supply השרים]. Nothing is so far known about Nathan's second son Sa'adya. Tobias Hakkohen the Ḥaber, the father of Yehuda who corresponded with Yehoseph b. Nathan, is probably identical with Tobias Hakkohen b. 'Āli the Ḥaber (see Bodl. $2834^{31 \cdot 32}$; 2878^{141}).

[1] This town is probably meant in verso, l. 4, 'the holy congregations that are במעטירה'. Just as Bagdād was styled עדינה (above, p. 174, note 1), so Damascus was given the poetical name 'the crowned (city)'.

[2] Wüst., III, 70, 73, bottom; cp. L.-P. 166.

to do the job showed a shrewd insight of human nature by refusing the task. He swore by the Torah that he did not know how to prepare the poisonous mixture. But Ibn Kirfa did as he was bidden, and Ḥasan soon died from the drink he was compelled to take. Still in the same year (1134) the Caliph had Ibn Kirfa arrested and executed. Abū Manṣūr was appointed chief physician and received as a gift all that his hapless colleague possessed (Wüst. III, 79–80, L.-P. 168).

Al-Ḥāfiẓ died in 1149 at the age of 75. During the next twenty years Egypt passed through a great crisis both internally and by the invasions of the Franks from Palestine. In Nov. 12th, 1868, Fusṭāṭ, for three centuries the metropolis of the country, was set on fire in order that the Franks should find no shelter there. A most glorious period of Muslim rule over the land of the Nile began with the famous Saladin who became Wezīr in 1169, and two years afterwards succeeded the last Fāṭimid Caliph al-ʿĀḍid (1160–71). The reign of this dynasty came then to an end after a duration of two centuries (L.-P. 169 ff., Wüst. 84 ff.).

The above physician Abū Manṣūr, so greatly honoured by al-Ḥafiẓ after his refusal to prepare the poison for his son Ḥasan, is no doubt identical with Samuel b. Ḥananya (p. 222), the famous Nagid who befriended Yehuda Hallevi during his visit to Egypt on his way to Palestine. Graetz (VI[4], 138–9) assumes that he became the political head of Egyptian Jewry soon after 1134. But so far we were able to trace his period of activity from documents dated 1142–50 (A. D. 17, 3). But he is also probably meant in the letter of Marḥeshwan 1141 (A. D. 16). It is unknown when Moses Nagid b. Meborak died.[1] Naturally Samuel, though a favourite of the Caliph, had to wait till a vacancy occurred. As we hear of no other Nagid between Moses and Samuel, the latter must have been the former's immediate successor. None of Moses' sons could attain the dignity since Samuel became very influential after the event of 1134 C. E.

[1] A Ketuba (T.-S. 8 J 33[1], vellum, top only preserved), dated 1437 Sel. (= 1125–6 C. E.), and probably drawn up at Fusṭāṭ, begins (l. 1): ... וחדוה וגילה לאדוננו משה נגיד הגולה. The bridegroom is El'azar b. Shemarya. The Nagid's name used to be inserted in the legal documents (see *infra*, p. 240). In the above Ketuba the Nagid Moses is no doubt identical with Moses b. Meborak. We thus learn that he was still alive in 1125–6 C. E.

When Yehuda Hallevi visited Egypt the Nagid was at the height of his power. It is noteworthy that Joshuʿa b. Dosa was then imprisoned, probably for some political offence. No doubt Samuel exerted his influence to obtain the release of this prominent co-religionist. It is difficult to ascertain whether the document of 1143-4, which states that the Bet-Dīn of Fusṭāṭ was under Joshuʿa's authority, is to be dated before or after the great poet's visit.

From the genealogies (A. D. 17, 1) we learn that Samuel's forefathers were all scholars. His fourth ancestor and namesake, Samuel, was a Ḥaber. The latter's son, Shemarya, was 'Sixth' of the academy, probably in Palestine towards the end of the eleventh century. But perhaps he was connected with David b. Daniel's school in Egypt. The Nagid's grandfather, Netaneel, was styled 'the great one of the school'. His father Ḥananya was an eminent physician. The Nagid's brother, Abraham, seems also to have been an influential doctor. It is remarkable that it is not stated expressly that Samuel himself was a member of this profession. But this is very likely since his great influence was probably due to his position as the Caliph's doctor, and he was known to the Muslims as the Abū Manṣūr of the poisoning affair of the Caliph's son. None of Samuel's offspring succeeded to the dignity of Nagid.

A. D. 18 contains an interesting letter to our Nagid from Elijah b. Kaleb b. Leon. The last two names point to Byzantine origin, and indeed it is evident that the writer was a stranger in Egypt. He was a scholar who seems to have landed at Alexandria not long before, and was proceeding to Cairo to see the Nagid. Evidently owing to lack of means he made his journey slowly from town to town and meanwhile corresponded with Samuel. Elijah was struck by the laxity of observance and the ignorance then prevalent in the Egyptian communities. He writes, I beg to inform you, in accordance with your request, that I have arrived here at Bēnhē. When I came to Alexandria and saw the people's doings, I ascribed them to be due to your living at too long a distance away to have a salutary influence over the congregation. I thought that perhaps those Jews nearer you were 'perfumed with your scent'. But behold they too (e.g. in Bēnhē) are still in their 'unclean state'. 'Men of knowledge are in their eyes as animals, the Torah and the Laws of no account to them. For a while my heart was in pain and I wondered about the difference I beheld here from other congregations of Israel. I inwardly mused why they (the Egyptian Jews) were so and how they possessed the callousness to eat without saying their prayers. But, I concluded, that was perhaps because scholars did not live among them. They are thus lax out of ignorance, and not out of presumption.' Here we have a not very flattering account of conditions in Egypt in the middle of the twelfth century. The paucity of scholars in this country was also noticed by Maimonides a few years afterwards. The eleventh century saw more of intellectual activity amongst the Jewry of this country, as we have discussed above, probably due to the spiritual instruction imparted by the academies of Babylon and of Palestine.

To return to our Elijah, who obviously had a grudge against the congregations he visited because he was not adequately supported. His remarks may thus be coloured by bias, and should not be accepted prima facie. The Nagid is requested to enable him to come to Cairo-Fusṭāṭ without delay, since he experienced many hardships on his journey from Alexandria. The messenger who brought the letter was originally hired for a journey from Maḥalla to Bēnhē, and Elijah had to pay him for the remainder of the way from that place to Cairo-Fusṭāṭ. The people showed him no respect whatever. The Nagid in his reply should let Elijah know how he could bring with him a number of books he possessed, and also whether to come as he was dressed. Many people frightened him into the belief that his speech and dress would expose him to danger. It is thus clear that he came from a Christian country. At that time the Franks threatened Egypt with invasion. Any traveller from a Christian land had to confront many risks of being suspected as a spy or being set upon by a hostile crowd. Elijah landed at Alexandria and spent there the whole summer very uncomfortably. His object was probably to find scope for his scholarship in Egypt. In the twelfth century we meet there several scholars from Christian countries, e. g. Isaac b. Benveniste of Narbonne (above, p. 218 f.), Joseph b. Gershon and Anatoli b. Joseph (Dayyanim in Alexandria in Maimonides' time, above, p. 175, and *infra*, p. 247 f.), and others. Egyptian Jewry became then dependent on abroad for its spiritual guides, whereas in the eleventh century and previously these would be obtained from former students of the Babylonian and the Palestinian academies.

While in the preceding letter Egyptian Jewry was painted in rather black colours, A. D. 19 informs us of a collection of money for the ransom of captives. It reveals the favourable side of this Jewry. No efforts were spared to redeem their unfortunate brethren who fell into captivity. This we have seen above (pp. 87 ff., 204–5) in the times of Ephraim b. Shemarya and Nahrai b. Nissim. No doubt all through the subsequent years 'the redemption of captives' was practised. But documentary evidence we have only for the time of Samuel Hannagid (and later on of Maimonides, *infra*, p. 244). Our fragment gives us the result of the collection in the provincial towns. The captives were from al-Rūm (Byzantium). At the instigation of the Nagid, Abū'l-Surūr b. Ṭarīf and Abū'l-Ma'āli (Samuel b. Yehuda)[1] were entrusted with this task. The collection amounted to 225 d. (at the rate of 40 dirhems per d.). The following is the detailed list of the contributions from the communities:

> Maḥalla 40¼ d., Miniya Zifta 37 d., Sambuṭiah 26 d., Damsīs 12 d., Samjūd 11 d., Milij 28 d., Damirah 14 d., Tinnis 3 d., Damietta 20 d., Benhē al-'Asāl 14⅛ d.

The Sheikhs Abū Sa'ad and Abu'l-Ma'āli (the latter probably identical with one of the treasurers of the fund) gave 20 d. The Alexandrian congregation is not mentioned in this list. Nor is it stated what the Jews of the capital contributed. But the amount required must have been considerable, since the provincial towns were asked to take a share.

A. D. 19[a] gives a calendar for the years 4914–16 A. M. (1153–6 C. E.) which a Jew (probably an elder in Fusṭāṭ) drew up for his own use. He first gave the respective details as to A. M., Sel., the year since the destruction of the Temple, the Shemiṭṭah, the Jubilee, the Solar Cycle, and also the month of A. H.

[1] The latter is probably identical with b. Asād, A. D., 17, 3 g. k. Abū'l Surūr b. Ṭarīf may be identical with the namesake mentioned in a document dated 1104 at Cairo (*J. Q. R.*, XX, 453).

wherein the Jewish New Year began. Then follow the dates of the New Moons, festivals, and fasts. But the chief interest of the calendar consists in the part which gives the names of the persons who supply the olive-oil for the 'perpetual lamp' in the synagogue. The writer of the calendar was one of them. During the three years the same persons, with a few new-comers, stood the expense, though each year in a different sequence. The list is defective for the first year. In the second year we have the Sheikh Abū 'Ali b. Ṣadaḳah supplying oil during Tishri (except New Year), the Sheikh Abū'l Ḥasan b. Ḥashūsh for Marḥeshvan, the Sheikh Abu'l Ridha for Kislev, Abū'l Ḥasan Abu Sa'ad for Ṭebet and Ḥanukah, the Sheikh Abu'lkhair Ṣadaḳah for Shevaṭ, the writer for Adar, his relation the Sheikh Abū 'Ali for Nisan and Passover, the Sheikh Abū'l Bayyan for Iyyar, the Sheikh Hilāl (Abū'l Najm) for Sivan and Pentecost, the Sheikh Abū'l Mufadhdhal for Tammuz and Ab, and X. for Ellul and New Year. In the third year we have the new-comers the Sheikh Abū Sa'ad (perhaps identical with the person mentioned in the preceding fragment, A. D. 19) and the heirs of a certain late Ḥaber, while the Sheikh Abū'l Mufaḍḍal is no longer mentioned. We have here a specimen of how the internal affairs of the synagogue (very likely in Fusṭāṭ) were arranged. Probably after three years another group of members were allotted the privilege of supplying the oil for its sacred use.

(4) The Nagid Samuel continued his beneficial activities till 1159. This is the latest date we could trace from documents. In the following year we find already deeds issued by the authority of Netaneel Hallevi, whom Benjamin of Tudela met in Cairo during his travels. Netaneel's period can be traced from 1160–5 C. E. (A. D. 20, 1). But during this time there lived in Fusṭāṭ a Nasi Daniel, by whose authority documents were also drawn up (in 1164/5, above, p. 175). It is evident that there existed a division of authority in the community which will be discussed in detail in the next chapter (see also above, p. 218). Samuel Hannagid is styled 'the help of the Nesiut', which clearly presupposes that he patronized a Nasi who probably lived in the capital. Likewise other people of that time held honorary titles bestowed by the Nasi (e.g. Moses 'the favourite of the Nesiut', A. D. 29, 3).

Towards the end of his life Samuel suffered from the denunciations of a co-religionist, named Yaḥya=Zuṭa=Sar Shalom, who usurped the chief communal office. The only source for the grave crisis which Egyptian Jewry went through is the Scroll of Zuṭa composed by Abraham b. Hillel (published by Neubauer, *J.Q.R.*, VIII, 543 ff., IX, 721, cp. also XI, 532; see also A. D. 19[b]). Zuṭa, the disturber of the communal peace, pretended to be indeed a scholar and 'head of an academy'.[1] But though he also went by the name Sar Shalom, his identification with the Egyptian Gaon Sar Shalom Hallevi is out of question.[2] The data discussed in A. D. 20 tend to show that there existed in Damascus a 'Palestinian academy' presided over by Moses Hallevi Gaon. A son of his, Netaneel, occupied the Gaonate in Egypt as 'head of the school of the Diaspora' (1160–5). He is never styled Nagid, though Benjamin of Tudela calls him שר השרים, which was the Nagid's usual title. After Netaneel we have a Sar-Shalom Hallevi b. Moses Gaon presiding in Egypt (Fusṭāṭ) over 'the Palestinian school' (from 1170–89). That he was a brother of Netaneel Hallevi b. Moses Gaon admits of very little doubt.[3] Both of them seem to have been generally recognized.

[1] The whole passage (ibid., VIII, p. 547, ll. 17 ff.–548, bottom) forms a genuine part of the scroll in all the fragments. Kaufmann's contention (ibid., IX, p. 168) that it crept into the Megillah 'from something like Ḥarizi's *Taḥkemoni*' is disproved by an examination of the MSS. This scroll has been re-edited and discussed by Kahana in *Hashiloaḥ*, vol. XV. But this publication is inaccessible to me.

[2] Pozn., *Babyl. Geon.*, 103–4, identifies them without much ado.

[3] T.-S. 10 J 20[21] contains a letter from Sar Shalom, beginning: עזרי מעם יי עושה שמים וארץ | מן שר שלום הלוי גאון יעקב החוסה | בשם יי ביר משה הלוי גאון יעקב | ביר נתנאל הששי בחבורה זצל. The letter is addressed to Netaneel החבר הרופא הנכבד. In his signature Sar Shalom also mentions his grandfather's name. Accordingly Moses' father was 'Sixth' of the school. His name, Nataneel, is additional proof that Netaneel Hallevi b. Moses Gaon is Sar Shalom's brother. Or. 5566 B, fol. 30, contains a letter from נתנאל הלוי בר משה הששי בה נט רה to Joseph Ḥakkohen b. Ḥalfon (so address verso). The title 'Sixth' evidently refers to Moses. It is doubtful whether this Moses is the father of Netaneel the 'Sixth' or he is identical with the later Gaon Moses, and accordingly Netaneel (the later Gaon) wrote this letter at a time when his father was still 'Sixth'. The former alternative is more probable. The above suggestion that Moses Hallevi was Gaon in Damascus, as the data discussed in A. D. 20 render it probable, would be assailed if a poem, attributed to Yehuda Hallevi (*Diwān*, ed. Brody, I, p. 105, no. 72), were really by him. Its heading in the MS. (see Neubauer's *Bodl. Catalogue*, I,

Thus, for example, Hillel b. Ṣadoḳ Ab (very likely the father of the author of *Megillat Zuṭa*) signs a Ketuba by authority of Netaneel Hallevi (A. D. 20, 1c). The correspondence of Sar Shalom Hallevi (A. D. 21–3) also gives the same impression.

It is therefore incumbent to dissociate the latter Gaon from Zuṭa, whom his parents called Yaḥya (probably being his Arabic name, while Zuṭa was his Jewish one) but who gave himself the well-sounding name Sar Shalom. By his actions he proved just the opposite. He first denounced the greatly esteemed Samuel Hannagid, with the result that he was in disgrace for sixty-six days. When the beloved Nagid had the advantage and returned to his exalted office, the whole Egyptian Jewry felt a great relief. Samuel died soon after 1159 (ten years before Saladin became the ruler of the country). Zuṭa, who became meanwhile greatly impoverished, made the demise of the Nagid the occasion for further denunciation. He informed the Caliph that 10,000 d. were in the Nagid's house (תחת ראשו, i.e. under his very pillow, ibid., p. 546, l. 12). But this proved a falsehood, and Zuṭa and his son incurred the Caliph's displeasure. The sovereign of the country was then al-Fāïz (1154–60). Not long after the Nagid's demise, his master, the Caliph, died, and was succeeded by al-'Āḍid, the last Fāṭimid ruler (1160–71). During his reign Zuṭa seems to have lived in obscurity. But with Saladin's

658, top, no. 412) reads וכתב אלי אלרי״ס הבה אללה בן אלששי. Brody's heading is (במצרים לר׳ משה (הבה̈ אללה בן אלששי; indeed the end of the poem shows that the person addressed was called Moses. Now the corresponding Hebrew name for Hibatallah is נתנאל. Hence probably the correct reading of the heading was משה בן הבה̈ אללה אלששי, i.e. our Moses b. Netaneel the 'Sixth'! The hero of the poem was evidently a renowned scholar (see ll. 3 ff.: אשר לבש במצרים מעיל הוד · ונשמע עד ספרד פעמונו · ורקח מרקחי תורה בצוען · והריחו בשנער קנמונו). Moreover, the ending ולמה יחרד העם לים סוף והמטה ביד משה גאונו (l. 19) seems to indicate that he went by the title *Gaon*, which would strengthen still more his identity with our Moses Hallevi Gaon b. Netaneel the 'Sixth'. Also the title al-Raīs would be shortened for Raīs al-Metibta ('head of the school', see *infra*, p. 262). Accordingly Yehuda Hallevi must have met this Gaon in Fusṭāṭ, where, in the poet's words, 'he put on the garment of glory', i.e. took up his exalted position. However, the very same poem is attributed in another source (see Steinschneider, *H. B.*, X, 98, note 3; cp. also Brody, *l. c.*, notes, p. 179) to Joseph ibn 'Aḳnīn as having composed it in honour of his great master Moses Maimonides. We must await further material to solve the problem.

accession in 1171 (*de facto* ruler since 1169), Zuṭa came again to the forefront. The author of the scroll indicates this in a general way (p. 546, l. 17 ff.), 'And it came to pass in those many days that the King of Egypt died and a new king arose over Egypt (cp. Exod. 2. 23, 8). And he (Zuṭa) obtained from him the dignity for an annual sum of 200 d.' The writer passed over the whole reign of al-'Āḍid. That by the 'new king' Saladin is meant, is evident from the intervention of Maimonides after Zuṭa's régime for four years. Maimonides arrived in Egypt in 1165 and it was only under Saladin that he began to wield any influence in the court. Egyptian Jewry was for a time relieved from Zuṭa's tyranny. But he succeeded for a third time to be the political head of this Jewry. By the aid of a certain state official, who subsequently was transferred to Palestine, Zuṭa and his son kept the community in awe for two years. Finally, his overthrow was brought about by R. Isaac (ibid., pp. 549–56).[1]

It is indeed remarkable that the documents of the Bet-Dīn from 1159 till the time of Abraham Maimuni (A. D. 33) contain no mention of a Nagid. Owing to the communal strife none seems to have been recognized. Certainly Zuṭa's claim was generally ignored. Just as Samuel Hannagid had charge of a school, though he never assumed the title of Gaon (see A. D. 17, 2), so our Zuṭa called himself Rosh Yeshibah. But his

[1] Zuṭa's final defeat probably took place still during Saladin's reign (1171–93). This ruler is evidently referred to in p. 549, ll. 11 ff., (i. e. Zuṭa and his son) ובראותם כי המלך [מלך] צדק · מחזיק הבדק [ומסיר החדק]: מעביר הפחד ולא יקח שוחד . . . R. Isaac is probably identical with R. Isaac b. Sason, Maimonides' colleague on the Bet-Dīn of Fusṭāṭ (as already Harkavy suggested, see p. 543, top). The Megillah itself seems to have been written (or copied) in 1196, three years after Saladin's death. Accordingly in the introductory poem (p. 545, ll. 3–4), ויהי מקדמון · בימי מלכות הארמון · היה מלך אוהב ממון · ויתן לו באלף דרכמון וכו׳, Saladin cannot be meant, as Neubauer thinks (ארמון is to mean 'Armenian', alluding to Saladin who was a Kurd, note 3). It more likely speaks of Zuṭa's first acts during Samuel Hannagid's lifetime in the reign of al-Faïz (1154–60). The author indicates this period as 'the time of the kingdom of the Temple' (i. e. Jerusalem), viz. when the Crusaders were the lords of the Holy Land. (If we read האדמון for הארמון, we shall have a still more explicit allusion, since אדמון = אדום ! A different explanation is given by Kaufmann, *Z. D. M. G.*, LI, 451–2). As is well known, Saladin's Holy War (1187–92) resulted in restoring the Muslim rule over Palestine except a narrow strip of the coast from Tyre to Jaffa.

ignorance was too glaring, and his pretensions to scholarship and literary accomplishments gave the author of the Scroll scope for biting ridicule. The deeds emanating from the courts during this period are issued by authority of either the Nasi (e. g. Daniel, 1164–5), the Geonim Netaneel (1160–65) and Sar Shalom (1170–89), or Maimonides (1171 C.E., A. D. 20, 5[a]). This very insertion of 'by the authority of' (מרשות) in documents and also in prayers recited in the synagogue became a subject of dispute. Maimonides was consulted about this problem (A. D. 20, 7) as well as a contemporary Dayyan Yeḥiel b. Elyāḳim, as will be shown presently.

To return now to the Geonim Netaneel and Sar Shalom. The data concerning them are collected in A. D. 20. They seem to have had the right of appointing Dayyanim, Readers, and even Mohelim for the provincial communities. Benjamin of Tudela reports this about Netaneel (A. D. 20, 2). About Sar Shalom's similar privileges we read in his correspondence. A. D. 21 is an epistle from him to the community of Ḳalyūb. Moses b. Levi, a Reader and Shoḥeṭ, received authorization from the Gaon. The congregation is enjoined to treat him well. His father Moses, also a Reader, held the title 'the beloved one of the Yeshiba'. Sar Shalom styles himself 'the descendant of Geonim'. In A. D. 22 he reminds a patron of his, Moses Hakkohen b. Ḥalfon, to send him a cloak, as is the latter's custom whenever he returns safely from his business travels. A. D. 23 is from Moses b. Elijah Hallevi, a communal official in a provincial town in Egypt, to the Gaon. Herein we find again that the latter authorized persons as Mohelim for the various communities. The writer is very much grieved on account of Sar Shalom's anger with him. A Jew in his town had a boy for circumcision and chose a certain Yefet to perform the rite, as he did it gratuitously. But another person, Yefet b. Solomon, the physician (called Abū'l-Ṭafāl), came and produced a document of authorization from the Gaon to the effect that he only should be the Mohel in the whole district. The writer declared the document as a forgery, with the result that the rejected Mohel slandered him to the Gaon. From the pitiful letter it is evident how Sar Shalom held his subordinates in dread. By his policy of authorization he tapped a source of income. This Mohel, for example, must have paid a certain sum to the Gaon, and in his turn claimed gratuities for the performance of the rite.

The following list of the principals of the Egyptian school can now be construed :

David b. Daniel, Nasi and 'head of the academy of the Diaspora' (שלגולה) about 1083–94
[Joshua b. Dosa ?, no Gaon] before 1121
Masliaḥ Hakkohen, Rosh ישיבת גאון יעקב 1127–38
Abraham b. Mazhir, Rosh ישיבת גאון יעקב after 1141
[Moses Hallevi b. Nataneel the 'Sixth'?, see above, p. 234, note 3, end.]
Netaneel Hallevi, 'head of the academy of the Diaspora' 1160–65
Sar Shalom Hallevi, Rosh ישיבת גאון יעקב 1170–89

(About a Joseph b. Jacob ראש ישיבת גאון יעקב in 1211, see A. D. 29, 1.) The grandson of Maimonides, David, bore the title ראש ישיבתה של תורה, by which also went his grandson Joshu'a, as well as the latter's son David (A. D. 33, 4, 6).

So far no holders of the dignity of Ab in the Egyptian schoo are known. It is also doubtful whether it possessed a college c seven scholars, as was the case in Palestine.[1] The literar achievements of the Egyptian Gaonate were still poorer tha those of the Holy Land. High-sounding titles and exaggerate eulogies were the fashion of the time. But no proof is availabl of the scholarly eminence of the persons thus eulogized. Whe so much time and energy were spent on communal strife an

[1] As regards the school in Damascus, Benjamin of Tudela (*Itinerary*, ed. Adle 31) found there the Gaon 'Azarya (or Ezra), his brother Sar Shalom Ab, and Josep החמשי בישיבה. As Pozn. (*R. É. J.*, XLVIII, 164, note 2) rightly suggests, f החמשי we should read השלישי 'the Third'. (Also more appropriate would b בחבורה than בישיבה.) Whether there existed four more dignitaries numbere from four to seven is unknown. Benjamin mentions also Masliaḥ ראש הסדר הדרשן who may have held some office in the school. Meir פאר החברים and Josep b. al-Plat יסוד הישיבה were probably patrons of the academy and received the respective titles in recognition of their services (see also A. D. 20, 7). In the Bagda school (in the twelfth century) we hear of no numbered scholars heading th college (חבורה). On the other hand, the school was divided into ten sectio (ישיבות), the heads of some of them held the titles חבר, יסוד (סוד) הישיבה ראש הסדר, and פאר החברים respectively (see Benjamin's *Itinerary*, 39, and c Pozn., *Babyl. Geon.*, pp. 16, note 1, 17, note 4, 18, notes 2, 4). The inner organizati of both these schools is on the whole still obscure (cp. also *infra*, p. 278 f.).

competition for advancement, no adequate attention could be paid to study and genuine literary work. No wonder therefore that in Spain the whole institution of the Gaonate was held in very little esteem in the twelfth century. Maimonides gives us his experiences in Palestine and in Egypt in a characteristic passage in his Mishnah commentary on Bekhorot.[1] We have also read (above, p. 230 f.) how a scholar from a Christian country was impressed by the religious knowledge and practice of a part of Egyptian Jewry. On the other hand, it should be added, Yehuda Hallevi greatly eulogized a number of learned and intellectual co-religionists whom he met in the land of the Nile. But the persons who gave themselves the imposing titles in connexion with the Yeshiba seem not to have deserved them by reason of their intellectual eminence.

(5) Before proceeding to deal in the next section with the period of Maimonides, we shall introduce here a scholar from Aleppo, Yeḥiel b. Elyāḳim, who settled in Egypt and after some vicissitudes became Dayyan in Cairo-Fusṭāṭ (A. D. 24–5). A. D. 24 is an epistle from Yeḥiel to Yefet the Teacher, probably in Cairo-Fusṭāṭ. The writer was travelling in Egypt. He left on Wednesday al-Maḳs (the port of Cairo) in a boat which safely reached the Miniyat Zifta district on the following day. Probably Yeḥiel intended to preach there and in this way benefit by the local Jews. But the place was in confusion. The people were in hiding from the tax-collectors, and our scholar was there a forlorn person. He requests Yefet to inquire after the welfare of his household and to continue teaching his boy Elyāḳim to read 'from the four sides, from above and below' (ll. 10–11). Probably the meaning is that the boy be taught to read from whatever side the page faced him. By getting used to this way

[1] 4[4]: ואל תטעה בכל ענינים האלו שכללתי במאמרי זה אלו השמות הידועים בארץ ישראל ובארץ המערב שקורין קצת בני אדם ראש ישיבה ואחרים אב בי"ד ועושין חילוק בין ראש ישיבה גאון יעקב ובין ראש ישיבה של גולה וכותבין לבני אדם שלא ראו אות (אותם .r) בראש ישיבה או זולתן מן השמות לפי שאלו הדברים פטומי שמא בעלמא והולכין אחר הכנוין והיחוסין וכבר ראיתי בארץ ישראל אנשים נקראין חברים ובמקומות אחרים יש מי שנקרא ראש ישיבה ואפי' בי בי רב דחד יומא ליתיה. . . . By ארץ המערב Egypt is meant in juxtaposition with Palestine (see above, p. 30, note 3, and p. 83).

of reading *four persons* could use one and the same book. We must bear in mind that books were then expensive and rare, as each copy had to be written by a professional scribe. Yeḥiel also instructs the teacher Yefet to make the boy familiar with the 'blessings', while his mother was to see that he said them as the occasion arose. Yeḥiel was poor, yet his children were very dear to him. He owed a loan to a certain man. If he be pressing for payment, the Sheikh Isma'īl al-Ṭulaṭuli had promised Yeḥiel to advance the money till he returned from his journey. Greetings are sent to X. 'the disciple' b. al-Dayyan, to a young man Abu'l-Bayyān, an orphan, to the Sheikh Samuel Rashīd, to a certain Joshu'a and his brother. The Sheikh Abū'l-Faraj, a companion of Yeḥiel, sends greetings to his family. This letter is of interest for the social life of those times. From another epistle (note 1) we learn that Yeḥiel was acting as minister at weddings in provincial towns. A person from Ḳalyūb invited him to come and officiate at his son's wedding.

A copy of an interesting legal decision by our scholar we have in A. D. 25, 1. Yeḥiel alludes to his having left his native place (i.e. Aleppo) for Egypt, where he observed strife in the communities about the mention of מרשות ('by authority of So-and-so', e.g. the Nagid, Gaon, or Nasi) in documents, at wedding banquets and similar functions, during the morning service in the synagogue and also before the preacher began his discourse. Maimonides was also consulted concerning that problem (A. D. 20, 7). The congregation that put the question to him bound itself by a ban not to make use of that formula at all. Yeḥiel, however, decided in favour of the formula. From the standpoint of the Law (דין) there was nothing against it. He is spoken of as Dyyan in Miṣraim (Cairo-Fusṭāṭ). In other epistles (nos. 2 and 4) he is styled הרב המובהק. A certain Ḥananya b. Yehuda requests him to come to Jerusalem to settle there some dispute. Benjamin of Tudela found in the Holy City, when still under the Crusaders, a community of 200 Jews. On the other hand, Petaḥya found there only one Jew. But soon after Saladin's conquest of the city (October 2, 1187), it received a new influx of Jewish inhabitants.[1] As will be shown

[1] Indeed Ḥarizi found there, besides pilgrims from France, two organized communities recruited from Ashḳelon and the Magreb. See *Taḥkemoni*, ed. Kaminka,

in the next chapter, a new office was created in Cairo to represent the Palestinian Jewry. Its holder was called 'the Nagid of the land of Israel and Yehuda' (נגיד ארץ ישראל ויהודה). The letter here probably dates after 1187. The Nagid is also mentioned (l. 16). A correspondent of Yeḥiel was Yehuda the Teacher b. Aaron the physician ('Ammāni). The latter is very likely identical with the Alexandrian Dayyan eulogized by Yehuda Hallevi (no. 4). We found him there in 1129 (A. D. 14, 2). When his son Yehuda corresponded with Yeḥiel, Aaron was no longer alive. This Yehuda was also a correspondent of Abraham Maimuni.

(5) In conclusion of this section three private letters from the Genizah are discussed as they are of interest for the ordinary life of the people (A. D. 26–28). A lady, by name Maliḥa, writes to her brothers Abū Sa'id and Solomon (A. D. 26). If the epistle is her own composition, it would do her much credit. It is written in good Hebrew with Paiṭanic embellishments. Maliḥa seems to have been away with her little daughter, Zoi, for several years in Byzantium. Perhaps she was married to a Byzantine Jew. Anyhow she desires now to return to Egypt, but is afraid to undertake the journey by herself. She would have joined the bearers of the letter. But after consulting a 'scroll of the law' for augury, she received an ill-omened reply. She demands therefore that one of her brothers should come to Byzantium and fetch her home. She alludes to 'our lord the Fourth', evidently

353 : ומשם נסעתי אל ירושלים · ונפתחו לי השמים · ואראה מראות אלהים · ויפגעו בי מלאכי אלהים · הם חסידי עליון · הבאים מארץ צרפת לשכון בציון · ובראשם הרב החסיד רבי יוסף בן הרב רבי ברוך · יהי לאלהיו ברוך · ואחיו החכם רבי מאיר · בנר שכלו חשכים מאיר · ושם מן האשקלונים קהל מעולה · ובראשם השר רבי סעדיה איש ימיני והוא משכיל ונחמד · ושכלו לא ימד · ושם מן המערבים קהלה חשובה וטובה · ובראשם רבי אליה המערבי · הוא בעל חסדים · ומרבה צדקות למרודים . . . See also Makamah, 28 (p. 245), and Gr., VI[4], 305–6. Probably the fragment inserted in A. D. 25, 3, dates from the time when the Jerusalem community was reorganized after 1187. The writer, Yeḥiel b. Isaac, inquires of a Rabbi (probably in Egypt) how to dispose of the sum of money the latter gave for the erection of a ritual bath. Yeḥiel established such a one in his own house. In the Shiloaḥ no bathing is permitted by the non-Jews. The fragment contains only the end of the epistle (wherein other details were probably mentioned) and the postscript. Yeḥiel sent previously another epistle to the Rabbi through a non-Jew from Fusṭāṭ whose father resided in Jerusalem.

a relative of hers. She thus came from a learned family and it would not be unusual for her to have possessed a good knowledge of the Hebrew language.

In A.D. 27 we have a letter from a husband to his wife in Cairo-Fusṭāṭ, dated Rosh Ḥodesh Kislev at Sammanūd. The epistle, written in Hebrew, is addressed to the Reader Abū'l Bayyān, who probably would translate its contents to the woman. Why her husband did not write to her directly in Jewish Arabic, which was the native language of the Egyptian Jews, is difficult to say.[1] He was a scribe who, owing to lack of employment, travelled in the provincial towns to find work. He just left Cairo-Fusṭāṭ on Thursday and spent the Sabbath in Benhē. His wife is requested to look after their boy. A certain Isaac b. Baruk is also mentioned.

Finally we have a letter from the wife of Solomon the scribe to her husband. The handwriting is probably from the thirteenth century and even later. The lady calls herself דונו סורו, Donna סורו, which would point to Italian origin. Her husband left his home for the purpose of obtaining release from taxes. A certain Solomon, the physician, is to intervene for him. Meanwhile his wife was told that he intended leaving for Turkey. This she absolutely vetoes. Several letters sent by her and her children were left unanswered by her husband Solomon the scribe. If he persists in his intention, their family concord will be broken. There is one daughter grown up and suitable for marriage. Their married daughter is in certain circumstances and must not be inflicted with pain. People will scandalize them by saying: There is a respectable man leaving his wife and family and wandering about in the world.

III

(1) The period of Maimonides has been the subject of numerous studies. It is not intended to write here a new life of the great sage.[2] Only additional material, which the Genizah furnishes,

[1] Perhaps the letter was purposely addressed to a well-known person in the town to make it easier for the bearer of the letter to deliver it.

[2] The latest biography is by Eppenstein in *Mose ben Maimon*, II, 1 ff. See Poznański's review in *Z.f.H.B.*, 1917, 59 ff.; that Maimonides was Nagid (ibid., p. 61) is mentioned nowhere. The title אלריים was given to several other

will be discussed. Maimonides' activity in Egypt really falls within the reign of Saladin and his successors and hence beyond the scope of the present treatise. Moreover, the data given here are very scrappy and allow as yet no connected account.

In 1211, a few years after Maimonides' death, we find in Fusṭāṭ an eminent scholar Joseph Rosh Hasseder b. Jacob Rosh bē Rabbanan (b. ʿAli Rosh Haḳḳahal). As shown in A. D. 29, 1–2, Jacob (also styled הדיין) was probably a native of Babylon. He was the author of a work codifying the laws of Sheḥiṭa. It is unknown whether he left his native country for Egypt, where his son resided. Joseph wrote a commentary on the Hafṭarot. The colophon of this work is of interest since it tells us about the Bible commentaries of Saʿadya, Aaron b. Sarjadu, Samuel b. Ḥofni, Isaac b. Samuel the Spaniard, Berakeel, and Joshiah b. חסכוי, which Joseph read and utilized. He was also the author of an Arabic commentary on the Mishnah, wherein very likely he followed in the footsteps of Maimonides. On the whole he showed little originality in his literary work, extensively drawing upon his predecessors. It may be assumed that he was personally acquainted with Maimonides. As to his title Rosh Hasseder, it should be noted that Joseph ibn Aḳnīn, Maimonides' favourite disciple, was styled likewise.

In the second half of the twelfth century we hear of an ʿObadya (al-Raīs Abū'l Ridha), 'Nagid of the land of Israel and Yehuda' (A. D. 29, 3). He was a member of a scholarly family, patrons of the 'academy' (probably of Egypt). Nothing further is known of this Nagid's activities. The character of his office will be discussed in the next chapter (see also above, p. 241). Perhaps Joshiah Hannasi corresponded with him (A. C. 20, 3) when writing to נגיד התעודה · נגיד ארץ ישראל ויהודה.[1]

dignitaries (see *infra*, p. 262). Also Abū'l Barakāt b. El'azar was no Nagid (see *infra*, p. 250).

[1] ʿObadya's son was perhaps Joseph with whom Ḥarizi came into contact in Cairo-Fusṭāṭ, and benefited by his generosity. See *Taḥkemoni*, ed. Kaminka, 353: ומאציליהם החסיד הנכבד השר הנעלה רבי יוסף בן השר הגדול רבי עובדיה · היה אביו מבחר הנסיכים · ואומן בחיק המלכים · והבן אין ערוך אליו · בצדקתו וכשרון מפעליו. The fiftieth Makamah also contains a poem in his honour (see *Catal. of Montefiore Library*, p. 107: וכתבתי לר׳ יוסף מקור התושיה · בן השר המצרי עובדיה זל). It is true that Ḥarizi does not mention ʿObadya by the title Nagid, but neither does he style Abraham Maimuni as such.

A correspondent of Maimonides was probably X. al-Fayyumi b. Sa'adya (A. D. 29, 4). The sage is styled 'the teacher of righteousness' (מורה צדק, see also A. D. 30) by reason of his works that were a guide to Israel (see also *infra*, p. 267). His son (i.e. Abraham) is also greeted (l. 15). The writer flatters his correspondent as the author of 'beautiful poems' (l. 5). But we know that Maimonides' fame was not due to his achievements in this branch of literature. As was the fashion of the time, he would compose his Hebrew letters in rhymed prose. An admirer might have regarded them as poetry. But the sage's whole bent lay in a direction quite removed from the imaginative flights of the muse.[1] The writer of our epistle is much pressed for time and only sends a few lines in order to keep up the friendship with his distinguished correspondent. He may be identical with the father of Netaneel b. Fayyūmi, the author of the theological work, Bustan al-'Uḳul (ed. Levine, New York, 1908).[2]

Having completed his Mishnah Commentary in 1168, Maimonides was soon recognized as a scholar of renown. Already in 1711 a Ketuba drawn up in Fusṭāṭ is issued by 'his authority' (A. D. 20, 5[a]). He thus had charge of the local Bet-Dīn. He is styled 'the great Rabbi in Israel', a title he already then fully deserved. Two years later he took an active part in obtaining the ransom-money for Jewish prisoners who probably hailed from Christian countries. Possibly on this occasion he wrote the circular letter to the communities of Damirah, Jaujār, Sammanūd, Damsīs, and Sunbāṭ (A. D. 29, 5). He imparted in Egypt instruction to a number of disciples and seems to have been at the head of a school. But Talmudic studies were pursued only to a small extent (A. D. 29, 4). It should, however, be borne in mind that our sage was a very busy man. What with his official duties as court physician, his large private clientele and his own studies, very little time for teaching was left to him.

1 See Gr., VI[4], 267. Yet he composed a number of verses, see Bacher, *Mtschr.*, LIII, 581 ff. Cp. also Harkavy, חדשים גם ישנים, VII, 52 (in *Hebrew Graetz*, IV).

2 That the book was composed by the father of Jacob to whom Maimonides sent his Iggeret Taimān, as Livine takes it for granted, cannot be ascertained from the work (see also *Arab. Lit.*, § 147 a; Eppenstein, *Mose b. Maimon*, II, 1914, p. 45).

An interesting letter from a correspondent in Kalne (Raḳḳah, where Benjamin of Tudela found about 700 Jews)[1] to his friend in Egypt we have in A. D. 30. The date of the epistle is either 1505 Sel.[2] (1194 C. E.) or three years later (if the correct reading is 1508 Sel.; 1540 Sel. is very unlikely). The writer first salutes 'our master' Moses 'the teacher of righteousness' (l. 45, most likely Maimonides) and his son (i.e. Abraham), then R. Ḥalfon and his son, R. 'Āli and his son-in-law, the profound scholar Mishael (very likely b. 'Uzziel, see Steinschneider, *Arab. Literatur*, § 167), his sons and nephew, a certain scholar X., further, all the 'disciples', headed by Joseph and X., and finally R. Menaḥem (see *infra*, 247, note 1, end). The writer had thus several acquaintances in Cairo-Fusṭāṭ, where he probably stayed for some time. Business took him to Raḳḳah. But he was displeased with his surroundings as they offered him no intellectual scope. He would have liked to leave his place of residence, where he was even the owner of whole streets, and return to Egypt in the hope of becoming famous in poetry as before. But first he must arrange his private affairs and provide maintenance for his children (l. 15 ff.). His friend's letters that reached him on Sivan 20th quite overwhelmed him by reason of their beauty of poetic diction. His correspondent's identity cannot be ascertained. He inquired about the excellent glosses by which 'our master' (רבינו, no doubt Maimonides, as he was the only person styled so in our epistle) elucidated the Halakot (l. 24 ff.). Probably reference is made here to the sage's explanations of certain passages in his Mishnah Torah.[3] The writer of our epistle states that he asked R. Joseph about them and he knew nothing of the whole affair. Very likely Joseph b. Aḳnīn, Maimonides' favourite disciple, is meant, who lived in Aleppo since about 1187

[1] *Itinerary*, ed. Adler, 33: ומשם יום אחד לראקיה היא סלכה (v. l. כלנה is more correct) בתחלת ארץ שנער החולקת בין ארץ התוגרמים ומלכות שנער · ובה כמו תש יהודים ובראשם ר׳ זכאי ור׳ נדיב והוא סגיא נהור ור׳ יוסף · ושם כנסת מבנין עזרא בעלותו מבבל לירושלם. About Raḳḳah see Le Strange, *Palestine under the Moslems*, 518.

[2] אתֹקֹהֹ; the ה is doubtful, and can also be taken as ח or ם.

[3] A number of these are to be found in his responsa to Jonathan Hakkohen of Lunel, and also to the Dayyan Pinḥas b. Meshullam of Alexandria, see *Ḳobeṣ*, I, 6ª ff., 26ª.

(see Munk, *Notice sur Joseph b. Jehouda*, 53, and Pozn., *Babyl. Geon.*, 30 ff.). It seems that Joseph sent to Maimonides (?) a request for the correct text of certain passages (l. 27 f.). That our writer had connexions with Aleppo we learn from the next lines (28 ff.). His Egyptian correspondent gave him some directions about certain Talmudical commentaries. He forthwith sent a messenger from Kalne to R. Samuel and R. Abraham in Aleppo. But meanwhile the former arrived at Kalne by another route and had with him only the Commentary on Berakot. (Probably the work of either R. Nissim or R. Ḥananel is meant here.) This R. Samuel inquired after the welfare of their Egyptian friend and congratulated him on his marriage.

Then follow details of business transactions between the two correspondents. The writer in Kalne does not desire to part with a certain headdress since he possesses in his whole stock none like it. He regrets to have taken a sum of money from R. 'Āli for a garment of foxes' fur. If possible let him refund himself from the bearer of the epistle. A certain thing is with Abū'l-Zahaḳ in Damascus. His correspondent authorized him to take 7 d., but of this sum he had so far received 50 silver pieces (very likely dirhems). From the whole transaction hardly any profit will accrue to him. Here we have a typical letter, written in rhymed prose and dealing with literature and business simultaneously. While following their material pursuits in life these two friends keep their spiritual needs in the forefront. In showing us that the Jew of those times was not merely intent on money-making, this letter has a peculiar interest of its own.

We insert here an epistle (A. D. 30[a] recto, by appearance dating from the beginning of the thirteenth century) addressed to a certain scholar R. Yehoseph. The writer, who lived in Damascus, reports of the movements of Rabbi Joseph, who is perhaps identical with ibn Aḳnīn. Owing to sickness and the dangers of the road the writer could not as yet return to the place of residence of R. Yehoseph. Yet he is longing for the congenial company of learned people. During the summer he hopes to be able to make the journey. The previous winter R. Joseph was ill in Baalbec[1] but he could not visit him on his sick bed.

[1] בעלת. See Benjamin of Tudela (*Itinerary*, ed. Adler, 31): ומשם חצי יום לבעלבך והיא בעלות (v. l. בעלת).

data are also discussed bearing on Joshu'a's son, David, who for a time occupied the dignity of Nagid and presided over the school. But certain unknown circumstances compelled him to leave Egypt for Damascus and Aleppo.

A number of fragments, attributed to Abraham Maimuni, are critically analysed in A. D. 34. As a result only one of them is a genuine product of the Nagid, while another forms the end of an epistle sent to him soon after his father's death (nos. 4 and 1). The remainder, except one coming from a Nasi who perhaps resided in Bagdād (no. 3), deals with the Bagdād academy (nos. 2 and 5), a subject not of direct connexion with our theme here, though Egyptian Jewry kept up relations with the centre of learning that was re-established in the twelfth century in the capital of 'Iraḳ.

(3) In conclusion a number of prominent Jews in Egypt are introduced who were not dealt with in the preceding pages. A. D. 35, 1, mentions Sar Shalom, 'head of the congregation', who is also styled 'the mighty dignitary', (Ab)-Bet-Dīn and 'Alluf of the academy'. Menasse, a grandson (or descendant) of Shema'ya (perhaps Shema'ya Gaon, see A. C. 28, 1–2, and Pozn., *Babyl. Geon.*, 110) requests a Reader X. b. Ṣadoḳ Hassopher to use his influence on Sar Shalom that the latter send an epistle in his own handwriting to the Alexandrian community on behalf of this Menasse. Evidently he was about to go there in order to take up a communal position. He hopes to be there before New Year. Let Sar Shalom write to the local Reader and congregation in favour of Menasse. He encloses some remarks about the dealings of the people of Ṣahragt. If his friend thinks it advisable, let him show them to Sar Shalom. If our Menasse was a descendant of Shema'ya Gaon, then it is possible that he lived in the second half of the twelfth century, and hence Sar Shalom can be identical with Zuṭa. But the handwriting has an earlier appearance. Also the title 'Alluf of the academy' held by Sar Shalom, and also by the Reader X. b. Ṣadoḳ, points to an earlier time when the Babylonian schools existed in the eleventh century, though it is likely that the title was also bestowed by the Bagdād Geonim in the following centuries.

An important elder was Ḥalfon b. Isaac (no. 2). Both father and son were given honorary titles, viz. 'the generous one of the congregations' and 'the desire of the congregations' respectively. Ḥalfon was also a patron of the academy and was styled 'the favourite of the school'. His acquaintances were two namesakes, Ḥalfon Hallevi b. Nataneel and Ḥalfon Hallevi b. Menasse (b. al-קטאיף). A very important Katib in the time of Maimonides was Abū'l Barakāt Yehuda Hakkohen b. El'azar (no. 3). It is impossible to identify him with Netaneel Hallevi Gaon (as Pozn., *Babyl. Geon.*, 103, does) as is evident from the difference of their names as well as their fraternity. Abū'l Barakāt's son, El'azar, was also an important state official, going by the name Sa'ad al-Mulk 'the happiness of the kingdom'. In a document of 1176 C. E. we read also about an eminent physician Yeḳutiel whose father Moses was a Katib and also 'superintendent of the merchants' (different namesakes are evidently those mentioned in a document of 1093 C. E., see A. B. 2, note 3). In no. 4 we hear of a Shemarya Nagid (b. David?), but nothing further is known about his exact time and activities. If he be identical with the Nagid to whom Ḥarizi's *Taḥkemoni* is dedicated (by the copyist?)[1], then we have a *terminus a quo*. The names of a few Jewish physicians in Egypt are given in no. 5, viz. Ephraim b. Yefet (in Fusṭāṭ, 1066 C. E.), Elijah styled 'the important dignitary' (his son Levi was also apparently a state official), and Zekarya b. Elijah Rosh Haḳḳahal (both father and son seem to have been influential persons).

From the good wishes of winning favour with 'the king and the dignitaries', it appears that Abraham b. El'azar (no. 6) was in the employment of the state. Likewise in no. 8 a great dignitary, a Levite, is saluted, and the hope is expressed that he find favour in the eyes of 'the king, the Wezīr, the Court ladies, the eunuchs, the lords of the realm, and all the men of the government'. The person addressed seems also to have been a scholar. Finally we hear of a number of Dayyanim in Fusṭāṭ and elsewhere (no. 7). As in the whole of this section, it is only fragmentary and disconnected material that could be offered here in the hope that the gaps will be filled up as further Genizah finds are made accessible.

[1] Bodl. 2517 contains Ḥarizi's *Taḥkemoni* with a dedication to a Nagid Shemaryah b. David.

CHAPTER VI

The Communal Organization.

We have reviewed the life of the Jews in Egypt and in Palestine during more than two centuries. A large number of communal officials and dignitaries as well as other persons bearing honorific titles have come to our notice. It is therefore necessary to attempt to reconstruct, in more or less systematic a manner, the communal organization which these Jewries developed. Without such a discussion this treatise would lack the *finale* which is required by way of summarizing and also supplementing what is to be learned from the preceding investigations.

1. The leading political position in the community was held by the Nagid. The origin of this office is still obscure (see Berliner, *Magazin*, XVII, 50–8, Neubauer, *J. Q. R.*, IX, 552, and Gottheil, *J. E.*, V, 68–9). Sambari (in Neub. I, 115 ff.) indeed tells us that the daughter of the Bagdād Caliph al-Tai (who ascended the throne in 363 A. H. = 973 C. E.) married the King of Egypt. On her arrival in 366 A. H.[1] she began to inquire into the constitution of her new country and discovered that the Jews had no political head corresponding to the Exilarch in Babylon. Her husband thereupon sent to 'Iraḳ for a member of the Davidic family, whom he appointed as Nagid over the Egyptian Jewry. Sambari in his account copies almost verbally David b. Zimra's well-known responsum about the Negidut office (שו"ת רדב"ז, III, no. 509).[2] But it is remarkable that none

[1] ובשנת שסו לחשבונם היא שנת ד׳ אלפים ותשמה לצירה באה המלכה לארץ מצרים וכו׳. But 366 A. H. = 976/7 C. E., whereas 4745 A. M. = 985.

[2] Frumkin, אבן שמואל, p. 18, quotes this responsum, and remarks, quite unwarrantedly, on the passage: ’מפני כי קרוב למלכות הישמעאלים נשא מלך מצרים אחד הנקרא אצלם אל כאליפה‘ (הוא הכליף אל אדהיד האחרון לבית פאטימי). Frumkin thus makes the Negidut to have originated in the reign of the last Fāṭimid

of the Negidim, known to us, claimed Davidic descent. As if to prove his assertion, Sambari (ibid., 116 and 133) states that the Nasi Yehuda b. Joshiah, the contemporary of Maimonides (above, p. 175), was also Nagid. But this is not confirmed by any other source and is not probable. On the other hand we have found Nesiim in Egypt who were contemporaries of Negidim of non-Davidic descent. Together with Meborak Nagid we have David Hannasi b. Daniel, while the former's son Moses Nagid and likewise Samuel Hannagid b. Ḥananya were the patrons of Nesiim, as can be gathered from their respective titles 'the standard of the Nesiut' and 'the help of the Nesiut' (דגל הנשיאות and עזר הנשיאות, see A. B. 20, II, 1; A. D. 8 and 17; cp. also above, p. 233).

The Negidut was probably a sequel of the conquest of Egypt by the Fāṭimids in 969. An exilarch living in Bagdād could naturally no longer wield any authority over the Jews of the new empire. Moreover, it became a political contingency to make these independent from a dignitary appointed by the 'Abbasid Caliph of Bagdād. The first Nagid was most likely Palṭiel, who is reported to have had such a large share in the conquest of the country of the Nile (above, p. 16). The *Aḥima'aṣ Chronicle* indeed states that he was the head over all Jewish communities within the Fāṭimid realm.[1] His successor was his son Samuel. But after the latter's death the office seems to have been divided. We find thus in the first half of the eleventh century the Negidim Abraham b. 'Aṭa and Jacob b. 'Amram in Ḳairowān (see *J. Q. R.*, N. S., IX, 162–3, and above, p. 144). Probably the communities of Ifrikiyya were represented by the Nagid, who resided in Ḳairowān. Till about 1044 North Africa, under rulers of the Sanhāja Berbers, seated at Mahdiya (near Ḳairowān), acknowledged the suzerainty of the Fāṭimid Caliphs. But then Mo'izz, the ruling governor, joined the orthodox Sumnites and accepted a new investiture from the 'Abbasid Caliph in 1046. After some warfare, Mo'izz maintained his independence in

Caliph al-'Āḍid (1160–71, see above, p. 229), nearly two centuries after the real creation of the office! And Gottheil (*l. c.*) makes of this an 'Egyptian Calif 'Aḍud al-Daulah (977–82)', quoting our very Frumkin!!

[1] Neub., II, 130: ר׳ פלטיאל המנגן (r. המנגד) לקהלות עם אל · הדרים במצרים ובארץ ישראל · בפלירמו ובאפריקא ובכל ממשלת ישמעאל.

Mahdiya, and henceforth the rulers of Egypt had no authority farther west than Barḳa (see L.-P. 137–8).

We have to deal here with the Egyptian Negidim. A highly interesting account of the installation of a Nagid has been published by Mr. Elkan N. Adler in *J. Q. R.*, IX, 717–18.[1] The new Nagid recounts how still in the lifetime of his predecessor he distinguished himself as a scholar and preacher. The Caliph designated him as the political head of Jewry, while still several years previously the Nasi Ḥasdai honoured him by the bestowal of the title 'crown of the lords' (עטרת השרים). Since then it became evident that he was to be the successor of the Nagid. His authority has been confirmed by the Nasi as well as by the Gaon of Palestine. Had not the government taken the initiative by bestowing upon him the dignity, the support of the Gaon alone would have sufficed. But now his position has been doubly strengthened since the academy accepted the candidate chosen by the government.

The Nasi Ḥasdai probably resided in Egypt. He cannot be identical with the Exilarch of Babylon, as Kaufmann thinks. As the fragment dates most likely from the Fāṭimid period, it is obvious that the Bagdād Exilarch would have no influence whatever in the matter of appointing the chief political representative of Egyptian Jewry. We have found above several Nesiim in Palestine and Syria towards the end of the tenth century and onwards. Likewise it is likely that members of the Davidic family resided in Egypt prior to David b. Daniel. We have seen above (p. 111 ff.) that during Solomon b. Yehuda's Gaonate a Nasi settled in Jerusalem who previously stayed for some time in the country of the Nile. The authority of these Nesiim was more of a moral than a political character. When the writer of the above account states that he was holding the dignity 'by permission of our lord the Exilarch under whose royal sceptre we and all Israel belong and all of us hold fast to the true God and to the Nesiut',[2] we have to regard it as

[1] See also Kaufmann, ibid., X, 162–4, and Pozn., *Babyl. Geon.*, 112–13.

[2] P. 717: וכי אני עוצר בעם י״י אחריו ברשיון אדוננו ראש הגולה אשר אנחנו וכל בית ישראל באים תחת שבט מלכותו וכולנו מתחזקים באלהי אמן ובשער נשיאותו ירומם. This Exilarch is no doubt identical with הנשיא הגדול ראש גליות כל ישראל mentioned before. The lacuna between נשיאנו נסיכנו . . . חסדאי should be filled out by [מר רב].

a flattering literary flourish subject to much discount. As far as could be gathered from the fragments discussed above, the Nesiim had only a spiritual hold on the people. As descendants of King David, they would bestow honorary titles on distinguished members of the communities, as will be seen farther on. If a Nasi happened to be a scholar in addition he would be able to assert increased influence and authority.

Now the author of the above account was given by the Nasi the title 'the crown of the dignitaries' (עטרת השרים) several years before he became Nagid. Indeed we find the Negidim Meborak and his son Moses styled by this title (see A. B. 20, II, 1; A. D. 8). The Nagid usually went by the honorific name of שר השרים ('the dignitary of the dignitaries'), and thus are the very same Meborak and Moses addressed (*l.c.*). It is obvious that they have been given the former title prior to their having become Negidim. Moreover, Samuel Hannagid's son, Moses (= Yaḥya), is designated as עטרת השרים and as 'candidate for the Negidut', המעותד לנגידות (A. D. 17, 1). We may therefore safely assume that the *Nagid designate* used to be known in the community as 'the crown of the dignitaries'. By bestowing this title on the author of the above fragment, the Nasi indicated his desire that he should be the successor of the contemporary Nagid. Probably the writer is identical with Yehuda Nagid, Meborak's brother, who was also a scholar and held the title Resh Kallah. Both the Nasi and the Palestinian Gaon were in favour of his election. His predecessor Yehoseph Nagid, the grandson of the famous Palṭiel, was still in office during the lifetime of Daniel b. 'Azarya (above, p. 184). As the Gaon of Palestine is not styled here also Nasi, it is to be inferred that Yehuda became Nagid after 1062 C. E. when Elijah Hakkohen occupied already the presidency of the academy. Meborak was assigned for the Negidut office already in his brother's lifetime and is therefore styled עטרת השרים, and likewise his son and successor Moses. Samuel Hannagid's son, Moses, though made a candidate for the dignity, did not however actually succeed his father. This was probably due to the intrigues of Zuṭa, who denounced Samuel and caused his deposal for 66 days (above, p. 235).

We are thus able to give the following chronology of the

Negidim. Beginning with Palṭiel, the dignity was handed on to his son Samuel and the latter's son Yehoseph (died about 1065 C. E.). It was then transferred to the important court physician Yehuda b. Saadya (*c.* 1065–79), and subsequently to his brother Meborak (*c.* 1079–1110) and the latter's son Moses (died about 1140). On the demise of the last Nagid, the Caliph's favourite physician, Abū Manṣūr (Samuel b. Ḥananya), became the political head of the Egyptian Jewry (*c.* 1140–59). For the next half-century, till the elevation of Abraham Maimuni to the office in 1205, no clear information is accessible as to the holders of the dignity. An unscrupulous person (Zuṭa = Sar Shalom) appeared on the scene, but he was not recognized by the community. With Abraham Maimuni the Negidut again remained the privilege of one family for several generations. Most of the Negidim were court physicians and for this reason could use their influence on behalf of that section of 'the people of tribute' that was under their charge.

The Arabic title of the Nagid was Raīs al-Yahūd. His functions were to represent all the Jews, to serve them as legal authority and as judge in conformity with their laws, to watch over the contracting of marriages, the pronouncing of the ban, and the turning in prayer to the proper Ḳiblah. The Muhammedans looked to him for protection against Jews. The custom has been that the Raīs should be of the Rabbinite community to the exclusion of the other communities, though he sat in judgement over all the three sections, Rabbanite, Ḳaraite, and Samaritan.[1]

[1] Firkowicz (as cited by Gurland, גנזי ישראל, I, 61, no. 36) knows of a *Ḳaraite* Nagid Samuel b. Isaiah Iskandri, who died in 1062 C. E. A supposed colophon of a Book of Precepts, composed by Israel b. Daniel, is said to contain this information. Firkowicz writes: הוא שמואל הנגיד נמצא זכרונו בפנקס הספרים הקדמונים שהובא מירושלים מהקדשי קהל דמשק לגוזלווא (Eupatoria) וז"ל: הספר הי"ח ספר המצות שהקדיש מר׳ ורב׳ ישראל הדיין אסכנדרי בר דניאל המערבי בק"ק חברון תוב"ב שמכרהו בששה ועשרים שנה בשנת 457 לקרן זעירא אשע"ג לשטרות (H. 457 really = 1064/5 C. E.) בשנת פטירת כג"ק הדרת יקרת השר הגדול אלוף אחינו בני מקרא קהל עדת יפיפיה מצרים ואחיותיה אבלי ציון וירושלים מורנו ורבנו שמואל הנגיד ב"ר ישעיהו אסכנדרו רי"ת אשר עשה טובות רבות לישראל עמו גם לבני מקרא וגם לבני בירב (i. e. Rabbinites!) במצרים ויספדו עליו כל ישראל אחינו . . . We have seen in the text that through-

In short the Raīs of the Jews took the place of the Patriarch of the Christians: so Ḳalḳashandi (cited by Gottheil, *J. Q. R.*, XIX, 500–1; cp. also ibid., XVIII, 21). The Nagid would relegate some of his powers to subordinate dignitaries. The local Jewish courts in several provincial towns are stated, as we have seen before, to have been appointed by the Nagid by whose authority the documents are issued. On the other hand we have documents issued by Maṣliah Gaon, while in 1139 we have courts appointed by a dignitary Solomon who was no Nagid. Also Joshu'a b. Dosa had authority over the (or a) Bet-Dīn in Fusṭāṭ (above, p. 217 f.) in 1144, when Samuel b. Ḥananya was Nagid. It is therefore evident that some of the prerogatives of the Nagid were also granted to other communal leaders of eminence, either of scholastic or political standing (see farther on *sub* Dayyan al-Yahūd).

In the Hebrew fragments, discussed above, the Negidim are given several high-sounding titles such as 'the Mordecai of the (present) time' (i. e. champion of Jewry), מקל תפארה, צנצנת המן, גביר הגבירים, נגיד הנגידים, 'Nagid of God's people', 'Nagid of Israel and Yehuda', 'Nagid of the diaspora' (as if holding sway over the whole community of Israel), and finally שר השרים.[1] Corresponding to the last title was that of the Nagid designate,

out the whole of the eleventh century the Negidat was in the hands of the Rabbinites. Of a Ḳaraite Nagid there is no mention anywhere else. Moreover, had there been such a dignitary in the second half of the eleventh century, he would have certainly been mentioned in the memorial list of important contemporary Ḳaraites in Fusṭāṭ (discussed above, p. 176 f.). Firkowicz's statement is very likely fictitious; indeed other objections have been raised as regards the author Israel b. Daniel (see Pozn., *J. Q. R.*, XIX, 71–8, and in Luncz's *Jerusalem*, X, 110 f.).

[1] For these titles see A. B. 20, II, 1; 58, l. 14; A. D. 4, 6; 8; 16; 17; 19; 33, 4. As to צנצנת המן, cp. also Bodl. 1 containing a colophon, dated 1104 C. E., לנטע נעמן · צנצנת המן השר הטפסר. The jar of manna as well as Aaron's staff, placed before the Ark (Exod. 16. 33; Num. 17. 16 ff.), were metaphorically applied to a Nagid or another prominent man. Cp. poem 27 in Steinschneider's מורה המורה (קבץ על יד, I, p. 6): מקום זו צנצנת המן שבה הפקד המן שמשה האבילו · לבני ישראל במדבר ארבעים שנה הזילו · המן הוא דתו שלמד ודבר האל שנגלה לו · גם זה משה האיש (Maimonides) הרץ אחריו החנה על דגלו. Yet the underlying idea of these metaphors is still obscure. According to tradition (Yoma 52[b]) the jar as well as the stick were hidden together with the Ark in the time of king Joshiah.

'crown of the dignitaries' (עטרת השרים). He is also called מעותד לנגידות (p. 254), while a Nagid's son would be styled סגן הנגידות (A. D. 8). Individual Negidim, if very influential, held also other titles. Thus Meborak is called 'viceroy' (משנה למלך, p. 209), while Samuel Hannagid is eulogized as 'the right hand of the realm' (ימין המלכות, ימין המלוכה, p. 222, note 2; A. D. 17). Is the latter title a Hebrew adaptation of 'Amīn al-Mulk' (p. 227, note 1)?

Two Negidim only are so far called נגיד ארץ ישראל ויהודה as distinct from 'Nagid of Israel and Yehuda', viz. 'Obadya b. 'Ula in the second half of the twelfth century, and Hillel b. Moses in the thirteenth century (A. D. 29, 3, see above, p. 243). Now as regards the latter we know that in the thirteenth century the Nagid dignity was held by Abraham Maimuni and his son David, and also in the next century by their descendants Abraham and Joshu'a (died 1355, above, p. 248). One should therefore not identify the 'Nagid of the land of Israel and Yehuda' with the Egyptian Nagid. Very likely after the reconquest of Palestine by Saladin in 1187–92, an official was appointed to look after the interests of the Jews in Palestine and in Syria. Before the Crusades the Egyptian Nagid was the political head of these Jewries too. But during nearly the whole of the twelfth century the Holy Land was in the hands of the warriors of the Cross, and the Nagid could exercise no authority there. After Saladin's Holy War a new office was created for the political head of the Syrian and Palestinian Jewry. Ḳalḳashandi (*l. c.* 534) indeed speaks of a Raīs al-Yahūd in Shām, who probably went within the community by the name of 'Nagid of the land of Israel and Yehuda'.[1] Accordingly, 'Obadya b. 'Ula was the first holder of this dignity, and so far only another such Nagid, Hillel b. Moses, is known. Whether they resided in Syria or in Cairo at the seat of government, cannot be ascertained.

(2) Next to the Nagid stood 'the head of the congregations'

[1] That by 'the land of Israel' Syria was understood in those times is also evident from Abraham Maimuni's letter (in Munk, *Notice sur Joseph Ben-Jehouda*, 5, note 1), wherein he writes about Joseph ibn 'Aḳnīn who lived in Aleppo: (*sc.* יוסף) ורבי נכבד היה בכל ארץ ישראל בחכמת התורה ובשאר החכמות. Likewise the Gaon of Damascus in the time of Benjamin of Tudela was ראש הישיבה של ארץ ישראל (A. D. 20, 6).

(ראש הקהלות, very likely those of Cairo-Fusṭāṭ), who had authority over Rabbanites, Ḳaraites, and Samaritans alike. Such a dignitary we found to have been the court physician Jacob b. Isaac b. Moses (above, p. 83). That the 'president of the congregations' was not identical with the Nagid is clearly demonstrated by the affair which involved Moses Nagid b. Meborak and Yakin ראש הקהלות b. Netaneel (above, p. 212 ff.). Both were in office at the same time. Other 'heads of the congregations' in Fusṭāṭ were Meborak (b. 'Āli) and Abū'l Faḍl (the latter perhaps identical with Yakin b. Netaneel, see above, p. 147, and A. D. 4). Also Mebasser b. Jesse, Menasse Hallevi, and Jacob b. Abraham Dayyan were such presidents (see above, p. 148 and A. A. 16, 1), the last two probably in Fusṭāṭ. Aleppo also had 'a head of the congregation'. In the letter from Tadmor? (Palmyra?, above, p. 37, note 1) to Jacob b. Joseph, Ab at Aleppo, we find that a Sa'adael 'president of the congregations' (l. 42) is saluted. Very likely every large community, divided into sections such as Babylonians and Palestinians, Karaites and Samaritans, had a dignitary who represented politically the whole local Jewry.

(3) In addition, each section had a Raīs, viz. the ראש הקהל. We have seen that in the time of Ephraim b. Shemarya the 'head' of the Palestinians in Fusṭāṭ was Samuel Hakkohen b. Abṭalion, while his colleague over the Babylonians was Yefet Hallevi b. Tobias (above, pp. 95 f., 99, 137). Already in 750 we find in Fusṭāṭ Abū 'Āli Ḥasan of Bagdād styled ראש הקהל, corresponding to ראש הכנסת (archisynagogus) of the pre-Muhammedan period (above, p. 15). If such a Raīs was also a scholar, he would naturally act as Dayyan (שופט, Ḳāḍi). Thus Samuel Hakkohen b. Abṭalion, who was a Ḥaber, i.e. holding a Rabbinical Diploma (סמיכה), was for some time the judge of the community (above, p. 110). Similarly, the Rosh Haḳḳahal Sar Shalon was also Alluf of the academy and (Ab)-Bet-Dīn (above, p. 249). Without giving an exhaustive list of the 'heads of the congregation', as far as hitherto known, reference is made to Sa'adya Hakkohen b. Hillel (Bodl. 2834[32]), Moses b. Yefet הפרנס הנאמן ראש ה[קהל] (*J. Q. R.*, XVIII, 28), and Moses Rosh Haḳḳahal in 1165 (*J. Q. R.*, XIX, 723; his identity with Maimonides is improbable).

(4) Next to the 'head of the congregation' were the Parnasim. Under Samuel Hakkohen b. Abṭalion we find as many as four such officials (p. 96). The mode of election of all these dignitaries is unknown. Whether a Rosh Haḳḳahal had first to serve in the capacity of Parnās or not is obscure. But we have just heard of Moses b. Yefet 'the faithful Parnās' who also became 'head of the congregation'. The Parnasim had probably to supervise the charity collections and were the trustees of the legacies for the benefit of the synagogues.[1]

(5) In addition, several other titles, mostly honorific, were given to important members. Any person of standing expected to be styled 'elder', זקן, corresponding to the Arabic al-Sheikh. This title would be amplified by הזקן הנכבד, הזקן החשוב, הזקן היקר (see e.g. A. B. 2; A. C. 29; A. D. 17, 3; 19; 35, 2). Their Arabic equivalents would be al-Sheikh al-jalīl, al-najīb, al-'azīz, &c. But specific titles, probably publicly bestowed either by a Nasi, Gaon, or a whole community, were the following: (1) זקן הקהלה 'the elder of the congregation'. This title I have found only once.[2] (2) זקן הקהלות 'elder of the congregations', was the title of the influential physician Isaac Hakkohen b. Furāt (above, p. 84). Perhaps all the sections of the Fusṭāṭ Jewry honoured him at a public meeting in recognition of his services on behalf of his co-religionists. (3) His son Abraham, a still more important doctor, went by the name of שר העדה 'the lord of the congregation'. But its exact character is not clear to me. Tobias the Babylonian was also styled שר העדה (above, p. 130). Hillel, the father of Abraham the probable author of the Zuṭa Megillah, is once mentioned as סיר אלאהל 'the lord of the people', which is the Arabic translation of the above Hebrew title (A. D. 33, 1[c]). (4) The same Abraham Hakkohen b. Isaac was given the name הוד הזקנים 'the glory of the elders', probably by the Nasi and Gaon Daniel b. 'Azarya. The same title was held previously in Bagdād by 'Ali b. Faḍlān (above, p. 86). (5) סגולת קהל צוען ורצויו

[1] A fragment in T.-S. Box K 3 mentions אלעזר הפרנס השמָש בר כ̇נ̇ק̇ מרנא ור׳ הילל נע. Did this Parnās combine the duties of the synagogue attendant?

[2] T.-S. 13 J 10[9] contains a fragment of a poem: (ll. 4–5) יאוספו יקובצו בכלול · לשר יקיר וגדול בהמולה הוא אבי עוזר צדקה · בנו יוסף זקן כל הקהלה: The metre is — — ᴗ — — — ᴗ — — — ᴗ.

'the choice of the Fusṭāṭ community and its favourite' was the honorific name of the important Parnes, Abraham b. Mebasser (above, p. 96). (6) Finally, the eminent elder Ḥalfon b. Isaac is styled 'the desire of the congregations' (חמדת הקהלות), while his father was honoured by the title 'the benefactor of the congregations' (נדיב הקהלות, pp. 249–50).

Titles without specific connotation are such as גביר החסדים, ראש הנדיבים, הדר הנדיבים, הוד הנדיבים, כארם אלכניסה, &c., profusely and flatteringly given to charitable and generous members of the community (see A. D. 17, 1; 29, 3; 35, 3; *Saadyana*, 28, note 4). A priestly elder would be addressed פאר הכהנים, סגן הכהנים, נזר הכהנים (so Abraham b. Isaac, the physician). This would be varied as regards a Levite, viz. שר הלוים, פאר הלוים, נזר הלוים, הוד הלוים (see above, p. 225, note 1, end; A. B. 10; A. D. 22; 33, 1[e]; 35, 2; *J. Q. R.*, N. S., I, 50).[1]

Special honorary names were bestowed upon the most prominent members of the community, e. g. such as Abū Sa'ad and his brother Abū Naṣr, the sons of Sahl al-Tustari, David Hallevi b. Isaac in Fusṭāṭ, or Netaneel Hakkohen in Alexandria. Thus the first is called 'the elder of the house of Israel' (זקן בית ישראל), the second 'the glory of the house of Israel' (תפארת בית ישראל), the third 'the elder of the generation, the glory of both sections' (זקן הדור, פאר שתי הפאות; also גביר וסלר), while the last is styled Pashah (הפחה).[2] Usually a state official or court physician is designated 'lord' (שר, dignitary = Arabic Sayyīd).[3] The corresponding amplifications are שר התעודה, שר כל בית ישראל, שר בית ישראל; השר הגדול בישראל, השר האדיר בישראל, השר האדיר, השר האביר; השר הנאה, השר הנעלה, השר הנכבד, השר הכביר.[4] Twice there occurs the title שר מנוחה (above, p. 146; A. B. 65; A. C. 16, 2), and once שר המנוחה (A. D. 29, 3), 'lord of rest'. These dignitaries were probably 'quartermasters' of the army (cp. Jer. 51^{59}). But it

[1] T.-S. 8 J 21[2] contains a letter addressed to the physician Samuel השר היקר שר הלוים פאר הרופאים b. Netaneel השר היקר פאר הלוים. Ḥananya, the brother of the Bagdād Gaon Samuel Hallevi b. 'Āli is styled סגן הלוים (Benjamin of Tudela, *Itinerary*, ed. Adler, 39).

[2] Above, p. 112, and A. B. 12; 47.

[3] See e. g. A. B. 60; A. C. 9; A. D. 17, 3 g.

[4] See A. A. 16, I, 2; A. B. 17; 65; A. C. 16, 2; 21; 23[a]; A. D. 4; 11, 2; 16; 17; 26; 35; *J. Q. R.*, N. S., I, 57–8. Cp. also above, p. 220, note 1.

may be that they were connected with Palestine and especially with Jerusalem.[1]

Corresponding to the titles of the Nagid and the Nagid designate (above, p. 254), those of other influential dignitaries would be תפארת השרים, נזר השרים, חמדת השרים.[2] Certain elders in Fusṭāṭ in the period of Solomon b. Yehuda were called 'noblemen' (אלדסתארה, pp. 121, 139), and likewise the heads of the Ḳaraite community in the capital, Moses Hakkohen and his father Aaron, were both styled אציל (see A. C. 21, 1, which is the Hebrew for al-dastūr). Several times are mentioned persons who were known as 'the officials of the merchants' (פקידי הסוחרים), probably holding government positions as inspectors of the bazaars. Such officials we found in Fusṭāṭ and in Ramlāh (p. 81 f., and A. A. 7[a]). One such dignitary was also a Katib (A. D. 35, 3). Also in the letter from Tadmor (?) to Aleppo (p. 37, note 1) 'the officials of the merchants' are saluted. Whether such a superintendent had charge of the Jewish bazaar only (שוק היהודים)[3] cannot be ascertained. Joseph ibn 'Aḳnīn's father-in-law in Aleppo was a Katib of the Dar ذكاء, which Munk (*Notice sur Joseph Ben-Jehouda*, 15) translates as 'contrôleur de la boucherie juive'. This would be a more limited office than that of 'the inspector of the merchants' in general. The controllers of Sheḥiṭa in the Jewish bazaar were communal officials, appointed either by the Gaon (e.g. in Ramlāh) or by the local Haber of the community (e.g. in Fusṭāṭ, above, pp. 128 and 149). To complete the list of honorific titles, there are mentioned עוז התעודה 'the banner of the Jews and the joy of their glory' (so Moses Hakkohen the Ḳaraite, David b. Daniel's father-in-law), כליל היופי (p. 177 and A. C. 29; A. D. 17, 1). A scholar would be eulogized as אב החכמה, עטרת החכמה, מודע התבונה (A. D. 11, 2). It is difficult to ascertain in each case of these and similar titles whether they were granted publicly by a Gaon, Nasi, or community, or were merely flattering adjuncts by the

[1] Cp. Gen. 49. 15, and Deut. 12. 9. In Zeb. 119[a.b] there are mentioned several opinions of Tannaites as to the specific meanings of מנוחה and נחלה. R. Simon b. Yoḥai's view that both expressions refer to Jerusalem has been accepted by R. Ishmael's school (ibid., 119[b], top). Perhaps a Jewish government official in the Holy City would be styled שר מנוחה or שר המנוחה.

[2] A. D. 17, 1; 35, 3-4.

[3] About the Jewish market in Fusṭāṭ see Worman, *J. Q. R.*, XVIII, 28 ff.

writers of the respective fragments wherein these names are to be found. But it may be assumed that those recurring several times or inserted in the documents issued by the Bet-Dīn were permanent ones. On the whole the Jews followed the custom of their Arab fellow-citizens to address prominent men with a host of high-sounding and flattering titles.

The title Raīs (ראש, אלרים, אלרייס) was given to several persons and not only to the Nagid. It is a general designation for several dignitaries. Thus a Gaon, Raīs al-Metibta, would be styled al-Raīs (A. A. 23, note 1, and A. D. 20, 3, הראש המובהק). Both Shemarya and his father Elḥanan went by the name הרב הראש, probably by reason of their presiding over the Bet-Dīn (ראש בית דין, p. 26). Also Abū'l Faraj Joshu'a al-Ḳmūdi is alluded to in the poem (above, p. 23) as ראש to Israel, i.e. a leader of the community.[1] In short the expression אלרים or הראש would also apply to a ראש הקהלות, ראש הקהל, ראש כלה, ראש הסדר, ראש הפרק, ראש בי רבנן, and so on. The influential elder David Hallevi b. Isaac is styled (A. B. 17) הראש האדיר.[2] Samuel b. Ḥofni begins his letter to Fez (*J. Q. R.*, XVIII, 403) שמואל הכהן ראש הישיבה שלגולה בן חפני הראש אב הישיבה שלגולה בן כהן צדק ראש הישיבה שלגולה בן יוסף הנגיד נזר הישיבה שלגולה. Jehuda al-Barceloni in his Sepher Hashṭarot has preserved a formula of a diploma issued to the spiritual head (Rosh) of a community on his appointment. Very likely this specimen was found already in Sa'adya's 'Book of Documents'. The lines given below are copied from Brit. Mus. Add. 27181, fol. 27ª bottom.[3]

[1] Cp. also *Geonica*, II, 69, among the questions of Yehuda b. Joseph of Ḳairowān to Hai Gaon, no. 4, is concerning the head of the community who ordained a fast (גזר רייס אל מוצע עלי אל גמעה), and no. 5 mentions a ban pronounced by the same president on a certain person (אמר הדא אלרייס בנידוי אנסן). In A. C. 25, 1, l. 9, Ebyatar Hakkohen is styled al-Raīs the 'Fourth' (of the school).

[2] Cp. further, A. D. 3, 2; החזן משה בן הראש (*Yehuda Hallevi's Diwan*, ed. Brody, I, no. 38); al-Raīs Barakāt (Bodl. 2878[39]); the Sheikh Abū'l Faraj ibn al-Raīs (Bodl. 2878[102]).

[3] Cp. *J. Q. R.*, N. S., VII, 462, X, 362, and see Halberstamm's edition, p. 131: ויש לך שטר אחר אפטרופוס שאינו מעסקי משאות ומתנות אלא שבוררין להם הקהל אדם למנותו עליהם ראש וכותבין לו שטר ואע"פ שכתבוהו ראשונים בשטרי אפטרופוס אינו נקרא אלא שטר מינוי: וזה טופסו אנו זקנים וראשי קהל

(6) When a Gaon sent an epistle to a community he usually would send his compliments to several of its communal servants. But a comparison of several letters shows that no uniformity was preserved in the order and sequence. In addition to the data discussed by me in *J. Q. R.*, N. S., X, 362 f., bearing on the Babylonian Geonim, a few selections are given here from the fragments dealt with before. (1) In the letter from Palmyra (?) to Jacob b. Joseph at Aleppo (p. 37, note 1) the following are saluted in succession (besides the Ḥaber), 'the head of the congregations', the teachers, the Readers, the Parnasim, the charity treasurers, and all that busy themselves in communal affairs, the elders, and finally 'the officials of the merchants' (l. 42 ff.). Here the chief spiritual and communal leaders are mentioned first (viz. the Ḥaber and the president), then the minor spiritual dignitaries, followed by the same lay workers. The last-mentioned officials probably were in government employ (above, p. 261). (2) In the letter from Tyre to the same Jacob of Aleppo (above, p. 37, note 1) we observe the same division between clerical and lay workers, viz. the Ḥaber, scholars, disciples, Readers, are saluted, followed by the Parnasim and the trusted elders (for ההימנים read מהימנים). (Aleppo Jewry is probably meant above (p. 173), as having in her midst סנהדרין, Ḥaberim, scholars, and disciples). (3) Joshiah Gaon addresses the Damietta community as represented by 'Amram (the head) of the Bet-Dīn, the judge El'azar, and the Dayyan 'Amram, followed by X. and Yeshu'a (X. probably being Rosh Hakkahal and the latter the Parnes), and the other respected elders. Likewise in Rafaḥ the judge Solomon b. Sa'adya is at the head of affairs, supported by the elders and the congregation. The same Gaon, in writing to another community (probably Fusṭāṭ), salutes first the Readers and the qualified judges (המומחים), then the Parnasim and the communal workers, and finally the merchants (A. A. 19–20). (4) Solomon b. Yehuda in an epistle to Tomai (?) greets first the Reader, then the elders, old and young (ישישים, זקנים and

דמתא פלונית החתומים למטה כך היה שברוב עונותינו שחינו ונתמעטנו ונתדלדלנו עד אשר נשארנו מעט מהרבה ונשארו בני קהלינו בלא ראש ובלא אב ב"ד ולא מנהיג . . . ופייסנו ממרנא פלוני בן פלוני חבר עירנו לפי שהוא חכם ונבון וירא שמים ואמיד בממון ושונא בצע . . .

בחורים; Maimonides likewise uses this expression, A. D. 29, 5), and the rest of the community (A. B. 34, Address). Likewise, when writing to Alexandria, the Gaon salutes the respected elders headed by the Reader Solomon (A. B. 31, 4). (5) The Dayyan who sends the epistle to Mastaura on behalf of the Alexandrian community sends greetings, first in the name of his colleagues the Dayyanim, then the communal leaders (נקובי שמות וקרואי עדה), followed by the Readers, and finally the charity collectors (A. B. 18). (6) When Ephraim b. Shemarya is requested to collect donations from his congregation, naturally the would-be subscribers are saluted. Thus in the letter from Alexandria concerning the prisoners (A. B. 15), there are greeted the Ḥaber, then the benefactors, the elders, the Readers, and the Parnasim. Likewise in the letter from Jerusalem (A. B. 27). (7) Finally in the epistle from Ashḳelon to Fusṭāṭ (A. C. 14), the two communities of the capital are saluted as represented by the Ḥaberim, the Readers, and the elders. Samuel Hannagid in a letter to a provincial community mentions first the 'leaders' (אלמקדמין), then the judges and the Ḥazzanim (A. D. 17, 3 j). It is thus evident that no stereotyped form of address was adopted. Though in most cases the clerical servants of the community, the scholars, and the Readers were honoured by being mentioned first.

(7) We shall now deal with the chief spiritual leaders of a community, the Ḥaber (Dayyan) and the Ḥazzan. The procedure in Babylon during the Gaonic period was for the Exilarch or the head of the academy to appoint Dayyanim for the congregations under their respective jurisdiction. No doubt such people were students of the academy where they received the necessary qualifications for administering the Talmudic law. Such a Dayyan would choose two elders from among the people under his spiritual leadership as coadjutors in order to form a proper court (Bet-Dīn, see *J. Q. R.*, N.S., X, 377 ff., for a detailed account). Likewise in Egypt and in Palestine we find several communities represented by Ḥaberim who held a diploma from the Palestinian academy. To mention a few, we find Jacob the Ḥaber b. Joseph in Aleppo, Ephraim b. Shemarya in Fusṭāṭ, styled 'the leading Ḥaber' (החבר המנהיג, *J. Q. R.*, XIX, 251, l. 10), Nathan Hakkohen b. Isaiah in Tiberias (A. C. 13, 4),

Joshua b. 'Āli in Ḥaṣor (A.C. 15), Samuel b. Moses in Tyre (above, p. 167 f.). The duties that devolved upon a Ḥaber in a large community such as Fusṭāṭ could be gauged from the fragments bearing on Ephraim b. Shemarya. Nathan b. Abraham points out that a town that has no Ḥaber has its communal affairs neglected (p. 148). Naturally the Ḥaber would be at the head of the local Bet-Dīn. But not everywhere do we find congregations represented by scholars who held a diploma from the school. The 'judge' (שופט) was not always a Ḥaber. Daniel b. 'Azarya differentiates between the Ḥaberim and the 'judges' (A. C. 22, l. 11). The Ḥaber who wrote the epistle given in A. C. 32 (see above, p. 200f.) seems to have supervised the affairs of his whole district. When the 'judge' of Kalneh died and a dispute arose as to his successor, our Ḥaber was sent for to allay the conflict. Probably respected elders with a knowledge of the Torah, though holding no diploma of the school, would be charged with the administration of justice in their respective communities (see also *J. Q. R.*, N. S., X, 340). Several communities had a fully organized court. Thus, for example, in Damietta (p. 71) we have 'Amram Bet-Dīn (= Ab-Bet-Dīn or Rosh Bet-Dīn, see Bodl. 2874[31], Berakya ראש בי"ד), El'azar השופט and 'Amram הדיין. On the other hand, in Rafaḥ we find only mentioned Solomon השופט and the elders (A. A. 20). Very likely only the first was the recognized judge, while the Rosh Hakkahal and the Parnes acted as his coadjutors in lawsuits. The expressions Shofeṭ and Dayyan are synonymous. Thus Joseph הדיין in Alexandria (*J. Q. R.*, XIX, 250–4, l. 12, see above, p. 88 ff.) is styled השופט by his own son (in the signature).

The president of the court was called Bet-Dīn (shortened from Ab-Bet-Dīn). This is the case with Ephr. b. Shem., 'Āli b. 'Amram, Sar Shalom, Elḥanan b. Shemarya, Joseph Hakkohen in Alexandria, and several others.[1] It is clear that the expression should not always be connected with the office of Ab of the academy. Only when '(Ab)-Bet-Dīn' is qualified by the addition of, e.g. בסנהדרין גדולה (p. 37, note 1), does it become certain that the person referred to was second to the Gaon. A Dayyan

[1] See A. D. 35, 8; *J. Q. R.*, XIX, 724, no. 7; Jacob the Ḥaber b. Isaac Bet-Dīn; *J. Q. R.*, N. S., I, 58, l. 24, Isaac בית דין הנגון: cp. p. 50, ll. 15, 27.

would be complimented as מופלא[1] 'distinguished', similar to the expression ממחה (see Sanh. 87ᵃ top, where Rashi comments on במומחה לבי"ד, במופלא שבבי"ד). Likewise a president of the court is called 'Bet-Dīn Mufla' (so Ephr. b. Shem., A. B. 21), or 'Bet-Dīn Mumḥa' (A. A. 19). Ephraim is also addressed 'the Mumḥa of the great Bet-Dīn' (A. B. 23), which refers to his diploma from the central court of the academy. Indeed the Bet-Dīn, established at the synagogue of the Palestinians in Fusṭāṭ, is designated in a document of 1032 C.E. (*J. Q. R.*, XVIII, 13) הקבוע מפי בית דין הגדול. The Bet-Dīn of the school, as is well known, was called the 'great one'. When Maṣliaḥ settled in Fusṭāṭ as head of a school, he gave this name also to his court which was held in the very same synagogue (A. D. 14, 3; see *J. Q. R.*, XVIII, 14, בבי דינא רבה בשער הישיבה).

On the other hand we find a 'Great Bet-Dīn' in Cairo-Fusṭāṭ at the time when the academy still flourished in the Holy Land. Nahrai b. Nissim is addressed 'Bet-Dīn Haggadol', which seems to be shortened from 'Ab-Bet-Dīn Haggadol' (A. D. 3, 4). Now the Exilarch in Babylon, as is well known, had a supreme court of his own presided over by a judge called 'the Dayyan of the gate' (דיינא דבבא, see *J. Q. R.*, N. S., X, 338). It appears that likewise the Nagid in Egypt had such a Bet-Dīn, at the head of which stood a prominent scholar. Several times there occurs the title Dayyan al-Yahūd.[2] We venture to maintain that just as the Nagid was called Raīs al-Yahūd, the president of his supreme court went by the name of Dayyan al-Yahūd. The local courts of the congregations, whether in Cairo-Fusṭāṭ or in the provincial towns, were under the jurisdiction of this 'great Bet-Dīn'. Thus we find a Fusṭāṭ court mentioned as established

[1] See A. C. 16, 3; Bodl. 2878¹⁰⁶; *J. Q. R.*, N. S., I, 50, ll. 14, 26.

[2] A. D. 35, 4; Bodl. 2876⁵⁶; al-Raīs Abū'l Faraj b. al-Raīs Abū Zakari (a native of Alexandria), Dayyan al-Yahūd (i. e. Fusṭāṭ); the same person is mentioned in the Arabic address, *J. Q. R.*, XIX, 743, no. 89; cp. also Bodl. 2878¹⁰². In April, 1301 C.E., there took place serious riots in Cairo against Christians and Jews because of their alleged contravention of the restrictions imposed upon non-Moslems, 'the people of the tribute'. The representatives of Jews, who solemnly subscribe again to the enactments, are the Raīs (i. e. the Nagid, above, p. 255) and the Dayyan of the Jews (= Dayyan al-Yahūd, see Quatremère, *Histoire des Sultans Mamlouks*, II, 2, p. 178). Cp. also the Hebrew account of Sambari, Neub., *Med. Jew. Chron.*, I, 135–7.

by the supreme court of Meborak Nagid (דממנא מבי דינא רבה, *J.Q.R.*, XVIII, 13; see also A. D. 20, 3). Meborak was a Talmudic scholar, and he may have combined both dignities of Raīs and Dayyan al-Yahūd. He is perhaps therefore styled סנהדרא רבא. He himself had authority from the Exilarch (דממנא מבי ריש גלותא, *J.Q.R.*, N. S., I, 54, bottom). But when a Nagid had to employ a chief Dayyan, he probably left to him the supervision of the minor courts. This furnishes the reason why during the period of office of Samuel Hannagid, Joshuʿa b. Dosa is mentioned in a document of the Fusṭāṭ Bet-Dīn as having authority over it (see above, p. 218). He was probably the Dayyan al-Yahūd side by side with the Nagid, and likewise Solomon (in 1139), styled 'the superior and great dignitary' (p. 217, note 2). The Dayyan al-Yahūd seems to have been a recognized state official. He is therefore called השר הגדול or השר האדיר (cp. p. 260). Joseph b. Nathan (and likewise probably Joshuʿa b. Dosa) was even honoured by the Caliph with the title Amīn al-Mulk, 'the faithful of the realm' (p. 227, note 1). Also Ephraim Hakkohen (b. Abraham), whom Solomon b. Yehuda styles 'lord' and Dayyan, was very likely the chief Dayyan. For a time he was deposed and the Gaon wished him speedy return to his office (p. 132, see also p. 181 f.). To go back to the beginning of the Faṭimid reign in Egypt, probably Shemarya b. Elhanan was president of the Nagid's Bet-Dīn. He therefore went by the name of 'Ab-Bet-Dīn of all Israel' (של כל ישראל, *J. Q. R.*, N. S., VIII, 344). The Ab-Bet-Dīn of the *academy* also styled himself so,[1] just as both the courts of the Nagid and the school were designated 'great courts'. Another Dayyan al-Yahūd was probably Abraham b. Nathan Ab (p. 194), and coming to the second half of the twelfth century and onwards, the holders of the office in succession may have been Maimonides, Yeḥiel b. Elyaḳim of Aleppo, and also Anatoli b. Joseph (pp. 240, 247).[2] The title מורה צדק is so far only applied to Maimonides (p. 244), more by reason of his literary works than because of his having been a Dayyan. Other titles flatteringly

[1] See, e. g. A. A. 15; A. C. 5, note 9.

[2] Perhaps Moses b. Ṣadoḳ was also such chief Dayyan. He is styled השר האדיר הדיין המש[כיל] יסוד המשרה תפארת הישיבה (*J.Q.R.*, N.S., I, 49, l. 5-6; cp. also *R. É. J.*, LXVI, 65, l. 18 f.).

bestowed upon a Dayyan are דגל הדינים, תפארת הדינים (*Saadyana*, 82, note 6).[1] Isaac 'head of all the Dayyanim' (ראש כל הדינים, ibid.) is perhaps identical with Isaac b. Sason, the colleague of Maimonides, who held a prominent position in Cairo-Fusṭāṭ. He exerted himself especially to bring about the final overthrow of Zuṭa (p. 236, note 1). It may be that when Maimonides found the office of Dayyan al-Yahūd too burdensome for him owing to his heavy duties as court physician, he vacated it for his colleague Isaac b. Sason. But in 1171, when a document was issued by authority of Maimonides (A. D. 20, 5[a]), he seems to have been chief Dayyan, because as such he had the privilege of having the documents issued in his name. He was therefore also called al-Raīs, whereas the Negidut was only held by his son but not by the sage himself. Both he and Isaac b. Sason are styled 'the banner of the Rabbinites' (דגל הרבנים, p. 222, note 2), probably after their solemn injunction against following the Ḳaraite practice as regards the ritual bathing of women.[2] But also Meborak Nagid was styled so (A. D. 8).

(8) An important communal servant was the Ḥazzan, who, as we have seen (p. 263, 4), heads in some places the congregation. Ḳalḳashandi (*J. Q. R.*, XIX, 500) declares him to be the leading official after the Raīs al-Yahūd, and he differentiates between the Ḥazzan and the Reader (Sheliaḥ Ṣibbūr). The former 'must be well versed in preaching. He ascends the Minbār (=Almemar) and exhorts them (the congregation)', while the latter is 'the imām who leads them in prayer'. Indeed, Solomon b. Yehuda in a letter speaks of a חזן ודרשן תורתו (and so also Ḥarizi more than a century and a half later, see A. B. 34). It stands to reason that a learned Ḥazzan, favoured by a pleasant voice, would be able to address his audience. The Ḥaber of the community may have been an expert Dayyan and a profound Talmudist, but did not always possess the gift of preaching.

[1] An elder, trusted by the court to act as guardian to orphans (אפטרופוס) or as trustee of charitable legacies, would be styled נאמן בית דין (see above, p. 196, note 2; A. D. 29, 3.

[2] The Arabic original of this תקנה, inspired by Maimonides, and aided by the other Dayyanim, including Isaac b. Sason, is published by Friedländer, *Mtschr.*, LIII, 469 ff. The date is 1487 Sel. = 1176 C. E. About Maimonides' attitude towards the Ḳaraites, see also *Gr.*, VI[4], 287, 306.

But it is incorrect to make the Ḥazzan exclusively the preacher as distinct from the reader (as Ḳalḳashandi does). The chief function of the Ḥazzan was to intone the prayers. Thus, for example, Revaḥ Hakkohen of Babylon, when making his pilgrimage to Jerusalem, passes Damascus and Tyre and is invited to recite the prayers in both places (above, p. 161). Likewise the Hazzan Solomon (Sabiḳ), who was reputed to have been under the ban, arrived at the synagogue of the Palestinians in Fusṭāṭ in order to act as Reader (above, p. 108). But in many cases no doubt the Ḥazzan was a scholar and also an author of liturgical compositions which he would recite during the service on Sabbaths and Festivals. Such learned Readers were, for example, Aaron הממחה b. Ephraim, Shelah הממחה, Revaḥ Hakkohen of Babylon, Moses b. Levi, X. b. Ṣadoḳ (A. B. 20, II, 5; A.C. 17, 3; A. D. 21; 35, 1). A Reader would be complimented as נזר החזנים (so Hillel Ḥazzan in a letter to him, Oxford MS. Heb. d. 76, fol. 63), פאר החזנים (A. D. 29, 3).

So far two scholarly readers were styled Rosh Happereḳ, viz. Nehemiah, the brother of Sahlān b. Abraham (p. 97), and Peraḥya b. Mumal (A. B. 71, ll. 4–5, where reference is made to his liturgical compositions which he recited in a powerful voice). The former, like his son Joshiah and his brother Sahlān, was apparently also an author of piyyuṭim.[1] Now this title Rosh Happereḳ (ראש הפרק) recalls the so-called archipherekitai in the time of Justinian (see Gr. v[4], 19, 412–13), who were the public exegetes of the Bible, using the Agadic method in their discourses. The son and namesake of the executed Babylonian Exilarch, Mar Zuṭra, settled in Palestine at the beginning of the sixth century and became Rēsh Pirḳa.[2] Brüll (*Jahrbücher*, V, 95), in dealing with Justinian's laws of 553, thinks that all the archipherekitai lived in Tiberias. But for this there is really no cogent proof. It is more likely that several communities in Palestine and elsewhere had such Agadists (רבנן דאגדתא) who preached to the people on the Sabbath as well as on other

[1] See Bodl. 2842, H, l 3, q 7: acrostic 'Nehemiah b. Abraham'. Probably Bodl. 2842, F, 21, 22, 24, 25, 28, 34; H a 28, 34, l 2, 4–7; q 8 and 2710, 1 are also by him. Bodl. 2842, H a 27 has the acrostic נחמיה בר אברהם מוטא חזק. What is the meaning of מוטא?

[2] See above, p. 58, note 1.

occasions. When Justinian prohibited the deuterosis, recourse was taken to piyyuṭim as its substitute in the service. Thus the Ḥazzan (in Talmudic times the synagogue attendant and also pupil teacher) took the place of the preacher by intoning the liturgical compositions, which were saturated with Halakah and Agada.[1] Thus Yannai's compositions were known as חזנות ינאי. Besides the above-mentioned persons in the eleventh century, there is no further clear evidence of readers and liturgical poets who were called Rosh Happereḳ. It may be that the title was revived by a Nasi or Gaon[2] in order to compliment therewith a learned Ḥazzan who was also a preacher and a writer of piyyuṭim. Perhaps the author of the Diwan, who lived towards the end of the tenth century somewhere in Syria, in styling his friend Joshu'a the Reader as ראש, referred to his title Rosh Happereḳ (p. 23).

Not fully a Ḥazzan but only a chorister was the משורר, probably required to intone the traditional melodies. A document of 1132 (Bodl. 2878[7]) states that the allowance for the wife and son of Ṣedaḳah the chorister (המשורר) b. Ṣemaḥ was fixed in the Palestinian synagogue of Fusṭāṭ before Maṣliaḥ Gaon. Of a משורר in Ḥebron (in the fourteenth century) we read above (p. 248). Other communal officials were the teachers (מלמדים), the scribes (סופרים), and also the 'constable' (שומר, see A. A. 16, I, 3; A. C. 8; A. D. 3; 24; Bodl. 2878[43]: Ibrāhīm אלרומי אלסופר). Now as regards the scribe, it is not always certain whether the person referred to was a professional scribe of documents issued by the Bet-Dīn (and of books, scrolls, Tephillin, and Mezuzot), or a government secretary (Katib). Only once we find the latter expressly called סופר המלכות (A. D. 35, 3; cp. also A. A. 1, l. 31). The 'constable' (שומר) was perhaps in charge of the market where Kosher meat was sold. Finally, reference should be made to the communal official called the 'Interpreter'. Bodl. 2806[24] contains an Arabic letter relating to a commercial transaction wherein is mentioned Ṣedaḳah Hakkohen b. David אלמתרגם,

[1] See Eppenstein, *Mtschr.*, 1908, 467–72.

[2] Both Sherira and Samuel b. Ḥofni refer in their responsa to dignitaries in their academies who went by this name (ראשי הפרקים, ראשי פרקי, see Eppenstein, *l. c.* 457), but their functions are obscure. Perhaps the above-mentioned people in Egypt were granted their titles by the Babylonian Academy.

who 'has to interpret the passage of the Pentateuch (סֿת) upon which an oath is taken'. As Arabic was the vernacular of the Egyptian Jews, a number of people were unable to understand Hebrew without translation. Probably this 'Interpreter' was attached to the Bet-Dīn, and among others his duty was to explain in Arabic the meaning of the Hebrew and Arabic formulae recurring in the legal documents issued by the court.[1]

(9) A few remarks are due here on the position held in the community by a Nasi, i.e. a descendant of David (see above, pp. 171 ff., 251–2, 254). In Babylon the Exilarch was from times of yore the recognized political head of Jewry. In the twelfth century the Exilarchate, after it had lost its authority for some time, was re-established with full powers. This we learn from the description of Benjamin of Tudela as to the influence wielded by the Bagdād Exilarch Daniel b. Ḥasdai (*Itinerary*, ed. Adler, 39–41). Political representatives were also the Nesiim of Mosul, the two cousins David and Samuel, whom Petaḥya found there during his travels. Every Jew had to pay a poll-tax, half of which went to the ruler and the other half to the Nesiim. To enforce their ruling, they disposed of a prison to confine therein the evildoers. In a dispute between Jew and Muslim, the latter, if guilty, would also be locked up (*Itinerary*, ed. Benisch, 8, 10). Benjamin of Tudela relates also of two Nesiim in Yemen, the brothers Shalmon and Ḥanan, who seem to have been actual rulers over the local Jewry (*Itinerary,* ed. Adler, 46–7). On the other hand, in Egypt the recognized political head of the Jews was the Nagid, and the Nasi's authority was more of a moral character by reason of his descent from David.

[1] In questions addressed to Sherira and Hai from Ḳairowān we read of complaints that in *most cases* the signatories of documents were unable to read them and understand their purport. Of course they could read the Hebrew script, but the language was unfamiliar to them. See *Gaonic Responsa*, ed. Harkavy, no. 231: דהא רוב החתומין על השטר וזימנין דהוו כולהו לא ידעי למקרא שטר ולמיקם על ענייני דיליה . . .; No. 238: אי נמי שאר שטרות דחתמין ביה עמי הארץ דלא ידעי למיקרייה ולמיקם על עניניה מאי אית למעבד בהו ורוב השטרות בעונות הכין משכחינן להו. Cp. also Bodl. 2878^{138}: a letter from Palṭiel to his father Joseph התרגמן. He is mentioned in a document, dated Iyyar, 1457 Sel. (1146 C.E.) at Fusṭāṭ (T.-S. 13 J 2^{25}), as אלשיך אבו יעקוב רבנא יוסף התרגמן הנכבד בן רבנא אבון השר הנכבד בעודו זֿל.

A Nasi would honour his friends by bestowing upon them titles such as ידיד הנשיאות, חמדת הנשיאות, חדות הנשיאות, דגל הנשיאות, רצוי הנשיאות, עזר הנשיאות, סגולת הנשיאות, נזר הנשיאות.[1]

(10) The last section deals with the academy and those connected with it. It is beyond the scope of this treatise to discuss the inner organization of the Babylonian Gaonate (see especially Eppenstein, *Mtschr.*, 1908, 338 ff., and Pozn., *Hakkedem*, II, Hebrew part, 91–6). The Palestinian Geonim also presided over a college of seventy ordained scholars, called the Sanhedrin after the ancient example. A student that was ordained in the school received the title of החבר בסנהדרין גדולה, or shortened החבר. The first seven scholars of the academy were numbered, viz. Gaon, Ab-Bet-Dīn, Third, Fourth, Fifth, Sixth, and Seventh (השלישי בחבורה, or shortened השלישי, and so on).[2] We have come across no dignitary named 'the Eighth' or after any later number.[3] Probably the seventy members of the Sanhedrin (or חבורה) sat in the school in seven rows of ten each, as was the case in Babylon, and the above dignitaries were the heads of their corresponding rows. Accordingly the Gaon, besides being Rosh Yeshiba, was also head of the first row, while the Ab represented the second one, and so on. In the Babylonian academies there were seven Rashē Kallot, each of whom was appointed over one row. But the whole title of Rosh Kallah was unknown in the Palestinian school, since only Babylon had bi-annual meetings during the so-called Kallah months, Elul and Adar (see Ber. 57ᵃ, and Nathan's Report in Neub. II, 87–8). Probably at a full meeting of the school in Jerusalem (or Ramlāh), the first row was occupied by the Ab and the other dignitaries, in all six in number. Who completed the number of ten is obscure. In Babylon we know

[1] See above, pp. 97, 194, 225, note 1, end, 252; A. C. 17, 1; 23, note 4; A. D. 29, 3. Or. 5542, fol. 33, contains a letter to Yefet b. Sason wherein are mentioned רבנא הלל נזר הנשיאות ראש כלה נט רח and the Exilarch. Addressed (verso) to Abū'l 'Āli Ḥasan b. Surur b. 'Āli, evidently the Arabic names of Yefet b. Sason.

[2] The first four officials are mentioned very frequently. As regards the 'Fifth', cp. Bodl. 2877⁶: שילא החמישי; the 'Sixth' is mentioned several times (above, pp. 108, 149, 191, 234, note 1); *J. Q. R.*, XIX, 730, no. 26: Abū Sa'ad the 'Sixth'; the 'Seventh' we find above, p. 183 (cp. p. 192, note 1): Solomon b. Ḥayyim השביעי; cp. also A. C. 26, l. 43; Bodl. 2878¹⁶: Solomon Hallevi b. Moses השביעי; Nathan the 'Seventh' (*infra*, p. 278, note 6).

[3] See also *infra*, p. 277, note 1.

that the first row was occupied by the seven Rashē Kallot and three Ḥaberim. The functions of the latter are not clear. Perhaps they formed the Bet-Dīn attached to the school, and hence one of them was the Ab-Bet-Dīn (or דיינא דבבא). But as regards Palestine no definite information is as yet available on this point. It may also be that the seven dignitaries of the academy had no connexion with the same number of rows of the school, in spite of the Babylonian parallel. It is known that the Gaon of Palestine claimed as his prerogative the fixing of the calendar (עיבור שנה, see especially above, p. 50 ff.). Elijah Hakkohen, reports the *Megillat Ebyatar*, convened a meeting at Ḥaifa in the year of his death (1083 C. E.), and there 'sanctified the year', re-affirming at the same time the succession of his son Ebyatar as Gaon. Now the fixing of the calendar (עיבור שנה) was determined upon in Talmudic times by *seven scholars* summoned by the Nasi (see Sanh. 10^b bottom, 11^a top). The suggestion may therefore be ventured that the first seven members of the Sanhedrin of the school in Palestine were those that fixed the Calendar.[1]

Be that as it may, the Gaon, Ab, and Third usually determined the policy of the school on various occasions. Thus, for example, the Fusṭāṭ congregation of the Palestinians demand that the letter, proving the annulment of the ban imposed upon the Ḥazzan Solomon (Sabiḳ), should be signed by these three officials (above, p. 109; see also Bacher, *J. Q. R.*, XV, 83). When the Ab was away in Egypt for several years, Solomon b. Yehuda is constantly aided by the 'Third' in managing the affairs of the school (see pp. 127 f., 129, 132). Ginzberg (*Geonica*, I, 12, note) suggests parallels in the triad of the Tannaitic Sanhedrin, Nasi, Ab-Bet-Dīn, and Ḥakam (חכם), as compared with Gaon, Ab, and Resh Kallah in Babylon and Gaon, Ab, and 'Third' of the Palestinian school. But on the one hand the latter had seven dignitaries

[1] In Yer. Sanh., 18^c, top, it is decided that Ḥaberim may participate in the sanctification of the new month, but not in declaring a leap-year (הדא אמרה שחבירים נכנסין לקידוש החדש: חברים מהו ליכנס לעיבור שנה? נישמעינה מהדא מעשה בר"ג וכו' ואפילו כן לא עיברוה בההוא יומא . . .). In Talmudic times the Ḥaberim were the disciples not yet ordained (see above, p. 54, note 2). But in our period the Ḥaber was a scholar with a diploma from the academy. Moreover, the first seven members were the foremost savants of the school, and corresponded to the seven elders (זקנים) in the time of R. Gamliel.

numbered in succession, while on the other hand the existence in the Babylonian academy of a chief Resh Kallah as distinct from the seven Rashē Kallot, mentioned before, is very problematic (see ibid., p. 8, note, and Pozn., *J. Q. R.*, N. S., III, 403).

A glowing description of the Palestine academy we read in the Targum on Canticles 7^3 (see Marx, *J. Q. R.*, N. S., I, 66). The head of the school is surrounded by seventy scholars who study the Torah and are maintained by 'tithes' and donations.[1] The Ab-Bet-Dīn administers justice and wields coercive powers. The 'scribes' (ספריך) are full of wisdom, whereby they calculate the calendar. 'They declare leap-years and fix the new moons at the gate of the house of the great Sanhedrin.' These 'scribes' (different from the seventy scholars, חכימין, mentioned before) may be identical with the dignitaries, known as 'Third', &c., who together with the Gaon and the Ab fixed the year's calendar, as suggested above. The Nasi is mentioned last (ורב בית בא (= אבא) לבית יהודה). Another proof that there lived in Palestine descendants of David whose activities were different from those of the Gaon. Only once were the Nesiut and the Gaonate combined in one person, viz. in Daniel b. 'Azarya.

Another important description of the Palestinian Gaonate is to be found in the remarkable poems, published by Schechter under the title 'The Oldest Collection of Bible Difficulties, by a Jew' (*J. Q. R.*, XIII, 345 ff.). Bacher (ibid., XV, 83) and Porges (ibid., XX, 197) have already dealt with this point. But the whole attitude taken up by the author has not yet been fully understood. From a sceptic (according to Schechter), who hurled his literary shafts into the camps of both Rabbinites and Ḳaraites, he has become (according to Porges) a partisan of the priestly brothers Joseph and Elijah in their struggle with Daniel b. 'Azarya about the succession to the Gaonate. But, needless to say, this conflict did not involve the problem of Bible exegesis. When it is stated in the *Megillat Ebyatar* that Daniel received the help of כת הצלע in Jerusalem, the Ḳaraites are meant who took an active share in the communal life (see above, p. 178). These

[1] The 'tithes' need not be taken literally. Above (p. 172) we have read how the bogus Nasi Shem-Tob opened up for himself a source of revenue by imposing 'tithes', i. e. fixed contributions, similar to the חומשים 'fifths', levied by the Babylonian schools (*J. Q. R.*, XIX, 105, cp. p. 401; N. S., VIII, 347, l. 3).

sectaries evidently resided in a special quarter which was identified with the Biblical צלע האלף (Josh. 18. 28). Munk (*Notice sur Abou'l Walid*, 14, note 3, end) has pointed out that Yefet b. 'Āli read צלע האלף היבוסי, taking these three words as one name for that part of Jerusalem belonging to the tribe of Benjamin. Yefet also quotes a couplet from an elegy by the poet Meborak b. Nathan ואבכה מול קבר זכריה בן יהוידע אשר קברו בצלע האלף נודע,[1] and he further states that in his time this tomb was shown in the '*quarter of the Orientals*' (ḥirat al-Musharikat). As the earliest Ḳaraite settlers in the Holy City hailed almost exclusively from Babylon and Persia, it is natural that the district wherein they settled was named the 'quarter of the Orientals'. It was identified with the Biblical צלע האלף. This suggested to the Rabbinites to dub this sect as כת הצלע 'the sect of calamity' and, by way of a pun, כת הצולעה 'the lame sect' (also הצולעה, without כת).

Now the Ḳaraites, who styled themselves בעלי מקרא, claimed a monopoly of a thorough knowledge of the Scriptures. Those in the Holy City, in their antagonism against the adherents of Tradition, would insinuate that the members of the school, engrossed as they were in the study of the Talmudic literature, were not their equals in the proper understanding of the Bible. Our author, who left an Eastern country[2] for the West (נוכח מבוא השמש, most likely Palestine) in order scientifically to study the Sacred Writings, takes up the challenge on behalf of Rabbinism. It almost seems as if he studied under Ḳaraite teachers in the Holy City who were renowned for their Biblical scholarship.

[1] This couplet is also cited by Salman b. Yeruḥam in his commentary to Lam. 2. 20 (see Pozn., Luncz's *Jerusalem*, X, 96).

[2] *J. Q. R.*, XIII, 365, l. 16 ff.: סבותי ימים ואיים וארץ גזרה · ובידי כסף לאנשי האלהים להביא תשורה למלמדי ומשכילי מצוה ותורה בגבורה . . . נער בן שמונה עשרה יצאתי ממגורי · מארץ תובל מבית הורי · ועזבתי את כל יגיע אבי ואת כל יקרי · והלכתי נוכח מבוא השמש למורי · חכמת המקרא לדרשה וכו׳. The native country of our author was then identified with the Biblical תובל (Gen. 10. 2). Now it is mentioned together with משך, which was regarded to be the same as the country of Khurasān (see Sa'adya in his Pentateuch translation, ed. Derenbourg). Hence תובל must be a neighbouring district. See, however, Schechter, ibid. 352, note 5. The Ḳaraite Jacob b. Reuben (to Ezek. 38. 3, see Harkavy, *Altjüd. Denkmäler*, 280, col. 2) identifies תובל with Slavonia (משך כורוסניים ותובל היא שקלבינאה).

But their instruction did not help him satisfactorily to explain the difficulties in which Scripture abounded.[1] He therefore became convinced of the futile claims of Ḳaraism to found the structure of Judaism on the Biblical text alone without the aid of Tradition and Agadah. Question upon question of Biblical difficulties are enumerated which the Ḳaraites, in spite of their vaunted knowledge, are unable to solve. And yet they assert that none of the Rabbinites can meet them in argument. These sectaries claim the Bible as their 'inheritance'.[2]

[1] See *J. Q. R.*, *l. c.*, l. 21 ff. Schechter (p. 353) has already suggested this, but he maintained that our author was a Rabbinite who joined afterwards the Ḳaraites. But in my opinion in his young days, on arrival at Jerusalem, he may have studied the Bible under Ḳaraite teachers. Afterwards, however, he emphatically repudiated their teachings.

[2] Ibid., p. 364, l. 21 ff.: קנוא קנאתי לקדושה עדתי ('the holy one, (viz.) my congregation') · ובאפי עלתה חמתי · על הצולעה (for כת הצולעה) היושבת המתרפקת לעמתי (i.e. in Jerusalem) · ומלין תפציר על חכמי אומתי (i.e. Rabbinites) · לאמר אפס משיב ועומד למגמתי · מאהלי בן ברוקה (A prominent Tannaite, R. Yoḥanan b. Beroḳah, is mentioned as the representative of Rabbinism. Of course this is done for the sake of the poetic scheme, about which see Porges, *l.c.*, XIV, 129.) כי · מצאנו חכמה פלילה (referring to הצולעה) תאמר לנו המקרא נחלה (as their name בעלי מקרא implies) ואין מי יעמוד בחכמי גורן עגולה · חבורת הצדק הקדושה: שוקדים על דלתות תלמוד ומשנה . . . ובמקרא לא יספנו דעתם לכוונה. (They do not pay proper attention to the study of Scripture; for the meaning of ספן, cp. Jastrow.) כי בלבם חרושה ('silent', owing to ignorance). Several other allusions to the Ḳaraites are to be found in these homes. Ibid., p. 358, l. 9 ff.: צבא יצבאו כלם על הפתרון · יחוגו וינועו כמלאי שכרון · זה אומר בכה וזה אומר בכה (i.e. no two commentators agree) . . . בחקים ומשפטים נוקשו ונכשלו ואזעק ואומר אהה: רוגנים ובוגדים מכחישי מצח על דבר כזב . . . תקעו חצוצרה ברמה שופר בגבעה · יאוספו עמים על הצולעה: להוציא מלבה תעתועה דברי בלעה . . . באזני אמרתי (r. שמעתי) קול מלים · לאמר נדע המקרא בכל פעלים · לא יותר דבר מראש ועד ישלים. On p. 362, l. 1, משכילי עם הואילו פנו אלי is probably another direct challenge to the Ḳaraite scholars who styled themselves משכילים. See further, p. 367, l. 3 ff.: אמרתי אשימה לרוחי מעצר . . . והנה רשע לנגדי מלים יפצר לדבר אל יי תועה . . . והנה זאת הרשעה . . . על קדושי יי הרחיבו פה בפער · ויאמר לבנות לה בית בארץ שנער (a clear reference to the Ḳaraites who originally hailed from Babylon) · כי משם יצאו מרעה אל רעה · דבה יוצאו על צדיק בגאוה ובוזה · מחללי

Our author also describes the academy of Jerusalem. At its head is the Gaon, whose decrees go forth to 'all Israel scattered in the four corners' (of the earth). There are '*seven Ḥaberim*, who understand the ancient things (i. e. the laws of Tradition), to teach in Israel' the Torah of Moses. Adopting the image of the Menorah (in Zech. ch. 4), he pictures the Gaon and his two chief assistants, the Ab on his right, and the 'Third' on his left. The 'elders' of the congregation (of the Rabbinites in Jerusalem) wield the power of excommunicating those who disobey their ruling.[1]

Patrons of the school, wherever their residence may have been, were given various titles, usually at the great public meeting on Mount Olivet on Hoshana Rabba. If the person honoured was a scholar, the Palestinian Gaon would make him a Ḥaber. In Babylon the corresponding honorary degree would be Alluf (= Resh Kallah). The title Ḥaber was amplified into החבר המעולה בחבורה (shortened into החבר המעולה or המעולה בחבורה), ראש החברים, פאר החברים, נזר החברים, הוד החברים. An aspirant to

---

מועדי יי נוגי ממועד בדאגה ורגזה. (Here, again, those sectaries are meant who impart to the festivals a mournful aspect, keeping them as days of mourning for the destruction of the Temple, as the Ḳaraite ritual clearly shows.) Against these sectaries our author took up the issue on behalf of Rabbinism. Ibid., l. 16 ff.: זה אלהים חילי נתן לי לשון למודים · וישם פי כחרב וחצים חדים · להגיד על פניהם דרך (supply אשר הם) צועדים · ולהחריש (supply הדברים) אשר הם בודים.

[1] Ibid., 364, last line ff.: ראם קרניו בהם ינגח לצים (i. e. heretics) · אל כל ישראל אשר בארבע פנות נפוצים · גזרותיו ודתותיו יצאו אצים נחוצים · גאון יעקב אבן הראשה · קרן שבעה עינים על אבן אחת חקוקים · שבעה החברים משכילי הדברים עתיקים · שבעה אלה עיני יי משוטטים בכל הארקים · ללמד בישראל משפטים וחקים · (it seems that they made pastoral tours) צפירת מנורת זהב ועל ראשה גלה (i. e. the Gaon) ועליה. שבעה נרות (i. e. 7 Ḥaberim) ושני בני היצהר מימינה ומשמאלה . . . הוא אב בית דין מימין הגאון והשלישי משמאלו לתהלה · ושבעה רועים ושמונה נסיכי חבורת הצדק הכלולה המלמדים בישראל (i. e. the traditional Torah, as Ezra did, Neh. 8. 8) תורה מפורשה. The phrase '7 shepherds and 8 dignitaries' is modelled after Mic. 5. 4. We know only of seven Ḥaberim, of whom the first three were the Gaon, Ab, and Third. פנו וראו אז (r. אבן) הבדיל ביד הזקנים · להבדיל מקהל יי כל סרבים וסלונים · וכל הממרים ולתורתם שמוע מאנים · מחוץ לעדת יי מושבם כמצורעים.

this title was styled מעותד לחבורה.[1] The Babylonian title אלוף ישיבה (once there occurs the title אלוף שתי ישיבות, i.e. of Sura and Pumbedita (Bagdād), p. 167) was apparently amplified into אלוף הבינות (thus Meborak Nagid, and two other persons Ephraim and Solomon, above, p. 210 and A. A. 16, I, 2).

Other titles bestowed upon benefactors and well-wishers of the academies, whether of Palestine, Babylon, Damascus, and Egypt, are the following:

[2] אהוב הישיבה, the beloved of the school.
[3] בחיר הישיבה, the chosen one, &c.
[4] גדול הישיבה, the great one, &c.
[5] דגל הישיבה, the banner, &c.
[6] חמדת הישיבה, the desire, &c.
[7] חכם הישיבה, the scholar, &c.
[8] ידיד הישיבה, the friend, &c.
[9] יסוד הישיבה, the foundation, &c.
[10] משוש הישיבה, the joy, &c.
[11] נאמן הישיבה, the faithful one, &c.
[12] נזר הישיבה, the crown, &c.
[13] סגולת הישיבה, the choice, &c.
[14] סגן הישיבה, the adjutant, &c.
[15] סוד הישיבה, the counsel, &c.

[1] Above, pp. 210, 225, note 1, end: A. B. 21; 25; 34; A. C. 9; 13, 4; A. D. 1; 29, 3.

[2] A. D. 16; 21; 35, 2. Cp. also the book-list in *ZfHB.*, XII, 123, l. 4 (cp. note 2), Abū'l Fadhail אלאהוב = אהוב הישיבה.

[3] A. B. 20, II, 4; A. D. 4, 2; 17, 3[h]; Bodl. 2876[11]; cp. also *J. Q. R.*, N. S., VII, 478, note 22.

[4] So Nahrai b. Nissim, p. 206. Also Sherira styles thus Shemarya b. Elḥanan (*J. Q. R.*, VI, 223, l. 15). T.-S. 13 J 18[15] contains a letter, dated Marḥeshvan, 1459 Sel. = 1147, to Ḥalfon Hallevi השר הנכבד b. Joseph גדול הישיבה.

[5] A. D 29, 3; *J. Q. R.*, XIV, 451, note 6.

[6] Above, p. 196; A. D. 1; 29, 3. Also Abraham חמדת הישיבה b. Nathan the 'Seventh' (see Margol., *Catal.*, III, 559, III; Bodl. 2878[29]).

[7] Above, p. 209.

[8] A. B. 69; A. C. 16, 2; A. D. 3, 2, where Joseph al-Rumi אלידיד = ידיד הישיבה.

[9] Above, p. 194; A. C. 17, 1; 26[a]; 28, 3; A. D. 6; 20, 7. See also above, p. 238, note 1.

[10] Probably = אבי הששונות, see above, pp. 144, 183; A. B. 5; 15; 20, II, 1; 62; A. D. 4, 1; Bodl. 2878[8].

[11] Bodl. 2878[43].

[12] So far only the grandfather of Samuel b. Ḥofni held this title (above, p. 262).

[13] A. B. 40 (סגולת ישיבת צבי); A. C. 24, 5, *Saadyana*, LV, l. 17; *J. Q. R.*, XIX, 732, no. 35. Perhaps the person Yehuda אל סגלת, to whom Yehuda Halevi addressed a poem (*Diwan*, ed. Brody, I, no. 29), held the title of סגולת הישיבה.

[14] See above, p. 97; A. C. 28, 3; A. D. 4, 1. Also Joseph b. Berakya in Ḳairowān (see Pozn., *Babyl. Geon.*, 17, note 2).

[15] See note 9.

[1] עוז הישיבה, the strength, &c.
[2] עזר הישיבה, the help, &c.
[3] פאר הישיבה, the glory, &c.
[4] רצוי הישיבה, the favourite, &c.
[5] רצוי שתי הישיבות, the favourite of both schools.
[6] תפארת הישיבה, the pride of the school.

A leading scholar was styled הרב; thus, e.g., Shemarya b. Elḥanan (A. A. 6, l. 10; 7, fol. 55ʳ, l. 11). A certain Jacob b. Samuel b. Abraham (of Byzantine origin) adds הרב to his own signature as well as to those of his father and grandfather (A. B. 20 II, 5). This title was amplified into הרב הגדול, הרב הגדול בישראל, and especially הרב המובהק, which became customary in Egypt in the period of Maimonides.[7] The Nagid Meborak, just as his grandfather, and also Maimonides were styled צורבא מרבנן (above, p. 222, note 2, and A. D. 4, 1). Another flattering designation of scholars and patrons of students (תלמיד) would be הדר התלמידים, תפארת התלמידים, פאר התלמידים.[8]

Finally, the titles ראש בי רבנן and ראש הסדר are to be mentioned. The former was held in Ḳairowān by Ḥushiel and his son Elḥanan (*J. Q. R.*, N. S., IX, 161). In Egypt so far four persons are known who went by this name, viz. the two contemporaries Abraham b. Nathan Ab and Isaac b. Samuel (al-Kinzi, the Spaniard), the latter's son Yehoseph, and Jacob the father of Joseph Rosh Hasseder (A. C. 17, 1; 26ᵃ; 28, 5; A. D. 29, 1). The first two persons were also designated Rosh Hasseder, which title should not be identified with that of Resh Kallah and Alluf (see *ZfHB.*, X, 144, note 1). It originates from the time when Babylon had not yet a properly organized Yeshiba. Thus Rab was called Rēsh Sidra (*Seder 'Olam Zuta* in Neub. II, 77). Samuel b. Ḥofni mentions (in a letter to Fez, *J. Q. R.*, XVIII, 404, l. 9) the ראשי הסדרים of his school. But their function is obscure. It is also unknown whether this honorific name as well

[1] *R. É. J.*, LXVI, 66 (l. 37), 70.
[2] Above, p. 146.
[3] *J. Q. R.*, N. S., I, 48–9.
[4] See above, pp. 149, 196, note 2.
[5] A. D. 4, 6.
[6] See above, p. 267, note 2.
[7] A. B. 20 II, 1; A. C. 28, 3; A. D. 3, 3; 25, 2, 4; 29, 1; 31; 32; *J. Q. R.*, XIX, 728, no. XVII.
[8] A. B. 2, note; A. C. 16, 2; A. D. 2; 24; 35, 2.

as the title Resh bē Rabbānan were granted both by the Babylonian and the Palestinian schools or only by the Geonim of 'Iraḳ. However, in Damascus school the bearer of this title was also called 'the preacher' (הדרשן, above, p. 238, note 1; Samuel b. Ḥofni in his letter mentions the ראשי המדרשים next to 'the heads of the Sedarim'). Indeed we found such a Rosh Hasseder travelling about in Egypt on a preaching tour (p. 101 f.). But the material at hand does not yet render it possible clearly to define the functions of these 'heads of the Sedarim'. Elḥanan b. Shemarya styled himself 'Rosh Hasseder of all Israel' (שלכל ישראל). Several other people in the country of the Nile went by this title.[1]

From the above remarks it is evident that the ages we are dealing with here were not sparing in flattering eulogies of their scholars and communal leaders. Public recognition of services for the common weal is quite in place if practised with discretion. But this multitude of titles with extravagant meanings probably led in many cases to vainglory. By too frequent use they became commonplace and soon lost all real significance. However, in Arab society the same practice was in force. It was the fashion of the time and Jewry followed in its train.

[1] Yehuda Hakkohen, Sahlān b. Abraham, Abraham b. Nathan Ab, the Nagid Meborak, Isaiah (A. D. 11, 1), Joseph b. Jacob (A. D. 29, 1). Cp. Bodl. 2834[14].

ADDENDUM

The new material as to the relations of R. Yehudai Gaon (760 C. E.) with the scholars of the Holy Land (referred to above, p. 57) is now published in *R. É. J.*, vol. LXX, 1920, p. 113 ff., under the title *Les Chapitres de Ben Bāboï et les relations de R. Yehoudaï Gaon avec la Palestine.* The point dealt with above (p. 42, note 1) is fully discussed ibid., pp. 123 and 126. Finally about the settlement of Babylonian Jews at Jerusalem early in the Arabic period (above, p. 45, note 2, beginning) see ibid., pp. 124 and 126.